Religion, Anthropology, and Cognitive Science

CAROLINA ACADEMIC PRESS
Ritual Studies Monograph Series

Pamela J. Stewart and Andrew Strathern
Series Editors

ﻹ

Religion, Anthropology, and Cognitive Science
Harvey Whitehouse & James Laidlaw

Resisting State Iconoclasm Among the Loma of Guinea
Christian Kordt Højbjerg

Asian Ritual Systems
Syncretisms and Ruptures
Pamela J. Stewart & Andrew Strathern

The Severed Snake
Matrilineages, Making Place, and a Melanesian Christianity in Southeast Solomon Islands
Michael W. Scott

Embodying Modernity and Post-Modernity
Ritual, Praxis, and Social Change in Melanesia
Sandra C. Bamford

Xhosa Beer Drinking Rituals
Power, Practice and Performance in the South African Rural Periphery
Patrick A. McAllister

Ritual and World Change in a Balinese Princedom
Lene Pedersen

Contesting Rituals
Islam and Practices of Identity-Making
Pamela J. Stewart & Andrew Strathern

The Third Bagre
A Myth Revisited
Jack Goody & S.W.D.K. Gandah

Fragments from Forests and Libraries
Essays by Valerio Valeri
Janet Hoskins & Valerio Valeri

RELIGION, ANTHROPOLOGY, AND COGNITIVE SCIENCE

edited by

Harvey Whitehouse
OXFORD UNIVERSITY

James Laidlaw
UNIVERSITY OF CAMBRIDGE

CAROLINA ACADEMIC PRESS
Durham, North Carolina

Library of Congress Cataloging-in-Publication Data

Religion, anthropology, and cognitive science / edited by Harvey White-
house, James Laidlaw.
    p. cm. -- (Ritual studies monograph series)
Includes bibliographical references and index.
ISBN 978-1-59460-107-1 (alk. paper)
1. Ethnology--Religious aspects. 2. Culture and cognition. 3.
Religion. I. Whitehouse, Harvey. II. Laidlaw, James. III. Title.
IV. Series.

BL256.R584 2007
306.6--dc22

2007021262

CAROLINA ACADEMIC PRESS
700 Kent Street
Durham, North Carolina 27701
Tel: (919) 489-7468
Fax: (919) 493-5668
www.cap-press.com

Printed in the United States of America.

Dedicated to the memory of Alfred Gell

CONTENTS

PART THREE
SOCIAL ANTHROPOLOGY, RELIGION, AND THE COGNITIVE SCIENCES

Ritual Studies and Cognitive Science: Anthropology's Shifting Boundaries[1]

Andrew Strathern & Pamela J. Stewart

Harvey Whitehouse and James Laidlaw's edited collection, *Religion, Anthropology, and Cognitive Science*, is a valuable contribution to the literature on the Anthropology of Religion and Psychological Anthropology in general. We are delighted to include the work in our *Ritual Studies Monograph Series*[2]. Both editors are well known scholars whose own work has added considerably to theoretical debates on the analysis of religion and ritual, and this co-edited volume is a further impressive testimony to the energy of the discussions which their work has evinced in this domain of theorizing. Their current aptly named and carefully assembled collection poses problems and proposes solutions within the rapidly developing domain of studies of cognitive aspects of ritual and the cognitive explanation of "religion" as an overall category. The volume as a whole is marked by cutting-edge scholarship and debate in this domain, largely, although not exclusively, stemming from innovative recent work on cognitive theory and modes of religiosity (see for example Whitehouse et al. 2002). One of the most interesting meta-features of this highly interesting and engaged volume is that it contains vigorous discussion of the

---

1. Substantial parts of this Preface were composed while we were Visiting Research Fellows at the Institute of Ethnology, Academia Sinica, Taipei, Taiwan (21 December 2006 to 8 March 2007). We thank the Director of the Institute, Prof. Huang Shu-min, for the renewal of our Visiting positions, and others of our colleagues in the Institute, particularly Dr. Guo Pei-yi, for their hospitality and help with the provision of an office during the time of our stay.

2. Other titles in the Ritual Studies Monograph Series are listed on p. ii of this volume.

relevant issues. James Laidlaw, as a Co-Editor for the volume, records his clear views about the limitations of the "cognitivist" approach to explaining ritual in the penultimate chapter; while Harvey Whitehouse surveys the terrain for a possible synthesis of cognitivist and interpretivist approaches in his own final chapter.

Whitehouse's synthesis turns on a very considerable expansion of the term "cognition" itself, so as to include many, if not all, of the factors of conscious reasoning and thought that Laidlaw sees as omitted from a more narrow version of the cognitivist paradigm, which stresses unconscious or habitual (non-reflective) cognitive patterns and foregrounds these as the causes of religious "beliefs". Whitehouse's expansion of the term cognition is a notable strategic move in response to Laidlaw's concerns and can be recognized as such. These matters come up in the Introduction by Laidlaw and Whitehouse, and their contrasting views on the potentialities of cognitive science in the anthropology of religions are admirably set out. Laidlaw in his sole-authored chapter further notes the historical complexity of the category "religion"; Bloch, in his chapter, goes further and considers it to be a general rag-bag category. Most of the contributors, as Laidlaw notes, go with a simple Tylorian "belief in spirits" definition that suits their invocation of the Hyperactive Agency Detection Device and Theory of Mind explanatory concepts (HADD and ToM). These and other debates need to be noticed by readers, so that they can register them and make up their own minds as they go along. Basically, in Laidlaw's view, cognitive science should be kept in its place, as a means of suggesting underlying universals; while Whitehouse has a more extensive vision of using cognitivist approaches to explain more and more detailed features of particular cases. The individual chapters in the collection provide a range of interesting perspectives on these topics.

These kinds of debates, on the use of models and findings from outside of a currently accepted notion of what constitutes "anthropology" have a long history, and were reviewed in the 1960s in a volume edited by Max Gluckman, called *Closed Systems and Open Minds* (1964). From its very beginnings as an academic discipline, in Europe, anthropology has existed in a condition of dynamic tension between defining itself as a separate subject and taking in ideas from a variety of sources as a means of enrichment. At any given time, anthropologists may have a certain "feel" for their approach to topics which suggests how this approach or perspective lends a distinctive character to their ways of looking at data. Considered over a longer period of time, however, it is quite evident that the approaches and perspectives in question change. Contemporary anthropologists discuss issues of globalization, transnational relations, ethnicity, nationalism, and the like which are in large part shared with sociologists, historians, and political scientists, Nevertheless, within these shared arenas, perspectival differences do tend to emerge, often deriving from the traditions of long-term study, close ethnographic description and analysis, and the ethos of participant observation, that form a part of anthropology's intellectual heritage. One axis of debate in theoretical terms has often centered on the matter of the relationship between anthropology and psychology. The propositions of the nineteenth century "armchair anthropologists" in Britain, such as Sir James George Frazer and Sir Edward Burnett Tylor, were quite often essentially of a psychological kind, dealing with supposed universal "mentalities" underlying the customary practices of peoples. This tradition was vigorously defended by R. R. Marett, a folklorist who extended his interests into contemporary ideas and practices and sought psychological ways of explaining them (Marett 1920).

The opposite tradition, of course, stems from the work of Emile Durkheim (1982 [1895]), although, as has recently been pointed out, Durkheim's sociological propositions can also be reframed as psychological (Throop and Laughlin 2002). The recent efforts to incorporate findings from cognitive science into anthropological theorizing, or, alternatively seen, to transform anthropology by subsuming aspects of it under cognitive science, have to be understood as the latest expressions of the dynamic tension we have referred to, between the impulse to embrace other disciplinary approaches or to draw a boundary around anthropological theorizing as such. This dynamic and productive tension is well exhibited in the debates between Laidlaw and Whitehouse in the present volume. The consequences of such a debate are not trivial, but relate to the future pathways or trajectories of anthropological thinking in general. One response to such debates is to oppose the widening of the anthropological enterprise. Another is to recognize that this process of widening and narrowing is continuous: what is accepted as "normal practice" by one generation may be rejected by the next, and so on. Even if, at any given time, we advocate, as Meyer Fortes used to do, that we "stick to our last", the last itself changes over time. And running through these debates has been an overarching question, whether anthropology can be a "generalizing science" or whether it is, and should remain, focused on ethnographic exposition and middle-level, grounded, theorizing based solidly on cultural and historical understandings. In Whitehouse's vision, we could, in a sense, "have it all": make anthropology a science, by borrowing from cognitive science, while keeping all of its historical and ethnographic specificities.

We point here briefly to some of the vital issues that are at stake in these kinds of discussions and which recur throughout the volume. One is the issue of conscious versus unconscious thought processes and how these may interact. Another, related, question has to do with evidence from language usages, as for example in Sørenson's discussion of Malinowski's work on Trobriand magic: how are we to know that Malinowski exaggerated the significance of language in this context? Language itself may be seen as an embodied form of action, closely tied in with gestures and emotional expressions, so that in a broader sense the opposition between language and other performative registers of magical activity is neutralized. Sørenson appears to recognize this point, or something akin to it, in referring to Malinowski's pragmatic view of language generally.

Sørenson also raises in his chapter another issue related to language usages which resonates with work that we have been engaged in on expressive genres (Stewart and Strathern eds. 2005a). Sørenson's focus is on usages in magical language, but the issues he raises can be extended also to the presentation of knowledge in balladic and epic forms that are striking parts of the cultural repertoire of aesthetic performance in two parts of the Papua New Guinea Highlands where we have carried out long-term fieldwork, the Hagen and Duna areas (see for example, Strathern and Stewart 2000a and Stewart and Strathern 2002a). Referring to the earlier work of Stanley Tambiah on Trobriand spells (Tambiah 1968), Sørenson asks why ritual forms of language should be deployed in order to convey practical kinds of knowledge that could, he suggests, be conveyed with greater facility outside of such ritual contexts. (Of course, their communication in ritual contexts does not preclude their transmission in other contexts of practical engagement also.) He himself seeks to understand, in the magical context, how features such as iteration and condensation could be especially appropriate to evoke the success envisaged in magic; and he seems to have answered his own question earlier when he notes how one Trobriand magician's spell encapsulates in itself a whole imagined narrative of agricultural activity in which both the dangers and the counteractions against these dangers are vitally delineated. In other words, the emotional power of the narrative, and its detailed exposition, together provide a model for all the practical actions needed to succeed in the agricultural cycle.

Sørenson's question, about why a ritual use of language is employed, is applicable also to verbal sequences in the Papua New Guinea balladic poetical forms which we have ourselves studied. In these, representations of practical knowledge also appear in highly condensed and imagistic forms which parallel in their characteristics the features that Tambiah in his classic formulation identified as belonging to Trobriand spells. We make two suggestions about this correspondence. The first is that such presentations of knowledge undoubtedly gain a greater salience in people's consciousness because of their aesthetic appeal. Listeners attracted to the poetic narrative are likely to register also the details of knowledge that the narrative purveys. Second, this process is underpinned by the systematic use of iteration, framing, and condensation which the poetic form itself generates, influencing the listeners at a sub-conscious level and further reinforcing the overt aesthetic appeal which is felt consciously (see Stewart and Strathern 2002b). Given these processes, we can understand better how the poetic forms adopted by ancient Greek and Latin authors to convey practical forms of knowledge would operate in similar aesthetic and computational ways to impress their messages on readers or listeners. Hesiod's *Works and Days* and Virgil's *Georgics* would belong to this genre (Strathern and Stewart n.d.).

Another point that is related to the question of cognition versus language is that language and cognition are not one and the same phenomenon, although they may be interdependent. And how do questions of doubt and uncertainty, so characteristic of human relations, and so productive of patterns of gossip and fears of witchcraft and sorcery (Stewart and Strathern 2004; Strathern and Stewart 2005, 2006), enter into the picture? Sperber's idea of semi-propositional representations is relevant here, but emotional aspects need to be added. In general, cognitivist approaches need to be put together with the kind of embodiment theory advocated by Thomas Csordas and many others (Csordas 2002; Stewart and Strathern 2001a). From the vantage-point of embodiment theory, for example, much more is involved in the actual processes of witchcraft suspicions and accusations than the tendency to think in essentialist categories. And an overall processualist approach to the study of witchcraft, and social life in general, is one that we have advocated repeatedly for some time (e.g. Stewart and Strathern eds. 2000a). It can be applied to Maurice Bloch's remarks about the inter-penetration of individuals as a general phenomenon in human society (not one limited to a particular geographic area, such as "Melanesia" or "South Asia"). Our concept of the "relational-individual," which we developed initially in order to deal with the complexities of debates about personhood in Papua New Guinea contexts, is a processual one, recognizing variations and fluctuations in stresses on the "relational" or the "individual" part of this composite notion, rather than arguing for the dominance of one aspect over the other (Stewart and Strathern 2000b; Strathern and Stewart 1998a). A related approach can be applied to the issue that Bloch mentions in passing, the analysis of kinship: the "tools" we use in investigating this topic need to be flexibly adjusted to the evidence rather than imposed upon it. Our relational-individual concept was designed to be one such flexible tool. Finally, here, and also drawing on Maurice Bloch's chapter, the task of "putting cognition and the social together" is absolutely decisive for the whole enterprise.

In his final chapter, Harvey Whitehouse engages in just such an exercise, via his analysis of the Kivung rituals in New Britain (Papua New Guinea). Whitehouse acknowledges the ways in which conscious reasoning operates in cultural contexts, and this in itself helps to narrow the gap between cognitivist and interpretive approaches to the analysis of rituals. He also stresses the complexity of the cognitive mechanisms that may underpin sequences of ritual action. The example he gives amply illustrates, from an established anthropological viewpoint, the kinds of social values that are likely to be important generally among the people in his area of study. The example also suggests that nuances and resonances from Christian ethnopsychology and ontology have been blended with ideas about sacrifice to the ancestors, although this is not Whitehouse's concern here. He focuses on a different point, that the rituals all exhibit the exercise of care in the face of danger through following rigid rules of conduct: a pattern which Whitehouse relates to the idea of a cognitive "hazard-precaution system" as hypothesized by Lienard and Boyer (2006). (In passing, Whitehouse also suggests cognitive parallels with obsessive-compulsive disorders (OCDs) among individuals: if these parallels exist, we should perhaps also note that the social contexts of rituals differ from those of individual OCDs..) Other aspects of the rituals, viz. the respect shown to ancestors, Whitehouse relates to the by now familiar "agency detection device" concept advocated by Stewart Guthrie and others in the present volume; and other aspects again he links to the pervasiveness of moral rules and consciousness of these rules in the construction of social life in general. And he relates others, finally, to the exercise of a "theory of mind" (ToM) capacity in humans, projected onto the ancestors. To this suite of explanations, Whitehouse further proposes to add conscious, historically situated factors which exhibit the "cross-domain analogical thinking system" pattern (CAT) also revealed in ritual practices. The question of belief in/knowledge of the ancestors which Rita Astuti tests experimentally in her chapter in this volume (chapter 7) can also be looked at in the light of the CAT principle: ideas about ancestors are based on an analogy with, or extension of, ideas about the living, so that the dead and the living are incorporated in a single domain of social relations. Ideas about dreams and the experience of encounters with the dead in dreams operate as crucial interpretive transducers which we can understand as bypassing or obviating formal issues of "belief" (see Lohmann ed. 2003 and Stewart and Strathern 2003, 2005b).

In our own research in the arena of the Anthropology of Religion in the Hagen, Pangia, and Duna areas of the Highlands of Papua New Guinea (see for example, Stewart 1998; Stewart and Strathern 1999, 2000a, 2000c, 2000d, 2001b, 2001c, 2002a, 2002c, 2005c; Strathern and Stewart 1997, 1998b, 1999a,

1999b, 2000a, 2000b, 2000c, 2003, 2004a, 2004b), we have been interested in the ethnographic documentation of the roles of ritual practices within the wider social framework of the groups enacting the practices, so that religious/ ritual practices are clearly seen as part of a fluid construction of social practice in general. Other scholars who have contributed to this arena of scholarship within the South-West Pacific (also referenced as "Melanesia") include: Barker (1990), Bashkow (2006), Biersack (1999), Clark (2000), Engelke and Tomlinson (2006), Gibbs (1994), Jacka (2001), Jebens (2005), Knauft (2002), Lattas (1998), Reithofer (2005), Robbins (2004), and many others.

It is possible to see aspects of the rituals that we have previously analyzed in our own fieldwork in Highlands Papua New Guinea in the light of Whitehouse's exposition. We will take a few details from the practices directed towards the Female Spirit (Amb Kor) in the Mount Hagen area. Agency detection is strongly at work in ideas about this Spirit. Signs of her coming to a particular man might be the appearance of menstrual blood near to his house; or the discovery of stones that were seen as marks of this presence. Precautions had to be carefully observed in setting up secluded sites for these stones to be installed in a clan area: both respect and fear were involved because incorrect ritual handling would lead to sickness and death in the community rather than health, fertility, and prosperity. The Amb Kor, like the ancestors, was also said to have thoughts and emotions like humans, but to be endowed with superior powers. For example, she was said to be jealous of the human wives of her male worshipers and if one of these human wives transgressively entered her secret enclosure she would turn their genital coverings round to their backs and drive them crazy. Rules, overseen by ritual experts, carefully regulated entrances and exits to the enclosure. Men should never enter or leave singly but always in pairs. At formal times of entry they might enter in single file, loaded with pork to be cooked, each one inspected by a ritual expert again to see that their gear was in order. This sense of order and predictability is, of course, proverbial in ritual; and Hageners themselves gave as its reason the simple view that if the rules were not adhered to, disaster would result. The behavior, in a sense, generated its own explanation. Finally, if asked about the meaning of various actions, participants who had knowledge of these would often say, in a manner reminiscent of the adherents of the Kivung movement, that the behavior was a kind of comparison or analogy: *to tendek etimin*, "they extend a comparison and do it", in the local Melpa language. *To* here corresponds to the *tok piksa* or metaphorical motif in Tok Pisin which Whitehouse refers to as operative for the Kivung followers. Regardless of the suggestions about the evolutionary development of this capacity, we agree with Whitehouse that it is of great significance in the interpretation of ritual. Indeed, without it the other mechanisms (agency detection, theory of mind, etc.) could not operate effectively, because the whole construction of rituals is built out of comparisons and analogies. And in this way we find a mechanism to reintegrate the analysis with structural and processual accounts, for the CAT system works precisely to provide mimetic moments and motivations for processes outside of the ritual context as well as within it, and these outside processes are those that constitute the overall social structure and the embodiment of identity. Thus, the pairing and gender complementarity that are marked ritual features in the Amb Kor complex are to be seen as a dynamic part of the wider contextual structuring of gender relations in the society at large (Stewart and Strathern 1999, Strathern and Stewart 1999b).

As a further general point, we applaud Lanman's insistence, in this volume, on the importance of combining interpretive and explanatory approaches. Lanman correctly argues that in the final analysis, "explanation and interpretation cannot escape each other" (Lanman, this volume). This is because explanations themselves depend on prior interpretations of the data; while interpretations depend on underlying assumptions of an explanatory kind, whether these are made explicit or not. Taken as a whole, this volume, for all its tendency to concentrate on specifically cognitive issues, should be seen as a constructive attempt to integrate together different traditions of anthropological work into a new paradigm that harnesses interpretive approaches to an explanatory project. Whitehouse's Kivung case study shows the way to such a possibility; while Laidlaw's astute caveats remind us of the need to recognize different kinds and levels of explanation, in particular of the need to acknowledge that some theories are better for explaining similarities and others for explaining differences. Both are important enterprises; the trick lies in combining them.

January 2007, Cromie Burn Research Unit

References

Barker, John (ed.) 1990. *Christianity in Oceania: Ethnographic Perspectives.* Association for Social Anthropology in Oceania Monograph Series No. 12. Pittsburh, PA: University of Pittsburgh Press.

Bashkow, Ira 2006. *The Meaning of Whitemen. Race and Modernity in the Orokaiva Cultural World.* Chicago and London: The University of Chicago Press.

Biersack, Aletta 1999. The Mount Kare Python and His Gold: Totemism and Ecology in the PNG Highlands. *American Anthropologist* 101: 68–87.

Clark, Jeffrey 2000. *Steel to Stone. A Chronicle of Colonialism in the Southern Highlands of PNG.* Edited by Chris Ballard and Michael Nihill. Oxford: Oxford University Press.

Csordas, T. 2002. *Body / Meaning / Healing.* New York: Palgrave Macmillan.

Durkheim, Emile [1895] 1982. *Rules of Sociological Method.* New York: Free Press.

Engelke, Matthew and Matt Tomlinson (eds.) 2006. *The Limits of Meaning. Case Studies in the Anthropology of Christianity.* New York and Oxford: Berghahn.

Gibbs, Philip 1994. Akali Andake: Reflections on Engan Christology. *Catalyst* 24(1): 27–42.

Gluckman, Max (ed.) 1962 *Closed Systems and Open Minds.* Chicago: Aldine Press.

Jacka, Jerry 2001. Coca-Cola and *Kolo.* Land, Ancestors and Development. *Anthropology Today* 17(4): 3–8.

Jebens, Holger 2005. *Pathways to Heaven: Contesting Mainline and Fundamentalist Christianity in Papua New Guinea.* New York and Oxford: Berghahn.

Knauft, Bruce 2002. *Exchanging the Past. A Rainforest World of Before and After.* Chicago and London: The University of Chicago Press.

Lattas, Andrew 1998. *Cultures of Secrecy: Reinventing Race in Bush Kaliai Cargo Cults.* Madison: University of Wisconsin Press.

Lienard, Pierre and Pascal Boyer 2006. Whence Collective Rituals? A Cultural Selection Model of Ritualized Behavior. *American Anthropologist* 108(4): 814–827.

Lohmann, Roger (ed.) 2003. *Dream Travelers. Sleep Experiences and Culture in the Western Pacific.* New York: Palgrave Macmillan.

Marett, R. R. 1920. *Psychology and Folklore.* London: Methuen and Co. Ltd.

Reithofer, Hans 2005. *The Python Spirit and the Cross. Becoming Christian in a Highland Community of Papua New Guinea.* Berlin: Lit Verlag.

Robbins, Joel 2004. *Becoming Sinners: Christianity and Moral Torment in a Papua New Guinea Society.* Berkeley: University of California Press.

Stewart, Pamela J. 1998. Ritual trackways and sacred paths of fertility. In J. Miedema, Cecilia Ode, and Rien A.C. Dam eds. *Perspectives on the Bird's Head of Irian Jaya, Indonesia,* pp. 275–289. Amsterdam, The Netherlands and Atlanta, GA: Rodopi.

Stewart, Pamela J. and Andrew J. Strathern 1999. Female Spirit Cults as a Window on Gender Relations in the Highlands of Papua New Guinea. *The Journal of the Royal Anthropological Institute.* [Sept. 1999] 5(3):345–360.

Stewart, Pamela J. and Andrew Strathern (eds.) 2000a. *Identity Work: Constructing Pacific Lives.* Pittsburgh, PA: University of Pittsburgh Press.

Stewart, Pamela J. and Andrew Strathern 2000b. Introduction: Narratives Speak. In *Identity Work: Constructing Pacific Lives*, pp. 1–26. Pittsburgh, PA: University of Pittsburgh Press.

Stewart, Pamela J. and Andrew Strathern 2000c. Introduction: Latencies and Realizations in Millennial Practices. In, P.J. Stewart and A. Strathern (eds). Millennial Countdown in New Guinea, *Ethnohistory* Special Issue 47(1): 3–27.

Stewart, Pamela J. and Andrew Strathern 2000d. Naming Places: Duna Evocations of Landscape in Papua New Guinea. *People and Culture in Oceania* 16:87–107.

Stewart, Pamela J. and Andrew Strathern 2001a. *Humors and Substances: Ideas of the Body in New Guinea.* Westport, CT and London: Bergin and Garvey.

Stewart, Pamela J. and Andrew Strathern 2001b. Foreword: Pentecostal and Charismatic Christianity in Oceania. Special Issue, "Pentecostal and Charismatic Christianity in Oceania" edited by Joel Robbins, Pamela J. Stewart and Andrew Strathern. *Journal of Ritual Studies* 15.2: 4–6.

Stewart, Pamela J. and Andrew Strathern 2001c. The Great Exchange: Moka with God. Special Issue, "Pentecostal and Charismatic Christianity in Oceania" edited by Joel Robbins, Pamela J. Stewart, and Andrew Strathern. *Journal of Ritual Studies* 15.2: 91–104.

Stewart, Pamela J. and Andrew Strathern 2002a. *Remaking the World: Myth, Mining and Ritual Change among the Duna of Papua New Guinea.* For, Smithsonian Series in Ethnographic Inquiry, Washington, D.C.: Smithsonian Institution Press.

Stewart, Pamela J. and Andrew Strathern 2002b. *Gender, Song, and Sensibility: Folktales and Folksongs in the Highlands of New Guinea.* Westport, CT and London: Praeger Publishers (Greenwood Publishing).

Stewart, Pamela J. and Andrew Strathern 2002c. Water in place: The Hagen and Duna people of Papua New Guinea. *Journal of Ritual Studies* 16.1 (2002) pp. 108–119.

Stewart, Pamela J. and Andrew Strathern 2003. Dreaming and Ghosts among the Hagen and Duna of the Southern Highlands, Papua New Guinea. In *Dream Travelers: Sleep Experiences and Culture in the Western Pacific*, Roger Ivar Lohmann (ed.), pp. 42–59. New York: Palgrave Macmillan.

Stewart, Pamela J. and Andrew Strathern 2004 *Witchcraft, Sorcery, Rumors, and Gossip*. For, New Departures in Anthropology Series, Cambridge: Cambridge University Press.

Stewart, Pamela J. and Andrew Strathern (eds.) 2005a. *Expressive Genres and Historical Change: Indonesia, Papua New Guinea and Taiwan*. For, Anthropology and Cultural History in Asia and the Indo-Pacific Series, London, U.K. and Burlington, VT: Ashgate Publishing.

Stewart, Pamela J. and Andrew Strathern 2005b. Cosmology, Resources, and Landscape: Agencies of the Dead and the Living in Duna, Papua New Guinea. *Ethnology* 44(1): 35–47.

Stewart, Pamela J. and Andrew Strathern 2005c. The Death of Moka in Post-Colonial Mount Hagen, Highlands, Papua New Guinea. In, *The Making of Global and Local Modernities in Melanesia. Humiliation, Transformation and the Nature of Cultural Change*, edited by Joel Robbins and Holly Wardlow, pp. 125–134. For, Anthropology and Cultural History in Asia and the Indo-Pacific Series, London, U.K. and Burlington, VT: Ashgate Publishing.

Strathern, Andrew and Pamela J. Stewart 1997. Introduction. Millennial Markers in the Pacific. In *Millennial Markers*. Stewart, Pamela J. And Andrew Strathern (eds.). Townsville: James Cook University, Centre for Pacific Studies, pp. 1–17.

Strathern, Andrew and Pamlea J. Stewart 1998a. Seeking Personhood: Anthropological Accounts and Local Concepts in Mt. Hagen, Papua New Guinea. *Oceania* 68(3): 170–188.

Strathern, Andrew and Pamela J. Stewart 1998b. Embodiment and Communication: Two Frames for the Analysis of Ritual. Social Anthropology (Journal of the European Association of Social Anthropologists) 6(2): 237–251.

Strathern Andrew and Pamela J. Stewart 1999a. *Collaborations and Conflicts. A Leader Through Time*. Fort Worth Texas: Harcourt Brace College Publishers.

Strathern, Andrew and Pamela J. Stewart 1999b. *"The Spirit is Coming!" A Photographic-Textual Exposition of the Female Spirit Cult Performance in Mt. Hagen*. Ritual Studies Monograph Series, Monograph No. 1. Pittsburgh.

Strathern, Andrew and Pamela J. Stewart 2000a. *Arrow Talk: Transaction, Transition, and Contradiction in New Guinea Highlands History*. Kent, Ohio and London: Kent State University Press.

Strathern, Andrew and Pamela J. Stewart 2000b. *Stories, Strength & Self-Narration. Western Highlands, Papua New Guinea*. Adelaide, Australia: Crawford House Publishing.

Strathern, Andrew and Pamela J. Stewart 2000c. *The Python's Back: Pathways of Comparison between Indonesia and Melanesia*. Westport, Conn. and London: Bergin and Garvey, Greenwood Publishing Group.

Strathern, Andrew and Pamela J. Stewart 2003. Divisions of Power: Rituals in Time and Space among the Hagen and Duna Peoples, Papua New Guinea. *Taiwan Journal of Anthropology* 1(1): 51–76.

Strathern, Andrew and Pamela J. Stewart 2004a. *Empowering the Past, Confronting the Future, The Duna People of Papua New Guinea*. For, Contemporary Anthropology of Religion Series, New York: Palgrave Macmillan.

Strathern, Andrew and Pamela J. Stewart 2004b. Cults, Closures, Collaborations. In, *Women as Unseen Characters. Male Ritual in Papua New Guinea*, Association for Social Anthropology in Oceania Monograph Series, edited by Pascale Bonnemere, pp. 120–138. Philadelphia, PA: University of Pennsylvania Press.

Strathern, Andrew and Pamela J. Stewart 2005. Witchcraft, Sorcery, Rumors , and Gossip: Terror and the Imagination—A State of Lethal Play. *The Central States Anthropological Society Bulletin* 40.1: 8–14.

Strathern, Andrew and Pamela J. Stewart 2006. *"Witchcraft and Rumor: A synthetic Approach"* Keynote presentation in Annual Ethnological Society meeting at the Institute of Ethnology, Academia Sinica, Taipei, Taiwan, 26 June 2005. *Newsletter of Taiwanese Anthropology and Ethnology* 39:3–34.

Strathern, Andrew and Pamela J. Stewart n.d. Bamboo Knives, Bows, and Waterfalls. The Presentation of 'Traditional' Knowledge in Melpa *Kang Rom* and Duna *Pikono*. For volume on Chanted Tales edited by Alan Rumsey.

Tambiah, Stanley 1968 . The Magical Power of Words. *Man* 3: 175–208.

Throop C.J. and C.D. Laughlin 2002. Ritual, Collective Effervescence and the Categories . Toward a New Neo-Durkheimian Model of the Nature of Human Consciousness, Feeling and Understanding. *Journal of Ritual Studies* 16(1): 40–63.

Whitehouse, Harvey, Brian Malley, Pascal Boyer, Fredrik Barth, Michael Houseman, Robert N. McCauley, Luther H. Martin, Tom Sjoblom, and Garry W. Trompf. 2002. JRS Book Review Forum of *Arguments and Icons: Divergent Modes of Religiousity*, Harvey Whitehouse. *Journal of Ritual Studies* 16(2): 4–59.

CONTRIBUTING AUTHORS

Rita Astuti is a Reader in Anthropology at the London School of Economics and Political Science. She has conducted extensive fieldwork among the Vezo of Madagascar and her writings have focused on issues of gender, ethnic identity and kinship. In her more recent work, she has combined anthropological and psychological methods to explore how Vezo children construct the adult understanding of the social and supernatural world. She is the author of *People of the sea* and of *Constraints on conceptual development* (with G. Solomon & S. Carey).

Justin L. Barrett earned degrees in psychology from Calvin College (B.A.) and Cornell University (Ph.D). He served on the psychology faculties of Calvin College and the University of Michigan (Ann Arbor), and as a research fellow of the Institute for Social Research. Dr. Barrett is an editor of the *Journal of Cognition & Culture* and is author of numerous articles and chapters concerning cognitive science of religion. His book *Why Would Anyone Believe in God?* (2004) presents a scientific account for the prevalence of religious beliefs. He is currently Senior Researcher at the University of Oxford's Centre for Anthropology and Mind.

Maurice Bloch is Emeritus professor of anthropology at the London School of Economics and Political Science. He is also occasional professor in the anthropology department of the Free University of Amsterdam. His two most recent books are *How we Think they Think* and *Essays in Cultural Transmission*.

Emma Cohen is a post-doctoral researcher at the Centre for Anthropology and Mind at the University of Oxford. She completed her PhD in 2005 at the Institute of Cognition and Culture, Queen's University Belfast, where she remained for a further 18 months as a research fellow. She has carried out ethnographic fieldwork on an Afro-Brazilian religious tradition in Belém, northern Brazil. Her first book, *The Mind Possessed* (in press, OUP), combines cross-cultural ethnographic analysis with perspectives and findings from the cognitive sciences, and contributes to the developing field of cognitive science of religion.

Stewart E. Guthrie (Ph.D. Yale 1976) is Prof. Emeritus of Anthropology at Fordham University and a founding member of the Society for the Anthropology of Religion. His fieldwork has been in Japan (e.g., A Japanese New Religion), with surveys elsewhere. The central propositions of his 1980 *A cognitive theory of religion* have been widely adopted in cognitive studies of religion: that our sense of unseen intentional agency stems from a better-safe-than-sorry perceptual strategy, producing hair-trigger judgments that agents (or their traces) are present; that these agents have humanlike mentality and communications; and that we bet on them because they provide the most significant and powerful interpretations possible. He elaborates these ideas in *Faces in the Clouds* and elsewhere.

James Laidlaw is a Fellow of King's College, Cambridge and lecturer in the Department of Social Anthropology at Cambridge University. He has conducted ethnographic research in India (on Jainism), and in Inner Mongolia (on Buddhism), and his latest research is on new Buddhist movements in Taiwan. His publications include *Riches and Renunciation* and (with Caroline Humphrey) *The Archetypal Actions of Ritual*, as well as the two-volume *The Essential Edmund Leach* (edited, with Stephen Hugh-Jones).

Jonathan A. Lanman is a post-graduate student at the newly formed Centre for Anthropology and Mind and the Institute of Cognitive and Evolutionary Anthropology at the University of Oxford. Before arriving at Oxford in 2006, he received an M.A. in Religious Studies from the University of Missouri, Columbia and Ph.D. candidacy from the Institute of Cognition and Culture at Queen's University, Belfast. His contribution to this volume is a condensed version of his Master's thesis.

Jesper Sørensen is Associate Professor in Comparative Religion at University of Southern Denmark. Trained in history of religion and cognitive semiotics, his principal research interests lie in the cognitive science of religion. His book *A Cognitive Theory of Magic* (2006) focuses on ritual, magic and the transmission of religious ideas. He is a founding member of the International Association for the Cognitive Science of Religion and has recently been an International Fellow at the Institute of Cognition and Culture, Queen's University, Belfast and a Visiting Professor at the Department of Psychology, Washington University, St. Louis.

Harvey Whitehouse is Professor of Social Anthropology at the University of Oxford and a Professorial Fellow of Magdalen College. After carrying out two years of field research on a 'cargo cult' in New Britain, Papua New Guinea in the late eighties, he developed a theory of 'modes of religiosity' that has been the subject of extensive critical evaluation and testing by anthropologists, historians, archaeologists, and cognitive scientists. In recent years, he has focused his energies on the development of collaborative programmes of research on cognition and culture. His books include *Inside the Cult* (1995), *Arguments and Icons* (2000), and *Modes of Religiosity* (2004).

Religion, Anthropology, and Cognitive Science

INTRODUCTION

James Laidlaw & Harvey Whitehouse

All anthropologists must be aware of the tremendous energy and confidence currently enjoyed in the fields of evolutionary science and cognitive psychology. Many are at least dimly conscious of the high-profile synthesis of these fields that goes by the name of evolutionary psychology;[1] fewer are really informed about its nature and scope or familiar with the arguments within the relevant scientific communities as to its validity or otherwise.[2] And fewer still realise that in the 'cognitive science of religion' there now exists a burgeoning research programme that draws directly on the intellectual currency of these endeavours, concerns itself with topics and questions that are central to anthropology, and includes as prominent participants an increasing number of anthropologists. This book is designed to present this field to social and cultural anthropologists and to others, such as historians of religion, who draw on anthropological theories and analyses.

The cognitive science of religion has claims on the professional interest of all anthropologists, and not only those with specific interests in religion, for it has implications for the most general questions in the discipline about the nature of human social life and of anthropological knowledge. Furthermore, it has attracted and is likely to continue to attract considerable attention and interest among a wide readership outside anthropology: academics right across the range of disciplines, potential students, public authorities and policy makers, and the educated general public. Several recent volumes have put forward

---

1. For some time, the central text was Barkow et al (1992), updated in Hirschfeld & Gelman (1994), Barrett et al (2002), and Carruthers et al (2005) but the new 'bible' of evolutionary psychology is arguably now Buss (2005). Blockbuster popularisations meanwhile include Wright (1994), Pinker (1997), and Buss (1999).

2. For general arguments against, see Rose & Rose (2000), for more focused ones Fodor (2001); for related critical discussion see Karmiloff-Smith (1996), Laland & Brown (2002), Sterelny (2003), Sterelny & Fitness (2003), and Buller (2005); for an anthropological debate, Whitehouse (2001); and for an anthropological/political attack, McKinnon (2006).

synoptic views by anthropologists (Boyer 2001, Atran 2002, Whitehouse 2004) and others (Hinde 1999, Barrett 2004, Pyysiäinen 2001, 2004, Tremlin 2006, Slone 2006).[3] The prestige of evolutionary science is likely to ensure continuing interest. In 2006 alone at least three much-hyped works of 'popular science' by best-selling authors (Dawkins 2006, Dennett 2006, Wolpert 2006) drew heavily on this field.[4] Academics in other fields, potential anthropology students, funding bodies, and the public in general will expect anthropologists to be interested in the big and important questions that lie behind such works,[5] to be able to give them informed and considered responses to the whole enterprise, and responses also to some at least of the specific arguments and claims, claims that we may expect (otherwise) to gain general currency.

So it is neither intellectually defensible nor professionally prudent for anthropologists to remain unacquainted with the cognitive science of religion. Whether one agrees or disagrees with its tenets and claims, it is part of the general intellectual landscape and offers answers (plausible or otherwise) to many questions that in some form or another are inescapable for any seriously reflective person, and with which anthropology, if seriously reflective, will always want to engage. Some anthropologists may conclude that the influence of evolutionary and cognitive psychology is wholly malign, that the important questions become distorted and malformed in their hands, and that the declared results and findings are therefore worthless. Others may become persuaded, as several contributors to this volume have, that in this new paradigm anthropology can be profitably integrated into a productive and truly scientific inter-disciplinary enterprise that will achieve, at last, genuinely cumulative scientific knowledge of religion. Others still may reach one of many possible more qualified views, which would require, among other things, an ability to tell good from poor versions of the ideas and applications of the methods. This volume is designed so as maximally to help anthropologists to come to an informed view, and it does so by focusing on cognitive approaches to issues that have attracted considerable attention in the history of anthropology.

---

3. In addition, the following collections of essays are relevant: Andresen 2001, Pyysiäinen & Anttonen 2002, Whitehouse & McCauley 2005.

4. All three works are not just ambitious and would-be comprehensive explanatory theories of religion, but also debunking attacks upon it. Whether this is mere coincidence, or to be expected in the light of some of the approach's basic postulates, which are likely to attract those who are hostile to religion, is a matter on which the editors of this volume differ.

5. See Bloch's (2006) eloquent complaint that too few anthropologists fulfil their responsibilities in this regard.

Anthropology and Religion

Anthropologists and other students of religion have produced many richly detailed descriptions of religious traditions, and their myriad offshoots and variants, around the world. The picture that has emerged from this work is one of considerable variability in cosmology, myth, ritual procedure, religious institutions, organisations, and roles, and in representations of deities, saints, ancestors, and other supernatural beings. True, some religious traditions, including those commonly referred to as the 'world religions', have spread more widely than others, often displacing, suppressing, assimilating, or blending with others, processes that have been greatly accelerated by those of colonization and globalization in recent centuries. But despite certain obvious homogenizing effects of these processes, they have in turn generated a host of new kinds of local innovation and differentiation and religious pluralism. All of this too has been well documented in the literature, as have processes of 'conversion' and 'syncretism'. Taken together with ethnographic evidence gathered in populations on or beyond the margins of these great waves of religious transmission and innovation, for instance in remote parts of Oceania, Amazonia, Asia, and Africa, it may seem that few areas of cultural innovation have given rise to diversity comparable to that which we find in religion.

Of course, patterns of kinship, marriage, production, inheritance, exchange, consumption, social organization, conflict, and technological innovation all show considerable variation as well. It might seem, however, that material constraints impose themselves rather more strikingly in the latter domains. The range of ways of producing and rearing offspring, of making a living, and of co-operating with or coercing one's fellows are in both obvious and non-obvious ways limited by biology and prevailing ecology. Religion might seem to tether the human imagination rather less closely. When the structural anthropologist Claude Lévi-Strauss shifted his area of interest, from early studies of kinship and social organisation to mythology, it was indeed on the grounds that the relative lack of material constraint would allow 'the structure of thought' to express itself more freely and therefore more perfectly (Lévi-Strauss 1970). Religion, perhaps like the arts and sciences, would seem to be limited only by our capacities to conjure up new ideas, within whatever framework we have learned from those around us. And ideas, we might think, are potentially unlimited, like the infinite range of possible sentences in a natural language.

But this emphasis, in anthropological and other studies of religion, on the *variety* of ideas and practices, has been balanced by the fact that scholars have repeatedly noticed many *recurrent* features of religious thought and practice across the world. Much effort has been expended in various quite different attempts in anthropology and comparative religion to delineate and characterise and in some cases to explain these patterns of recurrence. From these ambitions have arisen classifications of types of religion, and of rituals and ceremonies (from sacrifices to funerals), religious specialization (from shamanism to divine kingship), forms of theistic belief (from paganism to ancestor worship), religious organization (from totemism to ecclesiastical hierarchy), and so on. Even if much more energy has gone of late into more middle-range theoretical questions—the relation between scriptural orthodoxy and local practice *within* a world religion such as Islam, or what if anything cargo cults might have in common—the persistent use of these general classificatory terms, notwithstanding that many of them have been 'deconstructed' at some time or other, testifies to the resilience of the basic perception that there are obvious commonalities across religious traditions.

Some attempts by anthropologists to explain cross-cultural recurrence in the domain of religion have proven less empirically productive than others. The least successful have generally been the most ambitious. As is well known, various forms of universal evolutionism were fashionable until the early twentieth century (and of course remained so for much longer in the socialist world), with intermittent revivals since (cultural ecology, socio-biology, structural Marxism, and so on). Most theories of this kind, including the classics of Tylor and Frazer, were not remotely Darwinian, in that they did not propose mechanisms of selection but instead that all human societies passed through one or more series of evolutionary stages, entailing distinguishable levels of complexity.[6] Theories of this kind gave way briefly to the hypothesis that recurrent features of the religious repertoire spread among human populations through processes of diffusion. Clearly, religious ideas and practices do get passed on from person to person and from one generation to the next. In that sense, diffusion, or something like it, surely has contributed to the recurrence of religious forms across wide areas. But this leaves much to be explained. How does the transmission occur? Why are some religious innovations transmitted and others not? And how are we to explain patterns of *independent invention* across civilizations?

To address these questions, anthropologists have taken a range of very different approaches. Some have simply resisted addressing them explicitly in general terms at all, but where this is the case their proposals for how to understand particular cases have of course depended, willy-nilly, on implicit assumptions about general principles, types, and processes. Others have looked

---

6. See Ingold's (1986) discussion of evolutionary social theories.

for general mechanisms that might shape and constrain the innovation and transmission of religion at all times and places. Considerable effort in the history of the discipline has been devoted to the search for such mechanisms in the arena of the *social*. Are there general features of the way social relations are configured or reproduced that might account for regularities in religious thinking and behaviour? Might particular forms of social organization give rise to corresponding religious ideas and institutions? A very great deal of anthropological writing on religion—one way or another all that takes its bearings from Marx or Durkheim, and even some of that which is more indebted to Weber—has supposed so. For some in these traditions, the very idea of a social explanation of religion has involved the principled exclusion of psychology. This of course was an article of faith for Durkheim, and has been for many since. But others, especially those inclined to theorise in terms of culture rather than social relations or sociality, have looked to psychology as a source of inspiration. Is religion a response to some set of universal intellectual, cognitive, or emotional characteristics in our species? Traditions of intellectualist, phenomenological, structuralist, and Freudian analysis have all offered positive answers to this question. So does cognitive science, but in its own distinctive ways.

While Freudian psychologists, for example, have thought of religion as being a response to certain emotional needs, cognitive psychologists do not have to postulate any such needs. Religion is rather a range of *effects* of the way our brains are constructed. The defining and foundational premise of the cognitive-science approach is that the *mechanisms* by means of which humans learn, think, perceive, remember, and so on, affect the *content* of their thoughts and behaviour. The brain is understood to be a complex set of functioning mechanisms of information processing: the outputs (thoughts and behaviour) will depend upon the inputs (the environment as perceived and experienced) but also on the mechanisms that come in between. The mechanisms, in turn, may be explained as the product of evolution (which is where evolutionary psychology may come in), although even if no explanation for the evolution of a mechanism is available, its existence and functioning could in principle be described, and the hope and claim of cognitive science is that this provides an explanation for the representations and behaviour the mechanism delivers.

Virtually all cognitive scientists deny that any single or limited set of mechanisms are responsible for religion—there is no religious module in the brain. Rather, the effects we call religion are, they claim, explained severally by a wide range of different mechanisms, operating in the context of certain environmental inputs, and interacting with each other. These are the same general causes that explain other, non-religious, features of human cognition. The cognitive science of religion is thus theoretically and methodologically fully a part of the general enterprise of cognitive science, but has so far taken as its special subject matter—this is therefore how 'religion' is operationally defined for the purposes of much of the research initially undertaken—beliefs and behaviour concerning culturally postulated supernatural beings and entities. Since these entities, being supernatural, are particularly underdetermined by the usual 'inputs' to human cognition—the environment as experienced and perceived by the human animal—cognitive mechanisms are likely, according to this way of modelling human thought and action, to play an unusually large part in accounting for the 'outputs', and this is where the special challenges and opportunities lie for the cognitive science of religion. It is also why co-operation with anthropologists seems to some of its proponents to be apposite.

It should be noted at the outset that a central ambition shared by cognitive psychology and evolutionary psychology is that the social sciences in general, and for these purposes anthropology in particular, be formulated explicitly *as sciences* in method and theory, so that they play a more prominent role in the cumulative advances taking place across a broader range of sciences (e.g. Tooby & Cosmides 1992; Sperber 1996, 2001; Whitehouse 2002). Although this ambition runs counter to most of the main trends in anthropology over the last two to three decades (and for longer in some schools of anthropology) it is not of course a new one: many of the founders of the discipline shared a view that anthropology is or should be in some sense a 'science', either resembling or simply part of the natural sciences. Of course, they did not all mean the same thing by this, and since Evans-Pritchard at least there have been eloquent spokesmen for a contrary view. 'Cognitive anthropology' has been a minor tradition within anthropology that has persisted with this scientific ambition through decades that have been largely dominated by symbolic, interpretive, post-modern, post-structuralist, and phenomenological approaches in anthropology (see D'Andrade 1995).

The idea that developments in cognitive psychology might be fruitfully applied to culture in general and religion in particular has been around for quite a long time, although the first generations of cognitive anthropologists concentrated overwhelmingly on mundane knowledge rather than religion (e.g. Tyler 1969). So the focus of interest was first on trying to represent the organisation of kin terms—from the foundational papers by Lounsbury (1956) and Goodenough (1956), and their followers (Romney & D'Andrade 1964)—then on ethnoscience and the study of folk taxonomies (from Berlin et al 1968 through Berlin 1992) and colour terms (Berlin & Kay 1969). Occasionally, a cognitive analysis might deal with the organisation of a ritual (Metzger & Williams 1963) but generally this kind of early 'formal analysis' was applied to subjects other than religion, and even here the analysis was purely of the cultural knowledge of organisation of activities, with little attention to religious content or meaning. Subsequent developing interest in modelling the way humans learn—most productively through schema theory, and the concepts of mental models and connectionist networks—also concentrated on everyday processes, such as basic technical and co-operative production processes (e.g. Gladwin 1970; Hutchins 1983, 1994; Gatewood 1985; Lave 1988).

This line of research has developed, on the one hand, into the idea of 'cultural models' which has occupied a group of American psychological anthropologists over recent decades (see Holland & Quinn 1987, D'Andrade & Strauss 1992, Quinn & Strauss 1998), but this has not so far led to or included much sustained interest in religion. On the other hand, connectionism helped to attract Maurice Bloch to cognitive science, and convinced him of its importance for anthropology. Although prefigured in some of his earlier writings,[7] Bloch's renewed interest in cognitive science was very influentially declared in his 1990 Frazer Lecture, 'Language, Anthropology, and Cognitive Science' (1991). Bloch was already a distinguished anthropologist, well known on account of writings characterised by quite other (principally Marxist and Durkheimian) theoretical influences, and therefore had an established reputation among anthropologists who were not remotely interested in cognitive science as such. Moreover, Bloch had an established research interest in religion and ritual (see Bloch 1971, 1986, and the essays collected in 1989), resulting from his ethnographic fieldwork in Madagascar. So his 'conversion' (as it was seen by many, both friendly and hostile to cognitive science) attracted considerable notice, especially in the UK.

The approach Bloch was attracted to, and in particular a set of arguments for the special relevance of cognitive science for the anthropology of religion, already had powerful expression in France. In the mid 1970s, in *Rethinking Symbolism* (published in French in 1974, then in English in 1975), Dan Sperber developed a sustained and compelling critique of Freudian, symbolist, and structuralist approaches to religious symbolism, and outlined a cognitive approach, which he developed in subsequent publications (1982, 1985a). In

---

7. A fine example would be Bloch's seminal paper 'Symbol, Song, Dance, and Features of Articulation' (1974), which asked how ritual could have some of its observed effects and social importance other than through the creation and communication of shared meaning, which most anthropologists, following Durkheim, had assumed to be the case. In that paper Bloch drew on writings by philosophers and others in 'speech act theory' in a line of thought that has been developed further by others, e.g. Humphrey & Laidlaw (1994), Keane (1997), and, in a more exclusively cognitive vein, Sørensen (this volume).

these works Sperber developed the first account of what might be distinctive, in cognitive terms, about 'symbolic' representations. Then, in his 1984 Malinowski Memorial Lecture (Sperber 1985b), he set out his 'epidemiological' model of the transmission of cultural representations, and this has been foundational for the whole of the cognitive science of religion. Sperber provided an account of the shaping and constraining effects of evolved cognitive capacities on the spread of public representations and, crucially, combined this with a selectionist (therefore broadly Darwinian) model of cultural change. In so doing, he laid out a quite sharply delineated conception of what a cognitive anthropology of religion might look like (see also Sperber 1990, 1994, 1996, 2005). It is one that has been influential on a number of authors in the field, especially those with an anthropological training, including Bloch, and also Rita Astuti, Scott Atran, Pascal Boyer, Lawrence Hirschfeld, Brian Malley, and Harvey Whitehouse.

Sperber's influence on the study of religion also extended beyond anthropology. For instance, it provided inspiration to the collaborations of E. Thomas Lawson (comparative religionist) and Robert N. McCauley (philosopher). The first major work to arise from this alliance, *Rethinking Religion* (Lawson and McCauley 1990), deliberately played on the title of Sperber's earlier volume on symbolism and built on the latter's fundamental claim that the institutions of society (religious or otherwise) do not affect each other directly but only through the micro-mechanisms of cognition that mediate all forms of human interaction. The central argument of *Rethinking Religion* was that religious rituals, just like natural language in a Chomskean paradigm, conform to a set of underlying universal constraints on their forms. In time, Lawson and McCauley came to focus more specifically on the question of variable patterns of ritual transmission, bringing them into extended dialogue with the work of Harvey Whitehouse. In 1992, Whitehouse published an article in *Man*, arguing that the frequency of ritual performances had implications for the emotionality, memorability, and transmission of religious knowledge, laying the foundations for his subsequent theory of 'modes of religiosity' (1995, 2000, 2004). Lawson and McCauley had been thinking along similar lines and, a decade later, published an extended critique of the Whitehouse corpus, entitled *Bringing Ritual to Mind* (McCauley and Lawson 2002). In that volume they argued that while the 'modes of religiosity' theory might correctly account for major patterns of divergence in the social morphology of religious traditions, it ultimately rested on claims about major mechanisms of human memory and, consequently, about the effects of variable frequencies of ritual performance. Some rituals are performed only very rarely, and in some cases (such as rites of passage) people undergo them only once in a lifetime. Other rituals, however, may be highly routinized, being subject to repetition on a daily or weekly basis. In Whitehouse's theory of religious modes, ritual frequency affects the *way* participants remember what happened (or happens), and this claim forms part of a web of hypotheses concerning levels of arousal, systems of memory, modes of transmission, and divergent patterns in the scale and structure of religious traditions. According to McCauley and Lawson, however, ritual frequency constitutes the *unexplained independent variable* of the modes theory. If one could show why some rituals are rarely performed and others much more frequently repeated, they argued, then all (or most) of the other predictions of the modes theory naturally follow. But without an explanation for that single variable, at the base of the model (as McCauley and Lawson saw it), the modes theory is substantially incomplete. The missing piece of the jigsaw, they maintained, lay in considerations of what they call 'ritual form'.

According to Lawson and McCauley all actions, ritual included, involve certain essential ingredients: an agent (who acts), a patient (who/which is acted upon), an action (of course) and, sometimes, an instrument (by means of which the agent acts on the patient). In a very simple ritual, for instance, the priest (agent) may sprinkle water (action) on a person (patient) using a special receptacle holding the holy liquid (instruments). The 'ritual form hypothesis' proposes that, in all religious rituals, supernatural agents are invariably represented as playing a special role (indeed this is, without remainder, how Lawson and McCauley define and characterise religious ritual, see Laidlaw & Humphrey 2006), associating them particularly with one of the main 'slots' in the action scheme. In 'special agent rituals' this association with a supernatural being is strongest in relation to the agent 'slot' (e.g. the deity is seen as acting through the priest, as for instance in ordinations and weddings). In 'special patient' and 'special instrument' rituals the supernatural association is strongest in relation to the patient or instrument slots respectively (e.g. the deity is seen as the recipient of the ritual, as for instance in a sacrifice, or is somehow manifested in the instrument, as for instance in a blessing). According to McCauley and Lawson, all religious rituals belong to one of the three categories in their typology and this is what determines the frequency with which they are performed.[8] Special agent rituals are always relatively low

---

8. We should note that this claim is not uncontroversial, and applies only to the set of actions defined by their theory as religious rituals. Other analysts have suggested in different ways that not just action but also specifically *inter*-action (situations in which, so to speak, agents are mutually patients to each other) comes to take on distinctive features

in frequency because what the god has done cannot be undone (unless by further special agent rituals, such as rites of divorce or defrocking, that serve to reverse the effects of the original ceremony). By contrast, special patient/instrument rituals are usually relatively high frequency because the effects of actions performed by ordinary agents are impermanent (and also non-reversible). On the basis of these arguments, McCauley and Lawson proceeded to develop a series of further predictions concerning the relative emotionality and memorability of rituals, as well as their relative centrality in religious systems, thereby incorporating (as well as challenging, modifying, and extending in various ways) the principal claims of Whitehouse's modes theory. (For a detailed rejoinder, see Whitehouse 2004: Chapter 8).

The debate between Whitehouse and Lawson & McCauley is important in part because Whitehouse's data remain virtually the only body of first-hand ethnography of religion of any breadth and comprehensiveness (as distinct from relatively de-contextualised single-issue experiments) to have been published by an anthropologist in the form of an analysis in (substantially) cognitive-scientific terms (for some anthropologists' discussion and critique, see the essays in Whitehouse & Laidlaw 2004). Bloch and Astuti, having conducted and analysed their initial fieldwork in different terms, are now conducting more and are analysing and publishing within, though not exclusively within, a cognitive-science framework. Other leading theorists in the field (such as Boyer and Sperber), despite having conducted ethnographic fieldwork, have never published monographs analysing their own data in a sustained way using the cognitivist methods and conceptual frameworks they recommend.[9] A few anthropologists have nevertheless found it fruitful to incorporate insights from cognitive science into ethnographic analyses, sometimes as fairly important elements, but where the general theoretical orientation has been in other terms (e.g. Gell 1980, 1992, 1995, Barth 1987, Humphrey & Laidlaw 1994, Humphrey 1996, Lewis 1980, Stafford 1995). But,

---

when ritualized. See for example Bloch (ed. 1975), Humphrey & Laidlaw (1994), and Houseman & Severi (1998).

9. Although there have been very few if any studies in the cognitive science of culture that social anthropologists would recognise as a full-scale ethnographic monographs, there have been various collaborative projects, in which anthropologists have been involved, that have attempted to combine ethnographic and experimental methods. For instance, one such programme is using the *methods* of ethnography and scientific psychology, and the *theories* of experimental economics and evolutionary anthropology, to investigate both recurrent and variable features of patterns of human cooperation cross-culturally (e.g. Henrich *et al* 2004; see also e.g. H. C. Barrett 2004, Fessler 2004, Richerson and Boyd 2004).

in general, the cognitive science of religion has had relatively little to say about the relevance of its findings for the practice of ethnography.[10] And almost no full-scale published ethnographic monographs on religion are informed, overall, by the methods and theories of cognitive science. But of course this in itself does not mean they cannot be. If this situation is to change, we may expect it to do so imminently, as PhD students of the established theorists, and others, begin to publish the results of new research. The first of these to appear was Malley (2004), to be followed by Cohen (in press), and others expected thereafter.

To sum up the situation so far: within the large and loosely integrated fields of cognitive science and evolutionary psychology, there has emerged a relatively tightly-knit group of scholars engaged in what has become known as the 'cognitive science of religion'. This group of scholars enjoys an unusual measure of agreement on shared presuppositions, methods, and problems. Over the last twenty years or so they have succeeded in establishing not only a paradigm for their research, but also several institutional centres around the world, a journal and book series, and a substantial literature based on new empirical research that has given rise to a series of new research problems.[11] Yet despite this institutional success, and their shared sense of conceptual and empirical *progress* in the problems they have set themselves, some social and cultural anthropologists have remained actively resistant to the implications of cognitive research. Part of the reason for this lies in the fact that the data around which discussion is concentrated are not substantially derived from recognisably ethnographic literature: not, as just noted, from new research published in the form of ethnographic monographs, and not upon the existing great anthropological studies of religion which constitute the shared knowledge base of anthropologists. Instead, many of the data borrowed and generated by the cognitive science of religion come from research in experimental psychology carried out in Western settings.

---

10. Exceptions include Liénard & Anselmo (2005), Roepstorf *et al.* (2003), and Sousa (2003).

11. The institutions and projects include the Institute of Cognition and Culture at Queen's University Belfast, the new Centre for Anthropology and Mind at Oxford University, the Centre for Religion and Cognition in Groningen, the Culture and Cognition Program at the University of Michigan, the Religion, Cognition, and Culture Project at the University of Aarhus, the Mind and Society in the Transmission of Religion Project at the University of Helsinki. The *Journal of Cognition and Culture* is published by Brill and the Cognitive Science of Religion book series by AltaMira Press.

Anthropology and the Cognitive Science of Religion

One aim of the present volume is to provide an opportunity for that situation to begin to change, and to this end we asked some contributors directly to address the question of what cognitive science has to contribute to the problems that dominate the work of some of the great anthropological theorists of religion (such as Durkheim, Malinowski, and Evans-Pritchard) and also to some topics (such as the study of witchcraft, afterlife beliefs, ancestors, and deities) that have always loomed large in the anthropology of religion. In this way we hoped to help to encourage dialogue between cognitive scientists of religion and social and cultural anthropologists, and so to enable a process to take place in which each can explore whether and to what extent they might productively learn from the other. We asked the contributors, who with the exception of Laidlaw would all describe themselves as participants in the 'cognitive science of religion', to try to show how problems historically central to the anthropology of religion might be fruitfully addressed by means of cognitive theories.

Consider, for instance, the venerable intellectual tradition instigated by Emile Durkheim (1995 [1912]) that came to be known as the 'symbolist' perspective on religion. At the heart of that perspective is the idea that religion symbolizes the transcendental character of society. Society transcends us in at least three ways: it outlives us (individuals come and go but the institutions of society have at least notional continuity); it seems to create us rather than being our own creation (individuals are often endowed with established roles, offices, and statuses rather than having to invent them); it regulates our behaviour (individuals feel themselves to be constrained by laws and codes of conduct and often have little personal influence over the content of those rules). Durkheim's genius was to observe that these are the very same properties we attribute to religious entities and objects (which he referred to collectively as 'the sacred'). Just like society, sacred things (gods, totemic species, ancestors, ritual objects and so on) are widely attributed transcendental properties of permanence, creativity, and supervisory prominence. To put it crudely the gods are construed as immortal, the source of life, and the source of all authority. But if we accept this interpretation a number of questions present themselves. If all have the same functions, and these and only these properties are necessary to religion, why do religions differ in the dramatic ways they do? Why do people not dispense with religious constructs altogether and simply recognize that these properties belong to society rather than to some 'other world'? Durkheim's expectation, of course, like those of many others before him who had been inspired by Positivist versions of Enlightenment thought, was that this was indeed going to happen, and that modernity would see the replacement of traditional religions with new, rationally-based forms of social solidarity. With the possible exception of Marx's detailed script for the collapse of capitalism and its replacement by socialism (declining rates of profit, class polarization, system collapse, and violent revolution) this widespread thesis of 'secularisation' is perhaps the most spectacularly and comprehensively falsified empirical prediction in the social sciences. Cognitive scientists aspire to be at least equally definite about their predictions, but of course empirically correct.

Thanks to a growing body of scientific research on the way minds perceive, encode, recall, infer, calculate, and perform other astonishing feats of information processing, cognitive scientists have developed quite a rich picture of the strengths and weaknesses of human cognitive capabilities. Some things we appear to do brilliantly: for instance, we recognize faces and remember patterns of behaviour we have seen or heard on only a single occasion, perhaps days or weeks ago, perhaps under very different circumstances from those in which the remembrance occurs. Or we make astonishingly accurate and convergent interpretations of other people's emotional states based on cues so subtle that giving formal description of them and/or subjecting them to experimental measurement is extremely difficult. Even the world's most powerful supercomputers have difficulties performing tasks of this kind—and some of the computations that humans accomplish automatically and effortlessly cannot (yet?) be simulated by artificial intelligence at all. But at the same time even an average home computer can carry out tasks that are utterly beyond our mental faculties, such as the manipulation of large numbers by means of mathematical rules or the exact storage of lists of lexical items. Minds and computers are good at doing rather different kinds of things. If it seems ironical that this finding implies definite limits to the analogy between human minds and computers, since it has been by the rather determined pursuit of that analogy in the cognitive sciences, in the claim that the human mind may be understood as a computational 'machine' for information processing, that the finding has been arrived at, those cognitive scientists who have also embraced evolutionary psychology are not themselves perturbed. Their view is that the differences between human minds and computers are instructive in drawing attention to the fact that human minds have specialized capacities that differ not only from those of computers but also from those of other species (the minds of which in turn display a vast array of evolved specializations). Chimpanzees, for instance, have wonderful brains for performing acrobatics that would put Olympic athletes to shame—but they cannot throw

for toffee. Humans and chimps have similar brains but they also differ in striking ways (De Waal 2005). Species that are more distantly related to us, like
dogs for example, have specialized perceptual abilities that exceed our own in
striking ways (their olfactory and auditory faculties for instance are far more
acute than ours), yet dogs, unlike humans, cannot be taught to do long division or to compose poetry. These are commonplace observations that are intelligible without appeal to scientific evidence. Yet experimental psychology
has revealed a far more subtle and intricate picture of the strengths and weaknesses of human cognition than could have been recognized through intuition
or unsystematic observation alone (for a useful synthesis see Eysenck and
Keane 2005). And there are arguments to suggest that many of the specialist
capacities of human brains, like those of chimps and dogs, are the outcomes
of evolution under natural selection (see Buss 2005).

There is the possibility, moreover, that the findings of psychological science might not be actually inimical to social theory (as many social theorists,
from Durkheim on, have assumed they would be). As Maurice Bloch elegantly
argues (Chapter 2), distinctively human ways of forming and construing social relationships seem to dissolve or obscure the boundaries between individuals. Our mental states continually mirror the states of those around us
such that there is a profound interpenetration of cognitive processes. The line
of demarcation between what goes on in the head, and what goes on among
many individuals, is hard to draw. Knowledge of all kinds comes to be *distributed*,[12] enabling it to persist even when individuals die and new ones gradually replace them.

How are we to conceptualize the resulting entities: social groups, traditions,
offices, languages, and so on? They cannot be comprehended at the level of
discrete beings *and yet* these entities intuitively seem (however misleadingly)
to possess at least some of the powers of indivisible *agents*, in commanding,
forbidding, or constraining us to act in certain ways rather than others. If social institutions can somehow be reformulated as agents, this makes them
readily intelligible. Human minds are very adept at handling notions of agency
(intentions, beliefs, desires, memories, and so on). If we can conceive of

---

12. For treatment of this idea in cognitive science, see Hutchins (1994). The basic idea
has mostly been developed in quite other intellectual traditions, such as by the philosophers Hilary Putnam (1975) and Saul Kripke (1980), and in a different vein again by F. A.
Hayek, who observed, 'It might be said that civilization begins when the individual in the
pursuit of his ends can make use of more knowledge than he has himself acquired and
when he can transcend the boundaries of his ignorance by profiting from knowledge he
does not himself possess' (1960: 22).

groups or institutions as agents, sociological reasoning becomes a great deal simpler. We can imagine, for instance, that groups, classes, or offices have *collective* memories, interests, aspirations, and beliefs. Our ability to empathize with the mental states of others, to grasp salient features of their experience of the world, provides us with a formidable set of tools that we can now put to work on our concepts of super-agency, the realm of the social. And if we fall 'naturally' into thinking of institutions as super-agents, then we might also accord them immutable essences, as Emma Cohen argues (Chapter 5). Just as we think of persons as in some sense unique at the core regardless of the changes wrought upon them by time or even death, so we are prone to imagine that whole groups of people share common essences that mark them off from other groups. Thus, we are easily seduced into thinking that at the heart of the sub-clan or the ethnic group lies a substance that is (mystically) shared among all its descendants. But if collectivities are construed as living things they are also *transcendent* in the ways indicated above. How better to convey such an idea than to envisage the tribe as a totemic spirit or god, who is immanent in all its members? Thus, argues Stewart Guthrie (Chapter 1), the social is 'anthropomorphized' and venerated, laying the foundations for some very widespread elements of religious thought.

According to Guthrie, the symbolist strand of Durkheim's sociology of religion was broadly on the right track, in revealing the agentive (or quasi-agentive) character of sacred things and thus the fundamental similarities in the way we reason about religion and society. Durkheim, however, could not account for these similarities beyond saying that both social and sacred entities are experienced as existing somehow 'above' us. As Guthrie observes, a substantial body of research in experimental psychology suggests that such extended attributions of agency are common. Agents can be, and generally are, spotted everywhere: in the gnarled bark of a tree, in the striated patterns of a rock face, in the embers of a fire, and in the nightly spectacle of the Milky Way. The claim from cognitive science is that there are numerous complex mental mechanisms or tools that 'deliver' these impressions of agency. Some are dedicated to the discernment of facial features, others to patterns of intentional movement, others to representing stable beliefs, and still others to the attribution of features such as function and essence.

So, if true, what if anything does this add to Durkheim's story about sacred symbols? The answer is that it is too early to say. That we have a tendency to anthropomorphism is intuitively plausible, and now well documented, but in just what does it consist, and what is its relevance to the anthropology of religion? Guthrie and Barrett, in their contributions to this volume, both argue that our cognitive architecture predisposes us towards certain kinds of deity concepts. But they differ on what those are. Barrett says (citing Guthrie 1993) that natural selection has primed us to look for the kinds of agency that might have characterised our predators or prey in our evolutionary environment, and this is why, in defiance of formal religious doctrine, we drift towards rather common-sense ('theologically incorrect') deities. Guthrie, noting that we routinely detect agency not only in physical objects and events but even in abstract or sketchy signs (faces in the clouds and so on), suggests that this accounts also for the prevalence, *per contra*, of abstract, theological concepts of God (Guthrie 1993). How might we decide if one, the other, neither, or both of these suggestions are correct?

One hope lies in the incremental experimental method followed by cognitive science, and the fact that these hypotheses suggest a reasonably clear agenda for research that will confirm, refute, or revise them, at least with respect to the operation of the postulated psychological mechanisms.[13] The aim is that the cognitive tools mentioned above (and there are many other suggestions discussed in this volume) should in time be thoroughly tested and checked with findings across a range of disciplines. For instance, research indicating the existence of dedicated face-recognition tools comes already from a number of more or less independent sources. Studies of how adults decipher individuated faces from a plethora of potential cues have been augmented by extensive research on how those abilities *develop* from infancy (Gopnik et al. 1999), by descriptions of what happens in the *brain* when faces are recognized (Nelson 2001), by examining the effects of *neurological disorders* on the phenomenology of face recognition (Bruce and Young 2000), by theories about the *evolution* of our capacities (Alvarez and Jaffe 2005), by *comparison* between individuals (Ross and Turkewitz 1981), between populations (Gauthier et al. 2000), and between humans and other species (Plotnik, Nelson, and De Waal 2003). And the same is true, though to varying degrees, of the way the cognitive sciences are investigating other mental processes involved in attributions of agency: intention-tracking, essentialist thinking, teleological reasoning, and so on.

Those involved in this research hope that this will be replicated for the at-present still rather disorganised rag-bag of modules, mechanisms, tools, devices, and so on that are postulated in the literature, and some of which are cited in the papers that follow. To the sceptic, in some cases this situation can look rather suspect: mental entities are cited, and the principal evidence ap-

---

13. Matters of ethnographic and historical interpretation, such as what counts as 'monotheism', are different again, and a resolution of the difference between the two authors would involve such matters too.

pears to be the very effects these entities are adduced to explain. Even if this is agreed to be an indispensable method among experimental psychologists, to some outside observers it may appear to resemble the Scholasticism caricatured by Molière in *Le Malade imaginaire*, according to which opium causes sleep because it possesses the 'dormitive virtue', which feature is then defined as the tendency to induce sleep. Some of the modules and mechanisms cited are more or less universally accepted among psychologists now, and for some there is even independent neurobiological evidence; for others, things are much more unclear and there is serious disagreement about how best to explain the observed effects. The shared ambition is to secure findings that are recognized by human scientists across a range of disciplines: developmental and cognitive psychologists, molecular biologists, neurologists, evolutionary anthropologists, game theorists, linguists, philosophers of mind, paleo-archaeologists, zoologists and many others who share important methodological and metaphysical presuppositions in common.

It is important, of course, not to exaggerate the degree of consensus there is, especially as there is always a temptation to do this of fields that are somewhat distant from one's own. It is a truism of science studies that concepts become 'theory', and working hypotheses 'discoveries', when viewed from a distance across disciplinary boundaries. And some of the techniques and forms of reasoning used by cognitive scientists of religion, especially those deriving from evolutionary psychology and relying on hypotheses about adaptation and 'evolutionary environments', remain somewhat contentious (see Rose & Rose 2000, McKinnon 2006, Buller 2005).[14] Still, the situation is not so highly charged or politicised as it was, for instance, in the days of socio-biology (on which see Segerstrale 2000). If any area of our understanding of religion could indeed be formulated so as to benefit from this kind of pattern of incrementally cumulative research, this would be a gain for all of us.

Bloch's and Guthrie's (not by any means identical) ideas on how to recast Durkheim's analysis of the sacred in cognitive terms are certainly ambitious. Bronislaw Malinowski, that champion of empiricism and enemy of theoretical abstraction, provides Jesper Sørensen (Chapter 3) with more concrete problems to address. Whereas Durkheim grappled with the ontological status of the social, Malinowski's primary interests lay in explaining the behaviour of flesh-and-blood individuals 'on the ground'. As Sørensen explains, Malinowski (unlike Durkheim) appealed explicitly to the psychological theories of

---

14. It should be noted, however, that claims about the evolutionary origins of the cognitive mechanisms involved in religious transmission are not, for some practitioners at least (including Whitehouse), an essential component of the cognitive science of religion.

the day in attempting to map out the relationship between biology, mind, and culture. Moreover, many aspects of Malinowski's approach amounted to a kind of methodological individualism, highly consonant (for good or ill) with the approaches of evolutionary psychology. Yet Malinowski was also writing at a time when a now thoroughly discredited behaviourism was on the ascent in psychology departments. Sørensen claims that in seeking an explanation for magical rituals, for instance, Malinowski asked penetrating questions that were in principle answerable but which required a different as well as a more detailed understanding of human minds than was available to him at the time. Sørensen argues that cognitive psychology now provides a rich account of how we represent actions in general which, he suggests, could provide us with both the theoretical foundations and the methodological innovations necessary to account for some of the distinctive features of ritual. Nevertheless, as Sørensen also concedes, we have not reached the point at which Malinowski's questions have in fact been definitively answered. Research results in cognitive psychology suggest a range of possible answers but much of the empirical work of investigating each of these lines of enquiry has still to be undertaken. This sense of 'work in progress' is a recurrent feature of the cognitive science of religion.

These are just examples of some of the ways in which cognitive scientists are seeking to address topics at the core of the anthropology of religion. A weightier tome than this might have ventured into a range of other topics, by attempting to bring work on mythology in the structuralist tradition of Lévi-Strauss into dialogue with cognitive theories of narrative construction and transmission (Turner 1998, Lakoff and Johnson 1980, Strauss and Quinn 1998); or by attempting to reformulate anthropological models of religious identity formation in light of the latest theories from cognitive science on such diverse topics as coalitional thinking (De Waal and Harcourt 1992), reputation management (Fessler and Haley 2003), and punitive altruism (De Quervain et al. 2004); or by searching for ways in which cognitive science might throw light on the apparently very radically other forms of thought and sociality anthropologists report from parts of the world such as Melanesia (Strathern 1988, Mimica 1988, Wagner 2001) and Amazonia (Viveiros de Castro 1998; for Inner Asia see also Pedersen 2001). But these ways of thinking, researching, and writing are perhaps just too far from those of the cognitive scientists for it to be at all straightforward even to establish what precisely they and the anthropologists might be disagreeing about. And in any case we are limited by space and must allow select examples to illustrate the general thrust of cognitive theorizing and to bring out the more important general issues it raises for anthropology.

It has been a repeated complaint of cognitive scientists and anthropologists influenced by cognitive science, that although anthropologists working in one or more interpretive tradition routinely deny the relevance of psychological knowledge to their interests, their own practice equally routinely relies on fairly strong (and in some cases implausible) psychological assumptions (e.g. Bloch 1998). Jon Lanman (Chapter 4) attempts to develop this point and to suggest that it has real consequences for the quality of the interpretations such anthropologists produce. His paper is a discussion of the debate between Sahlins and Obeyesekere concerning Captain Cook's status in the eyes of native Hawaiians: was he taken to be a god (as Sahlins suggests) or was he understood to be a mortal, albeit of considerable strategic value (as Obeysekere maintains)? Sahlins and Obeyesekere argue for their respective interpretations not only in terms of fit with available historical evidence, but also in terms of the general virtues they claim for their theoretical approaches. Sahlins' interpretation appeals to a theory of 'mythopraxis' and Obeyesekere's to a theory of 'practical rationality', but according to Lanman both theories are founded on flawed assumptions about the nature of cognition. He argues that as a consequence both *interpretations* are unwarranted. On this view interpretive speculation must be 'constrained' by cognitive theories. While Lanman concedes that cognitive science is not (yet, in his view) able to provide us with any positive suggestions as to what in fact did happen between Cook and the Hawaiians, or how the Hawaiians' indigenous religious thought ought to be understood, he regards it as an advance that we can at least rule out—or regard as so unsubstantiated as not really to be worth further consideration—the interpretations put forward by these eminent anthropologists.

One reason anthropologists give for neglecting the writings of cognitive scientists is that the theories are often explicated and tested not on what the former regard as rich and rounded ethnographic description, but instead through experiments carried out in artificial conditions, on small groups of individuals (so rarely, of necessity, in conditions that are experienced by the subjects of the experiments as natural). And such experimental work is moreover mostly conducted in Euro-American cultural settings and, where not, in places where those conducting the experiments have only limited cultural and historical knowledge. In this area, Rita Astuti's contribution (Chapter 6), on the effects of highly variable environments on the acquisition and spread of religious representations, blazes a trail. The combination of ethnographic contextualisation and experimental method is something that many have promised but has seldom been achieved. Astuti shows that what people say about their religious beliefs is heavily influenced by the contexts in which they are asked about them. The point may seem obvious, but how many ethnographers attempt to vary in controlled ways the effects of differently contextualized questions, measuring the responses gathered by age, gender, and other relevant variables? Not many. Of course, Astuti's chapter makes other important contributions, and it seeks to challenge claims that other cognitive scientists have made about the origins of afterlife beliefs (cited by Barrett and Lanman). But her *methodological* innovations are important in their own right. By producing data in such precise and measurable form, Astuti may encourage both anthropologists and cognitive scientists to pay closer attention to the role of sociocultural ecology in the activation and expression of beliefs. This in turn could open the way to more thoroughgoing investigations of the *extended* and *distributed* character of human cognition, the fact that it is shaped by locally varied material culture, landscapes, and social relations as well as by universal intuitive biases. Anthropologists of all persuasions, and not just cognitive anthropologists, stand to learn from research of this kind.

Justin Barrett (Chapter 7) argues that the aims of cognitive theories of religion include accounting for conscious experience, for instance in the formulation, learning, and transmission of theological and philosophical traditions. For Barrett, there is a close relationship between the operation of largely implicit cognitive tools and the establishment of conscious (or 'reflective') religious ideas and commitments. He characterizes the relationship like this:

> Reflective beliefs typically come from the cumulative weight of non-reflective beliefs converging on the same candidate belief. The more non-reflective beliefs that converge on a single idea, the more likely the idea becomes a reflectively held belief. Put another way, the more outputs from various mental tools that are captured by a proposition, the more likely that proposition is to be reflectively believed. (p. 189)

Barrett's claims are bold. People cannot be taught to believe just any old thing, no matter how hard you try to drum or beat propositions into them. They will only end up believing things that resonate with their implicit assumptions about the world—and the more implicit assumptions a proposition is supported by, the greater its chances of being believed. Those implicit assumptions cannot be taught. According to Barrett, they are 'instinctive', in the sense that they 'are the sorts of beliefs that children rapidly and uniformly acquire by virtue of being the sort of animal that they are living in the sorts of environments they live in' (p. 187). So culture in general, and religion in particular, must consist largely of explicit beliefs that are supported by implicit mental tools. This still allows variation in the range of possible explicit beliefs, but the range of possible beliefs is really quite tightly constrained.

Note that Barrett's crucial claim is qualified: 'reflective beliefs *typically* come from ...' wherever-it-is they come from. He does not claim they *invariably* require support from tacit intuitive assumptions. So we could, at least in principle, find reflective religious beliefs that do not chime with our 'instinctive' beliefs (though whether Barrett's argument would allow that they could be widely distributed or socially important is worthy of closer scrutiny). Even a swift review of the burgeoning literature in the cognitive science of religion shows that while something like this caveat is included by other authors too, little has been done to flesh it out or to spell out its implications. The thrust of most cognitive scientists' endeavours has been and remains the attempt to construct a detailed account of those beliefs that can be explained because they depend substantially upon natural/universal cognitive biases operating outside conscious awareness. Some think that when this job has been done there will be very little left to explain, and that in any case what is left will largely be confined to the airy-fairy worlds of learned religious élites and theologians rather than the mental lives of rank and file worshippers.

As anthropologists, the editors of this book regard those last two suggestions with scepticism, for both are disinclined to minimize the distinctiveness of conscious experience,[15] and both see the ethnographic and historical record as providing evidence of much deeply counterintuitive (or imaginative) reflective thinking going on among even the most untutored of adherents to the world's diverse religious traditions. The fact, which cognitive-scientific studies have brought out rather vividly, that certain general kinds of concepts and representations recur very widely in different religious traditions, does not alter the fact that what religious thinkers, including very lowly everyday practitioners, actually *say* with these concepts differs substantially between different traditions. The ideas that dominate in local communities of Protestant Christians, Melanesian ritual experts, Shaivite Hindus, and Zen Buddhists really do differ profoundly, even if some of the concepts they have (e.g. concerning the special attributes of deities) resemble each other closely.

Directions for Cognitive Science and Anthropology

The two final chapters of this volume are the editors' respective responses to the situation cumulatively presented by the other papers, and their somewhat contrasting thoughts on what a sensible and productive future might be

---

15. For anthropological reflections on consciousness and self-consciousness, see Cohen (1994) and Cohen & Rapport (1995).

for the cognitive science and anthropology of religion. Laidlaw thinks that the relation between the two must remain that between different enterprises, with the cognitive science of religion being, fundamentally, a part of cognitive science and not in any interesting sense distinctive within it, but able, like the rest of cognitive science, to be in conversation with anthropology as a humane discipline; Whitehouse envisages an expanded, inter-disciplinary cognitive science of religion, whose theoretical presuppositions, language, methods, and criteria of validity are scientifically based, but into which more humanistic anthropological methods and ideas would be integrated.

According to Laidlaw (Chapter 8), cognitivists may be on solid ground in attempting to explain why concepts of witchcraft, sorcery, magic, ghosts, goblins, and gods are culturally widespread, but their methods cannot explain the *patterns* of their occurrence across time and space or their *variations*. Insofar as their methods are successful, they identify mechanisms which enable and/or dispose *all* humans to think in particular ways. But to show that we have a cognitive mechanism that enables us to think a certain way does not tell us who among us, or when or why or to what purposes, will use it. If religions everywhere really were all the same this would be less of a problem, but they are not. And the demonstration of a propensity, which, where it is more than impressionistic must take the form of establishing a statistical probability, by its very nature cannot be an explanation for why the feature in question is respectively present and absent in particular instances. So while specifying a connection to a relevant cognitive mechanism might be an interesting thing to tell us about a religious practice, or a part of a ritual for example, no such specification, however minutely detailed, will constitute an explanation *of the practice*, as an institutionalised historical particularity. For Whitehouse, by contrast, there is no principled reason why the cognitive science of religion should restrict itself to explaining the cross-cultural recurrence, all else being equal, of relatively simple and recurrent concepts of supernatural agency. That has certainly proved to be a fruitful starting point for some cognitive theories of religion but why, he would ask, should it be the end point? Whitehouse (Chapter 9) envisages the possibility of increasingly detailed accounts of the shaping and constraining effects of intuitive cognition on patterns of innovation and transmission with regard to religious concepts, based on close specification of the impact of local ecology (including particular institutional arrangements), ultimately contributing to a fuller account of cross-cultural *variation* in patterns of occurrence over time and space.

Laidlaw further objects that cognitive science cannot account for the traditions of conscious, reflective, and self-critical thought and practice we are also (perhaps primarily) referring to when we talk about 'religion'. Insofar as there are aspects of human thought that are not computational and not modular, he argues, the products of such thought are effectively outside the purview of cognitive science, because to that extent its defining move cannot be made: that is, *what* people think and say and do (the 'outputs', as it were) will not be predictable or explicable in terms of any *mechanisms* by means of which they represent and process information. And Laidlaw argues that religious traditions, as historical phenomena, are conspicuously and constitutively characterised by thought and practice of exactly this kind. Here, Whitehouse also disagrees. In his view, all human thinking, behaviour, and its products—whether viewed at the level of individuals or in terms of patterned distributions at the population level—are historical phenomena. It follows that all cognitive operations (whether we are talking about implicit processing or more explicit deliberations involving 'reason, will, and imagination') occur in historically constituted contexts. Whitehouse would argue that cognitive science offers a wide range of theoretical perspectives, of which modularity theory is only one. But even a massively modular mind can be seen as interacting with highly varied and complex environments, affording opportunities to investigate the role of cognition in generating *variation* in the beliefs and practices of religious traditions on the ground. In addition, even the most enthusiastic advocates of modularity theory would recognize that conscious reasoning can play a role in shaping attitudes, beliefs, and behaviour and thus in patterns of religious variation. A major challenge, according to Whitehouse, is to weigh the relative importance of explicit and implicit cognition in the transmission of religious knowledge.

The editors differ, then, in their view of the capacity of cognitive science to account for conscious, reflective thought, and in their view of the import of this for the contribution cognitivism might make to the study of religion. Whitehouse envisages a cognitive science of religion that embraces and includes many of the questions anthropologists have traditionally asked, and offers cognitively informed answers to those questions. And for him, the cognitive science of religion will prove its worth by embracing and including the traditional interests of anthropology and history, and providing better explanatory strategies than traditional interpretive methods have garnered in response to the questions anthropologists and historians have long been asking.[16] Minds, he would argue, do not exist in a vacuum, but develop through

---

16. Whitehouse would not argue that this should *replace* traditional forms of historiographical or ethnographic interpretation, which he regards as (often compelling) narratives about, rather than explanations of, human thought and behaviour, and the kaleidoscopic patterns and material effects that arise from them. For him, explanation augments

complex interactions with their varied and historically constituted environ-ments. For Laidlaw, while cognitive science has an important contribution to make in the understanding of human thought, including some forms and pat-terns of thought that are found in religion (beliefs in gods and ghosts, 'sym-bolic' representations, etc.), it is a mistake to think that 'religion' can be a suit-able object for 'a cognitive science'. Cognitive science already has its object— cognition: that is, thought, viewed in a particular and partial way—specified in its name. A 'cognitive science of religion', like an 'economic approach to marriage' or a 'Marxist perspective on art', will be necessarily tendentious. This does not preclude cognitive-scientific research continuing to make a contri-bution to the understanding of aspects of religion, and being of interest to an-thropologists, historians, and others. What it precludes, in Laidlaw's view, is a discipline or field that seeks to 'explain' religion, organized around cogni-tivist conceptualisations and methods.

Thus the editors have come (for the present at least) to sharply different views on the prospects for the cognitive science of religion and its proper re-lationship to anthropological and other forms of study of the same phenom-ena. But we agree that the issues on which we differ will only be clarified and settled as cognitive scientists seek to press ahead, as, on the evidence of this volume they surely will, with their engagement with the ethnographic and his-torical evidence on the variety and complexity of religious traditions.

References

Alvarez, Liliana and Klaus Jaffe. (2005) 'Narcissism Guides Mate Selection' in *Evolutionary Psychology*, 2: 177–194.

Andresen, Jensine (ed.). (2001) *Religion in Mind: Cognitive Perspectives on Religious Belief, Ritual, and Experience*. Cambridge: University Press.

Atran, Scott. (2002) *In Gods We Trust: The Evolutionary Landscape of Reli-gion*. New York: Oxford University Press.

---

narrative, the latter often filling in meaningful details that the former cannot embrace, ei-ther because of the limits of scientific methodology at a given stage of development or be-cause some aspects of complex systems (such as societies and cultural traditions) are too complex, or perhaps chaotic, ever to explain satisfactorily. Still, Whitehouse is optimistic that far more of the social and cultural world falls within the explanatory purview of cog-nitive theories than Laidlaw recognizes and, in this respect, he sees the differences between them as qualitative and tractable rather than absolute and irreconcilable.

Barkow, Jerome H., Leda Cosmides, & John Tooby (eds.). (1992) *The Adapted Mind: Evolutionary Psychology and the Generation of Culture.* New York: Oxford University Press.

Barrett, H. Clark. (2004) 'Descent Versus Design in Shuar Children's Reasoning About Dead Animals' in *Journal of Cognition and Culture*, 4: 25–50.

Barrett, Justin. (2004). *Why Would Anyone Believe in God?* Walnut Creek, CA: AltaMira Press.

Barrett, Louise, Robin Dunbar & John Lycett. (2002) *Human Evolutionary Psychology.* Basingstoke: Palgrave.

Barth, Fredrik. (1987) *Cosmologies in the Making: A Generative Approach to Cultural Variation in Inner New Guinea.* Cambridge: University Press.

Berlin, Brent O. & Paul D. Kay. (1969) *Basic Color Terms.* Berkeley: University of California.

Berlin, Brent O., Dennis Breedlove & Peter Raven. (1973) 'General Principles of Classification and Nomenclature in Folk Biology' in *American Anthropologist*, 70: 290–99.

Berlin, Brent O. (1992) *Ethnobiological Classification.* Princeton: University Press.

Bloch, Maurice. (1971) *Placing the Dead: Tombs, Ancestral Villages, and Kinship Organization in Madagascar.* London: Seminar.

——— (1974) 'Symbol, Song, Dance, and Features of Articulation or Is Religion an Extreme Form of Traditional Authority?' in *Archives Européenes de Sociologie*, 5: 55–81.

——— (1986) *From Blessing to Violence: History and Ideology in the Circumcision Ritual of the Merina of Madagascar.* Cambridge: University Press.

——— (1989) *Ritual, History, and Power: Selected Papers in Anthropology.* London: Athlone.

——— (1991) 'Language, Anthropology and Cognitive Science' in *Man* (NS), 26: 183–98.

——— (1998) *How We Think They Think: Anthropological Approaches to Cognition, Memory, and Literacy.* Boulder CO: Westview.

——— (2006) Where Did Anthropology Go? Or the Need for 'Human Nature'. In *Essays on Cultural Transmission.* Oxford: Berg.

Bloch, Maurice (ed.). (1975) *Political Language and Oratory in Traditional Societies.* London: Academic.

Boyer, Pascal. (2001) *Religion Explained.* London: Heinnemann.

Bruce, V. and Young, A. (2000) *In the Eye of the Beholder: The Science of Face Perception*. Oxford: Oxford University Press.

Buller, David J. (2005) *Adapting Minds: Evolutionary Psychology and the Persistent Quest for Human Nature*. London: Bradford.

Buss, David. (1999) *Evolutionary Psychology: The New Science of the Mind*. London: Allyn & Bacon.

Buss, David. (2005) *Handbook of Evolutionary Psychology*. London: John Wiley and Sons.

Carruthers, Peter, Stephen Laurence, & Stephen Stich (eds.), *The Innate Mind: Structure and Content*. New York: Oxford University Press.

Cohen, Anthony. (1994) *Self Consciousness: An Alternative Anthropology of Identity*. London: Routledge.

Cohen, Anthony P. & Nigel Rapport (eds.). (1995). *Questions of Consciousness*. Routledge: London.

Cohen, Emma. In Press. *The Mind Possessed: The Cognition of Spirit Possession in an Afro-Brazilian Religious Tradition*. Oxford: Oxford University Press.

D'Andrade, Roy. (1995) *The Development of Cognitive Anthropology*. Cambridge: University Press.

D'Andrade, Roy & Claudia Strauss (eds.). (1992) *Human Motives and Cultural Models*. Cambridge: University Press.

Dawkins, Richard. (2006) *The God Delusion*. London: Bantam.

Dennett, Daniel C. (2006) *Breaking the Spell: Religion as a Natural Phenomenon*. London: Allen Lane.

De Quervain, J.-F., Urs Fischbacher, Valerie Treyer, Melanie Schellhammer, Ulrich Schnyder, Alfred Buck, & Ernst Fehr. (2004) 'The Neural Basis of Altruistic Punishment' in *Science*, 305: 1254–1258.

De Waal, Frans. (2005) *Our Inner Ape: A Leading Primatologist Explains Why We Are Who We Are*. New York: Penguin.

De Waal, Frans & A. H. Harcourt. (2002) *Coalitions and Alliances in Humans and Other Animals*. Oxford: Oxford University Press.

Durkheim. Emile. (1995) [1912] *The Elementary Forms of the Religious Life*. New York: Simon & Schuster.

Eysenck, Michael, W. & Mark Keane. (2005) *Cognitive Psychology: A Student's Handbook, 5th Edition*. Hove and New York: Psychology Press.

Fessler, Dan M.T. (2004) 'Shame in Two Cultures: Implications for Evolutionary Approaches' in *Journal of Cognition and Culture*, 4: 207–262.

Fessler, Dan & K. J. Haley. (2003) The Structure of Affect: Emotions in Human Cooperation. In P. Hammerstein (ed.), *The Genetic and Cultural Evolution of Cooperation*. Cambridge MA: MIT Press.

Fodor, Jerry. (2001) *The Mind Doesn't Work That Way: The Scope and Limits of Computational Psychology*. Cambridge MA: MIT Press.

Gatewood, John B. (1985) 'Actions Speak Louder than Words' in Janet W. D. Dougherty (ed.), *Directions in Cognitive Anthropology*. Urbana: University of Illinois: 199–220.

Gauthier, I., P. Skudlarski, J.C. Gore, & A.W. Anderson. (2000) 'Expertise for Cars and Birds Recruits Brain Areas Involved in Face Recognition' in *Nature Neuroscience*, 3: 191–197.

Gell, Alfred. (1980) 'The Gods at Play: Vertigo and Possession in Muria Religion' in *Man* (NS), 15: 219–48.

———— (1992) *The Anthropology of Time: Cultural Constructions of Temporal Maps and Images*. Oxford: Berg.

———— (1995) The Language of the Forest: Landscape and Phonological Iconism in Umeda. In Eric Hirsch & Michael O'Hanlon (eds.), *The Anthropology of Landscape: Perspectives on Place and Space*. Oxford: Clarendon.

Gladwin, Thomas. (1970) *The East is a Big Bird*. Cambridge MA: Harvard University Press.

Goodenough, Ward. (1956) 'Componential Analysis and the Study of Meaning.' in *Language*, 32: 195–216.

Gopnik, A., A. N. Meltzov. & P. Kuhl. (1999) *The Scientist in the Crib: Minds, Brains, and How Children Learn*. New York: William Morrow

Guthrie, Stewart. (1993) *Faces in the Clouds: A New Theory of Religion*. New York: Oxford University Press.

Hayek, F. A. (1960) *The Constitution of Liberty*. London: Routledge.

Henrich, Joseph, Robert Boyd, Samuel Bowles, Herbert Gintis, Ernst Fehr, & Colin Camerer (eds.) (2004) *Foundations of Human Sociality: Economic Experiments and Ethnographic Evidence from Fifteen Small-Scale Societies*, Oxford: Oxford University Press.

Hinde, Robert. (1999) *Why Gods Persist: A Scientific Approach to Religion*. London: Routledge.

Hirschfeld, Lawrence A. & Susan A. Gelman. (1994) *Mapping the Mind: Domain Specificity in Cognition and Culture*. Cambridge: University Press.

Holland, Dorothy & Naomi Quinn (eds.). (1987) *Cultural Models in Language and Thought*. Cambridge: University Press.

Houseman, Michael & Carlo Severi. (1998) *Naven or the Other Self: A Relational Approach to Ritual Action*. Brill: Leiden.

Humphrey, Caroline. (1996) *Shamans and Elders: Experience, Knowledge, and Power among the Daur Mongols*. Oxford: Clarendon Press.

Humphrey, Caroline & James Laidlaw. (1994) *The Archetypal Actions of Ritual: A Theory of Ritual Illustrated by the Jain Rite of Worship*. Oxford: Clarendon Press.

Hutchins, Edwin. (1983) 'Understanding Micronesian Navigation' in D. Gentner & A. L. Stevens (eds.), *Mental Models*. Engelwood Cliffs: Lawrence Erlbaum: 191–225.

———— (1994) *Cognition in the Wild*. Cambridge MA: MIT Press.

Ingold, Tim. (1986) *Evolution and Social Life*. Cambridge: University Press.

Karmiloff-Smith, Annette. (1996) *Beyond Modularity: Developmental Perspectives on Cognitive Science*. Cambridge MA: MIT Press.

Keane, Webb. (1997) *Signs of Recognition: Powers and Hazards of Representation in an Indonesian Society*. Berkeley: University of California Press.

Kelemen, D. (2005) 'Are Children "Intuitive Theists"? Reasoning about Purpose and Design in Nature' in *Psychological Science*, 15: 295–301.

Kripke, Saul. (1980) [1972]. *Naming and Necessity*. Oxford, Blackwell.

Laidlaw, James & Caroline Humphrey. (2006) Action. In Jens Kreinath, Jan Snoek, and Michael Stausberg (eds.), *Theorizing Rituals, Volume 1: Issues, Topics, Approaches, Concepts*. Leiden: Brill.

Lakoff, George & Johnson, Mark. (1980) *Metaphors We Live By*. Chicago: University Press.

Laland, Kevin N. & Gillian R. Brown. (2002) *Sense and Nonsense: Evolutionary Explanations of Human Behaviour*. Cambridge: University Press.

Lave, Jean. (1994) *Cognition in Practice*. Cambridge: University Press.

Lawson, Thomas E. and Robert N. McCauley. (1990) *Rethinking Religion*. Cambridge: Cambridge University Press.

Lévi-Strauss, Claude. (1970 [1964]) *The Raw and the Cooked: Introduction to a Science of Mythology. Volume 1*. London: Jonathan Cape.

Lewis, Gilbert. (1980) *Day of Shining Red: An Essay on Understanding Ritual*. Cambridge: University Press.

Liénard P. & (photographs by) F. Anselmo. (2005) The Social Construction of Emotions: Gratification and Gratitude among the *Turkana* and

Nyangatom of East Africa. In Steven Van Wolputte and Gustaaf Verswijver (eds.) *At the Fringes of Modernity. People, Cattle, Transitions.* African Pastoralists Studies 2. Tervuren: RMCA.

Lounsbury, Floyd. (1956) 'A Semantic Analysis of the Pawneew Kinship Usage' in *Language*, 32: 158–94.

Malley, Brian. (2004) *How the Bible Works: An Anthropological Study of Evangelical Biblicism.* Walnut Creek, CA: AltaMira PRess.

McCauley, Robert N. and E. Thomas Lawson. (2002) *Bringing Ritual to Mind.* New York: Cambridge University Press.

Metzger, Duane & G. Williams. (1963) 'Formal Ethnographic Analysis of Tenejapa Ladino Weddings' in *American Anthropologist*, 65: 1076–1101.

Mimica, Jadran. (1988) *Intimations of Infinity: The Cultural Meanings of the Iqwaye Counting and Number Systems.* Oxford: Berg.

McKinnon, Susan. (2006) *Neo-Liberal Genetics: The Myths and Moral Tales of Evolutionary Psychology.* Chicago: Prickly Paradigm.

Nelson, C.A. (2001) 'The Development and Neural Bases of Face Recognition' in *Infant and Child Development*, 10: 3–18.

Pedersen, Morten. (2001) Totemism, Animism and North Asian Indigenous Ontologies. *Journal of the Royal Anthropological Institute*, 7: 411–427.

Pinker, Steven. (1997) *How the Mind Works.* New York: Norton.

Plotnik, Joshua, Peter A. Nelson, & Frans De Waal. (2003) 'Visual Field Information in the Face Perception of Chimpanzee' in *Annals of the New York Academy of Sciences*, 1000: 94–98.

Putnam, Hilary. (1975) *Mind, Language, And Reality: Philosophical Papers. Volume 2.* Cambridge: University Press.

Pyysiäinen, Ilkka. (2001) *How Religion Works: Towards a New Cognitive Science of Religion.* (*Cognition & Culture Book Series*; 1.) Leiden: Brill.

———. (2004) *Magic, Miracles, and Religion: A Scientist's Perspective.* Walnut Creek, CA: AltaMira Press.

Pyysiäinen, Ilkka, & Veikko Anttonen (eds.). (2002) *Current Approaches to the Cognitive Science of Religion.* London: Continuum.

Quinn, Naomi & Dorothy Strauss. (1998) *A Cognitive Theory of Cultural Meaning.* Cambridge: University Press.

Richerson, Peter J. & Robert Boyd. (2004) *Not By Genes Alone: How Culture Transformed Human Evolution.* Chicago: Chicago University Press.

Roepstorf, Andreas, Nils Bubandt and Kalevi Kull. (2003) *Imagining Nature: Practices of Cosmology and Identity.* Aarhus: Aarhus University Press.

Romney, A. K. & R. G. D'Andrade. (1964) 'Cognitive Aspects of English Kin Terms' in *American Anthropologist*, 68: 146–70.

Rose, Hilary & Steven Rose (eds.). (2000) *Alas, Poor Darwin: Arguments Against Evolutionary Psychology*. London: Jonathan Cape.

Ross, P. & G. Turkewitz. (1981) 'Individual Differences in Cerebral Asymmetries for Facial Recognition' in *Cortex*, 2: 199–214.

Segerstrale, Ullica. (2000) *Defenders of the Truth: The Sociobiology Debate*. Oxford: University Press.

Slone, D.J. ed. (2006) *Religion and Cognition: A Reader*, London: Equinox.

Sousa, P. (2003) The Fall of Kinship—Towards an Epidemiological Explanation' in *Journal of Cognition and Culture*. 3/4: 264–303.

Sperber, Dan. (1975 [1974]) *Rethinking Symbolism*. Cambridge: University Press.

——— (1982 [1979]) 'Is Symbolic Thought Prerational?' In Michel Izard & Pierre Smith (eds.), *Between Belief and Transgression: Structuralist Essays in Religion, History, and Myth*. Chicago: University Press.

——— (1985a [1982]) *On Anthropological Knowledge*. Cambridge: University Press.

——— (1985b) Anthropology and Psychology: 'Towards and Epidemiology of Representations' in *Man* (NS), 20: 73–89.

——— (1990) The Epidemiology of Beliefs. In Colin Fraser & George Gaskell (eds.), *The Social Psychology of Widespread Beliefs*. Oxford: Clarendon Press: 25–44.

——— (1994) The Modularity of Thought and the Epidemiology of Representations. In Lawrence A Hirschfeld & Susan A. Gelman (eds.), *Mapping the Mind: Domain Specificity in Cognition and Culture*. Cambridge: University Press: 39–67.

——— (1996) *Explaining Culture*. Oxford: Blackwell.

——— (2001) 'Conceptual Tools for a Natural Science of Society and Culture (Radcliffe-Brown Memorial Lecture 1999)' in *Proceedings of the British Academy*, 111: 297–317.

——— (2005) Modularity and Relevance: How Can a Massively Modular Mind be Flexible and Context-Sensitive. In Peter Carruthers, Stephen Laurence, & Stephen Stich (eds.), *The Innate Mind: Structure and Content*. New York: Oxford University Press.

Stafford, Charles. (1995) *The Roads of Chinese Childhood: Learning and Identification in Angang*. Cambridge: University Press.

Sterelny, Kim. (2003) *Thought in a Hostile World: The Evolution of Human Cognition*. Oxford: Blackwell.

Sterelny, Kim & Julie Fitness (eds.). (2003) *From Mating to Mentality: Evaluating Evolutionary Psychology*. Sydney: Psychology Press.

Strathern, Marilyn. (1988) *The Gender of the Gift: Problems with Women and Problems with Society in Melanesia*. Berkeley: University of California.

Tooby, John & Leda Cosmides. (1992) The Psychological Foundations of Culture. In Barkow et al (eds.), *The Adapted Mind: Evolutionary Psychology and the Generation of Culture*. New York: Oxford University Press: 19–136.

Tremlin, Todd. (2006) *Minds and Gods: The Cognitive Foundations of Religion*. New York: Oxford University Press.

Turner, Mark. (1998) *The Literary Mind*. New York: Oxford University Press.

Tyler, Stephen A. (1969) *Cognitive Anthropology*. New York: Holt.

Viveiros de Castro, Eduardo. (1998) 'Cosmological Deixis and Amerindian Perspectivism' in *Journal of the Royal Anthropological Institute* (NS), 4: 469–88.

Wagner, Roy. (2001) *An Anthropology of the Subject: Holographic Worldview in New Guinea and Its Meaning and Significance for the World of Anthropology*. Berkeley: University of California.

Whitehouse, Harvey. (1992) 'Memorable Religions: Transmission, Codification, and Change in Divergent Melanesian Contexts' in *Man* (NS), 27: 777–97.

———— (1995) *Inside the Cult: Religious Innovation and Transmission in Papua New Guinea*. Oxford: University Press.

———— (2000) *Arguments and Icons: Divergent Modes of Religiosity*. Oxford: University Press.

———— (2002) Conjectures, Refutations, and Verification: Towards a Testable Theory of Modes of Religiosity. *Journal of Ritual Studies*, 16: 44–59.

———— (2004) *Modes of Religiosity: A Cognitive Theory of Religious Transmission*. Walnut Creek, CA: AltaMira Press.

———— (2005) Emotion, Memory, and Religious Rituals: an Assessment of Two Theories. in Kay Milton and Maruska Svasek (eds.) *Mixed Emotions*, Oxford: Berg.

Whitehouse, Harvey (ed.). (2001) *The Debated Mind: Evolutionary Psychology versus Ethnography*. London: Berg.

Whitehouse, Harvey & James Laidlaw (eds.). (2004) *Ritual and Memory: Toward a Comparative Ethnography of Religion*. Walnut Creek, CA: AltaMira Press.

Whitehouse, Harvey & Robert N. McCauley (eds.). (2005) *Mind and Religion: Psychological and Cognitive Foundations of Religiosity*. Walnut Creek, CA: AltaMira Press.

Wolpert, Lewis. (2006). *Six Impossible Things Before Breakfast: The Evolutionary Origins of Belief*. London: Faber.

Wright, Robert. (1994) *The Moral Animal: Evolutionary Psychology and Everyday Life*. New York: Pantheon.

PART ONE

CORE PERSPECTIVES IN THE ANTHROPOLOGY OF RELIGION

CHAPTER ONE

ANTHROPOLOGY AND ANTHROPOMORPHISM IN RELIGION

Stewart Elliott Guthrie

Not only general theories but even definitions of religion, in anthropology as elsewhere, have remained elusive (Saler 2000 [1993]). Rappaport (1999:23), for example, while calling religion a human universal, also calls the concept "irreducibly vague." Theory of religion thus remains an open field. I shall summarize the major theories in anthropology and then argue that religion may best be approached cognitively. Specifically, it may be defined and explained as a system of thought and action for interpreting and influencing the world, built on anthropomorphic and animistic premises.

Central here is my account of anthropomorphism and animism, as residual, retrospective categories of perceptual and conceptual mistakes. They consist in thinking that we have detected human or other animal agency, or one or more of their characteristics, when in fact we have not. They arise inevitably, as by-products—namely, as false positives—of our scanning an uncertain world for what matters most. What matters most is agency, especially complex agency, and prototypically that of our fellow humans. We are unconsciously geared to detect such agents by varied perceptual sensitivities and by the conceptual framework called theory of mind (Hassin, Uleman, and Bargh 2005), and we have a low threshold for judging that we have detected them.

Together, these sensitivities and this framework bias us to interpret ambiguous phenomena as humans, as other complex animals, or as their artifacts or traces. When we are right in these interpretations, we gain important information, and when we are wrong we lose relatively little (Guthrie 1980, 1993, 1997, 2000, 2002, forthcoming).

Anthropology and Anthropomorphism in Religion, A Brief History

Anthropological theories of religion may be categorized into three groups. These are social-solidarity (or symbolist or social-functionalist), wishful-thinking (or emotionalist or projectionist) and intellectualist (or neo-Tylorian or cognitivist) theories. According to social-solidarity theories, society may be understood as a kind of organism, and features such as religious ritual may best be explained by their contribution to the organism's viability. According to wishful-thinking theories, religious ritual is best explained by its reassuring effect on the emotional lives of individuals. And according to intellectualist or cognitivist theories (one of which I shall advance), such ritual is best seen as an attempt to control or influence the world in general, and is based on a particular understanding of the world. These three groups are not necessarily mutually exclusive, but may be combined in various ways. Each group is illuminated by material from recent cognitive science.

Although its fortunes have waxed and waned, the social-solidarity theory of religion has been predominant in anthropology for much of the history of the discipline. Indeed, recognition of the capacity of religious symbols to unite members of society, and a corresponding use of such symbols by civil authorities, extends far back before the beginning of the discipline, both in the West and in East Asia. In China, for example, the Chou Dynasty explained its conquest, circa 1,000 BCE, to its new populations as reflecting its acquisition of the Mandate of Heaven. This assertion established a pattern of dynastic claims that lasted until modern times. Similarly, Confucius was made the object of a durable statist cult throughout East Asia. In the West, the opinion that religion supports (or at least primarily attends to) the social order dates back at least to Polybius (first century BCE). It continues through a line of writers up to Comte, Freud, and Durkheim in the nineteenth and early-twentieth centuries, to a long list of anthropologists including Radcliffe-Brown (1979 [1939]), Malinowski (1948), Turner (1969), Rappaport (1999), Whitehouse (2000), Boyer (2001) and Atran (2002), as well as the biologist Wilson (2002).

Despite variation in the social-solidarity view, Durkheim may be considered representative. With his abiding interest in how societies cohere despite conflicting individual interests, he famously saw religion as a means to that end. Three aspects of Durkheim's account of religion are especially relevant here.

The first two are aspects of his social functionalism, and are problems that suggest a need for amendment or for alternatives. The general problems of functionalism have been noted elsewhere (Douglas and Perry 1985 cite weaknesses regarding religion), and here I mention only two. The first problem is empirical, namely that the many cases in which religion divides groups provide evidence against the thesis that it necessarily unifies them. A recent scholar similarly refers to "religion's most distinctive and alarming feature, namely its capacity to fuel divisive conflicts" (Hart 1999: xix).

A second weakness is logical. Broadly, it is the question of immediate cause: how does any ostensibly functional feature of a society come to be adopted? That is, why should people do something that is good for the group, if they do not at the same time perceive it as good for them individually? (Wilson 2002 applies the principle of group selection to this problem in the case of religion, but fails to ground this application in a cross-culturally adequate conception of religion). A sense of the group as powerful may indeed arise from group experience (especially, as Durkheim says, from ritual). Nonetheless, how a sense of something sacred—a sense that might, as Durkheim claims, motivate individual behavior—arises, above and beyond the group itself, never becomes clear. Indeed (as Whitehouse 2000:4 notes), Durkheim's work is marked by a principled aversion to using psychology to account for social phenomena. But psychology is needed here, and even may be applied to the apparent naturalness of functionalism itself, since this recurrent feature of human thought probably reflects our perceptual and cognitive bias toward teleology (Dennett 1987, Kelemen 1999, 2004) more than it reflects anything about the world.

The third aspect of Durkheim's account seems less problematic and somewhat resembles the kind of cognitive approach I think is most promising. This is his claim that the features of the sacred actually are the features of human society. Thus the relation of the sacred to its worshippers is the same as that of society to its members: it is superior to them, has authority over them, protects them, makes demands of them, and punishes them for misbehavior. The sacred, then, sounds rather like an agent, even a humanlike one.

Durkheim, as is well known, denies that gods are necessarily features of religion. He asserts that the necessary feature is, instead, the concept of the sacred. His main evidence that gods are unnecessary is Buddhism, which he, with some others, maintains is a religion without gods. However, he is mistaken in this, as several writers have noted, since although some philosophical variants of Buddhism have no gods, just as demythologized Christianity and Judaism have none, Buddhism as popularly practiced is rich in them.

This issue may not matter for our purposes, however, since Durkheim's descriptions of the sacred and of totems make his separation of them from gods appear as a distinction without much difference. A society is to its members what a god is to his worshippers. In fact, a god is, first of all, a being whom men think of as superior to themselves, and upon whom they feel that they depend. Whether it be a conscious personality, such as Zeus or Jahveh, or merely abstract forces such as those in play in totemism, the worshiper, in the one case as in the other, believes himself held to certain manners of acting which are imposed upon him by the nature of the sacred principle with which he feels that he is in communion ... it imperiously demands our aid.... the totemic emblem is like the visible body of the god (Durkheim 1979:34 [1915])

The distinction here between "conscious personality" and "abstract forces," it seems, is not important to the worshiper. In one case as in the other, he or she is dealing with something superior that is capable of communion, imposes behavior, is imperious, wants aid, and has a body.

Despite Durkheim's claim that gods are not necessary in religion, his description of religion is not far from those given by many other scholars, in that it makes central more or less anthropomorphic beings—or at the least, anthropomorphic forces. Durkheim's description thus identifies anthropomorphism, as have many others, as a component central to religious belief and practice. What is missing is a persuasive explanation of why such ideas arise and how they affect practice.

The second group of theories holds that religion is wishful thinking. These argue that religion serves to mitigate human discontents, by envisioning alternative and more sanguine possibilities. If we can appeal to gods or look forward to a happy afterlife, in this view, our current misery will be alleviated.

As with social-solidarity theories, something like wishful-thinking theories dates back to antiquity. Euripides, for example, noted that fear and uncertainty lead to religiosity. Subsequently, Spinoza (1955), Hume (1957 [1757]), Feuerbach (1957 [1873]), Marx (Marx and Engels 1957:37–38), and Freud (1964 [1927]) among others elaborated on this theme. Anthropologists taking this view are a minority, but do include major figures such as Malinowski (1948), Kluckhohn (1942) and, in a particularly Freudian vein, Spiro (1966), Wallace (1966), and LaBarre (1972). As Freud has been the common denominator in most wishful-thinking anthropology of religion, I shall concentrate on his views.

Freud's views differ sharply from functionalism, including Durkheim's opinion that any phenomenon as widespread as religion can be no mistake. For Freud, it *is* a mistake and, on balance, maladaptive. An early essay (1907), for example, likens religious rituals to the rituals of neurotics. In a later work, Freud calls religions "illusions, fulfillments of the oldest, strongest, and most urgent wishes of mankind" (1964:47), and even delusions, "born from man's need to make his helplessness tolerable" (1964:25). At best, religions alleviate the existential anxieties of individuals and, by promising rewards and punishments in an afterlife, overcome selfishness and secure good social behavior. Overall, however, their delusional character means that they are poor guides to action. Hence we would be better off if we could let go of them.

Two features of Freud's stance are particularly relevant here. The first is his description of religious ideation, which resembles the one advocated in this paper: religion consists, in the first instance, in the "humanization of nature," that is, in anthropomorphizing. Religion postulates that "everywhere in nature there are Beings around us of a kind that we know in our own society" (1964:22–23). Here Freud follows a line of thought dating at least from Spinoza, through Hume and, probably most influential on Freud, Feuerbach (Harvey 1995).

The second feature, also following a thread in Feuerbach, is Freud's explanation of why people humanize nature and why this includes a life after death. They do so because it alleviates their fears. Humanizing nature gives them a potential ally, or allies, against the ills of existence. These ills include a nature that "rises up against us, majestic, cruel and inexorable" (1964:21); the inevitability and inexplicability of death; and injustice. Hence gods perform a "threefold task: they must exorcise the terrors of nature, they must reconcile men to the cruelty of Fate, particularly as it is shown in death, and they must compensate them for the sufferings and privations" (1964:24) of social existence.

How precisely do people arrive at conceptions of gods? They do it through projection. This concept again evidently is borrowed from Feuerbach, who meant by it, among other things, a human process of creating an external, objectified God in whom cherished but incomplete human virtues can be imagined as fully realized (Harvey 1995). In Freud, however, the term has other meanings, not necessarily coherent (Guthrie 2000). Best known is the specifically psychoanalytic idea that we are dimly aware of, but repress, internal impulses and desires that we find unpleasant and unacceptable. We exorcise these by "projecting" them onto an external object, usually another person, and thus imagining that they belong to someone else instead.

Another meaning of projection in Freud (1964) seems simpler: it is the direct expression of a deep-seated wish, such as that for a father figure, by imagining that the wished-for condition obtains. Simple as it appears, however, how this process works remains unclear. Harvey (1995:241) calls it a "theory-free theory," meaning that Freud does not say what psychic mechanism produces the projection.

Yet another problem with Freud's theory is that religious world-views often are not especially comforting, as varied writers have pointed out. Radcliffe-Brown, for example, writes that it is equally likely that religions give people "fears and anxieties from which they would otherwise be free" (1979:55); and Geertz writes that the "inadequacy of this 'theology of optimism' is radical ... religion has probably disturbed men as much as it has cheered them" (1966:18).

A last and broadest problem is that Freud's account establishes no relationship between religious and secular thought and action, and no general framework encompassing both. Instead, his account depends on the assumption that religious and secular thought and action constitute distinct, separate realms and operate by different rules. This is an assumption with Western precedent back at least to Schleiermacher (1996 [1799]), but one that does not work well in many non-Western societies. Most of the latter assume that religious and secular life are continuous and integrated, and indeed most have languages that do not distinguish them. For this reason among others, anthropologists tend to locate both religious and secular life within some larger framework of thought and action, in which principles of emotion, perception, and cognition are more or less uniform. In contrast, Freud makes religion an idiosyncratic and determinedly non-cognitive—even anti-cognitive—enterprise, the chief purpose of which is to deny reality. If, in this account, religious ritual has any meaning, it is that we go to considerable lengths to fool ourselves.

The third group of theories, intellectualism or cognitivism, emphasizes the human need to understand and act in a complex and uncertain world, and portrays religion as an attempt to answer this need. Tylor (1873), the earliest major anthropological writer on religion, was a powerful advocate of this approach. Once again, however, this approach considerably predates anthropology, extending at least back to Spinoza and continuing with Hume (who, Tylor wrote, produced the modern view of religion). Both Spinoza and Hume wrote that religion, as practiced by most people, consists in anthropomorphizing the world in an attempt to understand it, and in acting accordingly. Thus, for example, religious action is largely ritual, and largely symbolic, because its intended recipients are conceived as humanlike and hence as amenable to such action.

Hume's argument anticipates much of the modern intellectualist position, as it appears for example in Tylor and in Horton (1993). It is quite general: human understanding is limited, but the environment with which it must cope is unlimited. Facing the complexity of our environment, we grasp it only partially and superficially, as an audience in a theatre in which most of the action takes place offstage. In our anxiety and our lack of adequate models for what we perceive, we fall back on the model with which we are most intimately familiar: that of ourselves. This is the basis for notions of gods. Hume's theory thus combines what may be called the comfort and familiarity theories, both of religion and of anthropomorphism.

Although both the comfort and the familiarity theory doubtless have some element of truth, neither is adequate, nor are they adequate if combined (for an extended discussion, see Guthrie 1993). As noted above for Freud's theory, the comfort theory is contradicted by frightening religions. The familiarity theory, which identifies religion as anthropomorphism and attempts to explain what anthropomorphism is, does not explain why we anthropomorphize things and events that are as familiar to us as we ourselves: cats and dogs, stuck drawers and doors slammed by the wind.

Nor does either comfort or familiarity explain another phenomenon closely related to religion, which, Hume concedes, is puzzling. This is the sense that nature shows design, a sense that writers from at least Xenophon (ca 390 BCE) to present-day intelligent-design advocates have made the basis of an argument for the existence of a Designer. The sense of design, Hume writes, flows in upon us with a "force like that of sensation" (1947 [1779]: 154f). He remains skeptical of religion, but adds that a theory to explain the sense of design "would be very acceptable."

Tylor, the pioneer of the anthropology of religion, resembles Hume in his intellectualism and his conclusion that religious ideas are based on our experience with our selves and with other humans. As Evans-Pritchard notes, Tylor "wished to show that primitive religion was rational [and] that it arose from observations ... and from logical deductions from them" (1965:26). Tylor famously defines religion as a belief in spirit beings, and a spirit being as a "thin insubstantial human image, in its nature a sort of vapor, film, or shadow, the cause of life and thought in the individual it animates, independently possessing the personal consciousness and volition of its corporeal owner, past or present" (Lambek 2002:25).

Tylor's theory of religion is his theory of this belief in spirit beings and its application in action, including ritual. The belief originates as an explanation of two experiences: dreams and death (i.e., the deaths of others). Dreams give rise to the idea of the phantom—an image separable from its owner—and death gives rise to the idea of the "life," an animating force separable from the body. These two ideas, combined, make up the idea of the spirit being. The spirit being, in turn, explains death (which is the departure of the spirit), dreams (which are a visit from the spirit), and much else. Religious ritual is action addressed to spirit beings.

Criticism of Tylor's theory has varied, but has consisted largely of two claims: that he has no direct evidence that the process of explanation he describes actually occurs or has occurred in the past, and that his account makes religion a more rational enterprise than it really is. These criticisms seem fair but, as I shall suggest, may be partly countered—as may some of the criticisms of Durkheim and Freud—by recent work on cognition. However, despite Tylor's impact and despite the length of the tradition he continued, the intellectualist approach was largely abandoned through much of the twentieth century.

Perhaps the most careful elaboration of rationalistic intellectualism in anthropology is that of Robin Horton (1993). In several essays, Horton compares religion to science as an explanatory enterprise. He finds these two more similar than usually is thought. Both science and religion, he says, aim to reduce chaos to order and diversity to unity. Both use models drawn from common sense and modified (by abstraction, for example) to fit particular theoretical problems. Both science and religion thus are continuous with ordinary cognition (*pace* Atran 1994, who thinks continuity of science and ordinary cognition should seem ludicrous to an anthropologist). Last, both comprise theories at several levels, from relatively concrete and specific to relatively abstract and general. Religion and science differ primarily in that scientific ideas regularly are subjected to criticism while religious ones are not, and only secondarily that religion uses a personal idiom whereas science does not.

The fact that much religious action is ritual is not idiosyncratic, Horton continues, but instead reflects the fact that it is meant as communication with one or more social beings. To the extent that it is formal, it resembles communication with other social superiors, such as royalty. Scholarly preoccupation with the personal idiom—the anthropomorphism—of religion otherwise is a red herring and leads away from religion's more basic intellectual properties, such as its attempt to reduce chaos to order.

Horton's analysis undermines traditional scholarly contrasts between religion and science, such as "intellectual versus emotional, rational versus mystical, causally orientated versus supernaturally orientated, empirical versus non-empirical" (1993:220). While this result, together with his view of religion as an explanatory system in many ways resembling science, is persuasive, his description of personalism as mere idiom problematically suggests that choice of idiom is arbitrary and that religious systems could adopt a different idiom yet remain substantially unchanged.

In the view advanced in this paper, in contrast, personalism, or anthropomorphism, in human perception and cognition is fundamental. Convergent evidence, as I will suggest, indicates that we have multiple perceptual and conceptual sensitivities to potential signs of human presence and that we thus are primed to use humanlike models in preference to others. The reasons for this are deeply rooted. They have been selected, like most features of organisms, by evolutionary forces. This does not mean, however, that they necessarily are infallible in the interpretations of the world that they produce.

The New Cognitivism and the Anthropology of Religion

The past two decades of rapidly growing research on cognition have brought new information relevant to all three approaches to religion outlined above, especially to the intellectualist or cognitive camp. The new information that is most relevant bears on the kinds of features of living things, especially of animals and humans, that humans are predisposed to perceive; on how and why conceptions of humanlike beings, including spirit beings, arise and persist; and on the accessibility to conscious introspection of perceptual and other cognitive processes concerning these issues.

Evidence from several disciplines suggests that humans (and many other animals as well) are especially sensitive to features on several dimensions—morphological, behavioral, and mental—indicating the possible presence of other animals. Morphologically, animals across a range of phyla, including ourselves, are sensitive to elements of form characteristic of complex animals. These include markings that resemble eyes ("eyespots"; Altbacker and Csány 1990, Ristau 1998, Haley and Fessler 2005), bilateral symmetry (Washburn 1999, van der Helm 2000, Evans, Wenderoth, and Cheng 2000) and, at least for complex animals, faces (Brown and Dooling 1992, Johnson 2001, Emery 2004).

These features need not coincide with each other to trigger our sensitivities. Rather, each may appear by itself, like the smile of the Cheshire cat. Nor need they even be in normal relationships to be perceived as though they were. In the Thompson Effect, for example, a portrait may be inverted but with eyes and mouth altered to remain individually right side up, and yet be perceived as normal. This indicates that eyes and mouth are perceptually processed separately from the face as a whole (Gregory 1997:74). Thus this processing, like that of the other sensitivities mentioned and that of motion, probably is modular—that is, dedicated to a narrow range of inputs (such as two round, black dots separated by a particular, horizontal spacing) and outputs (such as a representation of a pair of eyes).

Behaviorally, motion, especially self-initiated motion, is the most salient feature of animacy (Michotte 1950, Guthrie 1993, Poulin-Dubois and Heroux 1994, Scholl and Tremoulet 2000, H. C. Barrett 2004). For humans, at least, most salient of all is motion that appears goal-oriented (Opfer 2000), as when one object follows another object that changes course. Sensitivity to motion, of course, is crucially adaptive for complex animals. As Gregory (1997:98) puts it,

> detection of motion is essential for survival of all but the very simplest creatures. Moving objects are likely to be dangerous ... or potential food, or a mate. They generally demand action of some kind, while stationary objects may be ignored with safety. Indeed, it is only eyes quite high up the evolutionary scale that produce signals in the absence of movement.

The salience of motion in primitive vision is preserved, incidentally, at the edge of the human retina. If an object beside us moves at the edge of our visual field, we see motion but can identify neither the object nor its color. When the motion stops, the object is invisible again (Gregory 1997:98). As motion is a more primitive percept than color or form, it, rather than any specific form, also must be the most basic sign of life; and indeed it generally is so regarded (Scholl and Tremoulet 2000). Nonetheless motion of most kinds (goal-directed motion may be the exception) is, like form, ambiguous, and some scholars think that neither it nor any "list of perceptually accessible features ... will always tell us what is animate and what is not" (Gelman, Durgin, and Kaufman 1995:182).

A last feature of animals may be called mental. This feature is agency: a capacity for intention, goal-directedness, and corresponding action. This capacity is not directly observable but must be imputed, as Gelman et al., above, suggest. Its imputation is central to theory of mind (Uleman 2005, Malle 2005). It requires that we produce a complex representation of the agent's ends and means, in a "coordination of multiple cues" involving conceptions of the agent's intentions, goal orientation, and essence (Poling and Evans 2002:107).

Of these last three features, conceptions of intention and goal orientation (i.e., teleological conceptions) appear earlier in development. According to Poling and Evans (2002), they are supplemented significantly by biological essentialism only by the age of ten or twelve. Since intention and teleology appear as aspects of theory of mind, this finding supports Carey's (1995) contention that children's naive understandings of animals and plants do not constitute a core ontological domain of biology (which Carey thinks does not exist), but instead are applications of a core domain of psychology to non-human animal behavior. That many young children, and some adults, cross-culturally do not consider plants alive (Cherry 1992) also is consonant with

Carey's contention that biology is not intuitive but is acquired. Accordingly, young children and many adults may attribute language and other human qualities to nonhuman organisms, or fail to attribute qualities such as metabolism, growth, and limited life span to them. This has implications for several theories of religion.

In searching for humans, the features of morphology to which we are sensitive are largely the same as those for other animals: bilateral symmetry, eyespots, and faces. In addition, bipedalism and the human upright stance make us especially sensitive to objects that stand up vertically in the landscape. We occasionally mistake, for instance, tree trunks, garbage cans, and other vertical objects, seen in dim light or at a distance, for humans (Guthrie 1993).

Behavioral features of humans which we are primed to see also resemble those of other animals. Motion, especially self-initiated and goal-oriented motion, is central. Since human behavior is more complex than that of other animals, however, the range of motions that may qualify as goal-directed is vastly greater, and indeed virtually endless. Similarly, the kinds of traces that human behavior leaves behind are innumerable. Because humans produce and use many kinds of intermediate means to their ends and often arrive at these ends circuitously, they create both intended and unintended artifacts. Thus the number of kinds of phenomena that may be produced by human action is indefinitely large, and very little can be ruled out a priori as stemming from such action (Guthrie 1993).

Moreover, tools play such a large part in human action that they arguably may be considered as extensions of humans themselves. Gell (1998) brilliantly describes artifacts as constituting a "distributed agency" that may carry out our intentions in our absence. For Gell, as Harrison writes, "personhood must be understood as extended or distributed among the many objects it fashions and employs in social action, not as something singular or discrete. Social agency, properly conceived, is not co-terminous with the human body" (Harrison 1998:2). Gell is primarily concerned with art works, which act in the artist's stead. He also offers a more somber example: a soldier who plants land mines may continue to kill long after he himself has moved on or is dead. Distributed agency thus, among other things, complicates what we search for when we search for humans and traces of humans. These cannot be restricted to what looks human. A mine, for example, may look like a scarcely perceptible disturbance of the earth or like nothing at all. At the very least, the diversity of forms and effects of human action means that the perceiver must consider an enormous range of things and events as possible products of human behavior.

That the ways in which human agency shows itself are diverse, even limitless, is echoed in the readiness, generality, and abstraction with which we actually conceptualize it. Wegner (2005:22) notes that humans have an "extraordinarily compelling inclination" to perceive causal agents and a "readiness to perceive minds behind events." Remarking that the adaptive importance of distinguishing a person from a lifeless object is clear, Malle asks how the mind knows which is which. He answers that "details aside, objects that are self-propelled are classified into the category of agent" and that this category "can be activated very easily" (Malle 2005:228). For example, it can be activated both by simple stimuli, such as geometric figures moving in two dimensions (Heider and Simmel 1944), and by complex ones, such as computers (Nass and Moon 2000). Indicating the great breadth and generality of our notion of person, Malle cites Tagiuri's proposal to use "the term person perception whenever the perceiver regards the object as having the potential of representation and intentionality" (Malle 2005:229). If such a notion of person perception appears too broad, recall Carey's (1995:279) observation that infants treat even a mobile as a social agent if it shows some interactivity (but see Gelman 2002 for a denial).

Finally, Kuhlmeier, Bloom, and Wynn (2004) report that while five-month-old infants recognize continuity as a basic principle of object motion, they do not expect humans to exhibit it. The authors suggest, therefore, that infants do not regard humans as material objects. This is consistent with a suggestion by Carey (2002) that although folk physics may be intuitive core knowledge even for young children, when it comes to children's expectations about human behavior, all bets may be off. Since human behavior arguably is the principal prototype for agency in general (Cherry 1992), it may be that infants do not regard any agents as material objects. It also is consistent with Scholl and Tremoulet (2000) who report work with both children and adults indicating that the nature of motion, not formal properties, produces perceptual animacy. They write, for example, that "animacy is perceived even when the simple 'actors' in an animation sequence are groups of items rather than unified shapes." That is, animacy does not require a solid body. Once again, this suggests that our expectations about the physical characteristics of human presence, as well as of traces of such presence, are open and flexible.

Regarding the mental aspects of humans, once more the features attributed to non-human animals are present in what we expect about humans: intentionality, teleology, and essentialism. The first two, at least, appear as central components of the fundamental human conceptual framework mentioned above, theory of mind (ToM). ToM is, of course, a major topic in current studies of human cognition. Here, however, we can be content with a sketch, emphasizing the aspects most relevant to anthropomorphism and animism in religion.

First, ToM, which produces our readiness and ability to construe other humans in terms of their mental conditions and qualities, is our principal means of understanding those humans. As such, it is foundational to social cognition and to human life. Second, it is "theoretical" in that it is causal-explanatory (Lillard and Skibbe 2005), explaining behavior in terms of mind. It even somewhat resembles scientific theories in that it "postulates unobservables, predicts them from observables, and uses them to explain other observables" (Malle 2005:225). Third, unlike scientific theories, it is unconscious (Malle 2005, Lillard and Skibbe 2005) and is applied to its objects, including inanimate entities, spontaneously and involuntarily (Abell, Happe, and Frith 2000, Lillard and Skibbe 2005:278–279). As are the mental processes of language, its processes appear largely innate (Bruner 1990, Fodor 1992, Baron-Cohen 1995) and largely inaccessible to conscious scrutiny and criticism. Fourth, ToM typically conceives its subject matter, mind, both as unobservable (Malle 2005, Lillard and Skibbe 2005) and as disembodied (Leder 1990, Lakoff and Johnson 1999, Bering 2002, Bloom 2004, Bering and Bjorklund 2004). Kelemen (2004:7–8) writes, for example, that even young children of three to four years conceive of intangible, agents that comprise little more than mind.

In sum, then, theory of mind represents crucial aspects of the world involuntarily, unconsciously, and largely innately. In this representation, the principal actors are conceived primarily in terms of their minds, not of their physical or other directly observable qualities. Moreover, minds are separable from bodies, and the category of agent is large and open-ended, extending even to biologically inanimate objects.

How do these recent findings from cognitive science bear on the three anthropological approaches to religion outlined earlier? Looking again at the four writers discussed—Durkheim, Freud, Tylor, and Horton—we see that the new material sometimes supports, sometimes modifies, and sometimes undermines them. Some of the new material is only tangential to claims made by these earlier writers, but is relevant to more recent cognitive accounts of religion.

Durkheim, we recall, has been faulted for his functionalism and his failure to show what makes religious thought and action plausible. In addition, some writers have rejected his claim that gods are unnecessary to religion, though his description of the sacred as social and as quasi-personal blurs this claim. The new cognitive material bears somewhat on his functionalism, in part by providing slight support but in larger part by providing an alternative explanation.

The support is that aspects of unconscious cognition, especially theory of mind, indicate that humans have well-developed unconscious capacities for social life. These capacities support both abstract conceptions of society and reifications of sociality in material forms—even in forms that are not, on first glance, obviously personal, ranging from geometric shapes to totems (Gell 1998). Bargh (2005:39) notes, for example, the "automatic activation of abstract, schematic representations of people and groups." These conceptions and forms often may, as Durkheim held, serve social cohesion.

More important, however, is the strength given to an alternate, purely cognitive position: that our predisposition to conceive the world in social terms, including teleological ones, is promiscuous (Kelemen 1999) and inevitably results in an over-extension of human-like social attributes to non-human and non-social features of the world. This over-extension may or may not be useful, and the now-plentiful psychological evidence of how and why it occurs robs Durkheim's social-functional explanation of its salience.

A last reflection on Durkheim from the new cognitivism is some slight support for his view that gods are unnecessary to religion and that a more abstract notion, the sacred, should be substituted for them. More precisely, the new cognitivism shows how diverse and how abstract our conceptions of persons, and hence of gods, can be. Recall Malle's (2005:229) citation of a proposal that person perception occurs whenever the object is seen as having the "potential of representation and intentionality." This modest requirement is met by Durkheim's description of the sacred. Although most conceptions of gods are more fully humanlike, and are bound, for example, to time and place as are humans (J. Barrett 2001), some theological conceptions of gods are not (e.g., Tillich 1948).

Freud also receives both support and subversion from the new research. The Freudian unconscious, with id, ego and superego striving in a complex and unpredictable hydraulic drama, has been broadly rejected as unfalsifiable (Uleman 2005). However, Freud's observation that religion involves the humanization of nature gains support from observations of how readily we apply theory of mind to everything. As Lillard and Skibbe note, we apply theory of mind without regard for domain specificity and may, for instance, "say of the sky, 'It wants to rain'" (2005:281). Still, no wishful thinking is required for this humanization. Rather, it results from a conceptual framework in which the main criterion for detecting agency is self-initiated motion, and in which the principal object, mind, is by nature invisible and may be disembodied, or may be embodied in any of numberless forms.

Tylor, too, is partly borne out and partly modified. A new recognition that the vast majority of mental activity, including cognition, is unconscious and inaccessible (Lakoff and Johnson 1999; Hassin, Uleman and Bargh 2005) means that Tylor's nineteenth-century rationalism must be modified. In it, observations of mysteries such as dreams and death were taken to be objects of explicit speculation and explanation, and the soul and spirit beings were the explicit theoretical entities postulated as explanatory.

According to the new cognitivism, in contrast, theory of mind leads us unconsciously, and incorrigibly, simply to assume agency in whatever phenomena we can. Mind, the essence of agency, is, as noted, conceived as invisible and intangible. Moreover, as Lakoff and Johnson (1999), Bering (2002), Bering and Bjorklund 2004, and Bloom (2004) hold, that the mind survives death is our default assumption. This assumption is produced neither by wishful thinking (as in Freud) nor by a need to explain any particular phenomenon (as in Tylor), but by a kind of cognitive economy: like the doctrine of conservation of matter and energy, it obviates the radical change from existence to non-existence. In Bering's view, we simply are cognitively unable to simulate nonexistence, since we have not experienced it.

Thus a mind something like Tylor's soul or spirit being, insubstantial and separable from the body, already is intuitively available for cultural shaping and application to the Tylorian problems of dreams and death. There is no need to create it for the purpose. Tylor's claim, then, that the notion of spirit being is a cultural universal is bolstered by the cognitive-science claim that the notion of mind is a cognitive universal.

Last among the older approaches to religion reviewed, Horton (1993) once again is both supported and modified by recent cognitive research. Like Tylor, he finds religious thought and action reasonable responses to observations about the world, and he sees conceptions of deities as abstractions from experience with humans. Unlike Tylor, he sees personalism (or in Tylor's terms, animism, and in my terms, anthropomorphism) as mere idiom, a superficial and virtually arbitrary choice of models. Again as with Tylor, Horton's view of deities as attempts to explain empirical data must be modified to fit new evidence that ToM broadly preconceives things and events as agents and as humanlike and that, at the perceptual level, we also are sensitive to signs of complex life. Most important, this evidence subverts Horton's assertion that personalism is only an idiom. Rather, it appears as deep-seated indeed.

Recent Cognitivism in the Anthropology of Religion

In the last quarter-century and especially in the last decade, scholars in several fields have returned to something like Tylor's view of religion as an attempt to explain or at least interpret the phenomenal world. However, whereas

Tylor relied on ethnographic and other descriptive reports and his own analysis of the logic they reflected, current work relies more heavily on the cognitive sciences.

The new cognitivist scholars of religion largely hold, as did Tylor, that religion may best be defined as thought and action concerned with spirits or deities. These are beings who are humanlike in their mental (and sometimes physical) characteristics, yet still usually are distinguishable from, and usually superior to, ordinary humans. Despite this agreement, current cognitivism may be divided approximately into two sorts. The first sort is concerned mainly with how religious ideas and behaviors arise. It maintains that they arise intuitively—that is, as products of "spontaneous and unconscious perceptual and inferential processes" (Sperber 1996:89)—and hence arise constantly (Guthrie 1980, 1993, 2001, 2002, forthcoming; Burkert 1996; Bering 2002; and Kelemen 2004. Heberlein and Adolphs 2004 say the same of anthropomorphism). They also transmit easily, since their bases are deeply familiar. We have intuitive ideas and perform intuitive behaviors, as Sperber says, without knowing why, or even that, we do.

Crucially, this first form of cognitivism furnishes an explanation for the most distinctive features of religious thought and action, namely systematized animism (both in the sense of belief in spirit beings and in the sense of attributing life to the biologically inanimate) and anthropomorphism. It holds that these phenomena constitute a category of interpretive mistakes, namely mistaking non-human and inanimate things and events for human and living ones. It further holds that these mistakes are not random but stem from our mostly-unconscious search, guided by our specific sensitivities and theory of mind, for all possible agents in a perceptually ambiguous world. Since theory of mind, in particular, represents agency as both invisible and polymorphic, all manner of phenomena are potential agents. Since most actual complex agents are adept at concealing their presence, our criteria for deciding that one is present, or has left traces, are lenient. As we thus are (again unconsciously) on a hair trigger for detecting friend or foe, predator or prey, we cannot prevent ourselves thinking we have detected one even when none is there (Guthrie 1993). In bear country, every dark, bulky shape in a thicket is cause for alarm.

Moreover, our obligatory response is general, not restricted only to fight or flight, and we are forced to it even by artifacts. Scholl and Tremoulet (2000:306) write that a perception of animacy is nearly instantaneous and "mandatory" on viewing even simple, two-dimensional animated displays (such as those of Heider and Simmel 1944). Complex artifacts, for example conveyances, may obligate us similarly. Emerson said that "it is impossible not to personify a ship," and Oliver Wendell Holmes that "a ship is the most living of the inanimate things" (Tamen 2001:83). Indeed anthropomorphization of vessels has been systematized and has become the basis of aspects of maritime law. Holmes writes, "it is only by supposing the ship to have been treated as if endowed with a personality, that the arbitrary seeming peculiarities of the maritime law can be made intelligible" (ibid.).

A second contemporary cognitive view of religion, part of an approach to culture called cultural epidemiology (Sperber 1985, 1996), holds that religious ideas resemble epidemic disease in their genesis and distribution. They arise only randomly and for obscure reasons, but once hatched spread quickly. They spread because they are memorable, and they are memorable because they combine an intuitive element, which makes them easy to grasp and productive, with a counterintuitive one, which makes them striking (J. Barrett 2000, Boyer 2001, Pyysiäinen 2001, Atran 2002).

A leading advocate of this approach is Boyer (1994, 2001). Boyer calls his key term, counterintuitive, "technical." It does not merely mean "strange … exceptional or extraordinary" (2001:65). Instead, it means contradicting intuitive ontological categories. *Animal, person,* and *plant,* for instance, ostensibly are ontological categories intuitively implying that their members have certain characteristic properties, including being alive, needing nutrition, and undergoing growth, aging, and mortality. Counterintuitive ideas include beings that belong to these categories yet fail to have one or more of these properties, and beings that do not belong to these categories yet have such properties. In addition, Boyer notes that models of humans are attractive because they have great potential for making inferences. Here he joins earlier cognitivist scholars of religion such as Spinoza (1955), Hume (1957 [1757]), Horton 1993, and most explicitly Guthrie (1980, 1993).

Several problems appear in the cultural-epidemiological account. One is the question of what is and is not counterintuitive, as this central term is used here. Boyer says that it should not be understood in its usual sense and that "counterontological" (2001:65) might be more descriptive of what he means. Ontological categories, however, evidently have no independent basis in science or in nature, but only in intuition: they are not "always true or accurate … They are just what we intuitively expect, and that's that" (2001:68). Thus, what is counterintuitive is whatever contradicts what we intuitively expect.

But what do we intuitively expect, and why? For the key domain of biology, we are said to expect the list mentioned above: life, having bodies, needing food, growing, aging, and dying. The most definite answer to why we expect it is given by some epidemiologists (Sperber 2001, Atran 2002) who say we do so because the domain and its entailments are modular and innate. However, the innateness both of this domain and of particular entailments is contested. Some researchers say that biology is, instead, learned (Carey 1985, 1995, 2000; Cherry 1992, Johnson and Carey 1998), and that what appears to the epidemiologists as an innate biology is instead an extension of an innate psychology, including theory of mind. If biology is learned, it is likely to be culturally variable; and intuitions and counterintuitions about it also will be culturally variable. If there is no innate biology, then we can have no innate counter-intuitions about it. Needless to say, we still can be surprised by unusual animate and inanimate objects; but that is much less than what the epidemiologists mean by intuitive biology.

Of several reasons for doubting that biology is a modular, innate domain (Carey 1995, 2002), I mention only two. The first is very general. It is what Carey and Spelke (1994) call the "problem of perception." The problem is, if biology is modular, how does the input module know which entities are organisms and which are not? Since modules by definition have a narrow range of input and since animals, for instance, are physically diverse (usually, for example, being camouflaged to invisibility unless and until they move), it is more likely that animals are identified by a module sensitive to intentional states. Such a module might respond to goal-directed motion. But this module would be psychological (involving, for example, theory of mind), not biological.

The second reason for doubt is more specific and is based on at least two kinds of empirical observation undermining an innate-biology domain. One is that children are poor biologists. Even Gelman, a scholar who is on the innatist side of this issue, writes that children have limited understanding of biological functioning (Gelman and Opfer 2002). Preschoolers deny that plants are alive (as do some adults, Cherry 1992) and cannot distinguish "not alive" from similar but distinct ideas such as inactive, absent, unreal, and dead (Slaughter, Jaakola, and Carey 1999, cited in Gelman and Opfer 2002). Even older children may not understand (contrary to a specific epidemiological assertion) that death is inevitable for living things and is permanent (Slaughter, Jaakola, and Carey 1999). Indeed, adults may not understand this either. Gelman and Opfer (2002) conclude that although the animate-inanimate distinction is fundamental, the question remains open whether it is wired-in and domain-specific or the result of experience. Hence the question whether there can be domain-specific biological intuitions also remains open.

A second kind of empirical observation, noted above in connection to theory of mind, is especially germane. It contradicts a central and distinctive claim of the epidemiologists: that a common religious conception—disembodied agency—is widespread because it is counterintuitive. As mentioned, two philosophers and a linguist (Leder 1990, Lakoff and Johnson 1999) hold that a conception of agency as essentially disembodied is, on the contrary, intuitive, and recent cognitive scientists (Bering 2002, Carey 2002, Bering and Bjorklund 2004, Bloom 2004, Kuhlmeier, Bloom and Wynn 2004) report experimental evidence to the same effect. This evidence is that young children, including five-month-old infants, have mutually exclusive conceptions of agents (prototypically humans) on the one hand, and of material objects on the other. That is, even young children are dualists. They conceive agents as essentially immaterial and therefore as independent of bodies; and they do so intuitively and even innately. These findings, of course, undermine the epidemiological view that religious conceptions of disembodied agents are successful because they are counterintuitive. It suggests, instead, the opposite: that such conceptions are widespread precisely because they are intuitive. Quite possibly they even are, as Bloom (2004) holds, innate.

Finally, the epidemiological approach to religion seems contradicted by Darwinian principles, which hold that major features of organisms evolve in ways useful to their possessors. As Darwin sanguinely puts it, natural selection "selects exclusively for the good of each organic being" (1858, in Young 1985:92). Cognition accordingly evolves in a way that produces useful information (H.C. Barrett 2004). Cultural epidemiologists, however, maintain that human cognition favors information that is, in some optimal measure, paradoxical and false or "counter-factual." So far, the evidence produced for such a tendency seems only to be that information that is novel is more memorable than information that is not; but this evidence merely supports basic information theory.

How believable such paradoxical and counter-factual information is remains to be explored. So does the question why natural selection should favor it. Some writers (e.g., Sperber 1996) describe the transmission of such information in biological metaphor, calling it "parasitic," but the attractiveness of this metaphor probably derives more from its animism than from its productivity.

The first cognitivist approach to religion described above appears more parsimonious, because it does not posit special features either in mind or in religion. Instead it merely applies convergent material from recent cognitive science to what is common in the analyses of such writers as Spinoza, Hume, Freud, Durkheim, Tylor, and Horton. It holds that religion in general, as well as animism and anthropomorphism in particular, are widespread because they are intuitive, in the sense described: as products of "spontaneous and unconscious perceptual and inferential processes" (Sperber 1996:89). In particular, they are products of theory of mind and of the related perceptual sensitivities, applied to an uncertain world. This theory and these sensitivities have evolved to detect and to comprehend, in perpetually ambiguous circumstances, agency conceived either as disembodied or as embodied in limitless forms.

Conclusion

Anthropomorphism and its sister phenomenon, animism, then, may in the first instance be understood as the inevitable occasional errors of perceptual and conceptual systems. They appear in religion, as in other thought and action, because they are plausible—if in retrospect mistaken—interpretations of, and means of influencing, things and events.

That they are errors does not mean, of course, that they do not have uses. As writers as diverse as Freud, Durkheim, and Marx have urged, religious thought and action often are tools for social control or emotional assurance. However, although such uses help explain why religious thought and action may be actively promulgated and may be shaped into particular forms, they cannot explain why such thought and action arise and are plausible in the first place.

They arise and are plausible for reasons that are cognitive: that humans face a world that is complex and finally inscrutable, and in which the most important components are human, are capable of concealing themselves, and are conceived as essentially unobservable. This is a world with which we are prepared to deal by theory of mind, by related sensitivities to such diverse phenomena as motion, faces, and apparent traces of design, and by corresponding capacities for social action. In this world and owing to these capacities, animism and anthropomorphism, both unsystematized and systematized as religion, inevitably arise again and again.

References

Abell, F., Happe, F. and Frith, U. (2000) 'Do Triangles Play Tricks? Attribution of Mental States to Animated Shapes in Normal and Abnormal Development' in *Cognitive Development* 15:1–16.

Altbacker, V. and Csány, V. (1990) 'The Role of Eyespots in Predator Recognition and Antipredatory Behaviour of the Paradise Fish *Macropodus opercularis L'* in *Ethology* 85:51–57.

Atran, Scott (1994) 'Core Domains Versus Scientific Theories: Evidence from Systematics and Itzaj-Maya Folk Biology' in Hirschfeld, L.A. and Gelman, S.A. (eds), *Domain Specificity in Cognition and Culture.* New York: Cambridge University. Pp. 316–340.

Atran, Scott (2002) *In Gods We Trust: The Evolutionary Landscape of Religion.* New York: Oxford University.

Bargh, John A. (2005) 'Bypassing the Will: Toward Demystifying the Non-conscious Control of Social Behavior' in Hassin, Ran R., Uleman, James S. and Bargh, John A. (eds.) *The New Unconscious.* New York: Oxford University. Pp.37–58.

Baron-Cohen, Simon (1995) *Mindblindness: An Essay on Autism and Theory of Mind.* Cambridge, MA: MIT.

Barrett, J. and Clark, H. (2004) 'Cognitive Development and the Understanding of Animal Behavior' in Ellis, B. and Bjorklund, D. (eds.) *Origins of the Social Mind.* New York: Guilford. N.p.

Barrett, Justin (2000) 'Exploring the Natural Foundations of Religion' in *Trends in Cognitive Sciences,* 4(1):29–34.

Barrett, Justin (2001) 'Do Children Experience God as Adults Do?' in Andresen, Jensine (ed.) *Religion in Mind: Cognitive Perspectives on Religious Belief, Ritual, and Experience,* Cambridge: Cambridge University. Pp.173–190.

Bering, Jesse (2002) 'Intuitive Perceptions of Dead Agents' Minds: The Natural Foundations of Afterlife Beliefs as Phenomenological Boundary' in *Journal of Cognition and Culture,* 2:263–308.

Bering, Jesse and Bjorklund, David (2004) 'The Natural Emergence of 'Afterlife' Reasoning as a Developmental Regularity' in *Developmental Psychology,* 40:217–233.

Bloom, Paul (2004) *Descartes' Baby: How the Science of Child Development Explains What Makes Us Human.* New York: Basic.

Boyer, Pascal (1994) *The Naturalness of Religious Ideas: A Cognitive Theory of Religion,* Berkeley: University of California.

Boyer, Pascal (2001) *Religion Explained,* New York: Basic.

Brown, S. D. and Dooling, R.J. (1992) 'Perception of Conspecific Faces by Budgerigars (*Melopsittacus undulatus*): I. Natural Faces.' in *Journal of Comparative Psychology,* 106:203–216.

Bruner, J. (1990) *Acts of Meaning,* Cambridge, MA: Harvard University.

Burkert, Walter (1996) *Creation of the Sacred: Tracks of Biology in Early Religions.* Cambridge, MA: Harvard University.

Carey, Susan (1985) *Conceptual Change in Childhood,* Cambridge, MA: MIT

Carey, Susan (1995) 'On the Origin of Causal Understanding' in Sperber, Dan, Premack, David and Premack, Ann (eds.), *Causal Cognition: A Multidisciplinary Debate,* New York: Oxford University. Pp.268–302.

Carey, Susan (2000) 'Science Education as Conceptual Change' in *Journal of Applied Developmental Psychology,* 1:37–41.

Carey, Susan (2002) Personal communication, at Harvard University Center for Basic Research in the Social Sciences, Experimental Social Science Conference, "Why Would Anyone Believe in God?" Cambridge, MA. Oct. 25.

Carey, Susan and Spelke, E. (1994) 'Domain Specific Knowledge and Conceptual Change' in Hirschfield, L.A. and Gelman, S.A. (eds.), *Domain Specificity in Cognition and Culture,* New York: Cambridge University. Pp.169–200.

Cherry, John (1992) *Animism in Thought and Language,* Ph.D. thesis, University of California, Berkeley.

Dennett, Daniel (1987) *The Intentional Stance,* Cambridge, MA: MIT.

Douglas, Mary and Perry, Edmund (1985) 'Anthropology and Comparative Religion' in *Theology Today,* 41(4):410–427.

Durkheim, Emile (1979)[1915] 'The Elementary Forms of the Religious Life' in Lessa, W. A. and Vogt, E. Z (eds.) *Reader in Comparative Religion: An Anthropological Approach,* New York: Harper & Row. Pp.27–35.

Emery, Nathan (2004) 'Comparative Psychology of Face Perception' Paper presented at European Science Foundation Workshop "Social Communication and the Face," Cambridge, UK, 20–23 September.

Evans, C. S., Wenderoth, P.M. and Cheng, K. (2000) 'Detection of Bilateral Symmetry in Complex Biological Images' in *Perception,* 29:31–42.

Evans-Pritchard, E. E. (1965) *Theories of Primitive Religion,* Oxford: Oxford University.

Feuerbach, Ludwig (1957) [1873] *The Essence of Christianity,* New York: Harper and Row.

Fodor, Jerry (1992) 'A Theory of the Child's Theory of Mind' in *Cognition,* 44:283–296.

Freud, Sigmund (1907) 'Obsessive Actions and Religious Practices' in *Collected Papers* Vol. 2. London.

Freud, Sigmund (1964) [1927] *The Future of an Illusion,* Garden City: Anchor.

Geertz, Clifford (1966) 'Religion as a Cultural System' in Banton, Michael (ed.) *Anthropological Approaches to the Study of Religion,* London: Tavistock, Pp.1–46.

Gell, Alfred (1998) *Art and Agency: An Anthropological Theory,* Oxford: Oxford University.

Gelman, Rochel, Durgin, Frank and Kaufman, Lisa. 'Distinguishing Between Animates and Inanimates: Not by Motion Alone' in Sperber,

Dan, Premack, David and Premack, Ann. (eds.) *Causal Cognition: A Multidisciplinary Debate,* Oxford: Oxford University, Pp.150–184.

Gelman, S.A.and Opfer, J. E. (2002) 'Development of the Animate-Inanimate Distinction' in Goswami, U. (ed.) *Handbook of Childhood Cognitive Development,* Oxford: Blackwell, Pp.151–166.

Gregory, Richard (1997) *Eye and Brain: The Psychology of Seeing,* 5th ed, Princeton: Princeton University.

Guthrie, Stewart (1980) 'A Cognitive Theory of Religion' *Current Anthropology,* 21(2):181–203.

Guthrie, Stewart (1993) *Faces in the Clouds: A New Theory of Religion.* New York: Oxford University.

Guthrie, Stewart (1997) 'Anthropomorphism: A Definition and a Theory' in Mitchell, R.W., Thompson, N.S. and Miles, H.L. (eds.) *Anthropomorphism, Anecdotes, and Animals,* Albany: State University of New York. Pp.50–58.

Guthrie, Stewart (2000) 'Projection' in Braun, W. and McCutcheon, R.T. (eds.) *Guide to the Study of Religion, London: Cassell. Pp.225–238.*

Guthrie, Stewart (2002) 'Animal Animism: Evolutionary Roots of Religious Cognition' in Pyysiäinen, I, and Anttonen, V. (eds.) *Current Approaches in the Cognitive Science of Religion,* London and New York: Continuum. Pp. 38–67.

Guthrie, Stewart (Forthcoming) 'Gambling on Gods' in Wulff, David (ed.) *Handbook on the Psychology of Religion,* New York: Oxford University. N.p.

Haley, K. J. and Fessler, M.T. (2005) 'Nobody's Watching? Subtle Cues Affect Generosity in an Anonymous Economic Game' in *Evolution and Human Behavior,* 26:245–256.

Harrison, Simon (1998) 'The Extended Agency of Alfred Gell' in *Anthropology Today,* 14(4):2–3.

Hart, Keith (1999) Foreword, in Rappaport, Roy, *Ritual and Religion in the Making of Humanity.* Cambridge: Cambridge University. Pp. 14–19.

Harvey, Van A. (1995) *Feuerbach and the Interpretation of Religion.* Cambridge: Cambridge University.

Hassin, Ran R., Uleman, James S. and Bargh, John A. (eds.) (2005) *The New Unconscious.* Oxford: Oxford University.

Heberlein, Andrea and Adolphs, Ralph (2004) 'Impaired Spontaneous Anthropomorphizing Despite Intact Perception and Social Knowledge' *Proceedings of the National Academy of Sciences of the United States of America* 101(19):7487–7491.

Heider, Fritz and Simmel, Marianne (1944) 'An Experimental Study of Apparent Behavior.' *The American Journal of Psychology* 57:243–259.

Horton, Robin (1993) *Patterns of Thought in Africa and the West*, Cambridge: Cambridge University.

Hume, David (1947) [1779] *Dialogues Concerning Natural Religion*, 2nd ed. N. Kemp, ed. New York: Library of Liberal Arts.

Hume, David (1957) [1757] *The Natural History of Religion*. Stanford: Stanford University.

Johnson, Mark H. (2001) 'The Development and Neural Basis of Face Recognition: Comment and Speculation' in *Infant and Child Development*, 10:31.

Johnson, S.C. and Carey, S. (1998) 'Knowledge Enrichment and Conceptual Change in Folkbiology: Evidence from Williams Syndrome' in *Cognitive Psychology* 37:156–200.

Kelemen, Deborah (1999) 'The Scope of Teleological Thinking in Preschool Children' in *Cognition*, 70:241–272.

Kelemen, Deborah (2004) 'Are Children 'Intuitive Theists'? Reasoning About Purpose and Design in Nature' in *Psychological Science*, 15(5):295–301.

Kluckhohn, Clyde (1942) 'Myths and Rituals: A General Theory' in *Harvard Theological Review*, 35:45–79.

Kuhlmeier, Valerie A., Bloom, Paul and Wynn, Karen (2004) 'Do 5-Month-Old Infants See Humans as Material Objects?' in *Cognition*, 94(1):95-103.

La Barre, Weston (1972) *The Ghost Dance: Origins of Religion*. New York: Dell.

Lakoff, George and Johnson, Mark (1999) *Philosophy in the Flesh*. New York: Basic.

Lambek, Michael (ed.) (2002) *A Reader in the Anthropology of Religion*, Malden, MA: Blackwell.

Leder, Drew (1990) *The Absent Body*, Chicago: University of Chicago.

Lillard, Angeline S. and Skibbe, Lori (2005) 'Theory of Mind: Conscious Attribution and Spontaneous Trait Inference' in Hassin, Ran R., Uleman, James S. and Bargh, John A. (eds.) *The New Unconscious*, Oxford: Oxford University. Pp. 277–305.

Malinowski, Bronislaw (1948) *Magic, Science and Religion and Other Essays*. Garden City, NY: Doubleday and Company.

Malle, Bertram F. (2005) 'Folk Theory of Mind: Conceptual Foundations of Human Social Cognition' in Hassin, Ran R., Uleman, James S. and

Bargh, John A. (eds.) *The New Unconscious,* New York: Oxford University. Pp.225–255.

Marx, Karl, and Engels, Freidrich (1957) *On Religion.* Moscow: Progress.

Michotte, A. (1950) *The Perception of Causality.* New York: Basic.

Nass, Clifford and Moon, Young Me (2000) 'Machines and Mindlessness: Social Responses to Computers' in *Journal of Social Issues,* 56:81–103.

Opfer, John E. (2000) 'Developing a Biological Understanding of Goal-Directed Action' Ph.D. thesis, University of Michigan, Ann Arbor.

Piaget, Jean (1929) *The Child's Conception of the World,* London: Routledge and Kegan Paul.

Poling, Devereaux A. and Evans, Margaret E. (2002) 'Why Do Birds of a Feather Flock Together? Developmental Change in the Use of Multiple Explanations: Intention, Teleology and Essentialism' in *British Journal of Developmental Psychology,* 20:89–112.

Poulin-Dubois, D. and Heroux, G. (1994) 'Movement and Children's Attribution of Life Properties' in *International Journal of Behavioral Development,* 17:329–347.

Pyysiäinen, Ilkka (2001) *How Religion Works.* Leiden: Brill.

Radcliffe-Brown, A. R. (1979) [1939]. 'Taboo' in Lessa, W.A. and Vogt, E.Z. (eds.) *Reader in Comparative Religion: An Anthropological Approach,* New York: Harper and Row. Pp.46–56.

Rappaport, Roy (1999) *Ritual and Religion in the Making of Humanity.* Cambridge: Cambridge University.

Ristau, C. (1998) 'Cognitive Ethology: The Minds of Children and Animals' in Cummins, D. and Allen, C. (eds.) *The Evolution of Mind,* New York: Oxford University. Pp.127–135.

Saler, Benson (2000) [1993] *Conceptualizing Religion: Immanent Anthropologists, Transcendent Natives, and Unbounded Categories,* New York: Berghahn.

Scholl, Brian J. and Tremoulet, Patrice D. (2000) 'Perceptual Causality and Animacy' in *Trends in Cognitive Sciences,* 4(8):299–309.

Schleiermacher, Friedrich (1996) [1799] *On Religion: Speeches to its Cultured Despisers,* Cambridge: Cambridge University Press.

Slaughter, V., Jaakola, K. and Carey, S. (1999) 'Constructing a Coherent Theory: Children's Biological Understanding of Life and Death' in Siegal, M. and Petersen, C. (eds.) *Children's Understanding of Biology and Health,* Cambridge: Cambridge University.

Sperber, Dan (1985) 'Anthropology and Psychology: Towards an Epidemiology of Representations' in *Man* (N.S.) 20:73–89.

Sperber, Dan (1996) *Explaining Culture*, Oxford: Blackwell.

Sperber, Dan (2001) 'Mental Modularity and Cultural Diversity' in Harvey Whitehouse (ed.) *The Debated Mind: Evolutionary Psychology versus Ethnography*, Oxford: Berg. Pp.23–56.

Spinoza, Benedict de (1955) *The Chief Works of Benedict de Spinoza*, New York: Dover.

Spiro, Melford (1966) 'Religion: Problems of Definition and Meaning' in Banton, M. (ed.) *Anthropological Approaches to the Study of Religion*, London: Tavistock. Pp.85–126.

Tamen, Miguel (2001) *Friends of Interpretable Objects*, Cambridge, MA: Harvard University.

Tillich, Paul (1948) *The Shaking of the Foundations*, New York: Scribner's.

Tylor, E. B. (1873) *Primitive Culture*, London: John Murray.

Turner, Victor (1969) *The Ritual Process*, Chicago: Aldine.

Uleman, James S. (2005) 'Introduction: Becoming Aware of the New Unconscious' in Hassin, Ran R., Uleman, James S. and Bargh, John A. (eds.) *The New Unconscious*, New York: Oxford University. Pp.3–15.

van der Helm, Peter (convener and chair) (2000) Principles of Symmetry Perception, Invited Symposium, 2000 International Congress of Psychology, Stockholm, Sweden.

Wallace, Anthony F. C. (1966) *Religion: An Anthropological View* New York: Random.

Washburn, Dorothy (1999) 'Perceptual Anthropology: The Cultural Salience of Symmetry' in *American Anthropologist*, 101(3):547–562.

Wegner, Daniel M. (2005) 'Who Is the Controller of Controlled Processes?' in Hassin, Ran R., Uleman, James S. and Bargh, John A. (eds.) *The New Unconscious*, New York: Oxford University. Pp.19–36.

Whitehouse, Harvey (2000) *Arguments and Icons: Divergent Modes of Religiosity*, Oxford: Oxford University.

Wilson, David Sloan (2002) *Darwin's Cathedral: Evolution, Religion, and the Nature of Society*, Chicago: University of Chicago.

Young, Robert. M. (1985) *Darwin's Metaphor: Nature's Place in Victorian Culture*. Cambridge: Cambridge University.

CHAPTER TWO

DURKHEIMIAN ANTHROPOLOGY AND RELIGION: GOING IN AND OUT OF EACH OTHER'S BODIES

Maurice Bloch
In memory of Skip Rappaport.

Durkheim's work has always been criticised for his reifying of the social and situating it in an indeterminate zone between actors' consciousness and quantifiable facts. However, in this chapter, I am not concerned with arguing whether this criticism of the founder of French sociology's work is justified. My purpose is to show that it is possible to maintain some aspects of his conclusions about the nature of religion and of the social with quite different types of arguments to those he employed. My framework here is that of modern evolutionary natural science and our recent understandings of the specificities of the human mind/brain.

Such an evolutionist position tends to make social/cultural anthropologists most uncomfortable, although I hope that, as they read on and overcome their distaste, they find that an evolutionist perspective does not necessarily lead to the dangers which they fear from such a stance and that it can even be reconciled with some of their most cherished ideas, ideas which will thereby emerge as strengthened.

But since one might as well hang for a sheep as for a lamb, I begin my argument much further back than is usual in evolutionary anthropology with a consideration of the very earliest stages of life on earth, when unicellular organisms associated together to form multi-cellular units in the Cambrian era.

During this crucial transition, and for millions of years, it was far from clear whether those early multi-cellular organisms were one or many since they were in an in-between stage. This biological conundrum still exists, in varying ways and to varying degrees, for many subsequent and more complex forms of life. An extreme example would be coral, about which one can argue equally plausibly that the minute units of which it consists are separate organisms, or that whole coral branches, or even whole reefs, are one single animal.

The difficulty does not only apply in the case of such exceptional life forms or when we try to isolate the "individual". The problem of the unit, or level, on which natural selection acts, is a difficult issue with respect to all living things and it has become particularly acute in modern biology. Does natural selection occur at the gene level?, or on combinations of associated genes? or at the level of the individual?, or on a larger group which shares genes in differing degrees (Stotz, & Griffiths, 2004)?

This sort of question is particularly problematic when we are dealing with social species. Is it the bee or the hive which is the animal? After all, the bees in a hive are as genetically identical as are the different bits of our human body, and a hive possesses only one set of working reproductive organs.

The biological problems do not end there. When does an embryo become separate from its mother? Is a live spermatozoid a unit? More generally, how far are parents one with their children, and are descendants of individuals their continuation or a new unit? Are descent groups one body? Do members of one caste have unique distinctive types of blood? Are nations one people? Are we all the *children* of God in the *brotherhood* of Christ? Is society, as Durkheim claimed, more than the sum of the constituent individuals?

Here, those readers who have already given me up as some sort of biological reductionist, indifferent to the higher purpose of cultural anthropology, might summon a flicker of interest with these more familiar disciplinary questions. They may even begin to hope that I might have something to say about religion and ritual, which, after all, is what this book is about. I shall get there.... eventually. And, indeed, my prime purpose in this chapter is to consider the theoretical implications of the way I have just managed to *slither* from a discussion of the structure of coral to hoary classical subjects in anthropology and even to central tenets of some versions of the Christian religion.

But if the reader is totally unsympathetic to the approach I propose he or she will already have revelled in identifying a familiar sleight of hand, namely representing facts about the world as if they were just that, without having first recited the anthropologists' exorcism prayer: "*I humbly acknowledge that every thing I say is nothing but an epiphenomenon of my present cultural position and time and that this inevitably leads me to essentialising a particular cultural position and then mercilessly imposing it on defenceless people*". In other words, I have been guilty of suggesting that *my* scientific knowledge, a mere elitist manifestation of my own culture, is somehow the basis of the propositions made by those people around the world who say things like: "The members of our group, which has existed since the beginning of time, share a distinctive type of bone" or "Our lineage consists of one body" or "Initiation reunites us with our ancestors" or "Ask not for whom the bell tolls; it tolls for thee.".

I would have thus committed all the category mistakes in the book: especially in having forgotten the fact that the cultural creates an impenetrable screen between what is and our representations of it. Of course these familiar arguments are partly justified[1], perhaps as first steps when we teach an introduction to anthropology, but in this chapter I argue that when left in categorical form they, too, are just as misleading as the ethnocentrism anthropologists love to denounce.

We may start with a classic and familiar polemic as a way to introduce the basis of the theoretical position I shall adopt below.

In the bad old days, so the story goes, anthropologists used to think that kinship was based on the fact that people go in and out of each other's bodies. Indeed, they might have stressed that the physical separation from mothers takes quite a while, with intermediate phases such as breast feeding and child care. Some of these earlier vulgar anthropologists went so far as to suggest that the care given by fathers to infants was somehow the consequence of having gone into the mother during sexual intercourse. They argued that these "natural" foundations were the common base of all different kinship systems (Collier and Rosaldo 1987: p.31ff.)

Such naivety, however, was soon to be severely disciplined by developments in our subject. This was done, first of all, by people who stressed the old platonic point that humans (I don't see why this does not apply to other animals too) do not live in the world as God, or the scientists, see it, but *via* their understanding of it, and that therefore *the foundation, i.e.* going in and out of each other's body, is not directly any such thing for social knowledge. This correction was, however, soon deemed not to have been severe enough. It was not simply that people saw the world "through a glass darkly". It was that they did not see it at all. There was no such *fact* as that people went in and out each other's bodies. These were just accidental cultural representations of which my particular formulation is only one among many. Thus, to talk of different, culturally constructed, kinship systems as though these were cultural interpretations of a single reality was a fallacy. David Schneider in a wonderful

---

1. They are what would be used to dismiss as irrelevant studies such as those of Cosmides and Tooby (1992) about cheater detection.

metaphor explained that if you went out into the world with a kinship-shaped cutting tool you, of course, got kinship shaped pieces, by this he implied that if the tool had had any other shape than the Western-shaped kinship tool, which would be the case with the tools used by the "others", the shape you would have then got would then be quite different (Schneider 1984: 198).

I have always liked this metaphor of Schneider's because, as a child, I used to spend much time watching my grandmother making biscuits. She would roll out a large even pancake of dough on the marble of the kitchen table and, with a few ancient tin tools, she would cut out various shapes. This is exactly what Schneider has in mind. But the other reason why I like his metaphor, is that what is wrong with it is also obvious. The world in which people go in and out of each other, the denounced *foundation*, is not, as suggested by Schneider's analogy, inert, undifferentiated, and evenly flat, like biscuit dough. And its shape, although this does not determine the way it will be represented, it severely restricts what is likely. Plato used another culinary metaphor. For him the world was more like a roast chicken than pastry, and, unless you really wanted to make things difficult for yourself, you would "carve it at the joints", wherever these occurred on the animal you were serving up.

Indeed, it is the dialectic between the facts of sex and birth and the cultural representations of these phenomena that promises to advance our understanding of the nature of human beings, which of course also involves the cultural and hence historical aspect. But this examination is what the Schneiderian rhetoric makes impossible by refusing to allow us to ask what the representations "are about"; what the world is like; and, instead, replacing consideration by a trivial point about the fact that different languages will probably not all have a word for what anthropologists call "kinship".

And there is yet something else that is obscured by Schneider's figure of speech. The cutting tools, which represent concepts in the metaphor, also have to be explained. There is no doubt that these are the product of specific histories but they, nevertheless, have had to be usable tools by the minds of the human beings who employ them. Here the world, as it is, interacts once again in a challenging way with the representations that social or cultural anthropologists study. It is merely banal to stress that the world we live in is culturally constructed. What is of interest is the indirect relation of the construction with what is constructed and how the construction is used.

This chapter, however, is not going to advance on the implications of the link between the fact that we go in and out of each other's body in birth and sex and the cultural representations of this fact in kinship systems. Many, though I would not include myself among them, may feel that this topic has grown tiresome. I merely evoke the controversy to stress that, since all cultures interpret, and have to interpret, the fact that we go in and out of each other in sex and birth, they also have to interpret the consequent fact that for us, as is the case with coral, there is indeterminacy concerning the physical boundaries of individuals. The so-called "descent theorists" of my anthropological youth were fascinated with groups of people who declare themselves to be "one body", in other words corporate groups. These statements are so interesting, not because they are flights of fancy, but because they are in part motivated by the real fact of the indeterminacy and arbitrariness of the boundaries of biological units.

My focus in this chapter, however, concerns another real fact about human beings which although different from kinship matters is not altogether unrelated. This indeterminacy is not simply a result of the sexual character of our species and the way it reproduces itself. It is also due to another feature of *homo sapiens*. Individuals go in and out of each other because of certain characteristics of their nervous system. This form of interpenetration is as material as sex and birth, though, unlike sex and birth, it is, by and large, unique to our species (Povinelli, D. J., Bering, J.M., & Giamborone, S. 2000; Decety & Somerville 2003).

I have already mentioned above that, although the boundaries of individual units are arbitrary among all living forms, this ambiguity takes on a special, perhaps more extreme, form in social animals, since the social, of itself, and by definition, once again connects the individuals whom time and genealogical distance are separating. Such a process occurs in a variety of ways in different life forms. This is because the mechanisms that makes the social differ according to the species concerned. So, it is not surprising that the specific basis of human sociability is a product of those capacities of our species which make it distinctive (Humphrey 2002).

One thing that normal human babies do, at around the age of twelve months, but which our nearest relatives the chimpanzees never do, is to point at things, not because they want what they designate—they do do this, but chimps do that too—but because they want the person whom they are with to adjust his or her mind in harmony with their own, in other words, they want the person whom they are with to pay attention to the same thing as them, in other words to share intentionality (Gopnik 1993, Tomasello, M. and H. Rakoczy 2003, Tomasello 1999). This demonstrative pointing is one of the first stages of the development of that unique and probably most important of human capacity: the ability to "read" the mind of others, a capacity which is somewhat oddly referred to as "theory of mind" or ToM for short. This ability continues to develop from the age of twelve month on until it is mature, perhaps around four, when one can show that the child "knows" that other people act, not in terms of how the world is, but in terms of these other people's beliefs or concepts (Wimmer & Perner: 1983). By "know", I simply mean here, that the child and, of course, the adult, acts in terms of his or her reading of the beliefs of *alter* and is continually adjusting his or her behaviour accordingly. I do not mean that the person who does this is necessarily conscious of the process, a point to which I shall return in a moment. The whole process is going on in far too complex and too rapid a way for that to be possible. Nonetheless, the importance of ToM can hardly be overestimated. Those of you familiar with Gricean theories of linguistic pragmatics will realise that it can be argued, convincingly for me, that this continual mind reading is what makes linguistic communication, and indeed all complex human communication, possible (Sperber & Wilson 1986).

It would be legitimate to think that to talk of the "mutual mind reading" on which our social life is based is, at best, simply a metaphor, at worst, a mystification. However, I want to stress that the metaphor refers to an empirical phenomenon of interpenetration, even though, admittedly, we don't stick our finger into each other's brain, in some kind of mental intercourse.

Just how material the process of mind reading may be, has become clearer in the light of recent neurological findings. Thus many recent researchers have argued that the unique human ability to read the mind of those with whom we interact is ultimately based on a much more general, non human-specific, feature of the brain: the so called "mirror neurones" (Gallese & Goldman 1998).

Perhaps the term is misleading. What is being referred to is an observation that has been made possible by modern neural research. By mirror neurones is meant the fact that exactly the same neurones are activated when, for example, we see someone raising their arm to point at the ceiling, as when we perform the action ourselves. In other words, the action of *alter* requires from us a part of the same physiological process, the neural part, as the action of *ego*. Indeed, a moment's reflection makes us realise that, even without the arcane and somewhat contested biology of mirror neurones, the very nature of human communication *must* involve something like this (Decety & Somerville 2003)[2].

Let us consider a simple act of linguistic communication. Here I follow Sperber and Wilson's theory of relevance fairly closely (Sperber & Wilson 1986). For my message to come across when I say, for example, "Today we honour the memory of Roy Rappaport", a mechanism must occur which enables

---

2. Relevant here also is evidence of the importance of sharing of emotions, which points in the same direction as the evidence on ToM. I hope to consider this further in another publication. See De Waal 1996.

you to penetrate my brain and align yours so that its neuronal organisation resembles mine. In order to do this, you and I have had to use a tool, sound waves in this case, but it cannot possibly be the sound waves as such, which carried my meaning across. Sound waves, poor things, are just sound waves. The reality is that sound waves enable me to modify your brain, or mind, so that its neuronal organisation in part resembles mine, admittedly in a very limited way. And, of course, the ability to communicate in this way, to connect our neurones that is, is what makes culture possible since culture must ultimately be based on the exchange of information, which, of course, then may be combined with other information, transformed, or reproduced through time and across space in a unique human way.

The paralleled neuronal modification implied by communication has further important implications. Let us assume, for the sake of argument, that it is possible for an individual to create *ex nihilo* a representation. That representation could then be said to be under her control since the process which led to it would be hers alone. However, when the representation comes from someone else's brain, which in reality is always, though to varying extents, the case (i.e. when it has come *via* the process of communication I have just described) the representation of one brain colonises another, whether this be a conscious process, or the unconscious process that is the basis of all communication. In such a case, the created neuronal activity of one brain *is* the material existing in another. Brains of different individuals are thereby interpenetrating materially so that the boundaries, which we believe obvious, become porous.

What I am saying here is very similar to what some writers, especially Edwin Hutchins, have called "distributed cognition" (Hutchins 1995). However, I would distance myself from them on one minor point. Hutchins, in talking about this phenomenon, likes to refer to minds "not bounded by the skin" as though there existed some sort of extra-biological process. Personally, I am too literal minded to feel comfortable with such phraseology, which makes the process appear surreal. The process of interpenetration I have alluded to is straight-forward and biological.

My other difference with the proponents of distributed cognition is not a disagreement but rather that I would like to push their insights further. Hutchins is famous for his demonstration of the way the knowledge necessary to navigate a big ship is not held in the head of one person but is distributed in a group. In an action such as coping with an emergency, each individual does his job as best he can in the light of his own knowledge but in doing so he relies on others who he assumes know other bits of the knowledge necessary to navigate the ship but which he does not, and does not need to, know himself. This is what Hutchins calls distributed cognition. For this type of reliance on the knowledge of others to be possible, the different individuals need trust. Trust that the others know what they are doing and are well intentioned. This means that people can then act on what they know is incomplete knowledge, but which they trust is completed by the knowledge held by others, to the extent of acting on knowledge they do not fully understand. It is not simply that they rely on others, they rely on others at the very moment they are no longer able to rely on their own knowledge.

By using that formulation I deliberately align what I am saying with the point made by a group of philosophers who, following Hilary Putman and the "deference" theorists, stress how social life is based on trust of others, basically on the default assumption that these others with whom we are in contact are normally competent and cooperative. In other words, because of our theory of mind adaptation, we continually interpenetrate as we communicate and also hold as true information which only makes sense because it is also contained or continuous with that in other minds (Putman 1975, Burge 1986, Orrigi 2000). This is the aspect of human cognition that is essentially social. Such a state of affairs makes it possible for the content of knowledge stored in an individual not to be understood by them, nor consciously thought to be understood, but this individual is likely to be aware of the solidarity on which the whole system of social cognition is based and this may be greatly valued. This is a point to which I shall return.

I started this chapter by arguing that for all living things the distinctness of the units of life is far from clear and that this includes humans. Furthermore, I argued that, for people, this fact is commonly represented culturally in kinship systems that in varied and specific ways are *about* this reality. Furthermore, for social animals the problem of the blurring of individual boundaries is compounded by the very nature of their sociality. Individuals in social species are, to varying degrees, materially continuous with each other. Since humans are social animals this problem applies to them. In our case, this state of affairs is brought about by the tool that makes human sociability possible: the hard wired human capacity referred to as theory of mind. Such an assertion, however, raises the same question that I touched on in the discussion of sex and birth: what are the cultural implications, if any, of this fact? This difficult question is precisely what is missing from much of the work of such evolutionists as Tooby and Cosmides and even Rappaport.

The parallel with kinship may advance the argument but at the same time it highlights an obvious difficulty. When anthropologists are studying kinship systems they are studying representations of phenomena having to do with obvious empirical processes, of which no one can be unaware: going in and out of each other's bodies. When we are dealing with the interpenetrations of minds, however, we are dealing with phenomena not so easily consciously perceived. Rather, the continual mutual reading of minds on which communication depends is like grammar, which is, and has to be, unconscious, if only in order to operate at the necessary speed. If that is so, how is it possible that an *awareness* of this process could occur, a necessary step for it to take explicit form in cultural representations? As a way to approach this question I shall ask the reader to accompany me on a detour, away from purely theoretical considerations, on a brief description of a particular case.

About a year ago, I decided to do what was, for me at least, a new type of field research in the remote Malagasy forest village where I have been working, on and off, for the last thirty years. There I carried out what is probably the most typical experiment used to demonstrate the development of children's understanding of ToM in front of whoever was available at the time; I then asked the adults watching to make sense of what they had just seen. In other words, I placed my informants in the place that professional psychologists normally find themselves in in the lab so that they, like them, would give me *their* interpretation of what was going on. The experiment in question is usually called the "false belief task". In the version I used, I showed a child two hats and, in front of them, and everyone present, I placed sweets under one of the hats. I then asked a member of the audience to leave the house and, showing the child what I was doing, I switched the sweets from under one hat, to place it under the other. I then asked the child—this is the key question— under which hat the person who had just gone out of the room would look for the sweets when he, or she, returned. The results in the Malagasy village were, as expected, much the same as those reported from all over the world. Children under the age of four say that the person who left the room will look under the hat where the sweets actually are, while older children say that the person will look under the hat where she saw them put, but where, of course, they were not. This difference is usually interpreted by psychologists to mean that the younger child has not yet understood, subconsciously that is, that other people do not necessarily know what they know, or to put it more theoretically and somewhat differently, that people act in terms of their, possibly false, beliefs, not in terms of what the world is actually like.

The adult Malagasy villagers' interpretation of the experiment was not all that different from that of professional cognitive psychologists. After a bit of prodding and reflection, the commonest explanation was that younger children have not yet learnt to lie and, therefore, they do not understand that other people can lie also. For reasons I cannot go into here, I take this to mean that the younger child is represented by them as a naïve empiricist, while they believe the older children and adults know that people can deceive and therefore look for the communicative *intention* of the speaker, since they do not simply trust appearances which could be manipulated by people.

I then used the discussion of the results of this experiment, which had just been conducted in front of the villagers present, as a springboard for a more general discussion about the nature of thought. During these continuation discussions, it was explained to me by the villagers that thought was an activity through which one matched one's action to one's purpose. Thought, they reasoned, is thus a feature of all animals: fleas, for example, also think, since they hide in order not to get caught. Humans, however, are superior to other animals in that they have an extra tool, language, which enables them to achieve the purpose of their thought more efficiently, especially through indirectness and deceit.

When I consider the very detailed information, on mind, on thought and on cognitive development, which I obtained through this work from the largely unschooled Malagasy in this remote village, I am, above all, struck by the familiarity of the ideas they expressed and their similarity with our own folk view. I am also struck by the correspondence of their views with those of the psychologists. And, indeed, when I look at the few other ethnographic studies of folk theories of mind and thought we possess, I find this general family likeness again and again (Gubser 1965, Rosaldo 1980[3]).

These similarities inevitably raise the question as to what causes these recurrences. The obvious answer would be that they are triggered by an awareness of the same actual universal human cognitive process. This explanation, however, runs into the difficulty discussed above, that mental processes such as the workings of mind operate below the level of consciousness, while what I was told in the discussions following the experiments was clearly explicit and conscious.

But is this difficulty as serious as it seems? Or, to put it another way, following the arguments of a number of cognitive scientists (Jackendorf 1994: Part 4, Block 1990, Humphrey 2000), is the barrier between the conscious and the subconscious as impenetrable as the objection suggests? The comparison with grammar, alluded to above, suggests otherwise. When we speak or comprehend others, clearly we do not consciously obey grammatical rules, nevertheless we can *become* aware of the existence of such rules when, for example, somebody makes a grammatical mistake. Indeed, it is probably as a result

---

3. Rosaldo's book in fact emphasises the alleged exotic character of Ilongot psychology, but I am struck that in matters of cognition at least their conceptualisation is very familiar.

of such mistakes that folk grammarians, the world over, are able to build their theories. Although these folk grammatical theories vary, probably because of a great variety of historical and cultural factors, it would surely be perverse not to accept also that their obvious similarities are caused by the way grammar actually works, and that this can, thus, to a degree, be accessed.

The situation with theory of mind is probably similar, perhaps also based on reflection caused by cases of faulty or difficult communication. For example, much of the general speculation about the nature of mind and thought in the data I collected was linked to explicit reflection on the abilities and limitations of a deaf and dumb man who lived in the village. It seems that the same kind of continual attempt to understand the psychology of thought and communication as was caused by my experiment is also caused in a similar way by this sort of more familiar, less artificial, more recurrent circumstance. This is probably why, once the initial resistance had been overcome, people were so willing, enthusiastic even, in engaging in the discussion of the experiment I had demonstrated. The intellectual challenge it presented was not after all as unusual or bizarre as it might at first seem from the outside. Of course, this more ordinary speculation was not done in the jargon of modern psychology but with the cultural tools available. But even these unsophisticated tools and vocabulary must have been developed in relation to the psychological processes that actually occur and are known to occur. It is not surprising, therefore, that similar ideas and representations should crop up, again and again, in different cultural and historical contexts. In claiming that, I am not arguing for any direct determinism between the actual working of the mind and people's theories about it. Many other factors are clearly involved in each case. Understanding and representing the working of the mind is difficult for the Malagasy, as indeed it is for any psychologist. It involves peeping past barriers of many kinds, by means of thought or practical experiments, but both Malagasy and psychologist do this and for neither party is it completely impossible.

To illustrate such complexity, and to begin to approach the subject of religion and ritual, which the reader may have good reason to believe I have forgotten all about, I return to my Malagasy example.

When people so emphatically insisted that thought always, directly or indirectly, was a matter of matching ends and means, I was naturally led to ask about dreams. Were these not a case of thought without a practical end in view? The commonest answer I was given to such a question was negative. Dreams, I was assured, were cases of other people entering you and thinking *through* you in order to achieve their ends. In this way, the local general cognitive theory was made coherent with a theory of interpenetration with which I had been familiar when I studied Malagasy ancestor worship, since, it is through dreams that ancestors manifest themselves most typically and it is through dreams that they make their desires known. This theory of dreams, however, is radically different from what is found in many other cultures, including, of course, that of professional psychologists.

This, however, does not mean that, as soon as we touch on phenomena which are usually labelled religious, we inevitably move away completely from concerns cognate with those of professional cognitive science. The idea that dreams are really other people, especially ancestors, thinking through you for their own ends, is part of that much more general idea that previous generations, dead forebears, living elders, or absent members of the family are speaking through you, as you consciously, or unconsciously, "quote" them. Thus, you should utter the words of other wise people because you trust and rely on them. Or, rather, these forebears are continually acting through you. Indeed, to allow that to happen willingly is to show respect and to act morally. Morality is thus experienced less as a matter of individual choice and more as one of submission and recognition of the presence of others who penetrate you. But, as soon as we rephrase the Malagasy concept of ancestors in this (I believe ethnographically accurately) way, we find we have been brought back into the familiar territory of the scientific theories of distributed cognition and deference theory to which I referred above. In the very area in which my Malagasy co-villagers could be represented as most exotic, in their beliefs in the power of ancestors, we find them very close to Hutchins and Putman. Even the belief in the penetration of the young by elders and ancestors turns out to be built on the implicit realisation of the reality of the effect of the interpenetration made possible by ToM: that is on the fact that knowledge is distributed.

The point I want to stress is that the theory of mind and the distribution of knowledge in society is neither unknown, nor fully known, to the Malagasy villagers. Furthermore, they are aware of the unsatisfactory partial nature of their knowledge, something that was often commented upon by them after the experiments. And, as a result of their realisation of the incompleteness of their knowledge, when the chance arises, as when I showed them the false belief task, or when they observed the deaf and dumb man, they eagerly seize the opportunity to find out more about their own mental processes and those of others. In that inquisitiveness they are no different from professional scientists and, like them, their knowledge is incomplete, but like them they are also *straining* to know more about a reality which, in the case of psychological processes, is common to all human beings and is partly accessible. Of course, as in the case of the scientists, but probably to a greater extent, there are also many other factors interacting with their theoretical speculation and representations, and this multiplicity of factors produces systems that are only partly scientifically motivated. However, it is the commonality of the enterprises and the reality of the world they engage with which explains the continuity of the scientific discussion of such things as theory of mind and of the cultural representations of largely unschooled Malagasy villagers and western scientists.

The bodily interpenetration of ToM is thus, to a certain degree, known by people such as Malagasy villagers and this knowledge combines in varying ways and in varying contexts with other types of knowledge. This element, therefore, not only leads to partial continuities between scientific and folk understandings of the interpenetration of individuals and of the consequent provisionality of levels of individuation. It is to these that I now turn.

A central implication of ToM is that all social relations imply interpenetration and, therefore, the arbitrariness of boundaries within the social fabric applies not just to people who are related, but between all human beings who are in contact. The awareness of this ensures that ideologies of individualism are always, to varying degrees, negated by ideologies based on the realisation of interconnection, as Mauss stressed in the essay on the gift (Mauss 1923-24).

Knowledge of interpenetration and of lack of clear boundaries, as well as the emotions which are an integral element of the way this is experienced: all this is what we mean by that most Durkheimian of words: solidarity. The presence of this sort of sentiment, at its most general, is difficult to put one's finger on, because it is rarely made explicit or the subject of reflexive discourse. However, from my reading of ethnography and from my own experience, it would seem that in most cultures a very common default assumption is that there is a potential moral obligation to any stranger whom one might come in touch with or, to put it in a different way, that the very fact of entering into a relationship implies being consubstantial and therefore morally obligated. Perhaps the most familiar manifestation of this phenomenon is the obligation of hospitality towards strangers, a moral imperative which recurs, admittedly in different forms, in so many unrelated cultures, but which, as far as I know, has been little theorised at a comparative level by modern anthropologists. A general unspecific morality is thus probably an epiphenomenon of the very nature of human communication.

There are, however, many instances of much more specific and elaborate awareness of the lack of boundary between individuals. Many of these seem to fall in the general area usually labelled as religion, though some are of a less amiable and more threatening form. I have already mentioned the Malagasy interpretation of dreams and its link with ancestor worship, which, in a variety of forms is found all over the world and which is so often linked to the lack of bodily differentiation within descent groups. Another example is witchcraft-like ideas. These often take the form of a belief in the secret and evil penetration of a consuming other within one's body made possible by the existence of communication. More obvious perhaps, are the beliefs in spirit possession that seem to crop up all over the world. These involve the total invasion and replacement of one individual's intentional mind by that of another. These are extreme representations of the colonising nature of social relations.

In a somewhat different way, the realisation of the interpenetration of individuals and therefore the context-dependence of boundaries are present in many political movements and religions. Ideas of a corporal unity beyond the individual are well documented in certain forms of Christianity, Islam, and devotional Hinduism. These ideas emphasise a different "brotherhood", as an alternative to the interpenetration of sex and birth, thereby at the same time emphasising the comparability of the two types of interpenetrations, as well as using one to challenge the other. These ideas become most explicit in the mystical forms of these religions, for example in Sufism or devotional Hinduism, where the themes of the interpenetration of the bodies of the devotees and the lack of boundaries of their bodies take extreme and dramatic form.

Perhaps, however, it is in ritual that the conscious and culturally encoded awareness of lack of boundedness between persons is clearest. This, of course, was one of Durkheim's central points, but what he stressed was the effervescence of highly dramatic rituals. There is no doubt that in many of the manifestations we would label as ritual a feeling of transcendence of individuality and even of dissolution of self into a greater whole occurs. Furthermore, this may well be part of the realisation of the real lack of boundary of human individuals. However, many rituals are simply not like that. A universal feature of ritual however is deference, if only because it is at the very core of the meaning of the word in English. Deference is, as noted above, the accepting of the content of other minds without necessarily knowing the whys and wherefores of the propositions and actions one performs oneself. As argued in different ways by Putman, Burge, and Hutchins it is characteristic of knowledge in society and implies cognitive interpenetration. Ritual is an extreme case. In ritual one accepts that the motivation for meaning is to be found in others one trusts (Bloch 2004) In other words, it is not only that one surrenders one's intentionality to others but also that one is aware of this happening. The recourse to ritual is therefore not only to be understood as recognition of neural interpenetration, a submission to other minds, but also as a celebration of this awareness.

Of course, these religious and ritual representations are not simply realisations of the fact that we interpenetrate each other as we interact and that, therefore, the boundaries separating individuals are provisional and alterable. In each and every case much more is involved, which may indeed be more important. By this I mean that the social, sexual and reproductive characteristics of the human species means that we go in and out of each other's bodies in at least three different ways and that this implies an indeterminacy of the level of relevant differentiation.

In the case of birth and sex the interpenetration is inevitably, though variously, cognised. In the case of ToM the matter is more complicated. The working of ToM is normally below consciousness and therefore so is the interpenetration it involves. However, since the boundary between the conscious and the subconscious is not sharp and because we have tools to traverse it, such as experiments, or the existence of deaf and dumb relatives, we are able to use our hazy awareness of the process to interpret and speculate about such phenomena as dreams, the relation with ancestors, and many other central aspects of human life. This knowledge—the raw material of interpenetration— becomes a resource and an idiom that may become central in many representations which we would label as moral or religious or ritual. It is this line of causation from the fact of interpenetration to its conscious representations by diffrent people in different ways that makes possible the *slither* I illustrated and mentioned earlier from the biological to the cultural, including the religious.

This causal chain outlined above centrally involves a direct connection between the social, the moral, and the religious and ritual, such an argument is inevitably reminiscent of the theories of Durkheim, alluded to at the beginning of this chapter. After all, his central theory in *The Elementary Forms of the Religious Life* is that religion, by means of ritual, is a projection of the intuition of the dependence of the individual on society, and of the individual's incompleteness: an intuition that leads, therefore, to the impression of the presence of a superior transcendental element, the religious (Durkheim 1912).

My admiration for this great anthropologist cannot but be heightened by the similarity of our arguments. Much of what I have said is what he said long ago, though from a totally different epistemological base. Thus, it is also essential to stress the profound difference between my argument and his, if only to clarify what I have been arguing.

Unlike him, I am not proposing, in any way, a general theory of "religion." The awareness of the provisional nature of individual boundaries occurs in many kinds of cultural representations that could never reasonably be called religious. For the same reason, I am not arguing that the interpenetrations of kinship and ToM are the *origin* of the religious. Any such claim would be meaningless, since for me what we call religion in anthropology is a rag bag of loosely connected elements, without an essence or core.

Most importantly, however, I differ from Durkheim in his understanding of causation. For him the social, which comes from we know not where, mysteriously causes the cultural and the empirical, and then gives us the tools to invent what is, irrespective of what the world is like. This idealist fantasy would only be worth elaborating as an example of a quaint archaic conceit if it did not actually, I believe, still resemble or underlie much contemporary anthropological theorising.

What I am proposing is more straightforward, more modest, more materialist, and anchored in evolutionary theory. The source of the social is to be found in the cognitive capacities of humans, although, of course, there is no unidirectional evolutionary line of causation between the social and the cognitive. Rather, as argued by Humphrey and Tomasello, they are part of a single process. This socio/cognitive, means that, even more than is the case for non-social animals, and differently than is the case for other social animals, the boundaries between individuals are, at best, partial. This fact, and our consequent bodily connectedness, which supplements and sometimes competes with the connectedness of kinship, is fuzzily available to our consciousness. It is this awareness that becomes a recurrent element in a great variety of representations in different cultures, representations which we must not forget are different kinds of phenomena from the simply psychological. But it is these awarenesses that Durkheim examined under the label "solidarity". And, furthermore, the types of solidarities he identified are often, though not always as he also stressed, manifest in what we call religion and ritual.

References

Bloch, M. (2004) 'Ritual and Deference' in Whitehouse, H. and Laidlaw, J. (eds.) *Ritual and Memory*, Oxford: Altamira Press.

Block, N. (1990) 'The Computer Model of the Mind' in Osherson, D.N. and Smith, E.E. (eds.) *Thinking: An Invitation to Cognitive Science*, Cambridge. MA.: M.I.T. Press.

Burge, T. 1979. 'Content Preservation' *The Philosophical Review*. 100.

Cosmides, L. and Tooby, J. (1992) 'Cognitive Adapatation for Social Exchange' in Barklow, J.H. et al. (eds.) *The Adapted Mind: Evolutionary Psychology and the Generation of Culture*, pp. 163–228. Oxford: Oxford University Press.

Decety, J. & Somerville, J.A. (2003) 'Shared Representations between Self and Other: A Social Cognitive Neuroscience View' *Trends in Cognitive Sciences*, 7/12.

Durkheim, E. (1912) *Les Formes élémentaires de la vie religieuse* Paris: Alcan (translated as *The Elementary Forms of the Religious Life*, (1915) London: Allen Unwin).

Gallese, V. & Goldman, A. (1998) 'Mirror Neurones and the Simulation Theory of Mind' *Trends in Cognitive Science*, 12: 493–501.

Gopnik, A. (1993) 'How We Know Our Minds: The Illusion of First Person Knowledge of Intentionality' *Behavioural and Brain Science*, 1: 90–101.

Gubser, N. (1965) *The Nunamiut Eskimos: Hunters of Caribou*, New Haven: Yale University Press.

Humphrey, N. (2002) *The Mind Made Flesh: Essays from the Frontiers of Evolution and Psychology*, Oxford University Press.

Hutchins, E. (1995) *Cognition in the Wild*, Cambridge, MA.: MIT Press.

Jackendoff, R. (1987) *Consciousness and the Computational Mind*, Cambridge, MA: M.I.T Press.

Mauss, M. (1923–1924) 'Essai sur le don. Forme et raison de l'échange dans les sociétés primitives' *L'Année Sociologique*, seconde série.

Origgi, G. (2000) 'Croire sans Comprendre' *Cahiers de Philosophie de L'Universite de Caen* n.34.

Povinelli, D.J. Bering, J.M. and Giambrone, S. (2000) Towards a Science of Other Minds: Escaping the arguments by analogy, *Cognitive Science*, 24: 509–54.

Putman, H. (1975) 'The Meaning of 'Meaning'' in Gunderson, K. (ed.) *Language, Mind and Knowledge*, University of Minesota Press: Mineapolis.

Rosaldo, M. (1980) *Knowledge and Passion. Ilongot Notions of Self and Social Life*, Cambridge: Cambridge University Press.

Schneider, D. (1984) *A Critique of the Study of Kinship*, Ann Arbor: University of Michigan Press.

Sperber, D. and Wilson, D. (1986) *Relevance: Communication and Cognition*, Oxford: Blackwell.

Stotz, K. and Griffiths, P. (2004) 'Genes: Philosophical Analyses Put to the Test' *History and Philosophy of the Life Sciences*.

Tomasello, M. (1999) *The Cultural Origins of Human Cognition*, Cambridge MA. Harvard University Press.

Tomasello, M. and Rakoczy, H. (2003) 'What Makes Human Cognition Unique? From Individual to Shared to Collective Intentionality' *Mind and Language*, 18/2: 121–147.

Waal, de F.B.M. (1996) *Good Natured: The Origins of Right and Wrong in Humans and Other Animals*, Cambridge, Mass.: Harvard University Press.

Wimmer, H. & Perner, J. (1983) ,Beliefs about Beliefs: Representation and Constraining Function of Wrong Beliefs in Young Children's Understanding of Deception' *Cognition,* 13: 103–128.

CHAPTER THREE

MALINOWSKI AND MAGICAL RITUAL

Jesper Sørensen

> By placing thus each of these strange and queer customs within its proper psychological and cultural setting, we can bring it near to us, we can perceive in it the universally human substratum. In other words, we have to carry out our analysis of primitive belief or superstition by means of universally valid concepts and thus make it amenable to scientific treatment. (Bronislaw Malinowski: *Culture as a Determinant of Behavior*, 1937, reprinted in Malinowski 1963)

Why relate Malinowski's anthropological theories to present day cognitive studies of religion, ritual and magic? Is there anything to gain by such an exercise? The general questions raised by Malinowski about 80 years ago are to a large extent still pertinent, even if most of his answers create more problems than they solve. Throughout his extensive publications, Malinowski repeatedly discussed the relation between human biology, psychology, and cultural forms, and he persistently argued for a scientific approach to cultural phenomena taking all these levels into account.

In contrast to his ethnographic studies, the general reception of Malinowski's theoretical work has not been positive. Edmund Leach, for instance, described Malinowski when theorising about culture as a "platitudinous bore" (Leach 1957). This kind of dismissal can, to a large extent, be ascribed to the general anthropological hostility toward psychological explanation and a growing focus on structural explanation. This chapter will take as its point of departure a belief that more rather than less psychological theory and methodology is needed in order to arrive at satisfactory explanations of cultural forms. Further, in line with recent interest in the evolutionary development of human cognitive capacities, functionalist explanations are not understood as belonging in anthropology's theoretical dustbin.

I shall begin with a short description of Malinowski's theories of culture and magic. I will then address how the cognitive science of religion might answer some of the questions raised by Malinowski.

A Theory of Magic:
The Function of Cultural Forms

In early anthropology, magic was a subject of serious concern, and there was much interest in the general question: why do human beings perform magical rituals? Because Malinowski understood magic as intimately related to its local pragmatic context, he reframed the problem of magic as: why do people perform apparently irrational magical actions in concert with certain types of rational and technical actions? In short, Malinowski answered the general question by pointing to the psychological effect of performing magical rituals. Humans perform magical rituals because it makes them feel less anxious and more confident. The rituals are therefore performed in relation to endeavours that for different reasons produce such anxiety. In order to appreciate what value (if any) these answers can have for a present-day cognitive approach, we need to unearth Malinowski's underlying theoretical assumptions. To do so two questions will be addressed: (a) Why do specific types of endeavours make humans feel anxious? (b) Why does the performance of magical rituals alleviate that anxiety?

Malinowski's understanding of human nature and how it affects human behaviour combined three explanatory levels and three different theoretical approaches:

1. *Homo sapiens* is an animal species. In order to explain species-specific behavioural traits, Malinowski applied behaviourist psychology as his principal theoretical tool.

2. Human behaviour is distinct from that of other animals in being culturally moulded. In order to explain this Malinowski defended a functionalist explanation of cultural and social institutions.

3. Humans always act on the basis of pragmatic concerns constrained by their surroundings. In order to understand this, Malinowski defended a pragmatic explanation of human behaviour.

By arguing that humanity is an animal species Malinowski emphasised that we are subject to a "biological determinism [that] forces upon human behaviour certain invariable sequences, which must be incorporated into every culture" (1944:79). As a biological organism, humans breathe, feel hunger, thirst, sexual appetite, fatigue, restlessness, somnolence, bladder- and colon-pressure, fright and pain. All these impulses produce actions that lead to their satisfaction (1944:77). Therefore, the most fundamental way of understanding a specific type of behaviour is to demonstrate its ability to satisfy one of a range of basic organic impulses—thus identifying its primary function. Malinowski, however, was very well aware that such a description does not tell us much about observed cultural behaviour. Practices aimed at satisfying these basic impulses simply vary too widely between cultures for that to be the case. So, even if biology determines the existence of specific behaviour in all cultures (e.g. eating), how this behaviour is performed is determined by learning in a cultural context.

Inspired by behaviourist theory, Malinowski argued that learning is based on processes of conditional reinforcement. Once a specific action sequence satisfies an organic impulse it will be reinforced—leading to the formation of behavioural habits (1944:134). Whenever impulses are not satisfied, however, the individual organism will search for other instrumental means to achieve satisfaction. This results in a 'proto-cultural' situation of behavioural differentiation whereby each individual adopts different instrumental means that are all reinforced into habits. Lacking symbolic communication, however, this behavioural differentiation is *not* transmitted from one individual to the next. In contrast to idiosyncratic behavioural patterns, 'culture' describes behavioural regularities transmitted within a social group, marking it off as different from other groups. Thus, the individualistic explanation of the formation of behavioural pattern was transformed into an argument for the behavioural differentiation of social groups—in this way accounting for the creation of culture.

Malinowski identified four strands of development that had to come together in order to start such a process of cultural evolution: (a) the ability to recognize instrumental objects; (b) appreciation of their place in purposeful sequences of action; (c) the formation of social bonds; and (d) the appearance of symbolic communication (1944:136). Thus he emphasised the crucial role of artefacts in satisfying human needs and the ability to communicate knowledge about this to other individuals forming part of a social group. Once this development started, Malinowski envisioned a type of "ratchet effect" (Tomasello 1999),[1] whereby culture becomes a "vast instrumentality" necessary for human survival by providing what will effectively become the only

---

1. Tomasello (1999) coined the term "ratchet effect" to describe the cumulative structure of human cultural evolution. Humans modify their tools and, in contrast to other primates, these modifications are preserved in the group by means of imitative learning. Thus human children are born into a world filled with artefacts all based on a long history of cumulative modifications.

means to satisfy physiological needs (Malinowski 1963:196). By codifying successful behavioural sequences as custom, humans bypass the slow and potentially dangerous process of learning methods of survival conditioned only by
direct stimulus-response. Instead culture enables humans to follow customary, i.e. historically tested, means of satisfying primary impulses. This advantage, however, comes at a price. By being embedded in a secondary environment, humans become dependent for their survival on cultural artefacts.
Thus, culture imposes a whole range of *secondary* impulses that humans must
seek to satisfy. In the words of Malinowski, the emergence of culture "creates
new problems, inspires new desires, and establishes a new universe in which
man moves, never completely free from his organic needs, but also following
new ends and stimulated to new desires" (1963: 201).[2]

To explain how culture moulds individual behaviour, Malinowski argued that
institutions form a second unit of analysis (beside individual behaviour). He understood institutions as stable groups of people organised around a regulation
of instrumental actions. The function of institutions is to ensure the satisfaction of basic human needs by means of a specific 'charter' that regulates behaviour in relation to pragmatic endeavours (1944: 52ff). Malinowski referred to
four dimensions of this regulation as the *instrumental imperatives*: economics,
social control, education, and politics (1963: 207). There is, however, no direct
one-to-one relationship between specific action-sequences and social institutions. Institutions regulate a range of different action-sequences and by doing
so they effectively constrain and connect individuals' actions in a framework
that transcends the individual. At the same time, each behavioural sequence is
regulated by a number of different institutions. The Trobriand institution of 'the
family', for instance, regulates aspects of numerous actions related to different
physiological needs: hunger, reproduction, shelter, protection etc. On the other
hand actions aimed to satisfy hunger are not only regulated by the institution
of the family but also by those of kinship, clan, chieftainship, and territory.

Thus, Malinowski argued that two major factors determine human behaviour: (a) biology determines a bottom-line range of specific behaviours necessarily present in all cultures to ensure the survival of the organism; (b) cultural
institutions determine actions by imposing a customary instrumental format
on behaviour, thereby imposing secondary needs and goals to guide human action. The question then arises as to why humans have such institutions as religion, myth and magic that lack any apparent function in relation to survival.

---

2. Malinowski's argument is still relevant in relation to recent discussions on the role
of culture in human evolution, and in particular on how human cultural differences orig-
inate and are sustained (see Boyd & Richerson 2002).

Malinowski understood culture as a coherent system of institutions that ensures that the collective activities necessary for the survival of the individual organism and the group are carried out. In order to achieve this, institutions are not only functional in relation to specific pragmatic pursuits. We also find mechanisms ensuring the overall stability and endurance of the institutions themselves. He described these apparently non-instrumental practices as the *integrative imperatives* of social institutions and this is the domain of myth, religion and magic (Malinowski 1963: 213ff). In short, myth is a narrative form that confirms social structures, dictates moral beliefs, defines ritual actions and explains what is not capable of being explained by profane knowledge. Religion appropriates inevitable crises of life into traditional ritual actions and the belief in Providence. Thereby the social and dogmatic structure is confirmed and, more importantly, the potential social disruption produced by the emotional impact of a crisis is managed.

On the topic of magic, Malinowski seemed to fluctuate between two different explanatory strategies. In relation to its function as socially integrative, he argued that the performance of magical rituals alleviates anxiety, instils confidence in participants' abilities, and enables concerted social actions by allocating authority. Thus, the instrumental actions necessary for the survival of both group and individual are dependent on the organising function of magic. Magical rituals, however, are often performed in solitude and in relation to individual actions. To explain this fact, Malinowski argued that magic has a more basic and instrumental grounding in the attempt to manipulate the environment. All technical pursuits involve the ability to foresee, to plan, and to calculate the result of action. This, however, also gives humans the ability to foresee potential failure and danger. Addressing this potentially disruptive uncertainty, magic is "the ritual act performed to bring about a practical result unachievable by man's unaided force" (Malinowski 1963: 190).

Thus, magic is a type of instrumental action addressing problems that might jeopardize practical pursuits. If this is the case how can we distinguish magical actions from non-magical instrumental acts? Malinowski insisted that participants never mix up technical and ritual actions. They are distinct due to their pragmatic setting, their constituent behaviour and especially by the role and type of language involved.[3] Profane activity, e.g. planting, is a rational be-

---

3. Language plays an important role in Malinowski's theory of magic not dealt with in this chapter. First, the use of special tropes in the spells marks off magic from other types of behaviour. Second, as the Trobrianders stressed the importance of the spell in magical rituals, Malinowski tended to exaggerate the role of language in his general theory of magic (Evans-Pritchard 1929). But, as Malinowski's theory of language is radically pragmatic

haviour guided by primitive but 'scientific' knowledge and learned by observation. In contrast magical activity, e.g. ritual chanting, is based on tradition, is impervious to observation, is prompted by emotional experience and exploits associations of ideas (Malinowski 1991: 19, 35, 87). So, even if the performance of magical rituals is judged to be indispensable to success, it never renders the performance of profane activities superfluous, and does not address aspects of an endeavour within the technological control of the participants.

We are now able to answer the questions posed at the beginning of this chapter. According to Malinowski, people perform magical actions because: (a) as the human ability to foresee the result of actions also involves representations of the potential risk of failure, certain types of human endeavour are correlated with disruptive feelings of anxiety; (b) this anxiety is alleviated by the performance of ritual actions that purportedly manipulate hidden forces and instil confidence in the performer; and (c) when performed in a social setting, magic will further social cooperation and allocate social authority. Malinowski's theory of magic is thus in line with his understanding of human nature and the evolution of culture. Human behaviour is still constrained by biological needs, but it has been radically remoulded through the development of cultural institutions and the ability for symbolic communication. The cost of this development is the need to ensure cooperation between individuals by empowering the institutions organising behaviour and the need to alleviate the uncertainty that follows from the ability to predict a negative outcome of actions. Magic, together with religion and myth, is the stable organisation of ritual actions and systems of beliefs that have this function.

A Cognitive Explanation of Magical Actions

As noted at the outset, many of the questions posed by Malinowski are still relevant to a modern scientific investigation of magic, but some of his answers only raise further questions. At a general level, Malinowski was right to argue that we need to take both biology and psychology into consideration when trying to explain cultural forms. Two qualifications are necessary, however. First, the role of psychology envisaged by Malinowski was restricted to the effects of emotions, and his description of these is somewhat limited. Further, Malinowski underestimates the role of biology and evolved psychological

---

("words in their primary and essential sense *do*, *act* and *achieve*" (1935b: 52)) the functional role of magical ritual can be described by reference to the effect of actions in general, without giving special head to the role of language.

mechanisms as being limited to a constraining bedrock of impulses in the creation of cultural forms. In contrast, proponents of the cognitive science of religion argue that our psychology involves much more than emotion, that it must be much more precisely described in order to generate explanatory theories, and that its influence on the creation of cultural forms is substantial. In short, the relationship between biology, cognition and culture is more complex and intertwined than could be appreciated in Malinowski's day.

At a more specific level, Malinowski was on the right track when he argued that magical rituals are performed in concert with technical actions aimed at the same goal and that ritual and non-ritual actions are easily distinguished by participant and observer alike. His explanations of why this is the case, however, raises a number of questions. First, some magical rituals do *not* enhance social cooperation and therefore cannot serve the integrative function attributed to them by Malinowski. Second, magical rituals do not always alleviate anxiety as claimed by Malinowski. Often they actually produce it, if only by their evocation of forces beyond the control of the participants. We should not assume *a priori* that people always represent potential supernatural dangers involved in an endeavour prior to their evocation in the ritual performance. Third, if the dangers addressed by rituals are not supernatural, it is not clear why the performance of ritual action should enhance participants' confidence in the success of their endeavour. Fourth, Malinowski pointed to a range of external features, such as language, that he claimed distinguish ritual and non-ritual actions. This, however, begs the question of how these features (and others) are represented in participants' minds and also that of how the representations of ritual actions influence representations of non-ritual actions.

In order to address these complex problems, I will focus on two specific questions. First, what cognitive features distinguish ritual from non-ritual actions? Second, how are intuitions about the efficacy of ritual and non-ritual actions formed and how are these intuitions related?

Cognitive Representations of Non-Ritual and Ritual Actions

The ability to distinguish actions from mere events and the formation of action representations are central features of human cognition. It allows us, for instance, to predict the behaviour of other agents (both humans and animals), to cooperate with as well as to cheat them, and to distinguish a potential predator from an inanimate object. It is thus fundamental in basic interaction with the surrounding natural world and allows for social cognition involving complex representations of other agents' intentions. Research into the cognitive architecture underlying representations of actions has exposed a very complex system. Even though inquiries are far from completed, a picture of the cognitive systems involved in human action representation is emerging. Two questions must be addressed in order to adequately describe cognitive representations of actions: (a) how do humans represent *agency* involved in actions? and (b) how do humans represent *causal relations* between actions and results? Investigations into both agency and causality are very complex and have a long history in both psychology and philosophy. The description below is therefore no more than a very condensed summary of some of the most fundamental aspects of the cognitive systems involved in human representations of actions.

Starting with representations of *agency*, at least four cognitive mechanisms seem to be involved:

1. Simple movements in perceptual space trigger representations of agency (Mandler 1992; Leslie 1994, 1995). In order for an organism to survive, agents in the immediate environment must be detected and classified and movement is the most basic information that might indicate the presence of an agent. Movement therefore attracts human attention.

2. Movement that is contingent on other elements in the environment, i.e. that appears to be responding to the surrounding environment, is an even better indicator that an agent is present. Numerous experiments have shown that subjects understand geometrical figures on a screen as agents performing actions if they seem to interact purposefully with their surrounding environment (Blakemore et. al. 2003; Johnson et. al 2001; Gelman et. al. 1995).

Both mechanisms described are triggered by available perceptual information and research suggests that humans are prone to perceive agents in many situations where none is in fact present (e.g. the branch scratching the window at night) (Guthrie 1993; Mandler 1992). One theory explains these findings as a result of a perceptual strategy claimed to have significant adaptive value in an evolutionary perspective (Guthrie 1980, 1993). Whether as hunter or prey, a fast recognition of agents in the surrounding environment is a prerequisite to survival. Whereas mistaking an agent for an object (a bear as a stone) is costly and potentially lethal, mistaking an object for an agent (a stone as a bear) is not very costly and at worst a cause of irritation or embarrassment. Therefore, in an evolutionary perspective, individuals who are susceptible to detecting agents would have a selective advantage over individuals without this ability, even though this susceptibility generates false positives. Nevertheless, the representation of something as a human agent entails more than perceptible relations between movement and the surrounding environment (Gelman et. al. 1995).

3. A defining character of agents is their ability not just to react to their surroundings but to instigate activity based on the mental representation of a *goal*. When perceiving the activity of an agent able to move by itself and reacting to its surroundings, the activity is automatically represented as controlled by an internal representation relating the action performed to its goal. Thus, we represent human activity as goal-directed, i.e. as informed by a *teleological agency* (Atran 2002; Leslie 1994).[4]

4. Humans are not only represented as performing goal-directed actions (e.g. giving someone money in order to get flowers) but as having a cognitive attitude towards the actions performed (reluctantly buying flowers on Mothers Day). This is the basis of the human ability to understand pretend play, where actions are performed without wishing their goal to be realised (Leslie 1994). Further, it is related to representations of other agents' knowledge of the environment. Around age four, children know that other agents' access to information about the world is limited and potentially misguided so they ascribe certain cognitive attitudes, e.g. beliefs, to these agents. Beliefs are important as they are represented as informing the agents' goal-directed behaviour. The ability to relate the simple action-gestalt produced by the above-mentioned three mechanisms to beliefs ascribed to a perceived agent facilitates the emergence of far more complex representations of intention. Individual actions are thus connected in behavioural sequences that are represented as guided by overarching representations of a goal of the concerted effort, or what can be called *intentional agency*.

---

4. Neurological findings indicate that the automatic ascription of goals to human actions is related to the firing of a group of 'mirror neurons' that are activated both when one is performing an action and when one is merely observing someone else performing a similar action (Gallese 2000a, 2000b, 2001, Lakoff & Gallese 2005). It is questionable, however, whether the activation of mirror-neurons alone can give rise to more complex notions of human agency (Jacobs & Jeannerod 2005).

The cognitive systems underlying our notions of agency constitute core elements of what is commonly referred to as Theory of Mind mechanisms, enabling us to understand other people's actions as guided by both desires and beliefs (Carruthers & Smith 1996; Leslie 1994, 1995). Distinguishing teleological from intentional agency, however, is critical when giving a cognitive explanation of action representations. It allows us to distinguish between representations of *proximate* intentions related to an action that is specified by concrete motor behaviour and *ultimate* intention specified by the goal of concerted series of actions.[5] Consider, for instance, the act of riding a bicycle to the baker to buy a cake. Buying the cake constitutes the ultimate intention that determines the relation between a concerted series of actions each specified by behavioural sequences with a proximate intention: putting money into your pockets, lifting a leg to get onto the bike, placing your feet on the pedals, finding the balance etc. It is important to recognise that no low level behavioural sequences are directly prompted by the ultimate intention. One can get to the baker in a number of ways. Getting there, however, will involve the activation of a sequence of actions all specified by different types of motor behaviour.

If we turn to the role of *causal* representations, the mutual relation between actions in a given sequence is causally specified by an ultimate intention. The temporal order of getting on the bike and pressing down the pedals cannot be reversed. We therefore have to distinguish between the causal properties of the overall action-sequence (getting to the baker) and the causal properties related to each of the sub-actions (e.g. pressing the pedals). If we start with the sub-actions, a number of unconscious reasoning processes specify the causal properties of each type of action. This causal reasoning is constrained by two factors. First, experimental psychologists have pointed to a number of innate or early developed proclivities in causal reasoning. For instance, 6 months old infants have expectations as to the causal properties of physical objects (Leslie 1994, 1995). It is argued that humans have a register of ontological domains used to understand the surrounding world, each leading to different causal expectations. Thus humans have different general expectations of the causal behaviour of physical objects, tools, animals, and human beings.[6] Second, during development, humans acquire causal information through repeated observation, i.e. by inductively relating specific

---

5. 'The distinction between proximate intention' and 'ultimate' intention is rather similar to that between of 'motor intentions' and 'prior intention' (Jacobs & Jeannerod 2005).

6. The literature treating theories of domain-specificity is vast. Relevant anthologies include Hirschfeld & Gelman (1994) and Sperber, Premack & Premack (1995).

causes to specific effects. As shown by numerous studies of conditional learning, the spatial and temporal relation between a cause and its perceived effect must be close in order for this associative learning to be effective. Based on these findings it is safe to say that humans have unconscious expectations to the causal effect of sub-actions and that this knowledge constrains how such actions are combined into action-sequences.

Causal representations of the overall action take into account the extent to which it is instrumental to the ultimate intention. The causal efficacy of riding the bike to the baker is judged by whether it really *gets* the agent there and, ultimately, whether she can buy a cake. Failure to achieve the intended goal will lead to representations of the causal factors responsible for this failure and representations of the possibility of amending this by changing parts of the behavioural sequence. Further, ultimate intentions can be embedded as instruments in more comprehensive intentional structures. Thus, if our cyclist is buying a cake in order to please a friend, a bottle of wine might serve the same purpose.[7]

Core elements involved in the cognitive representation of actions are modelled in figure 1:

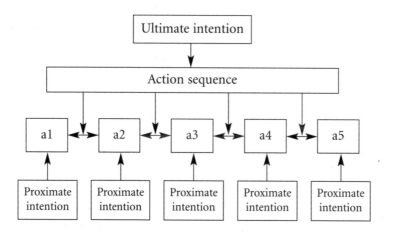

Figure 1: Elements involved in the representation of a non-ritual action-sequence: An ultimate intention specifies a possible action sequence that in turn specifies the causal relation between a number of individual actions each with their own proximate intention.

---

7. This is discussed in greater detail in Sørensen (forthcoming).

What can this tell us about the way *ritual* actions are cognized? When performing magical rituals people have more or less explicit ultimate intentions specifying why they perform the ritual and what effect its performance is likely to have. The magical rituals that form part of the agricultural cycle in the Trobriand Islands, for instance, are performed with two explicit instrumental goals: to protect the crop from pests and diseases and to ensure an abundant harvest. A given ritual action sequence is thus specified by an ultimate intention. If we turn our attention to the relation between the ultimate intention and the sub-actions, however, the picture changes. Unlike with ordinary actions, the ultimate intention does *not* causally constrain the actions performed in the ritual (Bloch 2004; Boyer 1994; Boyer & Lienard 2006; Humphrey & Laidlaw 1994; Lienard & Boyer 2006; Whitehouse 2004). Further, as the ultimate intention does not determine the actions performed, the causal relations between actions are replaced by a stipulated sequence (do *a*, then *b*, then *c* ...). To the extent that the ritual is represented as having a causal efficacy, individual actions are unlikely to be changed or omitted, as it is impossible to tell which are causally efficacious in bringing about the desired result. Thus the Trobriand spells must be correctly performed in order to have any effect.

These characteristics of ritual actions have four effects:

1. Ritual actions tend to expose what can be referred to as "goal-demotion" (Boyer & Lienard 2006; Lienard & Boyer 2006). Instead of specifying sub-actions in a causal relation to the ultimate intention, the correct performance of the ritual sequence becomes a goal in itself as only this can ensure their causal effect. The causal under-determination of the sub-actions is often emphasised by extreme iteration or other means to violate ordinary expectations relating actions to a goal specified by an ultimate intention. This entails a much greater focus on small elements in the behavioural sequence and on the ritual status of the agent performing the action (is he/she entitled to do so?).

2. As each action is underspecified by the overarching intention, our cognitive system must search for other clues to explain the purpose of the actions performed. In short, ritual actions provoke the activation of two different hermeneutic strategies both able to connect rituals with purpose or meaning. In the first, our cognitive system attempts to relate perceptual features of the actions to its purported goal and is therefore focused on the pragmatic *purpose* of the ritual action. For instance, Trobriand spells are often 'infused' into a material that is later brought into contact with the domain the spell is supposed to influence. Thus we find a widespread emphasis on relations of similarity

and contagion in magical rituals (Sørensen 2007). In contrast the second approach is focussed on the *meaning* of ritual actions in relation to some system of symbolic reference. Such understanding is context-distant and indifferent or even sceptical towards notions of ritual efficacy as it attaches ritual actions to prevailing dogmatic or ideological structures rather than its local, pragmatic context.[8] This difference in cognitive processing is basic to the distinction between 'magical' and 'religious' rituals. Contrary to most traditional theories of magic and ritual, however, it should be emphasised that all rituals in principle can provoke both hermeneutic responses and there is a dynamic tension between the two approaches in most religious traditions (Sørensen 2007, forthcoming).

3. As the ultimate intention does not causally specify the actions performed, the ritual action sequence can in principle be connected to any kind of ultimate intention. One cannot predict the intentions of the performers by watching the performance and one type of ritual performance can be related to many different types of ultimate intention. This accounts for the extreme variety of interpretations often given by ritual participants when asked why they perform a given ritual (Humphrey & Laidlaw 1994). In order to arrive at uniform interpretations of ritual actions other measures must be employed, such as extensive teaching of doctrines and sanctions following transgression of orthodoxy (Whitehouse 2004).

4. The lack of causal specification of ritual actions (how do they work?) and their intentional under-determination (why perform these particular actions?) has the further effect of making representations of superhuman agents highly relevant as their presence effectively address both of these questions. The more or less direct evocation of ancestors, gods or spirits can ensure that actions, which are otherwise not ascribed any particular efficacy, can be represented as efficacious actions when performed in a ritual context (McCauley & Lawson 2002). Further, if represented as instituting the rituals, superhuman agents specify a relation between the particular actions performed and an ultimate intention.

---

8. Obviously, participants might have no immediate representation of the purpose or meaning of a given ritual performance. It is questionable, however, whether ritual practices that are seen as neither doing anything or meaning anything will survive cultural transmission.

The transformation of actions representations in ritual actions is modelled in figure 2:

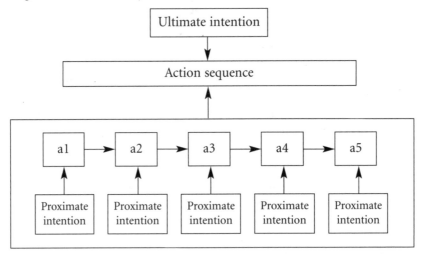

Figure 2: Elements present in a ritual action representation: The performance of a specific ritual action sequence is determined by some ultimate intention. This, however, does not specify the actions performed or the causal relation between them. Instead the sub-actions are frozen into a stipulated series of proximate intentions, whose performance only signals that the ritual action sequence has been performed.

Why Perform Both Ritual and Non-Ritual Actions?

Having outlined the cognitive mechanisms enabling people to distinguish non-ritual and ritual actions, we can now turn to the second question: why do people often perform both non-ritual and ritual actions in order to achieve the same goal?[9] If the hypothesis that it is the very existence of ritual actions that makes superhuman agents relevant is true, then belief in such entities cannot in itself explain the concerted performance of non-ritual and ritual ac-

9. When addressing the relation between non-ritual and ritual actions the proposed explanation will be mostly relevant to *prospective* rituals in contrast to *reactive* rituals. Whereas the former are directed to creating a new state of affair (e.g. an abundant harvest), the latter are concerned with reinstating a disrupted former state of affair (e.g. curing a disease). See Sørensen (2007), for a discussion of how this distinction creates different representations of events and actions.

tions. Further, as ritual actions are causally under-determined by their ultimate intention, they are clearly not regarded as just another practical method to achieve a result.

Based on his Trobriand material Malinowski identified a promising place to start this investigation by pointing out that not all actions are surrounded by magical ritual. Magical rituals surround only endeavours represented as imbued with significant uncertainty. Whereas dangerous deep-sea fishing has elaborate magical rituals to ensure the safety of the crew and the successful outcome, poison fishing in a safe lagoon has no ritual connected to it (1992:30f). Malinowski argued that the performance of the rituals makes people more secure and therefore has a positive effect on the actions undertaken. This account has been criticised because, even among the Trobrianders, not all endeavours entailing some level of uncertainty are surrounded by ritual actions and some activities with little uncertainty have elaborate magical rituals (Nadel 1957). In addition, it is far from obvious that the performance of ritual actions always have a reassuring effect. In contrast, ritual actions evoke representations of both positive and negative superhuman agents and may therefore evoke as much anxiety as reassurance. Further, even if Malinowski was right (as I believe he was) that uncertainty is a major motivation for performing magical rituals, uncertainty cannot be the only relevant parameter. We continually perform a wide range of different types of actions under conditions of uncertainty. A reasonable hypothesis is therefore that only actions both represented as uncertain and *important* are likely to involve concerted magical actions. Representations of importance, in turn, might be both culturally specified and a part of our evolutionary baggage. Thus, a promising hypothesis would be that actions directly involving basic biological functions, such as reproduction, sustenance, and health are more likely to provoke the auxiliary performance of ritualised action.

In order to explain why representations of uncertainty in relation to important pragmatic endeavours are likely to provoke the performance of ritual action, some basic premises should first of all be tested through psychological experiments. First, does the performance of ritual actions alleviate feelings of anxiety produced by uncertainty? Second, will performance of ritual actions induce a more positive judgement of the likely success of a pragmatic endeavour? Unfortunately, such experimental work has still to be done. But if it turns out that the performance of ritual actions in certain situations does alleviate anxiety and enhance expectations of success, the next natural question is, what underlying cognitive mechanisms can explain these effects. I suggest three possible lines of enquiry that may help answer these questions:

1. First, we need to know how uncertainty affects representations of actions. Uncertainty can be produced under a number of different conditions: (a) the successful outcome can be dependent on a number of variables beyond the control of the individual; (b) the outcome can be a result of a hierarchy of interdependent action sequences, allowing for many different things to go wrong in the process; (c) the actions can involve considerable risks to the performing agent and/or to the group of which he or she is a member.

Trobriand agriculture, for instance, combines the three conditions. It involves a number of important variables beyond the agriculturalist's control (weather, pests and diseases). It involves a large number of hierarchically and temporally organised action sequences spread out over considerable time. And it involves representations of a considerable risk (hunger) if the harvest fails. The magical rituals connected with the Trobriand agricultural cycle have different means to deal with this uncertainty. The most important spell, the *vatuvi* spell, is said on a number of occasions throughout the agricultural cycle.[10] It contains imagery that combines a projection of the desired overall result of the activities ('the swelling of my garden' = abundant harvest) with an exorcism of pests and diseases ('I sweep away grubs ...'). So, through the use of specific types of analogical imagery, variables beyond the control of the agents are transferred into a domain were they are objectified and manipulated. Different conceptual domains are blended in a ritual structure (Fauconnier & Turner 1998), whereby pests and diseases are transformed into objects that can be acted upon by 'sweeping', 'blowing', 'driving', 'sending', and 'chasing' (Sørensen 2007). Further, a long series of interdependent action sequences is transformed into a manageable sequence of stipulated actions postulated to secure its successful outcome. Representations of the interdependent action sequences constituting the agri-

---

10. The *vatuvi* spell plays a central role in several rituals performed throughout the agricultural cycle. Its initial part specifies the authority of the magician uttering the spell and contains imagery emphasising a desirable state of the yams gardens 'bulging' with tubers as if it were a pregnant woman. The central part of the spell takes approximately 45 minutes to pronounce and consists in a highly repetitive linguistic sequence in which different pests and diseases (blight, beetles etc) are expelled through by different types of actions (sweeping, blowing, chasing etc) all containing a schematic structure involving expulsion from a bounded area (Malinowski 1935a:96ff). The spell thus comprises the whole agricultural process in a highly condensed sequence involving both the desirable outcome as well as possible dangers involved.

cultural cycle (preparing the soil, planting, weeding, thinning, harvesting etc.) form a very complex network with numerous contingent variables. In contrast the ritual action sequence is represented as an efficient instrument independent from the contingent causal relations specifying other actions. Thus, it is likely that repeated explicit representation of the expected and desired causal scenario in a comprised form will increase expectations of its success.[11]

The imagery found in ritual actions often contains representations of force. Thus, pests and diseases are forced out of the garden in the *vatuvi* spell and such imagery of exorcism is widespread along with other basic image schemata of protection, inclusion, attraction, repulsion and expulsion (Sørensen 2007). Besides such direct expression of force-dynamic relations (Talmy 2000) force is iconically represented in the very form of the ritual. The longer the spell, the more repetitions involved and the more energy invested the stronger the ritual action will be represented as being. This points to the importance of bodily actions in ritual performance. Very few rituals are strictly oral. Most contain more or less stipulated sequences of bodily actions often iconically related to the purported goal of the ritual. This physical dimension of magical rituals gives a direct experience of actually doing something to effect changes to variables otherwise beyond the agent's control (Barsalou et. al. 2005). It is likely, but not experimentally proven, that such bodily experiences will produce more optimistic expectations.

2. A second line of inquiry might focus on how the performance of magical rituals provokes inferential processes in specific cognitive domains. There are two obvious candidate domains: the tool domain and the so-

---

11. This view has some similarity to that exposed by Tambiah (1968). He argues that magical rites attain a level of realism "by clothing a metaphorical procedure in the operational and manipulative mode of practical action" (1968: 194). Tambiah understands magical ritual as an *expression* and argues that the internal function of the ritual is to transfer information and store vital knowledge about pragmatic pursuits such as gardening. It is far from clear, however, why the enigmatic use of ritual language should be used to transmit information about gardening that people could more easily transmit in a non-ritual framework. Further, it is questionable whether iteration and redundancy will help convey information or whether such rhetorical strategies actually deplete words of ordinary meaning in order for other, more experiential structures to emerge. I believe that we need to focus on how the specific features of ritual action, such as condensation, redundancy and iteration, can evoke representations of pragmatic success not despite, but because of the special features. This, in turn, might help explain why the performance of magical rituals seem to be consistently connected to specific types of human activities.

cial domain. As ritual actions are causally under-specified they can be represented as instrumental in a whole range of different situations. Further, many magical rituals contain objects with specific powers that obviously will trigger inferences drawn from the tool domain. The same effect, however, can be produced linguistically by the use of non-sensical, foreign or archaic words and utterances. It is by the correct utterance of the word, whose meaning might be totally opaque, that the ritual has effect on the world. The proliferation and spread of both ritual objects and specific types of linguistic utterances testifies to the instrumental aspects of magical rituals. When ritual actions are understood as instruments, a whole range of cognitive mechanisms will trigger specific types of inferences. An instrument or tool cannot be changed to any large extent as it thus ceases to be a tool, it is generally 'made' by a human or superhuman being whose intentions specify the function of the instrument, and people will tend to focus on functional aspects of the instrument (in this case perceptual features that can relate the action to its purported effect) (Cosmides & Tooby 1994).

The wide proliferation of linguistic utterances in magical ritual points to another cognitive domain activated, namely that of social cognition. Physical things and animals are addressed as if they understand language, and a whole range of rhetorical strategies are involved including ordering, begging, describing, proscribing. This is, of course, even more the case when different types of superhuman agency are directly evoked in the ritual proceeding. By triggering social cognition, a whole range of inferential structures becomes involved: Theory of Mind mechanisms predicting intentions and beliefs of relevant agents; representations of relative social status; and representations of 'essence' due to membership of special social groups (Hirschfeld 1994; Leslie 1994). Rituals that trigger inferential processes from either the tool or the social domain thus have special salience. This, in turn, is likely to enhance successful transmission of rituals that excite either or both of these systems. Again, however, these speculations have yet to be experimentally demonstrated.

The activation of specific cognitive mechanisms can be investigated at an even more detailed level. Recently, Boyer and Lienard have proposed a selectionist account of cultural rituals. Accordingly, successful cultural rituals, i.e. rituals that become transmitted, are constrained by the extent to which they contain elements that trigger an evolved hazard precaution system. This consists in an Evolutionary Hazard Repertoire, originally evolved to detect potential environmental dangers and an Evolutionary

Precaution Repertoire that consists in a number of intuitively appropriate behaviours. The basic hazards are contamination, reproductive risks, social extrication, predation, and resource scarcity. Each hazard is further related to a repertoire of actions that are conjectured to have evolved to alleviate the danger, such as cleansing and protecting. The point is that even if these risks are not directly present, they are ritually mimicked and the intuitively appropriate actions are performed in order to create the necessary cognitive relevancy. The rituals humans perform are the ones that contain cues that activate this precaution system. This makes them attention-demanding and compelling and therefore easy to transmit (Boyer & Lienard 2006; Lienard & Boyer 2006).

In the present argument it cannot be decided in advance which of the many potential cognitive systems are activated by the performance of particular magical rituals. This needs to be investigated empirically and we are likely to find that different types of rituals trigger different types of cognitive systems. The importance of this research in relation to the question why people perform magical rituals in concert with non-rituals actions lies in a simple observation. By performing ritual actions more cognitive systems are triggered which, in turn, will make the overall action more relevant (Sperber & Wilson 1995; Boyer 2001). This heightened sense of relevance proliferates to the overall endeavour and it should therefore come as no surprise that magical rituals are performed in relation to actions that are both important and imbued with some degree of uncertainty.

3. Finally, the relation between ritual and non-ritual actions should be studied from the perspective of how these are represented *after* the event has taken place. As described above, the result of a non-ritual action sequence can to a large extent be explained by reference to the causal relations between the constituent actions. Thus, if a farmer does not weed the field and weeds overtake it, a small harvest might be expected to follow. When these actions are augmented by ritual, however, the number of possible *post hoc* rationalisations increases substantially. Now the meagre harvest is not only due to insufficient weeding but can be explained by insufficient positive magic, faulty ritual performance, evil magic performed by a rival etc. Thereby actions are related to a large number of explanatory event-frames, i.e. mental models of why and how specific events occur, and these will entail a greater explanatory flexibility in the social negotiations deciding the cause of specific events. This flexibility has the important additional effect that it spreads the responsibility for a successful outcome, not

only to include the agents involved in the magical ritual, but also to a range of superhuman agents made relevant by the ritual performance. Magical rituals in this way work as an incentive to embark on risky endeavours, as more people will have an interest in its successful outcome and given that various secondary rationalizations are available in case of failure thereby diminishing the potential embarrassment for individual participants.

These different lines of inquiry do not preclude each other. No 'magic bullet' will explain why magical rituals are performed in conjunction with ordinary actions. Instead of one cause, several causes all contribute to the relative stability of ritual practices when people embark on actions under uncertainty.

Conclusion

Malinowski argued that magical rituals serve an important function in human societies: they are a specific type of action that ensures that the human agent does not succumb to anxiety at the same time as it instils confidence in his or her own abilities. For this reason, magical rituals cluster around human endeavours perceived as carrying some type of risk. In this chapter I have argued that Malinowski's questions are still relevant, even if his answers need to be revised. We still need to address the question of why people perform both ritual and non-ritual actions in order to achieve the same specific goal. Cognitive studies of how humans represent actions allow us to distinguish representations of non-ritual and ritual actions based on (a) the relation between representations of intentionality and actions-sequence and (b) the causal expectations to the actions. In ritual actions, the action sequence is not determined by the intention of the agent. Further, there need not be any causal relations between the actions comprising the ritual. This makes rituals a peculiar type of action that will have specific cognitive effects. Moreover, a cognitive approach also allows the constructions of multiple models capable of explaining why the performance of rituals reduces (or might be expected to reduce) anxiety: it enables participants to interact with forces outside their control; it comprises long series of concerted actions into confined and stipulated series of actions; it activates several cognitive domains that make them highly relevant and compelling; and it enables a greater range of available models to explain the outcome of the pragmatic endeavour. Which of these models will survive thorough empirical testing remains to be seen, and perhaps the whole problem-complex will need further reshuffling in order to be explained. But the fruitfulness of the cognitive approach to classical anthropological problems such as magic does not only lie in the extent to which it can provide instant solutions. More importantly, it provides a theoretical and methodological framework that enables the construction of new hypotheses and the means to test them.

References

Barrett, Justin (2000) 'Exploring the Natural Foundations of Religion' *Trends in Cognitive Sciences 4* pp. 29–34

Barsalou, L. W. Barbey, A.K. Simmons, W.K. and Santos, A. (2003) 'Embodiment in Religious Knowledge' *Journal of Cognition and Culture* 5 (1–2): 14–57

Blakemore, S.-J., Boyer, P., Pachot-Clouard, M., Meltzoff, A., Segebarth, C. & Decety, J. (2003) 'The Detection of Contingency and Animacy from Simple Animations in the Human Brain' *Cerebral Cortex 13* pp. 837–844.

Bloch, M. (2004) 'Ritual and Deference' In *Ritual and Memory: Toward a Comparative Anthropology of Religion*, Walnut Creek: AltaMira Press

Boyer, P. (1994) *The Naturalness of Religious Ideas*, Berkeley: University of California Press.

Boyer, P. (2001) *Religion Explained: The Human Instincts that Fashion Gods, Spirits and Ancestors*, London: Vintage

Boyer, P. and Lienard, P. (2006): 'Why Ritualized Behaviour? Precaution Systems and Action Parsing in Developmental, Pathological and Cultural Rituals' *Brain and Behavioral Sciences.* 29(6) pp. 595–613.

Carruthers, P. and Smith, P.K. (1996) *Theories of Theories of Mind*, Cambridge: Cambridge University Press.

Cosmides, L. and Tooby, J. (1994) 'Origins of domain specificity: The evolution of functional organisation' in Hirschfeld, L. and Gelman, S. (eds.) *Mapping the Mind: Domain Specificity in Cognition and Culture*, Cambridge: Cambridge University Press.

Daprati, E.N. Georgieff, F. N. Proust, L. Pacherie, E. Dalery, J. and Jeannerod, M. (1997) 'Looking for the agent. An investigation into consciousness of action and self-consciousness in schizophrenic patients' *Cognition*, 65: 71–86.

Evans-Pritchard, E. E. (1929). 'The Morphology and Function of Magic'. *American Anthropologist* 31(4): 619–641.

Fauconnier, G. and Turner, M. (1998) 'Conceptual Integration Networks' *Cognitive Science* 22(2): 133–187

Gallese, V. (2000a) 'The Inner Sense of Action. Agency and Motor Representations' *Journal of Consciousness Studies, 7 (10)* pp.23–40

Gallese, V. (2000b) 'The Acting Subject. Towards the Neural Basis of Causal Cognition' in Metzinger (ed.) *Neural Correlates of Consciousness*, Cambridge: The MIT Press

Gallese, V. (2001) 'The 'Shared Manifold' Hypothesis. From Mirror Neurons To Empathy' *Journal of Consciousness Studies, 8 (5–7)* pp. 33–50

Gallese, V. and Lakoff, G. (to appear) 'The Brain's Concepts: The Role of Sensory-Motor System in Conceptual Knowledge' *Cognitive Neuropsychology, 21*

Gelman, R. Durgin, F. and Kaufman, L. (1995) 'Distinguishing between animates and inanimates: not by motion alone' in Sperber, D. Premack, D. and. Premack, A.J. (eds.) *Causal Cognition: A multidisciplinary debate*, Oxford: Clarendon Press.

Guthrie, S. (1980) 'A Cognitive Theory of Religion.' *Current Anthropology* 21(2): 181–203.

Guthrie, S. (1993) 'Faces in the Clouds: A New Theory of Religion' Oxford: Oxford University Press.

Hirschfeld, L. A. (1995) 'Anthropology, psychology, and the meaning of social causality' in Sperber, D. Premack, D and. Premack, A.J. (eds.) *Causal Cognition: A multidisciplinary debate*, Oxford: Clarendon Press.

Hirschfeld, L. A. and Gelman, S. (eds.) (1994) *Mapping the Mind: Domain Specificity in Cognition and Culture*, Cambridge: Cambridge University Press.

Humphrey, C. and Laidlaw, J. (1994) *The Archetypal Actions of Ritual: A Theory of Ritual Illustrated by the Jain Rite of Worship*, Oxford: Clarendon Press.

Jacobs, P. and Jeannerod, M. (2005) 'The motor theory of social cognition: a critique' http://www.interdisciplines.org/mirror/papers/2

Johnson, S. Both, A. O'Hearn, K. (2001) 'Inferring goals of a non-human agent' *Cognitive Development, 16* pp.637–656

Leach, E. (1957) 'The Epistemological Background to Malinowski's Empiricism' in Firth, R. (ed.) *Man and Culture: An Evaluation of the Work of Bronislaw Malinowski*, London: Routledge and Kegan, Paul.

Leslie, A. M. (1994) 'ToMM, ToBy, and Agency; Core architecture and domain specificity' In Hirschfeld, L. and Gelman, S. (eds.) *Mapping the Mind: Domain Specificity in Cognition and Culture*, Cambridge: Cambridge University Press.

Leslie, A. M. (1995) 'A theory of agency' in Sperber, D. Premack, D. and Premack, A.J. (eds.) *Causal Cognition: A multidisciplinary debate*, Oxford: Clarendon Press.

Lienard, Pierre & Pascal Boyer (2006)." Whence Collective Rituals? A Cultural Selection Model of Ritualized Behavior." *American Anthropologist* 108 (4)

Malinowski, B. (1935a) *Coral Gardens and Their Magic*, Vol.1. London: George Allen & Unwin Ltd.

Malinowski, B. (1935b) *Coral Gardens and Their Magic*, Vol.2. London: George Allen & Unwin Ltd.

Malinowski, B. (1944) *A Scientific Theory of Culture and Other Essays*, Chapel Hill: The University of North Carolina Press.

Malinowski, B. (1963) *Sex, Culture, and Myth*, London: Rupert Hart-Davies.

Malinowski, B. (1992) *Magic, Science and Religion and Other Essays*, Prospect Heights: Waveland Press Inc.

Mandler, J. (1992) 'How to build a baby II: Conceptual primitives' *Psychological Review* 99: 587–604.

Nadel, S. F. (1957) 'Malinowski on Magic and Religion' in Firth, R. (ed.) *Man and Culture: An Evaluation of the Work of Bronislaw Malinowski*, London: Routledge and Kegan, Paul.

Searle, J. R. (1969) *Speech Acts: An Essay in the Philosophy of Language*, Cambridge: Cambridge University Press.

Sperber, D. and Wilson, D. (1986) *Relevance: Communication and cognition*, Cambridge: Harvard University Press.

Sperber, D. Premack, D. and Premack, A.J. (eds.) (1995) *Causal Cognition: A Multidisciplinary Debate*, Oxford: Oxford University Press.

Sørensen, J. (2007) *A Cognitive Theory of Magic*, Walnut Creek: Altamira Press.

Sørensen, J. (forthcoming) 'Acts that work: Cognitive aspects of ritual agency' *Method and Theory in the Study of Religion*.

Talmy, L. (2000) 'Force Dynamics in Language and Thought' in Talmy, L. (ed.) *Toward a Cognitive Semantics*, Cambridge: MIT Press.

Tambiah, S. (1968) The Magical Power of Words, *Man* 3: 175–208.

Tomasello, M. (1999) *The Cultural Origins of Human Cognition,* Cambridge: Harvard University Press.

Whitehouse, H. (2004) *Modes of Religiosity: A Cognitive Theory of Religious Transmission,* Walnut Creek: AltaMira Press.

CHAPTER FOUR

How "Natives" Don't Think: The Apotheosis of Overinterpretation

Jonathan A. Lanman

The cognitive sciences, including the fledgling cognitive science of culture, offer a growing body of empirical knowledge concerning the human mind. What remains to be seen is how this knowledge will affect work in anthropology, history, sociology, and indeed any field that claims to study human beings and their actions. Are the findings of the cognitive sciences irrelevant to the concerns of these fields? Or, on the contrary, might they revolutionize the study of humanity?

In *Philosophy in the Flesh* (1999), George Lakoff and Mark Johnson argue that philosophy as a whole, not only philosophy of mind, stands to be revolutionized by the cognitive sciences. The latter, they argue, render *a priori*, intuitive, and introspective theorizing about the mind highly problematic in that many of those intuitive musings do not match empirical findings. As Lakoff and Johnson rightly state, "our understanding of what the mind is matters deeply" (3). And it matters to more than just philosophy. Our intuitive understanding of mind constitutes our intuitive understanding of persons, and our intuitive understanding of persons informs nearly all interpretation and explanation in the humanities and social sciences. As Harvey Whitehouse notes, "we are all psychologists of a sort" (2004: 168). So we are brought back to the questions: *What do the cognitive sciences mean for anthropology, for history?*[1]

---

1. These are very open questions that raise a plethora of substantive, methodological, and philosophical issues. One of the most obvious is the long-standing debate between *naturalists* and *humanists* over whether or not scientific understandings can say anything useful at all about the meaningful actions of human beings. This debate is made much more interesting in light of the fact that the understandings offered by the cognitive sciences di-

Naturalistic accounts such as those of Lakoff and Johnson certainly have the *potential* to transform the social sciences and humanities by transforming our intuitive, introspective notions of minds, persons, and their behaviors into scientifically grounded notions.[2] And, indeed, naturalistically inclined scholars have already attempted to reconstruct such centrally important concepts as *culture* (Shore 1996; Sperber 1996), *meaning* (Strauss & Quinn 1997), *religion* (Barrett 2004; Boyer 2001; McCauley 2004; Pyysiäinen 2004), and *religious ritual* (McCauley & Lawson 2002; Whitehouse 2004). But while such theories are gaining a wider and more appreciative reception, the naturalist project has by no means swept through the humanities and social sciences.

In this chapter, I will attempt nothing as grand as the naturalization of an important abstraction. Instead, I will highlight some of the consequences that naturalizing the mind has on our interpretations of human behavior. In general, I will argue that interpretative efforts that neglect to take into account

---

rectly concern the physical bases of mind and meaning, the very things that are thought to place the beliefs, desires, and reasons of human beings outside the ontology of science.

2. In the wake of claims from a variety of scholars in the humanities and social sciences that foundational epistemology and notions of certainty are highly problematic, many philosophers of science have embraced *naturalism*, a philosophical position which denies foundational epistemology and certainty but affirms normative epistemology and scientific progress, the babies thrown out with the bathwater by some humanities scholars (e.g. Clifford & Marcus 1986).

In short, naturalism holds that the sciences should be our "guides" in the areas of epistemology and metaphysics. In other words, "philosophy can use results from the sciences to help answer philosophical questions and can do this even in the philosophy of science itself" (Godfrey-Smith 2003: 149). Naturalism rejects foundationalism in matters of epistemology, not because foundations are not desirable but because they are impossible. The idea that we can be certain in our knowledge is untenable. Rather, "we can only hope to develop an adequate description of how knowledge and science work if we draw on scientific ideas as we go," leaving the account of knowledge that emerges "no more certain or secure than the scientific theories themselves" (Godfrey-Smith 2003: 150).

The science that has survived the demise of certainty is, of course, a different science than that postulated by the logical positivists in the 1920's. It is not in the business of producing absolute, universal Truth, but rather producing approximate truths, lasting only as long as it takes the creativity and collaboration of the scientific community to construct "truer" truths (Reyna 1994: 557). As philosopher Martin Hollis puts it, "Science is always open-ended, offering no certainties and no rest for the enquiring mind" (1994: 75).

Philip Kitcher's often cited essay "The Naturalists Return" (1992) and Peter Godfrey-Smith's introductory text *Theory and Reality* (2003) are fine introductions to this philosophical position.

Regarding "naturalization," intuitive philosophizing has given us many of our most widely-used abstractions (e.g. culture, religion, ritual, society). Naturalizing these concepts involves defining them according to scientific findings rather than intuition.

the explanatory progress of the cognitive sciences are problematic but that many of these problems can be addressed by a more collaborative effort between interpretive and explanatory approaches. More specifically, I will reexamine the debate between anthropologists Marshall Sahlins and Gananath Obeyesekere over the meaning of a variety of Native Hawaiian actions, including a particular ritual performance, in light of the findings of the cognitive sciences.[3] I will argue that these findings pose significant problems for both Sahlins' and Obeyesekere's interpretations. Findings of representational diversity in both populations and individuals problematize Sahlins' method of linking Hawaiian myths to individual thought and behavior. Findings concerning the "rational" abilities of human beings problematize Obeyesekere's claim of a universal "practical rationality." And while I will not claim that the cognitive sciences "resolve" the debate once and for all, I will claim that several larger anthropological questions the debate raises, such as how to ascertain mental representations from the existence of public representations, how public representations (e.g. rituals) can influence mental representations, and how cognitive and cultural factors interact to produce thought and behavior, can be more adequately addressed by taking the explanatory findings of the cognitive sciences into account.

Historical Sources and Ritual Actions

The debate between Marshall Sahlins and Gananath Obeyesekere, as found in Sahlins' How "Natives" Think: About Captain Cook For Example (1995) and Obeyeskere's The Apotheosis of Captain Cook: European Mythmaking in the Pacific (1997), concerns the interpretation of the Hawaiian response to Captain James Cook in 1778–1779, as documented in the journals of Cook and his crew. Sahlins and Obeyesekere disagree about what a variety of Hawaiian ac-

---

3. It might strike the reader as odd that distinguished anthropologists are debating "the meaning" of a ritual performance, given that work on symbolism and ritual have dispensed with the idea of a "deep" or "actual" meaning in both symbols and ritual actions (Sperber 1975; Humphrey & Laidlaw 1994). The answer to this riddle lies in the fact that it is not the meaning of the specific ritual actions, such as preparing food and sitting it in front of statues, that is the issue but the Hawaiians' decision to have Captain Cook participate. Thus, while it is nearly impossible to ascertain the intentions behind ritual actions (Bloch 2004; Humphrey & Laidlaw 1994; Whitehouse 2004), the debate between Sahlins and Obeyesekere is over the intentions of the non-ritual decisions/actions which led to Cook's ritual participation; the argument is over the mental representation of Cook in the minds of the Hawaiians which led them to include him in the ritual sequence.

tions reveal about their views of Cook, but both scholars single out a particular set of repeated ritual actions, performed for the first time just after the British anchored in Kealakekua Bay on January 17th, 1779, as of central importance in understanding the Hawaiian response. The following is a summary of the interactions between the Hawaiians and the British, including the crucial ritual sequence, about which Sahlins and Obeyesekere so vehemently disagree.

The meeting between the British ships, *The Discovery* and *The Resolution*, and 10,000 Native Hawaiians in Kealakekua Bay on January 17th was by no means the first contact between the British and the Hawaiians, nor even between the expedition and the inhabitants of Hawai'i proper. Cook and company had passed through the Hawaiian Islands early in 1778, coming ashore for a time on Kauai, where they engaged in trading with the natives, attended numerous religious ceremonies at a nearby temple, and witnessed nearly constant prostration on the part of the Hawaiians (Cook: 269–270).[4]

Even on the return passage through the islands in November-December 1778, the journals of Cook, Lieutenant King, David Samwell, and Heinrich Zimmerman document substantial contact with the Hawaiians off the coasts of both Maui and Hawai'i before the events in Kealakekua Bay, some shy in approaching and boarding the larger vessels, some not (Cook: 474–475; King: 496–498; Samwell: 1152, 1154; Zimmerman: 92–93). They even met with King Kalani'ōpu'u of Hawai'i in one such visitation off the coast of Maui, during which the king presented Cook with some small pigs (Cook: 476).

The meeting on January 17th, 1779, then, was not between total strangers. Yet, with little doubt, the gathering of thousands of Hawaiians in Kealakekua Bay on the 16–17th of January was a much more substantial affair than past meetings, with numerous Hawaiians filling the decks of the British ships, singing and jumping (Samwell: 1158).

In this raucous setting, Cook was sought out by a priest named Koa'a, who, besides giving the Captain a substantial gift of fruit, roots, and a large hog, wrapped Cook in a red cloth and held a small pig while repeating a long oration (Cook: 491; King: 504). That afternoon, after Cook and Lieutenant King had gone ashore, Koa'a led Cook by the hand to a nearby temple (Cook: 491).

The walk to the temple marks the end of the personal journal of James Cook, but the journals of Lieutenant King and David Samwell, among others, relate the events that followed. At the temple, Koa'a continued his re-

---

4. All references from the journals of Cook, King, Riou, Clerke, Phillip, and Samwell are as found in Beaglehole (1967).

peated praying and kept hold of Cook's hand. A procession of ten men brought a hog and a large red cloth before prostrating. Koa'a wrapped the cloth around Cook and saw that the hog was presented to him (King: 505). Koa'a continued to chant, repeating the word "Erono," or Lono, frequently, and led Cook to a variety of "images" around the temple, even having Cook prostrate towards and kiss one.[5] Lieutenant King and Koa'a, seated next to Cook, then supported his arms. Cook and King were then rubbed with chewed coconut wrapped in a red cloth, offered kava, and "crammed" with hog (King: 506).

This ritual sequence, with the offering of hogs, the supporting of arms, and the rubbing of the British with chewed coconut, was repeated numerous times during Cook's stay on Hawai'i (King: 509; Samwell: 1161–1162). In addition to these ceremonies, a priest greeted Cook whenever he came ashore and also sang to make onlookers prostrate in Cook's presence. More ceremonies, more hogs, more coconuts, all were given with "much indifference as to any return" (King: 510).[6]

Cook and company left Kealakekua Bay on February 4th, 1779, after the king and several chiefs had enquired about and desired their departure (King: 517). Yet, on the 11th of February, the expedition found itself back in Kealakekua Bay as a result of a storm damaging the mast of the *Resolution*. On their way into the bay, they came across several canoes, which brought "many of our old friends," including Koa'a, who brought presents once again and repeated his orating; some trading also took place (Samwell: 1190). Yet, as King notes, the number of Hawaiians greeting them was very small compared to the stagger- ing numbers of their first arrival in the bay (528). Heinrich Zimmermann also notes that the temperament of many Hawaiians had altered: "Upon our return we found the people quite changed, in fact we had noticed some discontent among them before our departure and very much less respect for us" (98).

This atmosphere of discontent intensified and resulted in the much-discussed death of Captain Cook, as the cutter of the *Discovery* was stolen and Cook led an armed group of marines to take Kalani'ōpu'u hostage, only to be brought down by an iron dagger in the back (Samwell: 1196; Phillip: 535).

---

5. The image is of Kū, the god of war, political power, and the king. Sahlins and Obeye- sekere debate its significance in determining how the Hawaiians conceptualized Cook (Sahlins 1995: 55; Obeyesekere 1997: 83–84).

6. Yet, not everyone had such indifference, as trading continued between the sailors and the Hawaiians through most of the British visit, save during *tapus* on trade, such as the one on the 24th of January for the arrival of the king, Kalani'ōpu'u (King: 511; Samwell: 1164).

The end of Cook was not the end of the interactions between the Hawaiians and the British. The following days were filled with a mixture of friendliness and violence between the expedition and groups of Hawaiians as the British attempted to make necessary repairs. Many Hawaiians did indeed fight the British, resulting in several Hawaiians being killed and one of the nearby villages being burnt to the ground (Clerke: 545; Zimmerman: 104). Yet, even during this violence, some Hawaiians came out under cover of darkness to trade with the British, and Hawaiian women, though not in as great of numbers, still came out to sleep on the ships each night (Clerke: 546; Zimmerman: 110).

Eventually, more Hawaiians than just the priests had made friends with the British, and both the chiefs and some common people put themselves in their "power," seeking to renew their former "confidence;" trading and gift-giving abounded (Clerke: 548; King: 565–566). By the time of the British departure on the 23rd of February, King notes, several Hawaiians wanted to remain friends with the sailors and the crew received "many affectionate farewells" as they sailed by the coast on their way out to sea (567).

Interpreting History

One can interpret history in both senses of the term "history;" one can interpret the sources and evidence concerning the historical past and one can also interpret the products of historians. Sahlins and Obeyesekere engage in both enterprises in their extended and ill-tempered debate. For Sahlins, the Hawaiians at Kealakekua Bay interpreted Captain Cook as their god Lono and treated him accordingly by including him in a series of rituals as Lono and continuously prostrating towards him. Sahlins also views Obeyesekere's alternative history as little more than "rhetorical politics" and its key thesis of a universal practical rationality as a type of "symbolic violence" against Hawaiian culture (1995: 2, 14). For Obeyesekere, the Hawaiians interpreted Cook as a powerful and terrifying foreigner who might help them in their own struggles and included him in a ritual that named him Lono, a powerful chief who would help them in their war against Maui. Obeyesekere dismisses Sahlins' account as a continuation of the Western notion of a "prelogical or childlike native ... given to unreflective traditional thought" and as part of a continuing culture of "terror" (1997: 16).

The above summary of the historical sources points to a much more complex and multi-faceted Hawaiian response to Cook than one might expect after viewing Sahlins and Obeyesekere's interpretations. Some Hawaiians welcomed the British back after their mast broke, others did not. Some obeyed *tapus* (taboos), others did not. Some fought the British, while others traded and expressed regret at the sailors' departure. And while it is the case that neither Sahlins nor Obeyesekere completely overlook this diverse response (they explicitly acknowledge it at times (Sahlins 1985: 121–122; Obeyesekere 1997: 91)), both scholars frequently use phrases such as *The Hawaiians viewed Cook as ...* or *The Hawaiians must have known ...* and both of their theses require some significant number of people to view Cook in the way they suggest. This scenario of empirical evidence complicating the more general pronouncements of Sahlins and Obeyesekere will repeat itself again as we examine the evidence from the cognitive sciences in relation to their respective explanatory frameworks.

Sahlins

Sahlins interprets the Hawaiian response to Cook as the response of a people to the arrival of one of their most important deities, Lono. He claims that Cook arrived at Hawai'i in conjunction with the annual ritual cycle of the Makahiki, a festival in honor of Lono, and that the Hawaiians both perceived and treated Cook as Lono. All was well as Cook's actions fitted with the Makahiki schedule. All was made most unwell, however, with his unexpected return on the 11th of February. His presence then conflicted with the mythic schemes of the Hawaiians, and he ended up dead on the Hawaiian coastline.

Sahlins' interpretation makes sense when we take into account the cultural context of the Makahiki, and Sahlins does a masterful job of relating this context. *Makahiki* can be loosely translated as "the rising of the Pleiades in the heavens corresponding with the time of the sun's turn northward, bringing warmth again to earth, the growth of plants, and the spawning of fish" (Beckwith 1951: 18). It is a festival in honor of Lono, god of fertility, cultivated plants, storms, rain, and numerous other phenomena (Handy & Pukui 1956: 31). The Makahiki lasts four-months and has a variety of stages, all of which are marked by appearances of Lono and the suspension of a variety of tapus. During these suspensions, the power of the human chiefs and king is "put in abeyance, making way for the temporary ascendancy of Lono during the annual renewal of nature" (Sahlins 1981: 18). This "abeyance" involves a tapu on war, the isolation of the king and high priest of Kū (another major Hawaiian deity) from the "revelries" of the people, and the procession of an image of Lono around the island, symbolizing the god's "appropriating" of the land. The festival is concluded by a mock battle between attendants of Lono and the attendants of the king and the symbolic "death" of Lono via the dismantling of his image. With the festival finished, the king takes back control of the island and reopens the Kū shrines (19–20).

For Sahlins, the opposition between the king and Lono is a manifestation of a major theme of Hawaiian religion and its view of "the human condition," the conflict between gods and humans for power. For Sahlins, this theme is essential in interpreting the rituals associated with Cook's reception, as well as his later death.

Sahlins notes that in the *Kumulipo*, the Hawaiian creation chant, "god and man appear together, and in fraternal strife over the means of their reproduction: their own older sister" (1985: 110). The resulting view of the "human condition," is that "men are sometimes (or even often) compelled to secure their own existence by inflicting a defeat upon the god, appropriating thus the female power—the bearing earth" (112). "Man, then, lives by a kind of periodic deicide" (113). Sahlins interprets the Makahiki as a powerful instance of this deicide. The Hawaiian chiefs and king, associated with Kū, god of war and political power, retreat from their positions and allow Lono, god of fertility, to renew the lands via his procession. They then return and, in mythic fashion, battle and kill Lono, taking back the "bearing earth" for humankind. This lengthy embrace and then killing of Lono is played out each year.

Sahlins notes a remarkable series of coincidences between the Makahiki schedule and Cook's arrival and actions in Hawai'i. The coincidences surrounding his arrival, combined with the mythic schemes of Lono and the Makahiki, led the natives to see and treat Cook as a manifestation of Lono. According to Sahlins, the British ships arrived very near the time of Lono's supposed arrival and circled the islands in a manner similar to the procession of Lono's image (1985: 121). When the priest escorted Cook to the temple, he anointed him with oil reserved for Lono (or at least Lono's image) and made him stand with his arms outstretched, again imitating the Lono image (1995: 55). The ritual sequence repeated with Cook was called the *hānaipū*, and was the same ritual sequence that would be repeated with the Lono image normally (1981: 21). Cook and company also departed the island nearly on schedule with Lono's departure and the end of the Makahiki (22).

Sahlins sees the diminished reception of the sailors upon their second arrival as a consequence of the Makahiki schedule as well, as "Cook's return out of season would be sinister to the ruling chiefs because it presented a mirror image of Makahiki politics. Bringing the god ashore during the triumph of the king, it could reopen the whole issue of sovereignty" (1995: 81). That issue of sovereignty was fully reopened as Cook attempted to take Kalani'ōpu'u hostage, and the Hawaiians responded by putting both men in their proper mythical and political place, the king in power and the god-image dismantled to return the following year.

Obeyesekere

Rather than focusing on how Cook's arrival coincided with the *mythological* politics of the Makahiki, Obeyesekere attempts to show how Cook's arrival connected with the *actual* politics of Hawai'i in the late 1770's. Obeyesekere bases this switch on his knowledge of the interaction between British colonialists and native Sri Lankans, specifically how Sri Lankans prostrated to them because of the power dynamics involved in the situation and not because they saw the colonizers as divine. The situation in Sri Lanka convinces Obeyesekere that the Hawaiian response to Cook "must be seen in terms of the power politics of that period" (1997: 9).

In the case of the island of Hawai'i in 1779, the power politics involved King Kalani'ōpu'u's war with Maui. Based on this ongoing war, and the assumption that the motives of King Kalani'ōpu'u resembled those of other Polynesian rulers who had attempted to convince Cook to help in their own wars, Obeyesekere interprets the actions of the Hawaiians in 1779 as an attempt to make Cook into a chief who would help them in their struggle against Maui (1997: 78).

Obeyesekere asserts, citing anthropologist Peter Buck (Te Rangi Hiroa),[7] that the Hawaiians calling Cook "Lono" repeatedly does not necessarily entail that they believed him to be a god. Rather, many "high chiefs" were recipients of names of gods and had ceremonies involving the sacrifice of pigs at the naming (1997: 75).

Obeyesekere also challenges Sahlins on the significance of the ritual Cook is put through at the temple. Obeyesekere stresses that, rather than being made into the image of the god, Lono, Cook was being "introduced to the Hawaiian deities," namely Kū, to whom the temple and the main priest, Koa'a, were devoted (1997: 83).

Rather than forcing Cook to imitate the image of Lono while he is chanted to and acknowledged as the god, the Hawaiians raised Cook's arms in the posture of prayer and chanted his prayers for him, as he was ignorant of Hawaiian religion (1997: 85). In addition to assuming this position of prayer, Cook was also made to prostrate himself to the image of Kū during the ceremony.

---

7. Sahlins and Obeyesekere play the identity politics game with Sir Peter Buck (Te Rangi Hiroa). Obeyesekere mainly uses his Polynesian name, Te Rangi Hiroa, and calls attention to his half-Polynesian heritage. Sahlins, as he does not regard him as a very credible source and wishes to show his colonial ties, dubs him "Sir Peter" (1995: 144).

Thus, for Obeyesekere, the ritual names him Lono, a high chief who will assist the fighters of Hawai'i in their war against Maui, not a land-renewing god (64). Cook arrived and was embraced as a possible war ally by the priests of the king. He was put through rituals that named him Lono, a chief.

For Obeyesekere, it was self-interest and annoyance that made the Hawaiians eager to see the British off at the beginning of February, not adherence to the Makahiki calendar. Cook's crew had made a significant dent in the food supply around Kealakekua Bay during their stay, and Cook himself had refused the king's requests to help him in his war with Maui (1997: 88). Cook had not renewed the land but had depleted it.

And it was, according to Obeyesekere, legitimate Hawaiian fears for their king's safety in the wake of his attempted kidnapping that resulted in Cook's death (1997: 89). Obeyesekere does concede, however, that Cook was deified after death, as it was possible in Hawaiian practice to turn chiefs into gods to attain their power, power that, in this case, Cook had refused to give them while alive (90).

Cook arrived and was embraced as a possible war ally by the priests of the king. He was put through rituals that named him Lono, chief. Yet, his men ate the Hawaiians' food, and Cook himself did not agree, either by outright refusal or indecision, to help with the conflict. Cook and company finally left Hawai'i but were forced to return for repairs to their mast. Many Hawaiians were not happy to see them return and inquired continuously as to why they had come back. Cook reacted unfavorably to the rising thefts and sought out the king to take as a hostage. Some Hawaiians had had enough of Captain James Cook.

Explanatory Foundations

The contributions of the cognitive sciences do not "resolve" the debate between Sahlins and Obeyesekere by confirming either of their interpretations. Rather, they complicate and enrich the debate, as well as larger anthropological questions the debate raises, by introducing very relevant and much needed explanatory frameworks on which to base such interpretations.

Explanation and interpretation cannot escape each other. All explanations depend on certain interpretations of evidence; all interpretations depend on explicit or implicit explanatory theories (Lawson & McCauley 1990; Atkinson 1978; Rosenberg 1995; Fay & Moon 1977; Martin 1994; Henderson 1993). If the explanatory base for an interpretation becomes defunct, so too does the interpretation that depends on it. I will argue here that the explanatory bases of both

Sahlins' and Obeyesekere's interpretations are defunct in light of the findings of the cognitive sciences; the implication is that so too are their interpretations.

Sahlins

The explanatory scheme supporting Sahlins' interpretation is his theory of "mythopraxis," which holds that Polynesian peoples relive, re-experience, and reenact mythic schemes in current events and that, through that reenacting, the meanings of the mythic schemes themselves change (1985: 145–151).

It is difficult to be precise about what mythopraxis involves because Sahlins is quite inconsistent on the issue of how *strongly* mythic or cultural schemes affect experience and determine action, both in his analysis of the Hawaiian material and in his "flights of neo-Hegelian abstraction" (Kuper 1999: 197). Sahlins oscillates between two quite different and inconsistent uses of the term. The first is a robust cultural determinism in which events are not unique but "are immediately perceived in the received order of structure," in which mythic schemes "are the true organization of historical practice," and in which people "act upon circumstances according to their own cultural presuppositions, the socially given categories of persons and things" (1985: 58, 76; 1981: 67). Thus, because the Hawaiians had mythic schemes of the human condition and the politics of the Makahiki in their heads, they thought James Cook was their god Lono and consequently included him in the *hānaipū* as the Lono image.

Sahlins' second, and much weaker, idea of mythopraxis holds that peoples' experiences and responses to historical situations can be quite novel and involve numerous interests and influences, merely entailing "specific understandings of the local cultural regime." Consequently, as Sahlins writes, "to say that an event is culturally described is not to say it is culturally prescribed" (1995: 251). Applied to the Hawaiian case, "we need not suppose that all Hawaiians were convinced that Captain Cook was Lono; or, more precisely, that his being Lono meant the same to everyone" (1985: 121). As Adam Kuper notes, Sahlins assumes the stronger version of mythopraxis in most of his writing, including his thesis of Native Hawaiians and Captain Cook, but retreats to the weaker version when denounced as a cultural determinist (1999: 199).

Sahlins frequently refers to "Hawaiian culture," "Hawaiian thought," and "Hawaiian cosmological schemes." He claims that these things cause Hawaiians to think of and behave towards Captain Cook in certain ways, most notably their installing him as the figure of Lono in the *hānaipū* ritual and killing him when he returns out of season. His authority for such a claim comes from his masterful knowledge of explicit Hawaiian statements and Polynesian ethnography recorded long after Cook's death.

One of the most crucial findings of the cognitive sciences, however, is that there is no obvious and necessary link between explicit discourse, whether in official texts or direct self-reports, and people's motivational states and behavior.[8] In other words, citing some text or tradition or people's own self-reports is insufficient in determining the thoughts of a person or the reasons for their actions. There is the middle-man of the mind to consider, and it is neither a simple container for culture nor a unified system that allows conscious access to most of its processes.[9]

By considering the mind, scholars in the cognitive science of culture have made two distinctions directly relevant to Sahlins' direct linking of explicit discourse and mental representations. The first involves a distinction between *cognitively optimal* and *cognitively costly* representations and the second a distinction between *theologically correct* and *theologically incorrect* representations.

Cognitively optimal representations are those representations that, via a variety of factors such as their relationships to intuitive inference systems and ontologies, are very easy to acquire, remember, and transmit (White-

---

8. For example, there are numerous studies in cognitive and social psychology documenting people explaining behavior by appeals to intentions, beliefs, and desires despite the fact that they are completely unrelated to the causal variables the experimenters have isolated. Numerous examples can be found in Timothy Wilson's *Strangers to Ourselves* (2002), including a study in which experimenters, aware of "ordering effects" on preference, set out four identical sets of panty-hose for shoppers to evaluate at a local bargain store. Most chose panty-hose further to the right, as the experimenters predicted; yet, no one could state that order influenced their choice. Rather, they constructed explanations about "superior knit" (102–103). The implication of such studies is that asking people why they have done something is not adequate in explaining why they have done that something.

9. The realization that the meanings and themes of texts, oral traditions, and the like are not directly internalized and utilized has been taken into account by several cognitively oriented anthropologists, some of whom were working with these ideas even as Sahlins developed his theory of mythopraxis. Dan Sperber has been working along these lines since the 1970's and, in the 1980's, made the crucial distinction between *public representations* and *mental representations* in his highly influential epidemiological approach to culture (1996). Maurice Bloch has written quite a bit on these matters as well, most forcefully in *How We Think They Think*, in which he notes that "what people say is a poor guide to what they know and think" and that "learning is not just a matter of storing received knowledge, as most anthropologists implicitly assume when they equate cultural and individual representations ..." (1998: 3, 10). More recently, cognitive anthropologists such as Bradd Shore, Claudia Strauss, and Naomi Quinn have also taken this distinction between culture in the world and culture in mind seriously in formulating more naturalized theories of culture which take psychology and neuroscience into account (Shore 1996; Strauss & Quinn 1997).

house 2004). Harvey Whitehouse's theory of 'modes of religiosity' has pointed out two distinct ways in which *cognitively costly* representations, which are more difficult to acquire, remember, and transmit, can be sustained in a population, involving the engagement of two distinct memory systems, semantic and episodic (2001, 2004). If the proper resources are not devoted to the process of sustaining the cognitively costly ideas, Whitehouse notes, we find most people's representations falling back to more cognitively optimal ones.

The relevance of this distinction resides in the fact that many of the representations Sahlins refers to in his interpretations (e.g. mythic and theological themes) come from the *Kumulipo*, an oral chant composed by a *Haku-mele* or "master of song" who collaborated with other elite Hawaiian priests in composing and memorizing the lengthy chant (Beckwith 1951). It would be difficult to classify this chant as cognitively optimal material, as learned priests had to devote significant time and resources in its composition and retention. And yet it is the themes and theologies of the Kumulipo that Sahlins places in the heads of Hawaiians that result in their viewing James Cook as Lono. It is very questionable whether or not the theme of "man vs. god over the bearing earth" and other complex theologies of the Kumulipo had been acquired and retained by any significant portion of the Hawaiian people at Kealakekua Bay.

In addition to this diversity within a population, there also exists representational diversity within individual minds. The view of early cognitive science, in which representations were thought to be stored as wholes and processed serially by a central processor, is no longer tenable; work in a variety of disciplines has shown a diverse array of storage and processing mechanisms operating in parallel.

One particular processing distinction relevant to the present discussion comes from *dual-processing* models of cognition (Tremlin 2005). A body of data supports the idea that representations are processed along two distinct pathways, one conscious, reflective, and slow; the other unconscious, reflexive, and fast. Justin Barrett's work on the phenomena of *theological correctness* suggests that many explicit and cognitively costly representations, such as the Copernican view of the solar system or the Trinitarian view of the Christian God, are too cognitively burdensome to be processed by the faster, unconscious pathways that constitute our intuitive reasoning (1996, 1999). In making fast, nonreflective judgments, the mind usually reverts to more intuitive, cognitively optimal representations, such as the Ptolemaic view of the solar system or a single-agent view of God.

The relevant point for the Hawaiian case is that, while the priestly elite surely possessed explicit, cognitively costly representations of the nature of divinity and nuanced interpretations of the Makahiki, these representations most likely would not have been employed in their quick intuitive assessment of the ontological status of James Cook.[10]

These findings present significant problems for Sahlins' mythopraxis. One cannot infer the thought or reasons of an individual or group of individuals from explicit verbalizations or texts. Citing the Kumulipo for the presence of a mythic theme concerning "man vs. god over the bearing earth" and noting the practice of the Makahiki does not go very far in explaining why some Hawaiians inserted Cook into the *hānaipū* or why they were more averse to the British upon their return and ultimately killed Cook, since it has not been adequately established how such traditions were represented and used in the minds of the Hawaiian people. It is no simple step from these public representations to their thought and behavior, as Sahlins' writing suggests. It is problematic to refer to explicit "Hawaiian theory" and "Polynesian thought" and use it to explain the empirical judgments of actual people since there is the open question of how much such theories and systems of thought were actually entertained by the majority of Hawaiians on the one hand, and in the quick empirical judgments and interpretations of the Hawaiian priesthood on the other.

The preceding comments addressed the stronger version of mythopraxis. Yet, Sahlins himself sometimes discounts such a strong version of mythopraxis, favoring a weaker version which also takes personal agency and interests into account (1995: 251). In this version, cultural schemes are not the "true organization of historical practice," but merely "find a place in the ordering of history" (1985: 76; 1995: 251). Do the findings of the cognitive sciences also call into question this weaker or milder version of mythopraxis? Not necessarily. The weaker mythopraxis, however, is problematic enough on its own. If one actually takes the milder mythopraxis to be Sahlins' actual theory, his thesis that the Hawaiians judged Captain Cook to be Lono disappears. Even if we agree with Sahlins that the ritual sequence the Hawaiians repeated with Cook was the *hānaipū*, this necessitates nothing in relation to the actual

---

10. The priesthood is, of course, not compelled in any way to act merely on their intuitive assessments. The British accounts suggest that there was ample time for the Hawaiians to reflect on the status of the British. Thus, the possibility indeed exists that they arrived at an "official interpretation" of Cook being a manifestation of Lono, as Sahlins suggests. However, as should now be clear, there is no reliable way of ascertaining whether or not such an official interpretation was reached or, if such an official interpretation was reached, if it coincided with the reflective beliefs of the Hawaiian priests themselves, as individuals. The point is not that interpreting Cook as Lono was impossible but that the explanatory claims about the mind that this interpretation assumes are fundamentally inaccurate; as a result, there is little to support that interpretation amongst the field of possible interpretations.

perception/conception of Cook in the minds of the Hawaiians, commoner or priest; the decision to carry out the ritual with Cook could have been motivated by any number of reasons besides their viewing Cook as a manifestation of Lono, including Obeyesekere's hypothesis that they were trying to honor Cook in hopes of enlisting his aid in war.

Sahlins' real thesis, however, is much stronger. His claim is that because of their mythic/cultural schemes, Hawaiian priests (if not the population as a whole) gave their "perceptions" of Cook the "empirical judgment" of Lono, and this explains their actions, including their including him in the *hānaipū* (1995: 162–163). This thesis is an example of strong mythopraxis, which holds that explicit cultural schemes direct peoples' thought and behavior. It is an example of an explanatory theory which appears highly implausible in light of evidence from the cognitive sciences. Given this, what is left of Sahlins' interpretation of the historical sources? Given that its explanatory base has been discredited, what is there to make us conclude that the ritual actions on Hawai'i were *about* a people embracing the return of one of their gods?

Obeyesekere

While Sahlins' explanation of mythopraxis highlights the importance of cultural information in determining thought and behavior, Obeyesekere's explanation stresses the importance of a universal cognitive capacity. The capacity that Obeyesekere posits is a universal "practical rationality." Practical rationality is not a new term and Obeyesekere briefly describes its original use and context in the works of Max Weber, as well as how he has altered it. Yet, he does not disclose all of his modifications, and, by the time Obeyesekere has made all his changes, the two notions are quite different.[11]

---

11. For Weber, the term is not "practical rationality" as much as it is that some actions can be interpreted as practically or "instrumentally" rational by sociologists. Practically rational action is one part of a four-part conceptual scheme for "social action," the other types of action being value-rational, affectual, and traditional (Weber 1968: 24–25). To be considered practically or instrumentally rational, an action must be "determined by expectations as to the behavior of objects in the environment and other human beings; these expectations are used as 'conditions' or 'means' for the attainment of the actor's own rationally pursued and calculated ends" (24). Or, put more succinctly, a practically rational action occurs "when the end, the means, and the secondary results are all rationally taken into account and weighed" (25). Weber is quick to point out that no social action is merely the result of one of these "orientations." Rather, "it would be very unusual to find concrete cases of action, especially of social action, which were oriented *only* in one or another of these ways" (26).

Most importantly, Obeyesekere changes "practical rationality" from a descriptive term to a universal neurobiological process that gives people, native and non-native alike, the capacity to reach beyond their culture and grasp the world as it really is in their "judgments" (1997: 20).

Although Weber does attribute "rationality" to human beings, he does not make practical rationality a universal cognitive apparatus. Rather, sometimes people behave in a way that an observer can interpret as being informed by consideration of means, ends, and consequences. Rather than calling actions practically rational, as a descriptor, Obeyesekere turns the concept into an ever-ready capacity with which all human beings are endowed by their common neurobiological heritage (1997: 230).

Obeyesekere also stresses that practical rationality is an attribute of *thinking* and not of *thought* (1997: 21). He claims that thought is associated with belief and that his use of the term is not about a type of belief but "reflexive thought processes ... that can exist in virtually any realm of belief" (229–230). Obeyesekere has, then, left the realm of practical action and entered the realm of reflective judgment of beliefs and perceptions, as practical rationality serves as a kind of judge of belief, a doorman of notions and beliefs that gives people "the ability to negotiate between received belief and actual experience" (234).

It is this new and, according to Obeyesekere, improved notion of practical rationality that informs his interpretation of the events of 1779. The Hawaiians, using their practical rationality, would assuredly see the "obvious contradictions" between their expectations of Lono's involvement in the Makahiki, presumably the procession of the icon and the sense of land renewal, and the arrival of ships full of British sailors seeking their food and women and protesting when the Hawaiians attempted to take iron nails from the ships (1997: 56). Cook's arrival would "violate common sense expectations," and, even though chiefs are also considered divine in Hawaiian thought, the people would make astute "distinctions" between the varieties of divinity (21). The Lono in Cook, the Lono in the sweet potato, and the transcendent being Lono were varieties of divinity that the Hawaiians themselves could easily distinguish. They would instantly realize that Cook could not be Lono, the transcendent being. The Hawaiians could not have interpreted Cook as Lono because the Hawaiians had eyes with which to see and rational minds with which to reflect. They must have grasped that Cook was a sea captain and not a god. They would also employ the same practical rationality to look out for their own best interests in their relations to Cook. They would accord him ritual honors and attempt to name him Lono, a powerful chief to help them against Maui, and, eventually, after Cook and his crew had caused a significant amount of harm to their society and were taking their king hostage, they would kill him.

In its application, Obeyesekere's practical rationality becomes a cognitive mechanism that allows individuals to negotiate between perceptions of reality and received cultural schemes in order to make both an ontological judgment in a situation (man or god), and a decision about how to act on that judgment according to their own interests. This ability allowed the Hawaiians not to place Cook in their mythic categories as Lono-returned, but to recognize what he was and treat him according to their own interests.

Obeyesekere's practical rationality bears a striking resemblance to what many philosophers and cognitive scientists call *traditional, standard,* or *ideal rationality*. Under the traditional account, people reason according to normative rational principles, except for the occasional "momentary lapse" or "performance error," and take action according to their best interests as they rationally weigh the means and ends of a given situation (Stein 1998).

Yet the traditional, ideal view of human rationality faces a fatal problem. The empirical study of the mind contradicts it in two ways. The first is very simple. There is no such thing as ideal rationality; there is no such thing as a voice of reason with which human beings are somehow endowed. The second is more subtle but no less important. The explanatory model of mind needed for ideal rationality to be plausible, which Pascal Boyer calls the "judicial model" of the mind, is just as much a fiction (2001: 302–303).

While evidence against ideal rationality has accumulated through the efforts of numerous researchers,[12] cognitive psychologists Daniel Kahneman and Amos Tversky's work is among the most widely cited. One of their most famous studies concerns how language "frames" people's rational decision making (1984). It might be thought that if people are rational, they reach beyond cultural-specific wording and grasp the true meaning of statements and states of affairs, as this allows them to act in their own rational best interests. Kahneman and Tversky show that this is clearly not the case.[13]

---

12. For an excellent review of this evidence and what it means for our human self-image, see Edward Stein's *Without Good Reason: The Rationality Debate in Philosophy and Cognitive Science* (1996).

13. One of their experiments involves giving people two problems concerning a deadly disease that could kill six hundred people. In the two formally identical problems, subjects get two options of fighting the disease. In problem number one, option one saves two hundred people while option two gives a one-third chance of saving everybody and a two-thirds chance of saving nobody. When given problem one, nearly all people choose option number one and avoid the risk of so many people dying. In the second, formally identical problem, option one has four hundred people dying while option two gives a one-third chance that no one dies and a two-thirds chance that all six hundred die. When given problem two, nearly all people choose option number two, taking the risk to save the most people.

Ideal rationality is not the only problem in anthropological conceptions of belief and behavior. The basic model of the mind that ideal rationality assumes is still widespread in anthropology and, as Boyer relates, problematic. Ideal rationality assumes the "judicial model" of mind, which holds that propositions and information exist in a person's mind and these propositions or pieces of information are then believed or rejected. This view requires two functional organs, a "Representations' Attorney" and a "Belief-Judge" (2001: 302–303). The Attorney brings up a representation with all its details and connections to other representations; the Judge, serving as the voice of reason, then reviews these representations and gives a ruling. Depending on the outcome of the ruling, some propositions or pieces of information are allowed to remain in the mind and trigger further inferences while others are dismissed (303).

While this account seems phenomenologically plausible, it is an inaccurate view of how our minds process information. The judicial model fails as soon as we examine the diversity and specialization of most of the information-processors in the mind-brain. In many cases, these processors are "their own Attorney and Judge at the same time" (Boyer 2001: 303). Most processors require no judgment before sending off lots of information to other systems for making inferences, never bothering to cohere and unify into something we would normally call a "belief." Instead, as Ilkka Pyysiäinen writes:

> We do not decide whether a belief is true before we start to employ it as a premise in reasoning. All that takes place in the mind is that given mental mechanisms send bits of information to other mental mechanisms, treating them as 'facts.' These implicit processes produce in us various kinds of intuitions about how things are in the world (2004: 114).

So while it may seem as if we have within us a strong, singular voice of reason overseeing our mental activity, study of the cognitive unconscious reveals that we have many voices relating information within us, and few of them operate according to the principles of logic and traditional reason.

The findings of the cognitive sciences pose serious problems for Obeyesekere's explanatory theory of a neurobiologically-instantiated, universal prac-

---

Problem one *frames* results in positive terms, saving people, and most subjects choose the sure thing. Problem two frames results in negative terms, people dying, and subjects take the risk. The experiment shows that by framing decision options in positive or negative terms, one can cause subjects to avoid risks or take risks, respectively. The subjects are not rationally evaluating the means and ends of the situation and deciding according to self-interests. They do not recognize the identical nature of the problems.

tical rationality that allows people to negotiate accurately between cultural schemes and experience. And because of the necessary connection between this explanatory idea and his interpretation of the Hawaiian ritual actions, these findings problematize Obeyesekere's interpretation as well. If the evidence points to the nonexistence of a practical rationality mechanism, what requires and inclines the Hawaiians to act in their best interests towards Cook by making him a chief? What requires them to get beyond whatever cultural frames and representations of Lono they might have in mind and see Cook for what he "really" was? And if the judicial model of mind is mistaken, as the cognitive sciences tell us that it is, why is it necessary to believe that the proposition "Cook is Lono" was ever brought to a practically rational "Belief Judge" by a "Representation Attorney" in the cognitive systems of the Hawaiians in the first place? With the existence of Obeyesekere's practical rationality and the judicial model of mind denied, we cannot assent to an interpretation of the Hawaiian ritual actions that depends on them.

Whither Interpretation?

What can we say about the Hawaiian interpretations of James Cook in 1779 from a naturalistic perspective? In short, nothing very conclusive. The fact that many grand interpretive/explanatory schemes in the human sciences, such as Sahlins and Obeyesekere's, attempt to say something strong about what a situation "means" for a certain group of people is probably part of the draw of such approaches. A strong, even if simple or inaccurate, explanatory scheme can lead to very intriguing interpretations, native people's perceiving a British sea captain as a god, for example. The findings of the cognitive sciences are exciting and expanding, but do not presently give us the tools to answer the question of whether or not actual Hawaiian people believed James Cook to be Lono.[14] The findings do, however, problematize the strong interpretive answers of Sahlins and Obeyesekere.

The debate between Sahlins and Obeyesekere is about more than the qualities of Cook in the mental representations of Hawaiians. Larger anthropological issues are also being considered and it is on these issues that the cognitive sciences and an interactionist approach to interpretation and

---

14. There are several reasons why the cognitive sciences are of less help in answering these questions. James Laidlaw, for instance, in his contribution to this volume, correctly points out that the cognitive sciences are presently focused on general explanations of widespread phenomena, rather than explaining specific instances and events.

explanation can help us move forward, as evidenced by the chapters by Astuti, Barrett, and Whitehouse. Some of the issues raised by the debate include: 1) *How do we ascertain individuals' mental representations when all of our evidence consists of public representations?* 2) *How can public representations, specifically ritual actions and discourse about ritual actions influence mental representations?* and 3) *What are the relative contributions of cognitive mechanisms and cultural information in determining mental representations and subsequent behavior?*

The Pursuit of Mental Representations

Anthropologists, psychologists, and all of us in our daily lives, attempt to ascertain the mental representations of others (e.g. beliefs, desires, opinions, attitudes), just as Marshall Sahlins and Gananath Obeyesekere attempt to ascertain the mental representations of Native Hawaiians. Yet, presumably, none of us have full epistemic access to the mental representations of others. We are constantly inferring them from a variety of public representations, such as self-reports, texts, and behaviors. And while it is true that our intuitive theory of mind allows us to understand each other in most everyday contexts and serves anthropologists well in adjusting to life in the field, intuitions are frequently complicated by scientific discoveries (e.g. objects that intuitively seem to be solid are mostly empty space, a group of people who intuitively share a common heritable essence (race) actually do not).[15] Ascertaining mental representations, however, has been the explicit scientific aim of psychological research since the cognitive revolution and the findings of the cognitive sciences both complicate and enrich our understandings of the mental representations of others.

Two noteworthy examples in this volume of how psychological research complicates and enriches our understandings of mental representations are the chapters by Rita Astuti and Justin Barrett. Inspired by the philosophical and methodological questions of Rodney Needham, Astuti asks how we can know the mental representations, specifically beliefs and knowledge, of others. Through ethnographic and experimental work among the Vezo of Madagascar, Astuti problematizes our intuitive notions about belief by suggesting that belief is not uniform but context dependent. Rather than having a belief set such as *Vezo thought* or *Hawaiian thought* in mind that is applied in all sit-

---

15. For a stimulating account of how we form intuitive racial-ethnic categories, see Gil-White (2001).

uations, contrary beliefs and representations can be utilized in different contexts. Consequently, referring to public representations such as texts and traditions as evidence of Vezo or Hawaiian thought and claiming that these representations result in people believing certain propositions in certain situations is unwarranted. Astuti's work has the potential to enrich our understanding of the mental representations of others by encouraging us to pay closer attention to relationships between certain contexts and certain beliefs and possibly establish patterns between types of contexts and types of beliefs.

Justin Barrett's distinction between reflective and nonreflective beliefs might also help us in our quest to ascertain the mental representations of others. Rather than simply viewing people as hypocritical or lying whenever their behaviors do not match their cognitively-demanding reflective beliefs, we recognize that different types of beliefs may be at work. One has to specify which type of belief one is examining in others, reflective or nonreflective. This type of distinction greatly enriches our efforts in understanding others through the adoption of the meticulous methodologies of the cognitive sciences in ascertaining nonreflective beliefs, on which the cognitive sciences put much of their focus. At the same time, it becomes a very open question as to what counts in a given situation as "belief." We have robust methodologies to ascertain nonreflective beliefs, but we only have people's statements about what they reflectively believe. If people's self-reports of their reflective beliefs do not match up with their behaviors and other beliefs, do they actually "believe" what they say or are such statements now to be labeled as merely customary speech behaviors? How would we know the difference? These are profound questions with substantial consequences for how we interpret the actions of human beings.

How Public Representations Influence Mental Representations

Anthropologists and psychologists alike are interested in how public representations (e.g. statements, actions) affect individuals' mental representations. Specifically in this volume, various authors have discussed how ritual actions and/or discourse about ritual actions affect belief. Applying these issues to the Hawaiian context, we might ask how the ritual actions of the Makahiki, as well as discourse about Cook's arrival and the Makahiki, affected Native Hawaiian beliefs about him.

Justin Barrett asserts four "dynamics" of rituals that influence religious beliefs: social testimony & conformity pressure, dissonance reduction, explicit transmission, and HADD (Hypersensitive Agency Detection Device) experiences. And while it may be that the former three of these dynamics are fairly intuitive, HADD dynamics between ritual and belief are not obvious but make sense in light of the research on agency and agency detection. Ritual contexts prime an individual's HADD to become even more hypersensitive than normal, which results in more events being attributed to supernatural forces, which sustains religious beliefs in an individual's mind.

Such an approach might help to account for general trends in thought and behavior across time and place, such as how people come to believe in gods and sustain that belief over time; in the Hawaiian case, they can help explain how rituals would help sustain the Hawaiian belief in Lono. Yet a much more detailed account is required to help in answering specific questions of a much shorter timescale, such as whether or not Hawaiians believed Cook to be a manifestation of Lono. Further work is needed to investigate the timescales and ritual frequencies required to spread and sustain different types of beliefs.[16] A large body of cross-cultural studies in this direction would potentially be applicable in evaluating a variety of claims, including whether the rituals involving Cook during his short stay in Hawai'i could have encouraged beliefs in his divinity.

Rita Astuti not only suggests that rituals can directly encourage religious beliefs but that discourse about rituals can as well. She claims that altering a narrative of a deceased Vezo man to include discourse about his family following proper ritual procedures after his death results in an increase in the number of people having reflective beliefs in the man's continued existence after death. Astuti's explanation for this is that by making the ritual context "relevant" to the participants, the altered narrative elicits different reflective beliefs than the original. This hypothesis is an intriguing example of Astuti's overall assertion of the context-dependency of reflective beliefs, and could potentially be applicable to the Hawaiian situation, as we might be able to ask if people's talk about the Makahiki might increase the likelihood of their viewing Cook as Lono. Yet, as mentioned above, getting at people's mental representations (specifically beliefs in this case) is fraught with difficulty. Before Astuti's claim of ritual discourse encouraging reflective belief in the afterlife can be accepted, some other interpretations of her data must be eliminated.

Another possible explanation for Astuti's findings lies in the distinction between reflective beliefs (mental representations) and self-reports of belief (public representations). In this case, there is a distinct possibility that what

---

16. Such an enterprise sounds very much like Harvey Whitehouse's modes of religiosity project, but would be distinct in that the phenomena in question are attitudes (beliefs) towards cultural information rather than knowledge of the cultural information.

caused the change in self-reports of belief was not an increase in actual reflective beliefs in the afterlife but something that psychologists strive to eliminate from their studies, social desirability. Social desirability effects, which involve participants adjusting their responses based on their desire to look good (to themselves or others) by producing socially acceptable answers, are well recognized in psychological research (Coolican 2004). In the Vezo case, the "ritual context" prime might actually be a "proper Vezo" prime that elicits representations of proper Vezo attitudes and behaviors. Having an anthropologist then immediately ask questions with an obvious purpose (finding out their afterlife beliefs) very well might encourage "proper Vezo" responses, either to give the anthropologist what she wants or to make themselves appear to be proper Vezo to others in general.[17]

Despite the concerns above, Astuti's chapter establishes a dialogue between the methodologies and findings of the cognitive sciences and ethnographic expertise, and constitutes progress in untangling these difficult general questions about how rituals and discourse about rituals can impact belief and other mental representations. And although this dialogue will most likely not answer with any certainty whether or not discussing the Makahiki resulted in Hawaiians viewing Cook as Lono, it certainly gives us a stronger explanatory base for such interpretive explorations.

Cultural and Cognitive Contributions

Besides being a debate about specific Hawaiian mental representations and about the politics of anthropological representation, the debate between Sahlins and Obeyesekere is also a debate about the importance of cultural information vs. the importance of cognitive mechanisms in determining thought and behavior. For Sahlins, cultural information concerning Lono and the Makahiki is of primary importance in understanding the Hawaiian response. For Obeyesekere, it is a cognitive process he calls "practical rationality." Most scholars would recognize that what actually caused the Hawaiian thoughts and behaviors in question would be some combination of cultural

---

17. To help rule out this alternative explanation and support her own interpretation of her findings, Astuti might do two things. 1) She could embed her key question(s) about the afterlife in a much larger set of questions about the narrative in order to minimize participant reactivity to the task. 2) She could also administer a social desirability scale, such as the widely-used Crowne-Marlowe Social Desirability Scale (1964), in order to identify individuals who have a tendency to produce socially desirable answers and control for this in her analysis.

and cognitive factors. Yet, saying anything more than that has proven difficult, as the unification of cultural and cognitive analyses will require a huge effort, one that has only just begun.

A very promising start in this effort has been provided by Harvey Whitehouse (this volume). Whitehouse's call to integrate what he calls "cognitivist" and "interpretive" approaches constitutes a move towards a framework for interpreting and explaining human thought and behavior that not only acknowledges the important roles of cognition and culture, but seeks to describe more precisely the ways in which they interact to produce specific human phenomena. By asking how discrete psychological systems, both relatively closed nuclear systems (such as theory-of-mind and the agency-detection-device) and relatively open global systems (such as semantic memory and the cross-domain-analogical-thinking system) are affected by types of environmental inputs, Whitehouse's model offers the possibility of explaining the pattern of cultural and cognitive factors at work in generating specific mental representations and behaviors. A vast amount of work must be completed before this framework can yield the fruit Whitehouse envisions, but the seed has been planted. With hard work and collaboration from both anthropologists and psychologists, the enterprise will flourish and surely enrich all discussions of the interplay between humanity's evolutionary heritage and the wider environment in generating thought and action.

Conclusion

I began this chapter with a question: *What do the cognitive sciences contribute to work in the social sciences and humanities?* The answer to this question is a developing one. There is a very real possibility that the contributions of the cognitive sciences will revolutionize the study of human thought and behavior through a naturalistic project. But even if this does not happen, the contributions of the cognitive sciences are very real and very relevant in at least two ways. First, with the acknowledgement of the constant interplay of explanation and interpretation in all discussions of human behavior, the explanatory frameworks that the cognitive sciences offer can become important bases for the construction and evaluation of interpretations. In this chapter, I have used these explanatory frameworks to evaluate the interpretations Marshall Sahlins and Gananath Obeyesekere give for Native Hawaiian behaviors in 1779 and have found them lacking in explanatory rigor. Second, although such specific questions as whether or not Hawaiians mentally represented Captain Cook as Lono currently lie beyond the grasp of the cognitive sciences (and anthropology for that matter), many general anthropological questions raised by the debate, such as how scholars can best ascertain mental representations, how public representations such as rituals can influence mental representations, and how culture and cognition interact to produce thought and behavior, do not. We can move forward in addressing these questions, but only with an interactionist account of interpretation and explanation, and only with a collaborative effort between the cognitive sciences, social sciences, and humanities.

References

Atkinson, R.F. (1978) *Knowledge and Explanation in History: An Introduction to the Philosophy of History*, London: Macmillan.

Barrett, Justin L. (1998) 'Cognitive Constraints on Hindu Concepts of the Divine' *Journal for the Scientific Study of Religion*, 37: 608–619.

———. (1999) 'Theological Correctness: Cognitive Constraint and the Study of Religion' *Method and Theory in the Study of Religion*, 11: 325–339.

———. (2004) *Why Would Anyone Believe in God?* Walnut Creek: Alta Mira Press.

Barrett, Justin and Keil, Frank C. (1996) 'Anthropomorphism and God Concepts: Conceptualizing a Non-natural Entity' *Cognitive Psychology*, 31: 219–247.

Beaglehole, J.C. (1967) *The journals of Captain James Cook on his voyages of discovery, III: The voyage of the Resolution and Discovery, 1776–1780*, Cambridge: Cambridge University Press.

Beckwith, Martha W. (1951) *The Kumulipo: A Hawaiian Creation Chant*, Honolulu: University of Hawaii Press.

Bloch, Maurice. (1998) *How We Think They Think: Anthropological Approaches to Cognition, Memory, and Literacy*, Boulder: Westview.

———. (2004) 'Ritual and Deference' in Whitehouse, Harvey and Laidlaw, James (eds.) *Ritual and Memory: Toward a Comparative Anthropology of Religion*, Walnut Creek: Alta Mira Press.

Boyer, Pascal. (2001) *Religion Explained: The Evolutionary Origins of Religious Thought*, New York: Basic Books.

Clifford, James and Marcus, George (eds.) (1986) *Writing Culture: The Poetics and Politics of Ethnography*, Berkeley: University of California Press.

Coolican, Hugh (2004) *Research Methods and Statistics in Psychology: 4th Edition,* London: Hodder and Stoughton.

Crowne, D. and Marlow, D. (1964) *The Approval Motive,* New York: Wiley and Sons, Inc.

Fay, Brian and Moon, Donald, J. (1994)[1977] 'What Would an Adequate Philosophy of Social Science Look Like?' in Martin, Michael and McIntyre, Lee (eds.) *Readings in the Philosophy of Social Science,* Cambridge: MIT Press.

Gil-White, Francisco. (2001) 'Are ethnic groups biological 'species' to the human brain?: Essentialism in our cognition of some social categories' *Current Anthropology,* 42, 515–554.

Godfrey-Smith, Peter. (2003) *Theory and Reality: An Introduction to the Philosophy of Science.* Chicago: University of Chicago Press.

Handy, E.S. Craighill and Pukui, Mary, Kawena (1991) [1956] *The Polynesian Family System in Ka'u, Hawai'i,* Rutland: Charles E. Tuttle Company, Inc.

Henderson, David K. (1993) *Interpretation and Explanation in the Human Sciences,* Albany: State University of New York Press.

Hollis, Martin. (1994) *The Philosophy of Social Science: An Introduction.* New York: Cambridge University Press.

Humphrey, Caroline and Laidlaw, James A. (1994) *The Archetypal Actions of Ritual: A Theory of Ritual Illustrated by the Jain Rite of Worship,* Oxford: Clarendon Press.

Kahneman, Daniel and Tversky, Amos. (1984) 'Choices, Values, and Frames' *American Psychologist,* 39: 341–350.

Kitcher, Phillip. (1992) 'The Naturalists Return' *Philosophical Review,* 101: 53–114.

Kuper, Adam. (1999) *Culture: The Anthropologists' Account* Cambridge: Harvard University Press.

Lakoff, George and Johnson, Mark (1999) *Philosophy in the Flesh: The Embodied Mind and Its Challenge to Western Thought,* New York: Basic Books.

Lawson, E. Thomas and McCauley, Robert, N (1990) *Rethinking Religion,* Cambridge: Cambridge University Press.

Martin, Michael. (1994) 'Taylor on Interpretation and the Sciences of Man' in Martin, Michael and McIntyre, Lee C. (eds.) *Readings in the Philosophy of Social Science,* Cambridge: MIT Press.

McCauley, Robert N. (2004) 'Is Religion a Rube Goldberg Device? Or Oh, What a Difference a Theory Makes!' in Brian Wilson and Timothy Light (eds.) *Religion as a Human Capacity: A Festschrift in Honor of E. Thomas Lawson*, Leiden: Brill.

McCauley, Robert N. and Lawson, E. Thomas. (2002) *Bringing Ritual to Mind: Psychological Foundations of Cultural Forms*, Cambridge: Cambridge University Press.

Obeyesekere, Gananath. (1997) [1992] *The Apotheosis of Captain Cook: European Mythmaking in the Pacific*, Princeton: Princeton University Press.

Pyysiäinen, Ilkka. (2004) *Magic, Miracles, and Religion: A Scientist's Perspective*, Walnut Creek: Alta Mira Press.

Reyna, Stephen P. (1994) 'Literary Anthropology and the Case against Science' *Man*, 29 (3): 555–581.

Rosenberg, Alex. (1995) *Philosophy of Social Science: Second Edition*. Boulder: Westview.

Sahlins, Marshall. (1981) *Historical Metaphors and Mythic Realities: Structure in the Early History of the Sandwich Islands Kingdom*, Ann Arbor: The University of Michigan Press.

———. (1985) *Islands of History*, Chicago: University of Chicago Press.

———. (1995) *How Natives Think: About Captain Cook For Example*, Chicago: University of Chicago Press.

Shore, Bradd. (1996) *Culture in Mind: Cognition, Culture, and the Problem of Meaning*, New York: Oxford University Press.

Sperber, Dan. (1975) *Rethinking Symbolism*, Cambridge: Cambridge University Press.

———. (1996) *Explaining Culture: A Naturalistic Approach*, Malden: Blackwell Publishers.

Stein, Edward. (1996) *Without Good Reason: The Rationality Debate in Philosophy and Cognitive Science*, Oxford: Clarendon Press.

Strauss, Claudia and Quinn, Naomi. (1997) *A Cognitive Theory of Cultural Meaning*, Cambridge: Cambridge University Press.

Tremlin, Todd. (2005) 'Divergent Religion: A Dual-Process Model of Religious Thought, Behavior, and Morphology' in Whitehouse, Harvey and McCauley, Robert N. (eds.) *Mind and Religion: Psychological and Cognitive Foundations of Religiosity*, Walnut Creek: Alta Mira Press.

Weber, Max. (1968) [1921] *Economy and Society: An Outline of Interpretive Sociology*, (eds.) Guenther Roth and Claus Wittich. New York: Bedminster Press.

Whitehouse, Harvey. (2000) *Arguments and Icons: Divergent Modes of Religiosity*, Oxford: Oxford University Press.

————. (2004) *Modes of Religiosity: A Cognitive Theory of Religious Transmission*, Walnut Creek, California: Alta Mira Press.

Wilson, Timothy J. (2002) *Strangers to Ourselves: Discovering the Adaptive Unconscious*, Cambridge: The Belknap Press of Harvard University Press.

Zimmerman, Heinrich. (1988) *The third voyage of Captain Cook*, Fairfield: Ye Galleon Press.

PART TWO

CORE TOPICS IN THE ANTHROPOLOGY OF RELIGION

CHAPTER FIVE

WITCHCRAFT AND SORCERY

Emma Cohen

On June 3, 2005, the UK edition of the BBC news website ran a story with the title, "Exorcisms are part of our culture"[1]. In it the reporter records details of a "deliverance" service in a London Pentecostal church that is predominantly frequented by members of the local African community. A pastor at the church described how "people are used by the devil to bring a curse or bad luck to other people's lives, even to kill them". Every Sunday, he performs a procedure used to exorcise people of evil sprits. In this church, 'deliverance' takes place when the pastor and elders whisper into the victim's ears, bidding the spirits depart. In another incident, reported on the same website on the same day, a very different technique was used: the report tells how a child was "beaten, cut and had chilli peppers rubbed in her eyes by her guardians to 'beat the devil out of her'"[2]. The guilty carers were imprisoned and the child was placed in foster care. The incident shocked and appalled the authorities and the wider British and African communities.

In many such situations, involving apparently extreme and cruel actions by those who are deeply committed to religious beliefs or radical political causes, questions often arise for those who do not share such attitudes and beliefs. How can these acts be understood? Are the participants and perpetrators insane, or immoral, or both? What explains the attraction of such practices, such as the weekly fresh public demand for deliverance? Are the congregations brainwashed and deluded by the persuasive words and charismatic appeal of a group of charlatans? Are they blinded by a religious fanaticism?

The purpose of this chapter is to consider aspects of these incidents from a perspective informed by recent discoveries in the cognitive sciences. A cognitive approach to human behaviours attempts to account for aspects of cross-culturally widespread features of human thought and behaviour by identify-

---

1. http://news.bbc.co.uk/1/hi/uk/4596127.stm (accessed 11/08/05)
2. http://news.bbc.co.uk/1/hi/england/london/4607435.stm (accessed 11/08/05)

ing and describing the cognitive structures and processes that facilitate their transmission. Cognitive scientists work from the assumption that the information processing devices of the human mind evolved in response to selective pressures in our ancestral environment (e.g. Mithen 1996). These devices form part of our universal biological heritage and are used to process information about the world we live in. The information that our minds process from the environment now often differs from the information that the mechanisms were selected for. Nevertheless, the capacities of these devices and their evolutionary history explain, in part, why aspects of human culture (e.g. religious ideas, social relations, moral proscriptions) across the world display fundamental continuities and are readily transmitted among and between generations.

This chapter contributes at least partial answers to the above common lines of questioning so often generated by situations in which other humans appear to be so different from oneself. It does so by considering the cognitive processes that underpin witchcraft beliefs and the apparently extreme reactions to them. Setting to one side personal moral objections to the cruel practices that may result from adherence to such beliefs, it seeks to understand the mind of the perpetrators, and to identify what mental structures are activated by such ideas and what makes the ideas compelling. This is not an interpretivist endeavour, however. It does not attempt to see and portray the situation from the Other's point of view, and thereby to draw attention to the moral innocence of these ideas and behaviours within the context of the Other's worldview. It simply attempts to portray a small part of what it is to be human in today's world, recognizing that our social cognition evolved in a context very different to the complex social world we now inhabit, and that this may sometimes predispose us to behave in certain ways. The final sentence on the moral acceptability of such beliefs and behaviours may be delivered without this knowledge. Nevertheless, by considering some of the mechanisms of the mind that are in part responsible for their cross-cultural prevalence, this account may be relevant to those seeking to identify fundamental causes for these behaviours and to influence their prevalence.

Typical reactions to witchcraft beliefs in the modern world echo scholarly reactions to early explorers' and missionaries' reports of religious practices in cultural contexts far from home. People were often defined by their exotic beliefs as irrational, if not insane, by turn-of-the-century 'armchair anthropologists'. One of the first British anthropologists to carry out long-term field research in Africa, however, was at pains to correct the assumptions that lay behind such reactions. "The Nuer", wrote E.E. Evans-Pritchard, "are undoubtedly a primitive people by usual standards of reckoning, but their religious thought is remarkably sensitive, refined and intelligent" (1956: 311). Elsewhere, he describes the reasons the Azande give for their behaviour as "intellectually coherent" (1976: 159). Beliefs in witchcraft, divination and magic, at least in Africa, could not be taken as indicative of illogical and irrational modes of thought.

Beliefs that specifically entertain the possibility of witchcraft activity are less common in the modern West than they were four centuries ago and in other parts of the world today. Nevertheless, the incidents reported on the BBC website are not isolated affairs. The vast ethnographic record of witchcraft, possession and exorcism practices worldwide strongly suggests that their presence is extremely widespread, if not universal (e.g. Bourguignon 1968; Cuneo 2001; Kapferer 1991; Luhrmann 1989). Michael Cuneo's (2001) ethnographic fieldwork and sociological analysis of exorcism in the United States of America show that the modern world has by no means discarded beliefs about possessing spirits. Indeed, their high incidence in some regions and regular recurrence across cultures and historical periods are suggestive of an underlying, perhaps universal, psychological predisposition to create and transmit such concepts.

The ethnographic facts demand an explanation that considers the pervasiveness of these beliefs cross-culturally. Questions that limit the scope of analysis to the behaviours of an apparent minority group within a cultural context that is unrepresentative of the incidence of organised witch and exorcism beliefs globally will ultimately fail to provide satisfactory answers. Parochial accounts must give way to, or at least be complemented by, accounts that can explain the recurrence of these beliefs across cultural contexts and throughout history. This chapter considers evidence that suggests that there are specialised cognitive structures that favour the spread of beliefs in witchcraft and witch spirits. These structures' outputs are not limited to the domain of "witch" concepts alone, however. They support mundane thinking, about other kinds of social categories, which is part of normal cognition and is fundamental to everyday perception and representation of the social world[3].

---

3. The approach adopted in this chapter thus diverges considerably from conventional anthropological treatments of witchcraft and sorcery in which these phenomena are described and accounted for primarily, or exclusively, in terms of local socio-historical processes (e.g. Stewart & Strathern 2004). I do not see these approaches as necessarily incommensurable. I do, however, attempt to offer an account that, although inevitably partial, explains certain cross-cultural and historical regularities among witchcraft and sorcery phenomena and between these phenomena and other similar widespread forms of thinking about the social world. These accounts may potentially inform one another in instructive ways, but at the very least can jointly provide necessarily more comprehensive theories of cultural transmission.

This kind of mundane thinking underlies intuitive explanations not only for others' behaviours, but also for personally significant events. The attribution of one's misfortune to the actions of another social agent, whether it is a spirit who is using the body of another person, or a non-agentive or unintentional force (e.g. as with notions about the 'evil eye'), or an enemy with an axe to grind, is intuitively compelling for several reasons. Common sense accounts, now supported by growing evidence from social psychology, tell us that people are quick to point the finger, slow to recognise their own flaws, or are simply "bad losers" when things go wrong. Such responses to misfortune are important for maintaining healthy levels of self-esteem (Blaine and Crocker 1993; Greenwald and Banaji 1995). Cognitive scientists of religion have added to the work of attribution theorists by identifying the likely mechanisms that underpin intuitions about causal associations between 'random' occurrences and the actions and intentions of other agents with special access to knowledge and special powers, e.g. gods, spirits, witches and sorcerers (Barrett 2004, Boyer 2001, Bering 2002). This chapter aims to develop this work, specifically by refining existing descriptions of the ways people represent the causal significance of different kinds of agency in explaining personally significant events.

The central claim of this chapter is that everyday reasoning processes underpinning pervasive concepts of race and gender are also activated in witch concepts. Notions about witches, race, gender, and other natural-like categories (e.g. ethnic categories) are characterised by "essentialist" reasoning (e.g. Hirschfeld 1996). Members of racial categories, for example, are perceived as such by virtue of possessing something inherent—the 'essence'—that defines category membership and that causes category-specific properties to emerge (e.g. features of appearance, behavioural characteristics) (Gelman 2004). As we shall observe, witch notions are often similarly 'essentialised'—witch essence separates those who are witches from those who are not. Furthermore, witch essence causes witchcraft to happen, sometimes without the volition or awareness of the witch.

The cognitive mechanisms engaged in attempts to account for events in terms of others' inherent essences (e.g. witchcraft) differ, therefore, from those that are operative in explaining one's misfortune in terms of the malicious intentions of others (e.g. sorcery). Both sets of mechanisms form part of ordinary cognitive equipment that is available to all human beings and that is crucial for inferring, acquiring and organising information about the social environment. Furthermore, because essences and intentions are hidden from view, it is often by means of ritual practices that the causes of unfortunate events are ascertained (e.g. oracular divination), and the situation resolved (e.g. counter sorcery, exorcism). This chapter seeks to describe fundamental aspects of cognition that undergird people's beliefs about witches and sorcerers, and that give rise to ritualized responses concerned with the revelation of these social threats. Without these universal features of cognition, such ritual practices would be meaningless, unnecessary and probably, therefore, absent from the cultural record.

Thinking about Persons and Things

Many events may potentially be explained in terms of both physical and social causes. If you wish to explain the event, 'Joan crashed her car", you might appeal to the laws of physics, ultimately reducible, for example, to the mathematics of momentum, gravitational forces, and so on. In addition, you might consider Joan's probable intentional states at the time and attempt to ascertain what she may have been trying to do immediately before the crash, or even whether she had intended to crash the car. You may also understand Joan's behaviour not only as dictated by her specific intentional states preceding the event, but as the effect of enduring and stable traits, e.g. perhaps she is generally clumsy, reckless, or easily distracted. Finally, Joan's behaviour may be perceived as the effect of her membership in a particular social category. Being female, for instance, may be perceived as having a causal association with poor driving skills. The causalities identified in the non-physical accounts (i.e. mental, trait and social) are not always independently generated, but may overlap. For instance, personality characteristics are often inferred from social category stereotypes (see Fiske 1995).

Research in cognitive and developmental psychology indicates that reasoning about social causes for events activates different cognitive processing mechanisms from reasoning about mechanical, physical causes. Evolutionary psychologists have argued that the mind is composed of a wide range of special-purpose processing devices, each of which is the evolved product of adaptation to specific challenges in the ancestral environment (see Hirschfeld and Gelman 1994). These devices are described as "providing the basis for competencies that children use to think about complex phenomena in a coherent manner using abstract causal principles" (Sperber and Hirschfeld 1999). Biological properties of living things (e.g. growth, reproduction, etc.), for example, are handled by our "naïve biology". 'Naïve psychology' represents a different knowledge structure from 'naïve physics' (Clark 1987; Hayes 1985). Studies from the field of developmental psychology have demonstrated that, from a young age, children grasp the causal importance of actions on the environment and intentions to their instantiation in action, and distinguish this causal sequence from the mechanical causation which underpins the motion of non-agentive objects (e.g. Gopnik, Meltzoff and Kuhl 2001). The relevant literature for this distinction has been summarised and discussed widely in writings on causal cognition, (e.g. Sperber, Premack and Premack 1995). I will therefore limit the following brief synopsis to the most relevant findings for our purpose here.

The mechanisms that enable us to make inferences about other people's intentions are widely referred to by psychologists as 'Theory of Mind' (ToM) (see Barrett, and Guthrie, both this volume). Since people's thoughts cannot be directly observed, they are necessarily inferred from their behaviours. It is in this sense that intentional states may be understood as "hidden" or non-observable. This is an important feature that we shall return to later in the chapter. The occult nature of the intentions of other agents, particularly one's enemies, in part create the demand for certain kinds of divinatory techniques encountered across the globe.

Psychologists have identified a number of other domains of knowledge that may be organised by distinct cognitive devices. There is some evidence pointing to the presence of systems dedicated to dealing with number (Gelman and Brennan 1994; Gelman and Gallistel 1978; Gelman and Greeno 1989). Anthropologist Lawrence Hirschfeld has argued for the domain-specific processing of *social-category information* (e.g. Hirschfeld 1994, 1996). That we process information about others according to categorical distinctions and group membership is well established within the fields of social psychology and social cognition. The rules that define these processes of categorisation and that underpin the selection of category content have been the focus of a long debate. As we shall see, however, some of the ideas and findings that have emerged may be important for explaining the causal attribution of personally significant events to the *un*intentional actions of others.

Thinking about Social Groups

To begin considering how we parse and understand the social environment it may be helpful first to glance around the place in which you are reading this book and consider how you might describe the physical objects. You will find yourself readily using category labels to describe objects that are similar to each other, but not necessarily identical. There are a few other books, perhaps, and a number of chairs. Perhaps you can hear cars and other vehicles outside. Are there any other people around? How would you describe them? We can, of course, describe any object—person or thing—by its physical appearance, and use the same description for another object judged to be similar in that respect. Both people and batteries, for example, may be described as 'fat' or 'small'. In this way we use the same descriptive labels across many different kinds of objects. Similarly, we often categorise objects into discrete kinds on the basis of surface or functional similarities, e.g. chair, book, etc.

But why do we have a stable and widespread *chair* category, but rarely, if ever, a category that combines the concept of 'battery' and the concept of 'person'? Perhaps it is because they don't have much in common. Yet batteries and people are similar in a variety of ways—both are smaller than mountains, both exist on this planet, both are physical entities that can be seen and touched, etc (Murphy and Medin 1985). The list of similar attributes could be extended much further, but, as Douglas Medin observed (1989), attribute matching is not categorization. Categorization processes are driven by basic explanatory reasoning about the relationships between attributes (e.g. between having wings and feathers, and flying) within a particular structure (i.e. bird). Hence, categories are not merely generated according to the sum of independently represented features. As Medin suggests, "Inference and causal attributions drive the categorization process ... Similarity may be a byproduct of conceptual coherence rather than a cause ... concepts are organized around theories and theories provide conceptual coherence" (in Hamilton 2005:121-2). Thus, while similarity of properties is an important feature of category membership, these properties are not represented as independent but are held together by inter-property relations. Knowledge (intuitive or scientific) of how the particular properties within a structure affect each other drives the selection of relevant similar attributes and promotes the establishment of categories.

Consider the following experiment carried out by Medin and Shoben (1988), revealing how theories affect judgments of similarity. Participants judged the terms *white hair* and *grey hair* to be more similar than the terms *grey hair* and *black hair*. But they judged the terms *white clouds* and *grey clouds* to be less similar than *grey clouds* and *black clouds*. These results suggest that the judgments about white and grey hair are theory-driven (i.e. according to the principles of aging) in a way that white and grey clouds were not. It seems, then, that what we know about the world and how it works (e.g. intuitive physics, biology, psychology) drives concept and category formation. The principles that are perceived to underlie correlated attributes determine which correlations are salient. This may explain why we have the categories we have and why some are more stable and pervasive than others.[4]

---

4. The prediction here is that categories formed from intuitive knowledge about basic physical, biological and psychological cause-effect relationships are likely to be found in all cultures, and should display a high degree of organizational similarity, e.g. taxonomies of

We are still some way from explaining the relevance of theory-driven concept and category formation to notions about witches, but we can now consider what all this means for the everyday understanding of the social environment more generally. Social perception is governed by heuristic principles that help to simplify the complex social world we inhabit. Impressions, for example, are the building blocks of mini-theories about individuals. It is on the basis of impressions about character that we may interpret and predict others' behaviours (Gilbert 1998). Without this capacity to form and subsequently access impressions, there would be little continuity between separate social encounters with a particular individual—each meeting would require us to abstract a character profile of the person from their actions. The ability to form and collate impressions rapidly on the basis of limited information provides us with well-organised, easily accessible person-schemas of individuals that we use to interpret and predict subsequent behaviour (Andersen et al 1995).

Stereotypes are schemas of social categories and as such constitute another set of guiding principles in social perception (e.g. Johnston & Miles 2003; Wittenbrink, et al 1997). They include the perceptions, beliefs and expectations that a person has for members of the target category and may have a strong influence on first impressions. A person will often assume that all members of the category share certain characteristics. Although this assumption is often false and produces biased inferences and errors of judgment, it reduces the cognitive effort that would be required for complex tasks of assessing others as individuals on the basis of their every action, thereby enhancing cognitive economy (but not necessarily empirically-determined accuracy). Stereotypes provide information about and shape attitudes toward target-category members without recourse to individuating information about any particular member. They may pick out correlations of believed/perceived/expected physical similarity, e.g. 'all Scandinavians have blond hair'. They may concern the correlation between a particular category of people (defined by intrinsic qualities) and occupation, e.g. 'male' and 'car dealer', or between a particular category of people (defined by extrinsic qualities) and character, e.g. 'second-hand car dealer' and 'untrustworthy'.

Why are social categories, defined by intrinsic or extrinsic qualities (e.g. by colour, occupation, gender), perceived as discrete, bounded entities? What holds them together? Consistent with the now widespread recognition that concepts are knowledge-based and embedded in theories about the world, a number of psychologists have seriously considered the possibility of such so-

---

living kinds. Other categories and sub-categories may have only limited relevance within a specific set of circumstances affecting a particular population, e.g. categories of infectious disease.

cial categories arising, not out of the matching of perceived attributes, but out of theory-like principles. The term, 'psychological essentialism', coined by Medin and Ortony (1989) refers to people's belief that the social (and biological) domain may be parsed according to fixed, internal essences[5]. The essence is sortal (i.e. it serves to define categories) as well as causal (i.e. it has consequences for category structure) (Gelman 2004). Hirschfeld writes, "Essential properties are those properties in the absence of which something would not be a member of that category" (1998: 54). So the notion of essence as a defining property is accompanied by notions of essence as the property that caused the thing to be the sort of thing it is. Hence, the thing that makes a leopard a leopard, and that causes the leopard to develop its species' characteristic spots, is represented as a kind of 'leopard essence'.

Not all generalizations and stereotypes are derived from essentialist reasoning, however. That a car salesman is likely to be untrustworthy appears to be what Hirschfeld has called an "empirical summary" (1995: 319)—a prediction based on behavioural regularities that are not perceived to rest on an underlying causation. Also, adults may consider occupation (an extrinsic quality) to be less important for identity (that aspect of the person which remains constant throughout life) than corporeal features such as skin colour and body build. Skin colour and body build, in turn, are conceptualised as having rather different causal significance for behaviour and identity. These distinctions between causal significance for identity of different social properties (i.e. between physical appearance and occupation, and between different aspects of physical appearance, e.g. skin colour and clothing) appear to emerge early in childhood. When making judgments about identity, preschoolers distinguish between the importance of biological properties and occupational categories. For example, children appear to distinguish between corporeal features (e.g. skin colour) and non-corporeal features (e.g. uniforms) as properties that determine enduring identity (Hirschfeld 1995). This research indicates that young children between the ages of 3 and 7 perceive the inheritance of physical and behavioural properties between generations and the natural changes that occur across the lifespan as lawful and non-random and that they attribute these processes to an intrinsic quality or essence. Tests regarding their knowledge of non-human kinds demonstrate similar reasoning processes (Gelman and Wellman 1991). Similar developmental findings have been reported in cross-cultural studies (Atran et al 2001; Astuti 2001)

---

5. Some have argued that in addition to humans and animals, tools and objects also are construed in terms of essence. Gelman and Bloom suggest that children are 'naïve essentialists'—"they seek to understand the superficial properties of objects in terms of deeper, more essential aspects of their nature" (2000: 100).

Hirschfeld interprets these results as pointing to an independent cognitive competence for essentialist thinking about natural-like categories in the social world (1996). Earlier models of the development of racial categories posited that, in the course of development, theory-like knowledge about biological species is transferred to the human social domain, thereby providing a theory (of essences) to explain observations of physical variation (Atran 1990, Boyer 1990, Rothbart and Taylor 1990). In other words, notions of essence and their contribution to growth processes and the inheritance of category-specific physical characteristics are put to the task of explaining observable differences of physically-defined social categories. The findings mentioned above by Hirschfeld and others suggest, however, that young children's thinking about race is essentialist from an early stage and not attributable to the observation of physical differences—children aged three weigh skin colour more heavily than body build when making judgments about a person's identity. Hirschfeld's most controversial claim, therefore, but one that empirical investigations so far appear to support, is that essentialist thinking about natural-like social categories[6] is underpinned by a domain-specific competence for the social domain.

If this is correct, our perception of others as members of natural categories develops early in childhood and delivers judgments that are theory-based, enduring and spontaneous. In a series of studies, Dunning and Sherman (1997) found that tacit inferences about natural-like and occupational categories creep into people's judgments and predictions of others' behaviours spontaneously and without prompting. In one study, results showed that participants inferred different information about a person's behaviour depending on whether the person was male or female. Those participants who scored low on a sexism scale made an equivalent number of gender-based inferences as those who scored more highly. Explicitly expressed commitment to gender egalitarianism, therefore, made little difference to the degree to which stereotype-driven tacit inferences were made.

Thinking about Witches, Sorcerers, Birth Signs and Spiritual Kinship

How does our natural propensity to partition the social world according to a commonsense social ontology inform our understanding of the spread of

---

6. Hirschfeld identifies four areas: age, gender, race or ethnicity, and kinship.

religious and magical notions about witches and exorcism? Over the last decade, scholars working within the area of cognitive science of religion have offered novel cognitively-informed hypotheses concerning the spread of religious concepts (e.g. about knowing gods, vengeful spirits, crying statues, sacred artefacts, etc.). This work proposes that the form and spread of such concepts are constrained by tacit, intuitive ontological knowledge about the world, which begins to develop from very early childhood. Dan Sperber (e.g. 1996), Pascal Boyer (e,g, 2001) and others (e.g. Barrett 2004; Slone 2004) have argued that this kind of intuitive ontological knowledge provides much of the information contained within notions of spirits and gods and special objects. The most easily transmitted religious ideas diverge only slightly from this basic knowledge about how the world works. Spirits and ghosts, for example, are only minimally counterintuitive in that they are largely consistent with the category of 'person', but they lack the property of physicality. Hence they can be reasoned about in much the same way as normal persons, e.g. they think, have feelings, know, see, etc. and act on the basis of their beliefs and intentions. Spirit concepts may also demonstrate counter-intuitive biology. For example, in some places it is believed that spirits never die, or never age, and so on. The successful transmission of such ideas depends upon the activation of a wide range of intuitive assumptions that are attached to a particular domain concept, (e.g. persons, objects) *and* upon the violation of one or more of those assumptions (e.g. invisible person, seeing stone). Little novel information has to be learned and rehearsed in memory as the new concepts already largely fit with intuitive knowledge. Violations of that intuitive knowledge arrest our attention and increase the salience of these concepts in certain situations (e.g. the 'ghost' concept may become relevant when things go bump in the night).

Psychological essentialism for social groups or 'naïve sociology' (Hirschfeld 1999) leads us to assume that the social world may be parsed according to natural-like categories, which have an underlying, non-observable reality. In many cases this reality, or causal essence, is in fact not a true natural reality, e.g. intuitive representations of race have no corresponding biological reality. But there is a *perceived* causal correlation, for example, between perceived racial differences and enduring traits. The putative causal essence, in these cases, is hidden from view, but it is what defines the person as belonging to the particular category, and guides expectations about the person's behaviours. As we have seen, such notions develop early in childhood, at least for notions of race, and for biological categories. Within the social domain, essentialist reasoning is the term used to describe processes of perception, representation and interpretation that follow from the parsing of categories according to a perceived reality or nature that cannot be directly observed. The ways in which essentialist categorization is employed is similar across different categories—membership in a group may have significance for identity and interpretation of the behaviours of any one member. Hence, if I tell person A that person B is a Blah, and that a characteristic feature of a Blah is a hook nose, and that Blahs are more violent than non-Blahs, certain inferences might be made readily and intuitively from this information without further explicit instruction. Person A, for example, may readily and intuitively assume that there is a causal (rather than accidental) connection between having a hook nose and being a Blah, and between the whatever-it-is that makes a Blah a Blah and Person B's violent behaviour, and that all Blahs look and behave in the same ways in these respects, and that Blah-ness is an enduring property without which a Blah would not be a Blah. Thus, on the basis of a partial description about the Blah category a host of assumptions about Blah essence may be mobilised. In this way the acquisition of ideas about essentialist categories requires only minimal novel input.

This may help us explain in part the pervasiveness of essentialist reasoning not only for gender, race and ethnic categories but also for traditional concepts about witches as natural-like categories, 'gods-of-the-head' (see below) and even zodiacal categories. The following section considers pertinent anthropological research on such categories and their description and use within specific cultures. As will become clear, there are aspects of these descriptions that point to widespread similarities for reasoning about certain categories, whether in the UK or Africa or anywhere else in the world, that are underpinned by ordinary cognitive function.

Evans-Pritchard offers a description of witches among the Azande as people who can "injure others in virtue of an inherent quality" (1976:1). Witchcraft substance, believed to take physical form in the abdomen of the witch, is hereditary, passed from mother to daughter and from father to son. The only way conclusively to confirm the presence of the witchcraft essence is by examination, usually post-mortem, but divinatory methods are also employed. Thus, nobody can really be sure who is and who isn't a witch, except by consulting the poison oracle. The poison oracle often surprises the suspected witch—although Zande are quick to accuse others of having consciously performed witchcraft following the oracle's verdict, they appear to be genuinely surprised when they are among the accused. Nevertheless, no one can prove that he is not a witch simply through introspection. Anyone may possess witchcraft substance without awareness and although it may remain 'cool', or inoperative, it may cause him to do things of which he has no consciousness memory. Indeed, the witchcraft act normally occurs when the witch is sleeping. Therefore, despite any offence that might be taken from the accusation, one should humbly accept the charge and perform the reconcilia-tory ritual gesture of blowing on the wing of a chicken, presented by the vic-tim. Evans-Pritchard sums up Azande ideas on the subject as follows: "A man cannot help being a witch; it is not his fault that he is born with witchcraft in his belly. He may be quite ignorant that he is a witch and quite ignorant of acts of witchcraft. In this state of innocence he might do someone an injury unwittingly, but when he has on several occasions been exposed by the poi-son oracle he is then conscious of his powers and begins to use them, with malice" (ibid, p.58).

Witchcraft essence is inherited and its intensity is variable according to the proximity of kin relations. Hence, all the sons of an identified witch may be sus-pected of possessing witch substance but their paternal cousins and distant kin may not. The substance is, according to this view, really an essence that defines members of a *witch* category. Although it may be expressed in terms of its phys-ical instantiation in the abdomen, one does not inherit one's father's substance as one may inherit his belongings. Witchcraft in this regard more closely resem-bles notions of kinship, as something 'in the blood', and constitutes a similarly natural-like category. It is a causal essence that produces observable effects ("one knows a witch by his red eyes" 1976: 2) and behaviours, but is ultimately only knowable through consultation with the oracles and post-mortem examination.

Similar beliefs about witches are held throughout many of the world's pop-ulations. Among the Akan of Ghana, witch essence is represented as a spirit that can be inherited at birth. It may also be passed on with belongings at death (sometimes impregnated in the belongings), breathed into another per-son, caught through contagion with objects onto which witches have trans-ferred their witchcraft, and it may be intentionally bought or acquired (De-brunner 1961). The Zulu witch, according to Berglund, may infuse her child with "certain medicines pertaining to witchcraft" (1976: 274) through inci-sions around the anus. The witchcraft, or *ubuthakathi*, is then developed through training later in life. This *ubuthakathi* is represented as an "incarnate power in men which may be geared toward harm and destruction" (ibid, p.266). Witches are thought to remain witches always and thus the only way to remove the witchcraft is to kill the witch. There are also elaborate ideas about the activities and superhuman capacities of witches among the Bare-'e-speaking Toraja people of Indonesia (Downs 1956). Here "witchcraft was said to be "a gift from the Gods" (*pombai lamoa*), and in general one was either a witch by nature or became one by contagion ... [I]n contrast to sorcery, witch-craft could not be learned, and ordinarily not cured" (ibid, p.41).

In medieval Europe, witches were often accused of wilfully entering into pacts with the devil. Writing in 1602, Henri Bouquet considered the importance of sexual intercourse that was believed to be a key characteristic of this relationship and that developed the bond between witches and the devil: "the Devil uses them because he knows that women love carnal pleasures, and he means to bind them to his allegiance by such agreeable provocations … there is nothing which makes a woman more loyal to a man than that he should abuse her body" (in Levack 2004: 80). Part of the abuse took the form of the 'marke', which, according to Richard Bernard (1627), the devil leaves on the witch and may appear as a "little teate, sometimes but a blewish spot, sometimes red spots like a fleabiting". He added that although witches have them taken away, "they grow againe and come to their old forme" (in Sharpe 2001: 120), an idea that corresponds to essentialist notions of 'witch essence' as the entity that not only sorts witches from non-witches, but that causes witch-typical properties to emerge and be sustained (Gelman 2004:405).[7]

Viewing witch beliefs within a cognitive and cross-cultural context can help us to begin to appreciate the implicit reasoning processes underpinning them. And it may help us to understand more fully the thinking behind the violent exorcism of the unfortunate young girl in London, described at the beginning of the chapter. People may be witches without being aware of it and without culpability. They may be born as witches, or may catch a spirit or essence of witchcraft through no fault of their own. Once someone is identified as a witch, however, he/she is a potential danger. Often this revelation alone is sufficient for people to take measures to eliminate the person or, if possible, the witchcraft. Witchcraft, whether it is called *ubuthakathi* (Zulu), *mangu* (Azande) or *ndoki* (West Africa), defines a particular social category as a natural-like type and is the substance and power that causes other category-typical activities and features to emerge (e.g. 'bewitching', red eyes, etc.). In this respect, the concept of witchcraft is a natural, but not an inevitable, product of normal cognition employed in the categorisation of the social domain into natural-like types (e.g. by gender, race, etc.). Beliefs in witchcraft essence are not universal (i.e. not all people everywhere entertain the possibility of a "witch" category), but where they do exist, they are the product of normal cognitive resources for parsing the social domain. Because the category label, *witch*, is underpinned by normal cognitive functions, which readily deliver a

---

7. Widdowson (1973) lists other characteristics that formed part of the witch stereotype at the time and which appear in modern folklore; "Extreme ugliness, bodily deformity of all kinds, birthmarks, warts and similar features" (1973: 202). He continues, "They are usually old, wrinkled, bent, crippled and reclusive. They often dress in dark, dirty, ragged clothes. They may mutter to themselves or display other signs of abnormal or antisocial behaviour" (ibid.).

vast array of assumptions and inferences based on perceived essence, there is reason to suppose that many other similar kinds of categories may be found across the ethnographic record. While basic notions about race and gender may be universal and develop early, other learned or perceived natural-like categories may harness exactly the same cognitive resources. Depending on their social surroundings, people may essentialise members of different caste groupings, religious traditions, accent and dialect groups and so on. Depending on the religious or cosmological beliefs they hold to, they may define themselves and others as members of a group by virtue of their zodiacal sign and the specific date and time they were born.

Similarly essentialist categories are found in Brazil, where I carried out eighteen months of fieldwork. Here people of the Afro-Brazilian traditions define themselves in terms of kinship with their *orixá* deities. As sons and daughters of particular *orixás*, they carry the essence of their *orixá* (called *orixá de cabeça*, or *orixá* of the head) and thus demonstrate predictable and typical character traits and physical features. Sons and daughters of Iemanjá, the *orixá* of the rivers and water, will thus have similar features of appearance and/or character and their behaviours may be attributable to their kinship identity with the *orixá*. I observed how people often perceived the influences of the *orixás* in the mundane features of personality and character, and predicted and interpreted people's actions as a direct effect of this identity. The *orixá* to which one belongs is normally identified through the divination techniques known as "the throw of the cowries", but this revelation is often preceded by much guesswork among community members as to the identity of the *orixá* that will be named for a given individual.

What is common to these modes of categorization (e.g. in terms of orixá kinship, star signs, and Azande and Zulu witch essence), is the assumption that there is something about membership of the category which is inherent and stable, which all members share, and which causes the emergence of other category-typical properties. It is the typicality of these properties that facilitates the prediction and interpretation of the behaviour of any one member without recourse to individuating information. These properties also facilitate the identification of members (e.g. being bisexual is not conclusive proof that one is the son of the *orixá*, Oxumaré, but it might be a good rule of thumb to work by and is indeed used as such by adepts and in popular Afro-Brazilian magazines, e.g. *Orixás*). The essence itself is ultimately unknowable. Just as one cannot be entirely sure that a dark-skinned person is 'black', so one cannot confirm on the basis of outward appearances and activities and behaviour alone the presence of witch essence, the spiritual kinship of the Afro-Brazilian religionist, or which sign the sun was in when a person was born.

Whatever this "something" is, and however it is described—as an essence, cosmological pre-determination, a physical substance, a biological association—it is perceived as a non-obvious, defining, determining, natural-like entity. It occurs without teaching or intention. You may be a witch and not know it until you go to live with the Azande, or be kin to an orixá and discover it only on reaching Brazil.

We can now begin to appreciate that there are potentially many ways in which to account for people's behaviours and for events in the world, e.g. through physical or mechanical causation, through intentional causation, and through the presence of causal essences in individual members of social categories. So far we have looked at only a few instances of social categories that are perceived as natural-like and at the ways in which membership in the category (and presence of the essence) may be implicated in unfortunate events (for themselves and for others. For a cognitive account of this, see Barrett 2004). Furthermore, only some aspects of these categories have been considered. It is worth emphasizing here that essentialism is not the only form of reasoning underpinning witchcraft notions, nor does it explain every aspect associated with belief in witchcraft. It is, however, a necessary part of conceptualising witches, as a generic category, and of organising knowledge about them and their activities. Reading further into the Azande and Zulu notions about witchcraft, it becomes apparent that there is much more going on than meets the essentialising eye in the identification of witches and the attribution of misfortune to their deeds. According to Evans-Pritchard, Azande are only interested in *particular* instances of witchcraft (who did what to whom) and not in the presence of witchcraft in general. Zulu train in the workings of witchcraft and learn how wilfully to use it against others. Azande often say that as one grows older, the witchcraft substance grows larger. Many witches are described in the local accounts as consciously and wilfully targeting their victims. There is clearly more at stake here than the presence of witch essence alone. Individuating information about skill, experience and intentionality in action is relevant and important for victims' decision making about how to resolve the situation, how to order their social relations, and how to avoid repeat incidents in the future.

Azande apply two models of causation simultaneously to witchcraft activity. Witchcraft exists by virtue of an essence that can work its effects through the unwitting behaviours of the witch. Yet these effects are also understood as being the outcome of intentional plotting by one's enemies. This latter aspect of witchcraft does not depend for its conceptual coherence upon essentialist forms of reasoning, but upon Theory of Mind. As noted above, reasoning about people's behaviours as the outcome of their intentional states requires a specific set of cognitive capacities that form part of normal cognition. These capacities handle the representation of other people's beliefs and desires. ToM identifies intentional states as the causal locus of people's observable actions and statements, and generates inferences about their specific character (see Barrett, and Guthrie, both this volume). Without ToM abilities we would be unable to detect sarcasm, to read between the lines of what people are saying, or to see any event or behaviour as the outcome of belief-desire psychology. We would represent the social world not as full of social actors—people consciously engaging with one another—but comprised of mindless automata.

It is ToM that enables people readily to grasp the threat of the sorcerer. Indeed, sorcerers normally require no special innate powers in order to act, but only knowledge of the ritual procedures and spells to bring about their desired effects. According to Berglund, the Zulu distinguish between *ubuthakathi* and *abathakathi,* translated as 'witchcraft' and 'sorcery'. There are two key distinctions of relevance to explaining the causal source of their special powers: while witches harbour a substance (identified by diviners), which is the defining criterion for the witch category and which 'never comes out of them', the power of sorcery may be used by anyone as and when it is needed. The two categories diverge along lines of inherence[8] and immutability, elements that are characteristic of essentialised social categories. Berglund writes, "Medicines can be obtained from a herbalist by practically anybody and the outcome of sorcery depends neither on the sorcerer nor on the herbalist who knows how to manipulate the power of medicines. In sorcery the power is in the medicines ... A manipulator can one day be the sorcerer who supplies medicines towards harmful ends and assists his client in the manipulation of the powers. But on the following day he is the herbalist who offers *imithi* to cure the harm of yesterday" (1976: 267). To put it crudely, a sorcerer may be defined by what he or she does (and knows), but a witch is fundamentally defined by what he or she is.

The clear-cut distinction between witchcraft and sorcery, as defined by the Zulu, is not a feature of all cultures where both kinds of activity may be found. Among the Azande, essentialist forms of reasoning and reasoning about people's intentions are combined in notions about witches' activities. That witchcraft activity is normally considered to be the result of both hereditary witch substance and malicious intent generates some degree of theoretical inconsistency in their accounts for specific instances. Evans-Pritchard observes, for ex-

---

8. The notion that there is an underlying reality that all members of a category share (Haslam et al. 2000:118)

ample, how the positive identification of witchcraft substance in one's forbears is of little interest to the Azande. "It is generally not even known, for it has no significance either to their sons or to other people since no one is interested in the question whether a man is a witch or not. To a Zande this appears an entirely theoretical question and one about which he has not informed himself. What he wants to know is whether a certain man is injuring him in a particular situation at a particular time" (1976: 63). Therefore, although it is impossible for someone who is not a witch—by essentialist definition—to perform witchcraft, further conditions of the social context may determine whether or not any particular witch is to be feared. A witch with neither enemies nor cruel intentions is still a witch, just as a lion without teeth is still a lion. This may be readily represented in essentialist terms, but the relevance of the category to everyday causal attributions for behaviours and events may be determined by other factors, which take into account individuating information such as intentions, beliefs and desires.

Both forms of causal reasoning capitalise on different structures of normal cognitive function. One facilitates the representation of essences as properties that define social groups and underpin certain group-level similarities. The other facilitates the representation of intentional states as the causal underpinning of individual's behaviours. Crucially, neither beliefs/desires nor essences can be observed directly. They are delivered as inferences, drawn from selected pieces of information. However people classify the hallmarks of misfortune caused by sorcery and of that caused by witchcraft, however they distinguish witches from non-witches, and however they rate the relevance of individuating information to a particular situation, the final decision is still only a supposition—the outcome of a series of provisional inferences. What we tend to find in these situations, however, is that confirmation of one's hunches is often afforded exclusively via divinatory procedures. Divination facilitates access to knowledge about people and events that is not afforded by normal human perception.

Revelation and Resolution

The techniques employed to obtain this knowledge often diverge in important ways from everyday methods of learning and discovery. By means of instruments (e.g. shells, astrological charts, etc), words (e.g. mediumistic messages) and behaviours (e.g. twitches), messages are believed to be conveyed that speak directly of specific events and situations. The procedure and the interpretation are not idiosyncratic, but follow established procedures and bodies of knowledge. For instance, in some Afro-Brazilian techniques of divination, cowry shells, thrown according to a prescribed method, become an instrument through which the divine will of the *orixá* deities can be ascertained and a person's *orixá*-of-the-head may be identified. The specific instruments and procedures followed in the divinatory technique are not wholly—perhaps not even partly—chosen for their technical relevance. Ask a diviner why shells and not stones are used, or vice-versa, and he or she will be unlikely to respond with reference to the technical functionality of the instrument. More often than not, the informant will be unsure, or may think the question rather silly, but may offer an account of their historical significance. In these respects such divinatory techniques may be considered to constitute forms of ritualised behaviour. Such behaviours are *inter alia* characterised by their irreducibility to technical motivations and goals, by repetition, by the strict adherence to procedural script, and by imprecision about when or by whom the procedure was originated (Boyer and Lienard 2006; Humphrey and Laidlaw 1994; Whitehouse 2004; Bloch 2004).

The perceived threat of witches (defined by essence) and sorcerers (defined by intentional action) arises from beliefs that both are dangerous by virtue of properties that cannot be ascertained through ordinary perception. There may be some tell-tale signs, but these are open to misinterpretation. One must confirm that these features are generated by the perceived, non-observable reality, or essence. In the case of witchcraft (and beliefs about *orixás* and the signs of the zodiac) there is no ordinary, tractable link between the essence and the effects that cause the perceived threat. In contrast with the diagnosis of bacterial pathologies, for example, it would not be possible even in principle to give a complete account of the causation entailed in witchcraft, whether it is said to be a physical substance in the belly or some other property. In the case of the sorcerer, intentions and secret actions of the sorcerer are often beyond any sort of conclusive verification. Were this not the case, there would be little need for recourse to ritual techniques to consult the gods and oracles. Ultimately, without the conceptual tools and cognitive mechanisms for representing the non-observable intentions of others and the essences of natural-like social categories, and for perceiving their effects upon the social world, there would be no demand for such revelatory knowledge.

Similarly, the procedures employed to resolve any situation that has negatively affected members of the society, (e.g. to eliminate the witchcraft, or reverse the sorcery) demand techniques that, although modelled on technical action, are fundamentally divergent from it. For example, if one believes that there is such a thing as witchcraft essence or spirits, and that witches are around, identifiable, and threatening, how should one protect oneself? How should one eliminate the essence? Shake it out? Ask it to leave? Get rid of the witch? All such courses of action may make perfect intuitive sense within the context of witch-infested societies.

In the perception of certain (groups of) members of the wider global community, each of these options may be morally objectionable to greater or lesser degrees. The moral implications of the ensuing actions fall outside the scope of this chapter and the cognitive mechanisms discussed here. Nevertheless, a pertinent observation from C. S. Lewis perhaps serves to bring some philosophical perspective on the matter. Drawing attention to a tendency for people to fail to distinguish "differences of morality and differences of belief about facts", he asserts, "It may be a great advance in knowledge not to believe in witches; there is no moral advance in not executing them when you do not think they are there" (2002: 15). Despite the intuitive appeal of essentialised social categories, the prevalence of the witch category is widely variable among individuals and communities, and throughout time. The apparent absence of witchcraft beliefs may be less a reflection of any such "advancement" of knowledge, however, and more an outcome of certain conditions in the environment in which we live that do not promote, or that directly inhibit, the generation of such beliefs. Indeed, psychological studies show that the acquisition of new or complex knowledge does not always influence real-time judgments delivered spontaneously by cognitive mechanisms. As we negotiate the social world around us, our cognitive systems deliver inferences about others faster that we can consciously monitor (see Gilovich, Griffin and Kahneman 2002). As noted at the beginning of this chapter, these outputs may in themselves be widely judged to be morally objectionable (e.g. racist thought). Nevertheless, the account here explains part of what sort of psychology lies behind concepts that inform the kinds of actions described at the beginning of this chapter. It argues that, contrary to possible initial interpretations of the evidence, the notions underlying these disturbing events are an evolutionary by-product of normal human cognitive function for the processing of social information.

Of course, it may be, as has been widely claimed, that the secular and ecclesiastical courts responsible for trials in the European witch-craze were really seeking out scapegoats for economic decline (Oster 2004), and that the diviners in the Africa, Asia and the Americas abuse their power in order to structure social relations as they wish. It may be that the 'belief' in witches was a powerful persuasion technique in the discourse of these perpetrators. Nevertheless, such accounts do not explain why specifically witch concepts are so readily and widely accepted and therefore become so persuasive in the first place.

Conclusion

In this chapter, we have considered some of the cognitive capacities that facilitate the spread of certain kinds of ideas about the causal source of humans' identities and behaviours. Psychological essentialism for social groups is an early-emerging cognitive bias that constitutes one of several kinds of tools for negotiating a complex social environment. I have argued that aspects of beliefs about the witch category, namely its discreteness, naturalness, stability, inherence and inductive potential (i.e. the capacity to infer from category membership that a witch is, for example, threatening and to predict any particular witch's likely activities), are supported by cognitive capacities that are dedicated to processing social category information and that give rise to essentialist forms of reasoning. Some aspects of witchcraft and of sorcery are underpinned by a different set of cognitive mechanisms, referred to as Theory of Mind. Both sets of capacities form part of our evolved biological heritage and as such are part of normal, universal cognitive functioning. Therefore, ideas about witches, star signs, and *orixás* of the head are delivered by normal, human cognition, as are ideas about sorcerers, divine retribution, and mischievous ghosts.

Anthropologists, social historians and sociologists have widely discussed putative causes for the rise and fall of witchcraft beliefs, witch hunts, and sorcery accusations. Few have attempted to render their hypotheses testable and to build upon scientific work developing in neighbouring disciplines. Few have endeavoured to identify the possible properties of human cognition that constrain the form and promote the transmission of such ideas, and that influence social perception. Few have considered in any scientifically tractable form how the natural, intuitive outputs of our cognitive predispositions and biases may be influenced by the cultural environment, and what specific aspects of the environment may be responsible for inhibiting or promoting such outputs.[9] This chapter is a tentative effort to return to explanation, and to take an initial step towards achieving these scientific objectives.

References

Astuti, R. (2001) 'Are we all natural dualists? A cognitive developmental approach' The Malinowski Memorial Lecture, 2000. *JRAI*, 7, pp. 429–447.

---

9. See Whitehouse (2004, Chapter 3) for a worthy attempt to consider the importance of certain ecological conditions for the propagation of different kinds of religious concepts.

Atran, S. Medin, D. Lynch, E. Vapnarsky, V. Ek, E.U. and Sousa, P. (2001) 'Folkbiology doesn't come from folkpsychology: evidence from Yukatek Maya in cross-cultural perspective' *Journal of Cognition and Culture*, 1, pp. 3–32.

Atran, S. (1990) *Cognitive foundations of natural history: towards an anthropology of science*, Cambridge England; New York; Paris: Cambridge University Press; Editions de la Maison des sciences de l'homme.

Barrett, J.L. (2004) *Why would anyone believe in God?* Walnut Creek, CA: AltaMira Press.

Berglund, A. (1976) *Zulu thought-patterns and symbolism*. London: C. Hurst.

Bering, J. (2002) 'Intuitive conceptions of dead agents' minds: the natural foundations of afterlife beliefs as phenomenological boundary' *Journal of Cognition and Culture*, 2, pp. 263–308.

Blaine, B. and Crocker, J. (1993) 'Self-esteem and self-serving biases in reactions to positive and negative events: an integrative review' In: R.F. Baumeister, (ed.) *Self-esteem: The puzzle of low self-regard*, New York: Plenum, pp. 55–85.

Bloch, M. (2004) 'Ritual and Deference' in: H. Whitehouse and J. Laidlaw, (eds.) *Ritual and Memory: Toward a Comparative Anthropology of Religion*, Walnut Creek, Calif.: Altamira Press, pp. 65–78.

Bourginon, E. (1968) *A cross-cultural study of dissociational states*, Columbus, Ohio: Research Foundation, Ohio State University.

Boyer, P. (2001) *Religion explained: the evolutionary origins of religious thought*, New York: Basic Books.

Boyer, P. (1990) *Tradition as truth and communication: a cognitive description of traditional discourse*, Cambridge: Cambridge University Press.

Boyer, P. and Lienard, P. (2006) 'Whence collective ritual? A cultural selection model of ritualized behavior. *American Anthropologist* 108:814–827.

Clark, A. (1987) 'From folkpsychology to naive psychology' *Cognitive Science*, 11, pp. 139–154.

Debrunner, H.W. (1961) *Witchcraft in Ghana; a study on the belief in destructive witches and its effect on the Akan tribes*, Accra: Presbyterian Book Depot.

Downs, R.E. (1956) *The religion of the Bare'e-speaking Toradja of Central Celebes*, s'Gravenhage: Excelsior.

Dunning, D. and Sherman, D.A. (1997) 'Stereotypes and tacit inference' *Journal of Personality and Social Psychology*, 73, pp. 459–471.

Evans-Pritchard, E.E. (1956) *Nuer religion,* New York: Oxford University Press.

Evans-Pritchard, E.E. and Gillies, E. (1976) *Witchcraft, oracles, and magic among the Azande,* Abridged with an introd. by Eva Gillies edn. Oxford: Clarendon Press. [1937]

Fiske, A. (1995) 'Social Cognition' in: A. Tesser, (ed.) *Advanced social psychology,* New York: McGraw-Hill, pp. 149–194.

Gelman, R. and Brenneman, K. (1994) 'First principles can support both universal and culture-specific learning about number and music' in L.A. Hirschfeld and S.A. Gelman, (eds.) *Mapping the Mind,* Cambridge: Cambridge University Press.

Gelman, R. and Gallistel, C.R., (1978) *The child's understanding of number,* Cambridge, Mass.: Harvard University Press.

Gelman, R. and Greeno, J. (1989) 'On the nature of competence: principles for understanding in a domain' in *Knowing and learning: essays in honor of Robert Glase,* Hillsdale, NJ: Erlbaum, pp. 125–186.

Gelman, S.A. (2004) 'Psychological essentialism in children' *Trends in Cognitive Sciences,* 8(9), pp. 404–409.

Gelman, S.A. and Bloom, P. (2000) 'Young children are sensitive to how an object was created when deciding what to name it' *Cognition,* 76, pp. 91–103.

Gelman, S.A. and Wellman, H.M. (1991) 'Insides and essences: early understandings of the nonobvious' *Cognition,* 38, pp. 213–244.

Gilbert, D. (1998) Ordinary Personology. in D. Gilbert, S.T. Fiske and G. Lindzey, (eds.) *Handbook of Social Psychology,* Boston: McGraw-Hill, pp. 89–150.

Gilbert, D. (2002) 'Inferential Correction' in Gilovich, T. Griffin, D. and Kahneman, D. (eds.) *Heuristics and biases: the psychology of intuitive judgment,* Cambridge: Cambridge University Press, pp. 167–184.

Gilovich, T. Griffin, D.W. and Kahneman, D. (2002) *Heuristics and biases: the psychology of intuitive judgement,* Cambridge, U.K.; New York: Cambridge University Press.

Gopnik, A. Meltzoff, A.N. and Kuhl, P.K. (2001) *How babies think: the science of childhood,* London: Phoenix.

Greenwald, A.G. and Banaji, M.R. (1995) Implicit social cognition: attitudes, self-esteem, and stereotypes, *Psychological Review,* 102, pp. 4–27.

Hamilton, D.L. (2005) *Social cognition: key readings,* New York: Psychology Press.

Haslam, N. Rothschild, L. and Ernst, D. (2000) 'Essentialist beliefs about social categories' *British Journal of Social Psychology*, 39, pp. 113–127.

Hayes, P.J. (1979) 'The naive physics manifesto' in Minchie, D. (ed.) *Expert systems*, Edinburgh: Edinburgh University Press.

Hirschfeld, L.A. (1994) 'Is the acquisition of social categories based on domain-specific competence or on knowledge transfer?' in Hirschfeld, L.A. and Gelman, S. A. (eds.) *Mapping the mind: Domain specificity in cognition and culture*, Cambridge: Cambridge University Press, pp. 201–233.

Hirschfeld, L.A. (1995) 'Do children have a theory of race?' *Cognition*, 54 (2), pp. 209–252.

Hirschfeld, L.A. (1996) *Race in the making: cognition, culture, and the child's construction of human kinds*, Cambridge, Mass: London, England: MIT Press.

Hirschfeld, L.A. (1999) 'Naïve Sociology' in: Wilson, R. and Keil, F. (eds.) *MIT encyclopedia of the cognitive sciences* [Homepage of MIT Press], [Online] Available: http://cognet.mit.edu/library/erefs/mitecs/hirschfeld.html

Hirschfeld, L.A. and Gelman, S.A. (1994) *Mapping the mind: domain specificity in cognition and culture*, Cambridge: New York: Cambridge University Press.

Humphrey, C. and Laidlaw, J. (1994) *The archetypal actions of ritual: a theory of ritual illustrated by the Jain rite of worship*, Oxford: New York: Clarendon Press: Oxford University Press.

Kapferer, B. (1991) *A celebration of demons: Exorcism and the aesthetics of healing in Sri Lanka*. Explorations in anthropology series, 2nd ed. Providence, R.I., USA; Washington, DC, USA: Berg; Smithsonian Institution Press.

Levack, B.P. (2004) *The witchcraft sourcebook*, New York: Routledge.

Lewis, C.S. (2001) *Mere Christianity*, Harper edn, San Francisco: Harper.

Luhrmann, T. M. (1989) *Persuasions of the witch's craft: ritual magic in contemporary England*, Cambridge, Mass: Harvard University Press.

Medin, D. (2005) 'Concepts and conceptual structure, in Hamilton' (ed.) *Social Cognition*, New York and Hove: Psychology Press, Originally published in 1989, *American Psychologist*, 44, pp. 1469–1481.

Medin, D. and Shoben, E.J. (1988) 'Context and structure in conceptual combination' *Cognitive Psychology*, 20, pp. 158–190.

Medin, D.L. and Ortony, A. (1985) 'Psychological Essentialism' in Vosniadou, S and Ortony, A. (eds.) *Similarity and analogical reasoning*, New York: Cambridge University Press, pp. 179–195.

Mithen, S.J. (1996) *The prehistory of the mind: a search for the origins of art, religion, and science,* London: Thames and Hudson.

Murphy, G.L. and Medin, D.L. (1985) 'The role of theories in conceptual coherence' *Psychological Review,* 92, pp. 289–316.

Oster, E. (2004) 'Witchcraft, weather and economic growth in renaissance Europe' *The Journal of Economic Perspectives,* 18 (1), pp.215–228.

Repacholi, B.M. and Gopnik, A., (1997) Early reasoning about desires: evidence from 14- and 18-month-olds. *Developmental Psychology,* 33, pp. 12–21.

Rothbart, M. and Taylor, M. (1990) 'Category labels and social reality: Do we view social categories as natural kinds?' in: Semin, G. and Fiedler, K (eds.) *Language and Social Cognition,* Sage.

Sharpe, J. (2001) *Witchcraft in early modern England,* Harlow, England: New York: Longman.

Slone, D.J. (2004) *Theological incorrectness: why religious people believe what they shouldn't,* Oxford: New York: Oxford University Press.

Spelke, E.S. (1990) 'Principles of object perception' *Cognitive Science,* 14, pp. 29–56.

Sperber, D. and Hirschfeld, L. (1999) 'Culture, cognition, and evolution' in: Wilson, R. and Keil, F. (eds.) *MIT encyclopedia of the cognitive sciences* [Homepage of MIT Press], [Online], Available: http://cognet.mit.edu/library/erefs/mitecs/cultureintro.html

Sperber, D. (1996) *Explaining culture: a naturalistic approach,* Oxford, UK: Cambridge, Mass: Blackwell.

Sperber, D. Premack, D. and Premack, A.J. (1995) *Causal cognition: a multidisciplinary debate,* Oxford England: New York: Clarendon Press: Oxford University Press.

Stewart, P. and Strathern, A. (2004) *Witchcraft, sorcery, rumors, and gossip,* Cambridge: Cambridge University Press.

Sternberg, R.J. and Talia, B. (2001) *Complex cognition: the psychology of human thought,* New York and Oxford: Oxford University Press.

Thomas, K. (1971) *Religion and the decline of magic: studies in popular beliefs in sixteenth and seventeenth century England.* London: Weidenfeld & Nicolson.

Whitehouse, H. (2004) *Modes of religiosity: a cognitive theory of religious transmission,* Walnut Creek, CA: AltaMira Press.

Widdowson, N. J. (1973) 'The witch as a frightening and threatening figure' in Newall, V. (ed.) *The witch figure,* London and Boston: Routledge and Keegan Paul, pp. 200–220.

CHAPTER SIX

ANCESTORS AND THE AFTERLIFE[1]

Rita Astuti

Anthropologists have long been troubled by belief. Perhaps the best illustration of their uneasiness is the opening page of Rodney Needham's (1972) *Belief, language and experience*, where the author recounts how he once dreamt that he was trying to converse with his Penan informants, but was dragged from his sleep by the failure to compose the following sentence: 'I believe in God'. Once fully awake, Needham concluded that it was actually impossible to translate this English proposition into Penan. This realization not only undermined his own habitual attribution of belief to the Penan (e.g., they believe in a supreme God, they believe that their God has certain features and possesses certain powers) but, more generally, triggered his suspicion towards anthropologists' confident attribution of belief to the various people they work with and motivated his elaborate study into the nature of belief.

Needham's investigation was self-consciously philosophical, and this same orientation has characterized the debates on rationality and on the interpretation of apparently irrational beliefs (e.g., Wilson 1970, Hollis & Lukes 1982). Arguably, the very abstract philosophical approach to belief has tended to obscure some important facts—for example, that ordinary people are likely to hold inconsistent sets of beliefs (Luhrmann 1989; Stringer 1996)—that are in fact highly relevant to the discussion of what it takes for anthropologists to attribute belief to others. My priority in this paper, therefore, is to investigate belief as an ethnographic phenomenon rather than as a philosophical conun-

1. This research was funded by the Economic and Social Research Council, UK (Research Fellowship R000271254, 2002–05). I wish to thank Maurice Bloch, Dan Sperber, Charles Stafford and Harvey Whitehouse for comments on earlier drafts of this chapter. I am indebted to Paul Harris for his collaboration on this project, to Nicola Knight for his assistance in data analysis, and to Sean Epstein for his help in the collection of data in Madagascar.

drum. This investigation is only a start, but it begins to reveal the complexities that lie hidden under the sort of confident attributions of belief that are so common in anthropology and that kept Needham awake.

The Ethnographic Background

The village of Betania, where I have conducted ethnographic fieldwork on and off since the late 1980s, has at present a population of about 1000 people. It lies a few miles south of Morondava, the main town in the area, which hosts governmental offices, a market, a hospital, a post office, and an airport. The livelihood of the village depends on a variety of fishing activities, and on the trading of fish at the Morondava market. Typically, men go out fishing daily with their dugout canoes and, daily, women sell the catch. With what they earn, women buy rice, the staple food, other essential foodstuff and a variety of luxury items. The development of tourism in recent years has made Morondava a much busier place than it was in the 1980s. This has created a new outlet for the fish caught by Betania fishermen, in addition to generating employment opportunities for some of the villagers. Nonetheless, most villagers still regard fishing as their most profitable, if erratic, source of livelihood, and for this reason, like other people who live on the coast and "struggle with the sea," they call themselves Vezo (see Astuti 1995a, 1995b).

Some of the resources that Vezo villagers earn from their skilful struggle with the sea are used to finance the work that living people perform for their dead relatives, such as the construction of family tombs and the erection of individual crosses that bear the name of the deceased (see Astuti 1994, 1995a). The work is a service that the living perform for the dead, but is not a service of a voluntary nature for if the living fail to provide the dead with decent "houses" or if they fail to honour them by erecting crosses, the dead can make one or more of their descendants ill or even take their life.

The demanding work that the living periodically perform for the dead is only one of the contexts in which Vezo villagers interact with their dead relatives. Many events in the productive, reproductive and social life of any Vezo family require that the dead be promptly informed, for example if one intends to move to a temporary fishing location, if one is moving into a newly built house or is launching a new canoe, if one is having a difficult birth or if a newborn is brought out of the house for the first time, if one is about to sit a school exam, if difficult words have been spoken which make people's heart heavy with anger, if the visiting anthropologist arrives or leaves, and so on. It is the responsibility of the senior head of the family (*hazomanga*, see Astuti

1995a) to call the dead and talk to them, asking for their protection or their forgiveness, and ensuring that they are kept well informed of life's events—for whenever the dead have reasons to be "surprised," they will want to ask questions, thereby causing trouble for the living.

The dead communicate with their living descendants through the dreams that they induce in them. This is because when a person dies, the breathing stops, the body becomes stiff, cold and soon begins to stink and to decompose. But when a person dies, the 'spirit'—known as *fanahy* up to the moment of death—permanently departs from the body. In its new disembodied, ghostly form, the spirit—now known as *angatse*—is invisible (*tsy hita maso*), and moves around like wind (*tsioky*). To be seen by living people, it enters their dreams, where it appears together with its original uncorrupted body, just as it was when the person was alive.[2]

In a sense, it is somewhat misleading to say that the spirit of the dead enters the dreams of the living, since these dreams are more like encounters between fellow spirits. During sleep, the *fanahy* of living people temporarily detaches itself from the body and wanders until waking time.[3] If one's *fanahy* travels to market, one dreams about the market; if it travels to sea, one dreams about the sea; if it is approached by the *angatse* of a dead relative, one dreams of that relative. Most of one's *fanahy*'s nocturnal activities reflect one's preoccupations during the day and especially one's thoughts just before falling into deep sleep. However, the encounters with *angatse* of dead people are different because they are originated by the will of the dead, rather than by the thoughts of the living. In this sense, *angatse* can indeed be said to force their way into the dreams of the living, in a way that is perhaps not so dissimilar from the more dramatic and complex forms of spiritual intrusion that go under the name of spirit possession.

Dreams about one's dead relatives must be promptly recounted to members of one's immediate family and to the senior person who has the authority to call upon the particular individual who appeared in the dream. The meaning of some of these dreams is plain and straightforward: the dead per-

---

2. When people recount their nocturnal encounters with *angatse*, they place great emphasis on the fact that they *see* the deceased and on the fact that the deceased appears exactly like s/he was before s/he died.

3. Because of the spirit's departure from the body during sleep, being asleep is like being dead (*olo matory naman' ny olo maty*, literally, people who are asleep are dead people's friends). Several adult informants told me that if a person's face is smeared with *tabake* (a yellow paste derived from medicinal woods) while she is asleep, the spirit will be unable to recognize the body it belongs to and will fail to reconnect with it, leading to that person's death.

son complains that she is hungry because her [living] son cannot be bothered to buy food for her, or she says that she feels cold because her house (i.e., the tomb) is falling apart; she might herself offer food to the dreamer or put her cold hand on the dreamer's forehead. All of these are bad, dangerous dreams, which have immediate effect on the dreamer (a fever, an ear-ache, some swelling), and which require immediate action (an offering of rice or even the slaughtering of a head of cattle) to appease the offended spirit. But dreams can be more ambiguous (e.g., the deceased simply appears, staring, but does not say anything) and may prompt no immediate action, until an illness calls for an explanation and the dream is promptly remembered and reinterpreted. In some cases—typically when children are involved—dreams are only revealed through divination. Given their lack of wisdom and understanding, children are not expected to recognize the significance of dreams, nor are they expected to remember or to recount them. But if children get ill and their illness persists and defies treatment with western medicines, parents will approach a diviner who will be able to see that the child had a dream in which the *angatse* of a certain dead relative touched her forehead or gave her food; an explanation will also be offered as to why the dead relative is angry—her children have forgotten her and they fight all the time, she feels lonely, she is "surprised" by a new residential arrangement she has not been informed of—and what actions must be taken to appease the *angatse* and restore the child's health.

This brief account of the interactions between Vezo villagers and their dead relatives is based on my observation of several "works" performed for the dead and on numerous instances when elderly *hazomanga* addressed invisible interlocutors, offered them cooked rice, tobacco, rum, or (more exceptionally) slaughtered a cow and offered bits of cooked meat. It is based on the reports and the interpretations of dreams involving dead relatives, and on the course of action that followed. It is based on diviners' diagnoses of unabating illnesses and on people's speculations as to why a healthy child suddenly died or a strong young man drowned at sea. And it is based on several conversations with my closest Vezo friends who, over the years, have helped me understand what was going on around me.

All of these sources appear to deliver one clear message: that Vezo believe that a deceased person's *angatse* continues to want, to feel cold, hungry, lonely or outright angry, and continues to monitor, judge and influence living people—in other words, that some of the person's sensory, cognitive and emotional (mental for short) faculties survive after death. Although this attribution of belief sounds like a plausible inference, common enough in anthropological interpretative practice, the experimental evidence I present next will call for some significant qualifications. Before I start, though, some terminological clarifications are in order.

What Works and What Doesn't

In his remarks on the verb "to believe," Pouillon (1982: 6) points out that "it is not so much the believer who affirms his belief as such, it is rather the unbeliever who reduces to mere believing what, for the believer, is more like knowing." When one says that, for example, the Dangaleat believe in the existence of their local spirits, it is because one does not believe that these spirits exist, and one assumes that to do so requires a special disposition, i.e., belief. These observations come with the proviso that in the case of Christian believers, for historical and ontological reasons, the believers themselves cannot avoid expressing their belief in the existence of God (see also Ruel 1982). Christians, therefore, most definitively believe in God. But, Pouillon asks (1982: 4), how can one tell whether Dangaleat believe in local spirits and in what way? What questions can one ask them, using what word in their language, in what context?

I am well aware that the same riddles apply to the Vezo. How can I tell whether the Vezo *believe* that the *angatse* survives after death or whether they just *know* it? How can I ask them? To address precisely this kind of questions, Bloch (2002) has turned to historical evidence from 19th century Highland Madagascar. He asks: What happened when Christian missionaries set out to convert the Malagasy? Which beliefs did they identify in Malagasy religion? Which beliefs were they able to eradicate? He notes: the missionaries—unquestionably experts in identifying Christian-like beliefs—targeted and successfully eradicated the "belief" in cult objects known as *sampy*, but they ignored the "belief" in the continuing existence of dead forebears, so that people's relations with the ancestors were not affected by conversion to Christianity. From this observation, Bloch concludes that for the Malagasy ancestors are not an object of belief in the Christian sense, for had they been so, they would have certainly been targeted by the missionaries.

Though convincing, Bloch's analysis leaves us with a negative conclusion: that the way Malagasy "believe" in the existence of their dead forebears is different from the way Christians "believe" in the existence of God. But it provides us with little evidence of how Malagasy do in fact represent to themselves the existence of their dead forebears. My intention in this paper is to begin to provide some of this evidence. But to be able to do this, I need to make the following stipulation: that I use the word belief in the simple sense of "holding something to be true." I shall take as evidence that people hold something to be true the fact that they use it is as a basis for novel inferences. For example, evidence that people believe that after death the body decomposes but the *angatse* survives can be found in the novel inferences they are prepared to make about which of a person's properties remain viable after death. From this perspective, whether Vezo believe in the survival of the *angatse* becomes a question that *can* be investigated empirically.

The experimental tool I have used to carry out this investigation was originally designed by developmental psychologists Paul Harris and Marta Giménez (2005) to study Spanish children's understanding of death and the afterlife. In the first instance, I used it to interview 23 Vezo men and women, aged between 19 and 62 years (mean = 33 years). I first asked them to listen to a short narrative about a fictional character called Rampy. They were told that Rampy was a very hard working man, who one day fell ill with high fever and was taken to the hospital by his wife and children. The doctor gave him four injections, but after three days he died. Participants were then asked a set of 14 questions, half of which were about the continued functioning of some of Rampy's body parts and bodily processes (e.g., now that Rampy is dead, do his eyes work? does his heart beat?), and the other half were about the continued viability of some of his sensory, emotional and cognitive functions (e.g., now that Rampy is dead, does he hear when people talk? does he miss his children? does he know his wife's name?).[4]

For want of a better, more intuitive phrase (such as the statement often heard during Vezo funerals: "when one is dead, one is dead!"), in what follows I shall refer to participants' *negative* answers (e.g., Rampy's eyes do *not* work or Rampy does *not* hear when people talk) as *discontinuity judgements*: judgments that state that life and death are *discontinuous*, that what works in life no longer works in death, that what was felt in life is no longer felt in death, and so on. By contrast, I shall refer to participants' affirmative answers (e.g., Rampy's ears work or Rampy knows his wife's name) as *continuity judgments*: judgments that state that life and death are *continuous*, that what works in life continues to work in death, that what was felt in life continues to be felt in death, and so on.

---

4. The complete list of properties was as follows: BODILY: Do his eyes work? Do his ear work? Does his stomach need food? Does his heart beat? Do his legs move? Does a cut on his hand heal? Does he age? MENTAL: does he see things around? Does he hear when people talk? Does he feel hungry? Does he know his wife's name? Does he remember where his house is? Does he feel cold? Does he miss his children? Participants were asked each set of 7 questions in one of two random orders. Half the participants received the bodily questions followed by the mental questions and half received the reverse order.

On the basis of the ethnographic evidence reported above, one would expect participants to judge that Rampy's bodily processes come to an end when he dies and that at least some of his sensory, emotional and cognitive functions remain viable, since these are the properties routinely attributed to the surviving *angatse* (as when people worry that their dead relatives might be feeling cold or that they will soon demand to hear the latest news). As expected, participants differentiated between bodily and mental processes: on average, they gave a smaller number of discontinuity judgments for mental than for bodily processes. However, the most striking finding was that just under half of the participants gave discontinuity judgments for *all* the mental processes they were questioned about. They reasoned, in other words, that death extinguishes the person and they made no room in their reasoning for the survival of the *angatse*.[5]

In view of this result, we can begin to qualify the conclusion reached above that Vezo believe that a person's mental faculties survive after death. As measured by my informants' judgments about the fate of Rampy, this belief is clearly present, but its spread is far from universal. As I show next, however, this first qualification does not go far enough.

To someone who has lived in Betania for extended periods of time and has seen people save significant sums of money to finance the construction of tombs and crosses that were meant to appease the anger of their dead relatives, and who has witnessed numerous monologues directed at a recently dead grandmother, at a long dead father or at long forgotten forebears, the fact that nearly half of the participants in the death interview failed to attribute any mental properties to the deceased is puzzling. In some cases, I knew for a fact that the people who emphatically stated that Rampy would be rotting under the ground with no possibility of seeing, hearing, feeling, knowing or thinking because his head would be filling up with worms, had encountered the *angatse* of a dead relative in a dream, which had prompted an offering of rice to the deceased, or had sponsored the repairs to the family tomb, following a sudden spread of illness in the family.

Many anthropologists might want to argue that the puzzling outcome of the death interview is an artifice of an inappropriate experimental tool which forces informants to give stark yes/no answers about a fictional character they do not know and cannot relate to in meaningful ways. Before embracing this line of argument, however, I shall explore a different possibility, which is motivated by the hypothesis that people will bring to mind the belief that a per-

---

5. Statistical analyses of the data presented here can be found in Astuti & Harris submitted.

son's mental properties survive after death when the belief becomes contextually relevant. From this perspective, the reason so many participants took such a radical annihilating stance towards Rampy is not that the task was in itself ecologically unsound, but that its narrative context did not make the representations of the survival of Rampy's mental properties relevant to them.

This hypothesis generates a straightforward empirical question: can a manipulation in the way the task is designed—specifically, a change of the narrative context in which the questions are asked—change the distribution of participants' discontinuity judgments? To pursue this question, I recruited a new group of 23 Vezo adults aged between 19 and 71 years (mean = 35 years) and asked them to listen to a different narrative about a different fictional character called Rapeto. They heard that Rapeto had lots of children and grandchildren who, on the day he died, were with him inside his house. Now that he is dead, his children and grandchildren often dream about him. Rapeto's family has built the cement cross for him, and they are happy because the work was well accomplished. The questions about Rapeto were identical to those about Rampy, but instead of being introduced by the statement that Rampy is now dead, they were introduced by the statement that Rapeto is now over at the tombs.

Of course, whatever difference we might find between the participants who heard the Rampy narrative (from now on referred to as the Corpse narrative) and those who heard the Rapeto narrative (from now on referred to as the Tomb narrative) could be caused by a cohort effect. Given the many variables that could potentially affect the way people reason in the task (including, perhaps, how recently they lost a close relative or have had a vivid dream about a dead relation), it is clearly impossible to control for everything. However, in recruiting participants, efforts were made to control for age, gender, education, and church attendance, making sure that the profile of the participants in the Corpse and Tomb conditions were as far as possible matched. Therefore, although it is impossible to entirely rule out a cohort effect, it is reasonable to suggest that if participants in the Tomb condition are found to respond differently from those in the Corpse condition, this is because of the different narrative contexts they were presented with.

We can think of the new Tomb narrative as a form of priming, intended to bring to the attention of the participants the ritual contexts in which the representations of the deceased's enduring mental properties are likely to be most relevant.[6] As it happens, the priming proved remarkably effective in that par-

---

6. To refer to the Rapeto narrative as a form of priming is not entirely correct because it implies that the Rampy narrative does not prime participants. Both narratives are in fact a form of priming in so far as they draw participants' attention to different aspects (i.e., or-

ticipants in the Tomb condition were less likely to give discontinuity judgments than their counterparts in the Corpse condition. In particular, the percentage of participants who judged that all mental faculties cease at death went down from 43 to 13.

To sum up: the brief evocation of the contexts in which the living work for the dead to honour and appease them had the critical effect of strengthening the distribution of the belief that a person's mental faculties survive after death. This means that Vezo adults are more or less likely to embrace this belief depending on the context that gives it relevance. The difference between the responses to the Corpse and the Tomb narratives suggest that Vezo adults do not believe that the deceased's mental faculties survive after death in the abstract, but when their attention is on tombs that have to be built, on dreams that have to be interpreted, on illnesses that have to be explained and resolved. By implication, this finding suggests that, depending on context, Vezo can summon up different, even contrary representations of what happens to people after death, a point that I have discussed more fully elsewhere (Astuti 2007) and to which I shall return later.

But there is yet another qualification that needs to be made. In both the Corpse and the Tomb conditions, the number of discontinuity judgments given by those participants who judged that the deceased would retain at least some mental properties ranged all the way between 0 (all properties remain viable) and 6 (only one property remains viable). This means that there was remarkably little agreement about the exact functions that the deceased would retain—for some, it was hearing, for others it was knowing one's wife name and remembering the location of one's house, for others still it was all of the above plus feeling hungry, and so on.

The overall distribution of participants' judgments, therefore, not only suggests that the belief in the survival of the *angatse* is deployed contextually, but also that it is appropriated by different people to compose very personal and idiosyncratic representations of what happens after death. This variability in people's representations of the afterlife was even more apparent in the course of the informal conversations that were sparked by the death interviews. For example, several people puzzled over the question of how exactly the dead manage to eat, drink or smoke what is offered to them. Some speculated that

ganic versus ritual) of the dying process. Nonetheless, the developmental data I present below suggest that the understanding of death as the end of both bodily and mental functions emerges before the understanding of death as the end of bodily functions and the preservation of mental functions. There are thus reasons to believe that the Rampy narrative primes a more intuitive construal of death than the Rapeto narrative, and this justifies its use as a baseline to assess the effect of the priming of the Rapeto narrative.

the dead feed by inhaling the smell and extracting the flavour from the food. Evidence for this is that, as they claimed, the meat that is distributed after slaughtering a cow that is being offered to dead people does not taste the same as the meat that one buys at the market for family consumption; the first type of meat is reportedly tasteless because all its flavour has been consumed by dead people's feasting *angatse*. Others were more tentative and rather unsure, wondering how dead people could possibly eat—since they don't have a body, they surely don't have a mouth! Maybe, all that happens is that they see the living throwing the morsels of food (which are likely to be eaten by passer-by animals) and that is all they care about—to be remembered and to be shown respect. The most radical position was that offering food or drinks or cigarettes to dead people makes no sense at all: has anybody ever tried to stuff food in the mouth of a dead person, or to get a corpse to puff a cigarette? The only reason people bother to cook meat and rice and to light the tobacco is that for a long, long time this has been the Malagasy way of doing things. In truth, what really happens is that the food is eaten by the living and the tobacco just goes to waste. As for the dead, well, the dead are just dead.

Apart from the variability in how they made sense of specific aspects of the *angatse*'s existence, people also clearly demonstrated to have very different degrees of interest in, and to have reached very different levels of elaboration of, the belief that a dead person's *angatse* survives after death. Some of my interlocutors were indifferent, even sceptical novices, while others were committed experts. Most strikingly, adults differed in the degree of sophistication with which they puzzled over difficult questions, some which I brought up and others which they had themselves considered and tried to answer: for example, is dreaming about a dead person in any way similar to being possessed by a spirit? Can a dead person appear simultaneously in different people's dreams? Can one dream about dead people one has never met? How exactly do *angatse* make people ill? Are dreams a necessary vehicle for their interventions? Are there ways of resisting these dreams? Do babies have *angatse*? Do animals?

Although difficult to quantify, some of this variation had to do with age, with older people (aged roughly 40 and above) being predictably more inclined to explain points of detail, to recount poignant personal experiences or to speculate about aspects of the relationship between the living and the dead that they did not fully grasp. When pressed by my relentless questioning, they hardly faltered, giving evidence that they had themselves, at some point, reflected about the hows and whys, and had come up with their own answers (different, perhaps, from those of a brother or a husband I had approached a few hours earlier). Younger adults (aged roughly 40 and below) tended to be less interested, to give more cursory and standardized answers to my questions, or to dismiss them altogether.

To illustrate: I never managed to get any of the younger people to seriously engage with the question of whether animals have *angatse*. The almost automatic answer they all produced was that they had never heard of anybody being visited in a dream by an animal—a patently absurd scenario! Admittedly, not many of the older people had much to say either about this topic, apart from pointing out that since animals do not talk, it is hard to know what might be going on with them. But in one case, a very old man took my question at heart and, having pondered over it in his mind, he suggested that *if* animals have a *fanahy*—and he guessed that some animals, like whales or dolphins, might—then when they die their *angatse* will probably wander around, just like the *angatse* of dead people. His insight was that the *angatse* of a dead animal is not going to appear in the dream of a human (as implied by the younger people), but in the dreams of its own children, whom it will miss very much. He was sure that mother-dolphins and mother-whales are capable of feeling something for their offspring, because they stubbornly look for them if they get separated. But he conceded that we shall never know whether dolphins and whales have dreams! Throughout the conversation, I felt that this old man was taking me to a level of understanding of what *angatse* are all about that was not to be matched by anyone else. Perhaps the reason for his sophistication is that, being the head (*hazomanga*) of his ancestral group, he dreams about his dead forebears almost every night. Understandably, the issue of what it means and what it feels to be an *angatse* is likely to be on his mind quite a lot.

There are two points I wish to draw out of these ethnographic observations. The first one is that the specific content and degree of elaboration of the belief that something survives after death varies greatly, between younger and older adults but also between one individual and the next. To be meaningful, the attribution to the Vezo of the belief in the survival of the *angatse* must take this variability into account. The second, related point is that if people are so inclined—and not everyone is—they can easily spend a lifetime trying to understand better and more. Both of these points raise the question of how this process of understanding might get started and how it might develop.

Developmental Insights

As reviewed by Harris and Giménez (2005), developmental psychologists of different theoretical inclinations have had a sustained interest in children's understanding of, and emotional reaction to death. Only recently, however, they have began to integrate the study of children's increasingly sophisticated understanding of death as a biological phenomenon (e.g., Slaughter, Jaakola & Carey 1999; Jaakola & Slaughter 2002; Slaughter & Lyons 2003), with the study of children's beliefs in the afterlife (e.g., Bering & Bjorklund 2004; Bering, Hernandez-Blasi & Bjorklund 2005; Harris & Giménez 2005). My investigation of how Vezo children come to believe that dead people remain an active presence in their lives has been inspired by this new line of research, particularly by Paul Harris's insights into children's ability to imagine outcomes beyond the realm of possibility (Harris 2000).

As a first exploration into Vezo children's understanding of the consequences of death, I recruited three groups of Vezo children—18 5-year olds,[7] 16 7-year olds,[8] and 28 9- to 17-year olds[9]—and asked them to take part in the Corpse task. A few changes in the basic design were introduced in an attempt to make the procedure as accessible as possible to the youngest children.[10] Irrespective of age, though, all the children were asked the same 14 questions about Rampy's bodily and mental properties that were used with adults.

The overall developmental trajectory that can be derived from the distribution of children's answers is as follows: 5-year olds made a random assessment of the consequences of death on either bodily or mental functions, and gave no evidence of understanding the consequences of death on either a person's bodily or mental functions.[11] By the age of 7, children reliably gave more

---

7. Mean age = 5 years 9 months; range = 5 years 6 months to 6 years 6 months. I made several attempts to work with younger children, aged 4 to 5, using a protocol similar to the one designed by Barrett & Behne (2005), which involved acting out the death of a toy-mouse which falls pray to a toy-cat. Unfortunately, I was unable to overcome children's shyness and their remarkable ability to remain silent, even when the questions were asked, in my absence, by a Vezo experimenter or by one of the children's own parents (the main problem, in this case, was that the parent had no patience for the child's "silliness" and prompted them to give the "right" answer).

8. Mean age = 7 years 1 month; range = 6 years 9 months to 7 years 7 months.

9. Mean age = 13 years and 3 months; range = 8 years and 11 months to 17 years and 2 months.

10. The 5- and 7-year olds were not told a story but were shown a drawing of a man called Rampy. After an initial warm-up session in which they were asked several questions about the drawing (e.g., is Rampy standing or sitting, are his trousers red or brown), children were told that Rampy had recently died, and they were shown a new drawing of the man lying flat on a bed, with a white cloth tied around his jaw. The 9- to 17-year olds were told the same narrative that was used with adults. While the story was narrated, they were shown the same drawings of live and dead Rampy that were used with the younger children, as this helped focus their attention.

11. The test questions were randomly interspersed with 5 control questions about factual details in the drawing the children were looking at (e.g., is there a bucket under the bed?) The few children who failed to answer the control questions correctly were excluded

discontinuity than continuity judgments, and did so for both bodily and mental functions. Conversely, if they judged that something survives, they were as likely to do so for bodily as for mental functions. Between the age of 9 and 17, children began to entertain the notion that, while the body most definitely perishes and rots away, some limited aspects of the deceased's mental life are preserved. This is shown by the fact that they were less likely to give discontinuity judgments for mental than for bodily properties. However, when we compare these older children with adults, we find that their endorsement of the belief that Rampy's mental life continues after death was somewhat weaker: first, the number of 9- to 17-year olds who gave only discontinuity judgments for mental properties was larger than the number of adults; second, those children who gave some continuity judgments tended to grant Rampy fewer mental properties than adults.[12]

This developmental progression suggests that the idea that the deceased's mental functions are preserved after death emerges only after children have consolidated their biological understanding of the consequences of death: that when a living organism dies, the functions that made life possible and that were sustained by life come to an abrupt end. Vezo children have at their disposal massive and readily available empirical evidence to support the construction of this view of the consequences of death—corpses that rot, do not move, do not speak, do not look, do not wake up, and are put away under the sand. As graphically put by a 9 years old boy: "the body goes bad, the skin is all decomposing and inside the tummy is full of worms ... and in the head there are all sorts of animals that go inside it, and there is nothing that they [dead people] need and they can't hear anything." Against this early-emerging assessment of the annihilating consequences of death, the realization that some sensory, cognitive and emotional faculties survive after death appears to *grow* with age. This finding converges with that of Harris and Giménez (2005),

---

from the study, as their failure suggested that they were not engaged with the task and/or were enable to cope with the test setting. By implication, we can assume that the answers to the test questions by those children who correctly answered the control questions reflect a genuine lack of understanding of what happens after death.

12. I have compared the test results of 7-year olds, 9- to 17-year olds and adults despite the fact that, as explained above, their test conditions were not identical. The reason the comparison remains valid is that all three age groups were prompted to focus on Rampy's dead body, whether by visual or verbal means, or both. The comparison would be invalidated if there were reasons to believe that 7-year olds would have given less discontinuity judgments for mental properties had they heard the Rampy narrative, or that adults' judgments would have been affected by the presentation of the line drawing of Rampy's dead body. Both of these eventualities seem highly unlikely.

and contradicts the claim put forward by Bering and his collaborators that young children have a natural disposition to make these attributions (i.e., to assume that faculties such as feeling, thinking, and knowing continue after death), a disposition which *weakens* with age as children learn to construe death as biological process (see Bering & Bjorklund 2004; Bering, Hernández-Blasi & Bjorklund 2005; Bering 2006).[13]

Undoubtedly, anthropologists are likely to find it self-evident that Vezo children gradually acquire supernatural beliefs about the ancestors. This is because they tend to assume that children *learn* beliefs in magic, spirits, or gods (see Mead 1932 for an illustration). However, the developmental data presented here suggest that Vezo children successfully acquire supernatural beliefs about the ancestors only once they have understood the biological consequences of death. Arguably, children do not need to understand that death brings to an end an organism's vital functions to learn to attribute all the relevant mental properties to dead people (e.g., knowing, remembering, feeling nostalgic, etc.) Indeed, ignorance of the biological consequences of death could facilitate children's assimilation of their elders' representations of the afterlife. But the results of this study suggest that Vezo children construct their understanding of the properties of the ancestors on their knowledge, not on their ignorance, of the biological consequences of death. And this suggests that *learning* about the ancestors is a much more complicated process than anthropologists tend to imagine. In this case, it would seem that instead of learning about the ancestors by learning about the ancestors (the standard anthropological model of cultural transmission), children may be learning about the ancestors in very unlikely places and at unlikely times, as when they play with small animals, pulling a lizard's leg or squashing a frog's head, and watching their "toys" die.

Granted that children first understand that death entails annihilation, they will eventually grow into the belief that death does not entirely extinguish the person. We must therefore ask what drives and sustains this growth.[14] If it is true that Vezo children have much evidence that supports

---

13. See Harris & Giménez 2005 and Astuti & Harris submitted, for the suggestion that the difference in the findings might be due to differences in design, specifically the fact that Harris & Giménez and Astuti & Harris use a story that involves the death of a person, whereas Bering and colleagues use a story that involves the death of a puppet-mouse (see Harris & Astuti 2006).

14. Developmental psychologist Paul Bloom (2004: 207) has argued that "belief in an afterlife is a natural consequence of our [i.e., members of the species *Homo Sapiens*] intuitive Cartesian perspective." My data do not bear on the hypothesis that humans are natural dualists, but they suggest that the conversion of dualism into a belief in the afterlife is

the realization that death extinguishes every aspect of the person, it is equally true that they have plenty of evidence that supports the opposite realization that something of the deceased survives after death. Like the Kwaio children beautifully described by Keesing (1982: 30–39), it is hard to imagine how Vezo children could escape the conclusion that the dead are a wilful and "lively" presence among the living, as they witness the monologues that elders direct at dead but clearly wanting interlocutors, or they share in the offerings of meat and rice given to them, or they suffer the illnesses, enjoy the recoveries or mourn the deaths that are caused by this or that angry *angatse.*

If this is the kind of evidence that fuels children's emerging awareness that something of the person survives after death, we might expect that children, like adults, will be more likely to bring to mind the belief that people's mental functions are not entirely extinguished by death when they are invited to think about tombs, crosses and the work that the living perform for their dead relatives to keep them happy. To explore this possibility, I invited a new group of 28 9- to 17 year olds[15] to listen to the same Tomb narrative that was used with adults.[16] Like adults, the children in the Tomb condition gave far less discontinuity judgments than the children in the Deceased condition. Thus, when primed to think about tombs and crosses, the majority of children judged that life continues after death. Such a dramatic effect confirms that, at least from the age of 9, Vezo children are well attuned with the ritual practices that concern the afterlife and that, from these practices, they infer that something of the person survives after death.

Note, however, that the early emerging representation of death as the annihilation of the organism will never be discarded, as revealed by the fact that in the Corpse condition older children and adults alike were more likely than in the Tomb condition to reason that all comes to a halt when a person dies. In other words, in the course of development apparently incompatible representations come to co-exist in people's minds. Such co-existence raises a further question for a future investigation, namely whether these representations can be distinguished in terms of the cognitive demands that they impose on their users. Following Barrett's distinction between basic and "theologically correct" concepts (1999), or Sperber's distinction between intuitive and re-

---

not automatic and does not come for free. Hence the question of what sustains it and makes it grow.

15. Mean age = 12 years and 11 months; range = 9 years to 17 years and 3 months.

16. Children in the Tomb condition were shown a drawing of live Rapeto and a drawing of his tomb and the cross bearing his name.

flective beliefs (1997), one could to test whether, in a cognitively demanding task where people are forced to reason quickly and on-the-fly (for example, a memory task), participants might only have access to the earlier, more basic representation of death as annihilation. This would indicate that bringing to mind the idea that the *angatse* of dead people survive the rotting of their bodies requires some effort, a certain amount of conscious reflection, and the mobilization of one's "theologically correct" and explicitly held reflective beliefs.

Conclusion

My investigation has challenged what at first sight seemed like a reasonable inference, based on sound ethnographic evidence: that Vezo believe in the survival of the *angatse*. The studies I have undertaken with Vezo adults and children have exposed several reasons why this attribution of belief needs to be significantly qualified. First, the belief is not held universally; second, the belief that some mental properties of the person survive after death is interpreted, understood, and elaborated in a great variety of ways by different people. And finally, and most significantly, Vezo believe in the survival of the *angatse* in some contexts and they do not believe in the survival of the *angatse* in other contexts. This does not make their belief in the power of the ancestors any less compelling, when it is believed; but it shows that the belief in the power of the ancestors is best approached in terms of when and where it is deployed, rather than in terms of whether it is held.

Where does this leave the anthropological study of belief? How do we know what our informants believe? It has become commonplace for anthropologists to warn about the ambiguities of the word 'belief' and the cultural specificity of the concept this word refers to. Such warnings seem to suggest that we have no way of finding out what goes on in the heads of our informants, and that therefore we are better off not trying. What I have shown here is that such pessimism is misplaced. The task is arduous and we shall never succeed completely. But we can move forward. Thanks to the studies described in this article, I feel we know *more* about what the Vezo "believe" than we did before. I trust that the reader will feel the same.

References

Astuti, R. (1994) "Invisible' objects. Funerary rituals among the Vezo of western Madagascar' in *Res. Anthropology and aesthetics*, 25, 11–122.

Astuti, R. (1995a) *People of the sea. Identity and descent among the Vezo of Madagascar,* Cambridge: Cambridge University Press.

Astuti, R. (1995b) "The Vezo are not a kind of people' Identity, difference, and "ethnicity" among a fishing people of western Madagascar' in *American Ethnologist,* 22, 464–82.

Astuti, R. (2007) 'What happens after death?' in Astuti, R., Parry, J. P. and Stafford, C. (eds.) *Questions of Anthropology,* Oxford & New York: Berg.

Astuti, R. & Harris, P. (submitted) 'Understanding mortality and the life of the ancestors in rural Madagascar'

Barrett, H. C. & Behne, T. (2005) 'Children's understanding of death as the cessation of agency: a test using sleep versus death' in *Cognition,* 96(2), 93–108.

Barrett, J. L. (1998) 'Theological correctness: Cognitive constraint and the study of religion' in *Method and Theory in the Study of Religion,* 11, 325–339.

Bering, J. M. (2006) 'The folk psychology of souls' in *Behavioral and Brain Sciences,* 29(5): 453–62.

Bering, J. M. & Bjorklund, D. F. (2004) 'The natural emergence of reasoning about the afterlife as a developmental regularity' in *Developmental Psychology,* 40, 217–233.

Bering, J. M., Hernández-Blasi, C., and Bjorklund, D. F. (2005) 'The development of 'afterlife' beliefs in secularly and religiously schooled children' in *British Journal of Developmental Psychology,* 23: 587–607.

Bloch, M. (2002) 'Are religious beliefs counter-intuitive?' in Frankenberry, N.K. (ed.) *Radical interpretation in religion,* pp. 129–146, Cambridge & New York: Cambridge University Press.

Bloom, P. (2004) *Descartes' baby: How the science of child development explains what makes us human,* New York: Basic Books.

Harris, P. L. (2000) 'On not falling down to earth. Children's metaphysical questions' in Rosengren, K. S., Johnson, C. N. and Harris. P. L. (eds.) *Imagining the impossible: Magical, scientific and religious thinking in children,* pp. 157–178, Cambridge & New York: Cambridge University Press.

Harris, P. L. and Astuti, R. (2006) 'Learning that there is life after death' in *Behavioral and Brain Sciences,* 29(5): 475–76.

Harris, P. L. and Giménez, M. (2005) 'Children's acceptance of conflicting testimony: The case of death' in *Journal of Cognition and Culture,* 5, 143–164.

Hollis, M. and Lukes, S. (eds.) (1982) *Rationality and relativism,* Oxford: Blackwell.

Jaakkola, R. O. and Slaughter, V. (2002) 'Children's body knowledge: Understanding 'life' as a biological goal' in *British Journal of Developmental Psychology* 20: 325–342.

Keesing, R. M. (1982) *Kwaio religion: The living and the dead in a Solomon island society* New York: Columbia University Press.

Luhrmann, T. (1989) *Persuasions of the witch's craft: Ritual magic in contemporary England,* Cambridge, Mass: Harvard University Press.

Mead, M. (1932) 'An investigation of the thought of primitive children, with special reference to animism' in *Journal of the Royal Anthropological Institute of Great Britain and Ireland,* 62: 173–190.

Needham, R. (1972) *Belief, language and experience.* Oxford: Blackwell.

Pouillon, J. (1982) 'Remarks on the verb 'believe'' in Izard, M. and Smith, P. (eds.) *Between belief and transgression: Structuralist essays in religion, history and myth,* pp. 1–8. Chicago: Chicago University Press.

Ruel, M. (1982) 'Christians as believers' in Davis, J. (ed.) Religious organization and religious experience, pp. 9–31. London: Academic Press.

Slaughter, V. Jaakola, R. and Carey, S. (1999) 'Constructing a coherent theory: Children's biological understanding of life and death' in Siegal, M. and Peterson, C. (eds.) *Children's understanding of biology, health, and ethics,* pp. 71–98. Cambridge: Cambridge University Press.

Slaughter, V. and Lyons, M. (2003) 'Learning about life and death in early childhood' in *Cognitive Psychology,* 46, 1–30.

Sperber, D (1987) 'Apparently irrational beliefs' in Sperber, D. *On anthropological knowledge,* pp. 35–63. Cambridge: Cambridge University Press.

Sperber, D. (1997) 'Intuitive and reflective beliefs' in *Mind and language,* 12 (1), 67–83.

Stringer, M. D. (1996) 'Towards a situational theory of belief' in *JASO, 27* (3): 217–234.

Wilson, B.R. (ed.) (1970) *Rationality.* Oxford: Basil Blackwell.

CHAPTER SEVEN

GODS

Justin L. Barrett

If I want to ensure a good harvest, I might take care in preparing my field, fertilize, use the best seeds possible, weed, and irrigate. I might also pray or conduct a ritual or in some other way try to get some supernatural help. If I wish to join a community or society, I might register or pay dues or even undergo an initiation ceremony. But I might submit myself to an initiation that appeals to ancestors, spirits, or gods.

Though many religious and non-religious actions bear similar motivations, religious actions (including ceremonies, rites, rituals, prayers, and so forth) typically include some kind of appeal to superhuman or supernatural agency. That is, religious actions might, for analytic purposes, be distinguished from other actions by their direct or indirect motivation through belief in superhuman agents.[1] Cognitive scientists of religion have begun to say much about how cross-culturally recurrent features of human minds inform and constrain religious actions, thereby predicting and explaining cross-culturally recurrent forms (e.g., McCauley & Lawson, 2002; Pyysiäinen, 2001, 2004; Whitehouse, 2000, 2004; Whitehouse & McCauley, 2005). Receiving less attention has been an explanation of how belief in these superhuman agents arises (Barrett, 2004). Though belief in gods (including ghosts, spirits, and other superhuman agents) is ubiquitous, a complete account of such beliefs remains a work in progress.[2]

---

1. Though what constitutes 'religion' or 'religious' actions may not be completely subsumed by appeal to superhuman agents, certainly any account of religion that ignores the role of superhuman agents would be easily criticised for being incomplete. Naturally, cognitive treatments of religion and culture extend far beyond superhuman agent beliefs (e.g., transmission of religious and mythical concepts generally, Boyer, 1994; scripturalism, Malley, 2004; magic, Pyysiainen, 2004; differences between lay beliefs and expert instruction, Slone, 2004; and ritual and social morphology, Whitehouse, 2000, 2004).

2. Note that religious beliefs are not alone in this regard. Many other common beliefs, such as why it is people believe in other minds or in the constancy of physical laws, like-

Below I sketch an account of why belief in superhuman agents is historically and cross-culturally so common by appealing to the naturally occurring properties of human minds operating in historically and cross-culturally common natural and social environments. After discussing the nature of belief generally, I propose some particular features of human minds that make belief in superhuman agents natural and then offer some suggestions for how religious actions and belief in superhuman agents may be mutually reinforcing.

How People Come to Believe

Before addressing how it is people come nearly universally to believe in superhuman agents (gods), we must have at least a preliminary sense for how it is people come to believe anything. Perhaps surprisingly, believing in gods arises similarly to other beliefs. Further, coming to believe in the existence of something or its properties is not a trivial matter of us simply perceiving the world and passively forming beliefs that perfectly map onto our environments. Rather, cognitive scientists, particularly those studying how infants and young children make sense of the world, have shown us that the mind is no brute all-purpose processing device. Instead, its normal functioning may better be likened to a workshop equipped with lots of specialized tools for processing particular classes of information. These mental tools arise with built in biases that influence which bits of information will be attended to and how that information will be represented (which might include its being distorted).

Two Types of Belief

1. Reflective Beliefs

When discussing why it is we believe any particular thing, I find it helpful to distinguish between two classes of belief: reflective and non-reflective be-

---

wise receive little attention from scientists. The prevalence of these beliefs, too, are problems to solve and appear to arise out of the naturally occurring biases of the human mind arising in course of cognitive development. Explaining belief in gods has received only modest attention from cognitive scientists of religion not because it is considered unimportant, but because much work in the area has focused on other problems such as recurrent forms of religious rituals (e.g., McCauley & Lawson, 2002; Whitehouse, 2004) or narrower projects concerning how cognitive structures inform expression in particular cultural contexts, (e.g., Barrett, 1998; Barrett & VanOrman, 1996; Cohen, this volume; Malley, 2004).

liefs.[3] Reflective beliefs approximate what we call *beliefs* in common usage. Reflective beliefs are those we hold consciously and may arrive at by using some deliberate reflection. When asked if we believe something in particular, a reflective belief is what we reply. So statements of belief (assuming no deception) may provide fair representations of reflective beliefs.

To illustrate, when people say they believe that Toyotas are more reliable vehicles than Yugos; that $E=mc^2$; that pumpkins are orange; that Michael Johnson holds the world record in the 200 meter dash; or that Harvey Whitehouse is six-feet, five-inches tall; they are expressing reflective beliefs. Note that reflective beliefs may or may not be true, empirically verifiable, or rationally justified. Whether a belief is reflective does not bear on its truth value.

2. Non-Reflective Beliefs

Non-reflective beliefs, in contrast, operate in the background without our conscious awareness. These beliefs may not be consciously accessible and do not arise through deliberation. Rather, our minds produce non-reflective beliefs automatically all the time. Though speech acts may give hints at the nature of non-reflective beliefs, other behavior may prove more informative.

Non-reflective beliefs may include such beliefs as the following. People act so as to satisfy their desires. Rainbows exhibit six bands of color. Raccoons and opossums are very similar animals. People from outside my group are more similar to each other than people inside my group. Animals have parents of the same species as themselves. My pants are blue.[4]

Like reflective beliefs, non-reflective beliefs may or may not be true, empirically verifiable, or rationally justifiable. Often, they match reflective beliefs, but need not. For instance, research suggests it is quite natural to assume non-reflectively (automatically and without conscious awareness) that members of other human groups (e.g., racial, regional, or national) are more alike than people within one's own group (Hirschfeld, 1996). We refer to this "belief" as a tendency to stereotype. Reflectively we may become convinced that

---

3. Dan Sperber makes a similar distinction he labels reflective and intuitive beliefs (1997). Some of the strongest evidence for non-reflective or intuitive beliefs comes from cognitive developmental psychology as discussed below

4. It is most efficient to present non-reflective beliefs in propositional forms but as many of these 'beliefs' arise preverbally, they are not cognitively represented as propositions but as information processing tendencies. When people reflectly report them (often when turning them into reflective beliefs), they may use propositional language. To stress this relationship between non-reflective and reflective beliefs, and for efficiency, I use propositional forms for both.

this non-reflective belief is flawed or accurate, but if so, the non-reflective belief nevertheless remains.[5] This fact gives us a hint as to the relationship between reflective and non-reflective beliefs.

Because non-reflective beliefs may be tapped independently of statements, we know a considerable amount about infants' non-reflective beliefs. Based on observing their eye gaze, for instance, we know that babies non-reflectively believe that solid objects cannot pass directly through other solid objects (Spelke & Van de Walle, 1993). They likewise non-reflectively believe unsupported objects fall (Needham & Baillargeon, 1993), inanimate objects must be contacted before they may be set in motion whereas people need not be, and so forth (Spelke, Phillips & Woodward, 1995). Note that these infant non-reflective beliefs tend to match adult reflective beliefs. This observation gives another clue to the relationship between these two types of beliefs.

Where Non-Reflective Beliefs Come From

Beliefs about the existence and properties of mundane, ordinary things come from numerous mental tools. These mental tools are inference systems that concern specialized domains of information and operate automatically and (typically) without conscious awareness. As such, they may be called intuitive inference systems.

The existence of such mental tools has been supported by research in the brain and behavioral sciences as well as evolutionary and developmental cognition (e.g., Gazzaniga, Ivry, Mangun, 1998; Pinker, 1997). Mind-brains are highly structured with numerous sub-systems designed to carry out particular tasks that are important for our species' survival.

These mental tools automatically and non-reflectively construct perhaps most of our beliefs about the natural and social world. Non-reflective beliefs arise directly from the operation of these mental tools on inputs from environment. The vast majority of these beliefs are never consciously evaluated or systematically verified. They just seem intuitive, and that is usually good enough.

To illustrate, let us consider four mental tools: Naïve Physics, Agency Detection Device, Theory of Mind, and Naïve Biology. Concerning itself with the properties of bounded physical objects, Naïve Physics generates the non-

---

5. Naturally, just which groups' members are non-reflectively believed to be more alike than one's own group varies by cultural context. Hence, Hirschfeld's work presents a fine example of how cognitive biases and cultural inputs work together to create beliefs, attitudes, and practices that cannot be explained by appealing to either cognitive or cultural factors alone.

reflective beliefs that objects: tend to move on inertial paths, cannot pass through other solid objects, must move through the intermediate space to get from one point to another, and must be supported or they will fall (Spelke, Phillips & Woodward, 1995). The Agency Detection Device automatically tells us that self-propelled and goal directed objects are intentional agents (Baron-Cohen, 1995). Theory of Mind gives us non-reflective beliefs concerning the internal states of intentional agents and their behaviors. For instance, agents act to satisfy desires. Actions are guided by beliefs. Beliefs are influenced by percepts. Satisfied desires prompt positive emotions (Wellman, Cross & Watson, 2001). Among others, Naïve Biology generates the non-reflective beliefs that animals bear young similar to themselves, and living things are composed of organic matter and not artificial substances (Simons & Keil, 1995).

None of these listed non-reflective beliefs are the sorts of things that children are taught through explicit verbal instruction. Indeed, if queried regarding these beliefs most children (and perhaps many adults) would think the questions very odd. These non-reflective beliefs are the sorts of beliefs that children rapidly and uniformly acquire by virtue of being the sort of animal that they are living in the sorts of environments they live in. They do not require special conditions or instruction. In this sense, then, they may be thought of as "instinctive" beliefs.

That these non-reflective beliefs arise so readily and robustly occasionally presents challenges to educators. Take two examples: beliefs about rainbows and the similarity between opossums and raccoons. Our color-perception faculty biases us to see a rainbow as exhibiting distinct bands of color, a process called categorical perception. So firmly entrenched (or so intuitive and obvious) is this belief about rainbows, that it makes teaching the truth about rainbows (that they exhibit a full color spectrum) difficult. Students may find the explanation unconvincing or quickly forget it as it conflicts with their intuitions. Similarly, cognitive research on folk taxonomies of animals shows a strong bias to consider animals with similar gross morphologies and ecological niches as similar. Hence, opossums and raccoons are intuitively or non-reflectively thought to be more similar to each other than either is to horses or dogs or cows (Atran, 1995). Biologists tell us otherwise. As marsupials, opossums are more similar to kangaroos than raccoons and raccoons are more similar to bears than to opossums.[6] This conflict between the non-reflective

---

6. Atran's animal similarity judgments are from studies concerning folk zoological taxonomy through which he found evidence that people in different ecological and cultural contexts use similar strategies for categorizing animals. Nevertheless, local experts may develop reasons for rejecting folk taxonomies. Like Hirschfeld's research on racism cited previously, Atran's work provides another example of how considering cognitive constraint

belief and the reflective belief undermines the ability to consistently acquire the reflective belief. These observations concerning the conflict between reflective and non-reflective beliefs, provide a third clue as to the relationship between these two classes of beliefs.

Where Reflective Beliefs Come From

As the examples already given demonstrate, non-reflective and reflective beliefs do not arise in isolation. Rather, non-reflective beliefs are the primary stuff from which our minds construct reflective beliefs. Specific mental tools generate non-reflective beliefs relevant to a given domain but then more general mental processes draw upon available non-reflective beliefs to form reflective beliefs. Returning to opossums and raccoons, if I were asked if a raccoon is more similar to an opossum or to a cow, I would be forced to form a reflective belief. If I had never considered these taxonomic relations, without conscious awareness of what I was doing, I would *read off* my non-reflective belief. In absence of salient, consciously accessible reasons to the contrary, I would simply adopt the non-reflective belief (raccoons more similar to opossums) as my reflective belief. This process of *reading off* mental tool outputs is the primary mode of reflective belief formation.[7]

Not every reflective belief arises from the output of just one mental tool. Some find support or counter-support from a number of mental tools. For instance, if I observe a boy run into a room, turn right avoiding a step-stool on the floor, then turn left and collide with his brother's carefully built model tower, I might form the belief that the boy wanted to topple his brother's tower. Why? Because his zig-zagging motion violates a purely mechanical (non-reflective) explanation of his action, the Agency Detection Device registers this action as self-initiated and goal directed, and hence, intentional. Theory of Mind tells me that intended actions arise from beliefs and desires. He wanted to do what he did. These non-reflective beliefs converge upon the reflective belief that the boy wanted to topple his brother's tower. In general, the more different non-reflective beliefs that converge on a particular reflective candidate belief, the more likely the reflective belief becomes held.

---

and cultural context yields a fuller account of thought and behaviour than either factor independently.

7. Boyer (2001) makes a similar argument. This tight relationship between non-reflective and reflective beliefs means that agreement between the two is likely to be common.

Certainly means of over-riding non-reflective beliefs sometimes become available. Most simply, we may "consider the evidence" for a given belief candidate. But the evidence (if available) is always filtered and shaped by the operation of mental tools. We never have direct access to evidence but only processed evidence—memories.[8] When asked "how many colors are in a rainbow?" I might recall the last time I saw a rainbow and what it looked like. These memories have already been influenced by non-reflective beliefs. Memory for a rainbow is really memory for how our perceptual and conceptual systems interpreted the visual stimulation. Cumulative memories of this sort impact what we learned about rainbows in science classes, perhaps rendering the actual nature of rainbows less salient than our perceptual experience.

To summarize, mental tools automatically generate tacit, non-reflective beliefs all the time. Reflective beliefs typically come from the cumulative weight of non-reflective beliefs converging on the same candidate belief. The more non-reflective beliefs that converge on a single idea, the more likely the idea becomes a reflectively held belief. Put another way, the more outputs from various mental tools that are captured by a proposition, the more likely that proposition is to be reflectively believed. Memories, already shaped by non-reflective beliefs, may contribute to the credibility of the belief as well. Without salient reasons for disregarding or overriding the non-reflective beliefs, they become reflectively held. This process takes place whenever conditions demand we form a reflective belief. Consequently, the bulk of explicitly believing we do comes from the non-conscious, automatic functions of mental tools in our minds.

This critical role of mental tools generating non-reflective beliefs applies to religious beliefs. Any account of why people believe in gods should start with how well such beliefs are supported by the non-reflective beliefs generated by naturally-occurring mental tools. Not all religious beliefs are anchored to non-reflective beliefs and arise because of them. For instance, that the Christian God is believed to be a trinity or non-temporal has little or no non-reflective foundation. Nevertheless, foundational religious beliefs such as the existence of gods that are intentional beings with beliefs, desires, and perceptual systems that guide their activities have a firm non-reflective foundation as I sketch below.

---

8. Even the claim of a science teacher at the moment of our attempt to form a reflective belief is only accessible as the interpreted memory of what was just said. What was said has already been processed by our auditory perceptual systems, our language processing systems, and any higher-order semantic processing relevant to the topic of the utterance. There is no such thing as pure experience from which to draw.

Why People Believe in Gods

In brief, people believe in gods because gods gain tremendous support from the natural and ordinary operation of mental tools. Note that because mental tools and their processing biases arise primarily as a consequence of biological endowment plus essentially universal features of human environments, the factors that prompt belief in gods in Melanesia are the same as those that prompt belief in Scandinavia. Below I sketch several ways in which god concepts receive this support. The first way concerns how god concepts are *minimally counterintuitive*.

Minimally Counterintuitive (MCI) Concepts

Recall the principle that the more non-reflective beliefs with which an idea agrees, the more likely it is to be embraced reflectively. Another way of expressing this is that concepts that are largely *intuitive* are generally more plausible. By *intuitive* here I mean conforming to intuitive expectations generated by mental tools. Conversely, concepts that are highly *counterintuitive* (again, in this technical sense) tend to be less plausible.

At first blush it might seem that god concepts are highly counterintuitive, but this is not necessarily the case. As Pascal Boyer has observed, most religious beliefs held by ordinary folk in real time thinking and problem solving are largely intuitive (Boyer, 1994, 2001). A statue that hears prayers may only involve a simple transfer of mental properties to an artifact. Except for this one transfer of property, the artifact meets ordinary intuitive expectations for artifacts (that is, non-reflective beliefs), and the mind of the statue meets ordinary non-reflective beliefs about minds. Anthropologists often come across artifacts that hear prayers but not artifacts that hear prayers not yet uttered or hear prayers no matter where you are or hear prayers but wholly misunderstand them, and so on. Such concepts would be highly counterintuitive. Similarly, ancestor-spirits, an extremely widespread form of god concept, seems to meet intuitive assumptions for people, except they do not have a material body. Compared to how massively counterintuitive concepts could be, successful religious concepts tend to be rather intuitive. They conform to non-reflective beliefs governing the sorts of things that they are—their intuitive ontology. Hence, general plausibility is maintained. But being only slightly or *minimally counterintuitive* provides god concepts with another asset: facilitated transmission.

For an idea to be "religious" or "cultural" it must be shared. If only one person has a belief in a particular superhuman agent, that is not a religious belief but an idiosyncratic one or an oddity. But when a group of people share the same beliefs in superhuman agents, then we have religious belief. Consequently, a crucial consideration pertaining to belief in gods is why some ideas or beliefs spread better than others do from person to person. If people remember and communicate ideas about a given god, that god will be more likely to be believed in than gods that are not remembered or communicated.

A critical factor affecting whether concepts become remembered and transmitted is their complexity. Concepts that are too complex cannot be easily remembered or communicated. But "complexity" is too vague a measure. Isn't the concept "dog" rather complex when one considers the amount of information packed into the label? More precisely, then, concepts that satisfy most mental tools' expectations or biases are most easily remembered and transmitted. That is, concepts that are largely intuitive spread well. Because the concept *dog* fits Naïve Biology's expectations on living things, dogs are readily remembered. Likewise, if I were to tell you about a dog that is like other dogs but the size of a small horse, you would probably find the concept easy to grasp, remember, and tell to someone else. An unusually large dog still fits Naïve Biology's expectations relevant to dogs.

Concepts that too greatly violate intuitive expectations generated by mental tools would be difficult to understand, remember, and communicate at a later time. For instance, a dog that experiences time backwards, is born of a rhino mated with a bullfrog, sustains itself on graphite, speaks Latin, and changes into cheese on Thursdays would be a difficult concept to transmit faithfully. Such a concept's primary limitation is that it so greatly violates mental tools' generated expectations (non-reflective beliefs) about dogs, that the conceptual structure of *dog* is undermined. We no longer have a portable concept but a laundry list of features that do not seem to hang together. Such a concept (if it can be called a concept) is massively counterintuitive—counterintuitive in the technical sense that it violates intuitive assumptions or non-reflective beliefs.[9]

But, as experiments have shown, not every counterintuitive concept is such a poor candidate for successful transmission (Boyer & Ramble, 2001). Those that violate a small number of intuitive assumptions can actually make for very strong candidates. Concepts that meet most non-reflective beliefs, but violate just a small number (e.g., one or two at a time) have been called minimally counterintuitive (MCI) concepts (Barrett, 2004; Barrett & Nyhof,

---

9. Science and theology both generate numerous massively counterintuitive concepts. Being counterintuitive in this technical sense does not imply being false, fictitious, or even unusual.

2001). A dog that speaks Spanish would be a minimally counterintuitive concept. A dog that gives birth to kittens would be MCI. A dog that can never die would be MCI. Such concepts enjoy good conceptual integrity and as such are easily remembered, recalled, and shared. Further, the counterintuitive feature may help the concepts to stand out against a backdrop of more mundane concepts, hence improving their salience and the attention devoted to remembering them. Experiments show that MCI concepts are transmitted more faithfully than ordinary or simply unusual ones (Barrett & Nyhof, 2001; Boyer & Ramble, 2001).

Note that whether or not a concept is *counterintuitive* in this technical sense is largely or entirely independent of cultural context. As described above, our mental tools function the way they do by virtue of our being members of our species and the sort of world in which we find ourselves. Hence, the non-reflective beliefs they generate remain essentially uniform across cultural context, as does whether a concept is counterintuitive.

But not all minimally counterintuitive concepts are strong candidates to be religious concepts (or any other cultural concepts, for that matter). Take, for example, a potato that vanishes whenever you look at it versus a potato that talks. Both potatoes are counterintuitive but the vanishing potato scores poorly in terms of *inferential potential*. That is, some concepts more readily generate inferences, explanations, and predictions than others do. Some concepts excite a greater range of mental tools and some mental tools more completely. Consequently, they touch on more human concerns and, due to the convergence of many non-reflective beliefs, carry more reflective credibility. Even if I had some evidence of a potato that vanishes whenever someone looks at it, not much follows from its discovery. A potato that talks? Now that sets the imagination running a bit, especially at suppertime.

Items such as vanishing potatoes do not populate religious belief systems. Rather religious belief systems center on counterintuitive *intentional agents*. Unlike other sorts of counterintuitive properties, the addition of (e.g., statues that hear prayers) or modification of (e.g., a person that reads minds) agency generates rich inferential potential.

Advantages for Agent Concepts

Compared with other minimally counterintuitive concepts, agents have more inferential potential—ability to inject explanation or meaning into a broad array of human concerns—and feed a large number of inferential systems or mental tools. I amplify this claim in three areas: the detection of agency; the role of agents in reasoning about fortune, misfortune, and morality; and the fate of agents after death.

Agency Detection

The mental tool responsible for agency detection is the Agency Detection Device (ADD). Research using moving dots on computer screens and other artificial displays, (e.g., Rochat, Morgan & Carpenter, 1997; Scholl & Tremoulet, 2000) supports the notion that the ADD is touchy or hyperactive. That is, given ambiguous inputs, ADD tends to find agency, even in situations where further reflection might lead to a different evaluation. To emphasize this hypersensitive character of ADD, I sometimes refer to it as the Hypersensitive Agency Detection Device or HADD.[10]

HADD and Objects

Anthropologist Stewart Guthrie has suggested that our tendency to find agency (especially human-like agency) around us has arisen for survival reasons. Historically, our best opportunities for survival and reproduction and our biggest threats were other agents. So, we had better be able to detect agents. Better to guess that the sound in the bushes is an agent (such as a person or tiger) than assume it isn't and become lunch. If it turns out you were too cautious (about the wind blowing in the brush, for instance), not much is lost (Guthrie, 1993). This hypersensitive agency detection device (or HADD) produces non-reflective beliefs that agency is present and then the Theory of Mind tool generates non-reflective beliefs about beliefs, desires, perceptions, and so forth of the alleged agent (Barrett, 2004).

It is HADD that makes us non-reflectively believe that our computers deliberately try to frustrate us, that strange sounds in a still house are evidence of intruders, and that light patterns on a television screen are people or animals with beliefs and desires. But more relevant to religious belief are situations in which a sheet on a clothesline or a wisp of mist gets recognized as a

---

10. Do not take this description to entail that HADD, or any of the other mental tools discussed, is error-prone. Quantifying just how accurate HADD is at detecting agency is dependent upon some principled (and agreed upon) criteria for where agency is and is not—criteria likely to remain unavailable. Perhaps the best available way to judge accuracy for HADD or any other intuitive system is by consideration of how often an individual explicitly over-rides his or her own non-reflective beliefs. But even on this count, it is likely HADD's 'accuracy rate' is very high.

ghost or spirit. This function of HADD, identifying objects as agents, has begun to receive a fair amount of attention from cognitive scientists (for a review see Scholl & Tremoulet, 2000). Receiving less attention are two other functions of HADD: registering an event as being caused by agency, and recognizing an object or pattern as being the consequence of intentional agency.

HADD and Events

An example of an event that may trigger agent detection might be the following. When walking through a reportedly haunted castle, a decorative sword falls and narrowly misses cutting off your arm, just after you scoffed at the idea of ghosts. (Foolish mortal!) Given that a physical object appeared to have moved in a way that was not readily explained by the non-reflective beliefs of Naïve Physics (because inanimate objects cannot move themselves), and the movement seemed to be goal directed (to answer your skeptical comment), your HADD might detect agency at play. HADD searches for a candidate agent. As the sword is not an agent in its own right, a non-reflective belief that an unseen agent must have moved the sword arises from HADD. Connecting this non-reflective belief in present agency to the reflective proposition that ghosts inhabit the castle makes acquisition of a reflective belief in a ghost perfectly natural given the circumstances. The sword falling is an event that HADD might detect as agency.

HADD and Traces

In addition to objects (such as wisps of fog or computers) and events (such as falling swords), HADD may find agency in *traces*, those physical changes that an agent may have left behind. Mysterious writing, tracks, or arrangements of objects could count as traces of agency. Crop circles, the intricate geometric patterns mysteriously left in crop fields around the world, present an excellent example of a trace that HADD typically identifies as caused by intentional agency. Indeed, crop circles are so compelling as agentive traces that the debate typically focuses only on what kind of agent (e.g., communicative space aliens or human pranksters) left the trace.

Contextual Factors

Do not let my tag "hypersensitive" on the Agency Detection Device lead you to believe ADD is always equally likely to detect agency. Rather, thresholds for HADD to register a non-reflective belief in agency vary as a function of context and personal relevance. In brief, contexts that possess more *urgency* cause

ADD to be more sensitive. By *urgency* I mean the salience of survival demands. ADD is more likely to find agency while you walk through the park at twilight when you already suspect an axe murderer is loose in your local park. The context has high urgency and so HADD invites more false-positives. "Better safe than sorry" definitely applies. Similarly, a very hungry subsistence hunter probably has a touchier ADD than the well-sated recreational hunter. Context matters.

HADD and Religious Events

Brute survival concerns do not exhaust the range of contextual factors that influence the likelihood of HADD generating an agency belief. The salience of explicit, reflective expectations for witnessing agency increases agency detection as well. Told that a particular religious event (e.g., a ritual or petitionary prayer) will cause a god to act in a particular way, I would be primed to find seek confirming evidence of the god's activity.

McCauley and Lawson observe that many religious rituals in which a god or representative of a god performs an action (e.g., as when a priest marries a couple, or a minister baptizes a person, or an elder initiates a youth), the ritual and surrounding trappings tend to be more elaborate and more emotional. One reason offered for this correlation is that the heightened sensory pageantry and resulting emotional arousal impresses upon the participants and observers that the gods are really acting because of or through the ritual (McCauley & Lawson, 2002). This observation leads me to speculate that the additional sensory pageantry excites HADD (perhaps through general arousal) and, in some cases, provides more potential events and traces that might be attributed to the gods.

HADD's Ability to Reinforce Belief

It might be objected that the Agency Detection Device's hypersensitivity sometimes erroneously registers agency around us, but we quickly override those non-reflective beliefs. Consequently, might HADD play only a very minor role in reinforcing beliefs in superhuman agents? Exactly how much of a role HADD plays is an empirical matter demanding further research. But that HADD's non-reflective beliefs frequently get overridden does not considerably mitigate HADD's probable role in encouraging beliefs in superhuman agency.

Consider the falling sword again. Someone with such a HADD-experience might initially think, "Ghost!" and run from the hallway. Upon calming down, the person might, for a number of other reasons, decide that he or she is not prepared to believe in ghosts in this case after all. Perhaps a return to the scene demonstrates that walking on that stretch of hallway obviously causes vibrations that radiate up the wall and could have shaken the sword loose. Further, the person discovers that the ghost that allegedly haunts the castle turns out to be a well-known pacifist that has never been reported to harm or even deliberately frighten anyone but instead whistles cheerful Irving Berlin tunes. These additional pieces of information might lead to an abandonment of this case of agency detection (even if one believes in ghosts).

But suppose that person, a day later, returns to the same castle and tells a friend that "of course there aren't any stupid ghosts in this castle" and then the person inexplicably trips over a bare stretch of floor. That person is more likely to return to non-reflective and reflective belief in ghosts than after the first HADD experience. Even though a single HADD experience might be overridden and not result in a reflective belief, these experiences will be remembered and cumulatively lend plausibility to reflective belief.

To illustrate this dynamic in another way, compare three people:

1. A person walks through a wood after having been told that forest spirits dwell in it. Something ambiguous happens prompting this person to have HADD experiences. The experiences will be likely to reinforce the belief in forest spirits.

2. A second person walks through a wood and has the same HADD experiences as the first person but does not successfully identify an agent that accounts for them, and so does not form a reflective belief in an agent. But after the fact, the person hears that forest spirits dwell in that stretch of woods. Memories for the HADD experiences might be triggered and evaluated as evidence for reflective belief.

3. A third person walks through the wood, having heard that it is populated by forest spirits but has no HADD experiences at all.

Clearly, the first two people are considerably more likely than the third to form a reflective belief in forest spirits. HADD would play a pivotal role in belief formation or encouragement.

It might be that HADD rarely generates specific beliefs in ghosts, spirits, and gods by itself, and hence does not serve as the origin of these concepts. Nevertheless, HADD is likely to play a critical role in spreading such beliefs and perpetuating them. A belief in forest spirits would be likely to disappear if the community of adherence never had HADD experiences that suggested forest spirit activity. Ritual systems typically presume that the superhuman agents act and that their actions are somehow detectable. Christians devoted to their faith are those who (at least occasionally) see events and traces as consequences of God's activity. That is, members of the community have HADD experiences that become identified with God's intentions.

Connecting Agency with Fortune, Misfortune, and Morality

Detecting events as the consequence of agency receives even more importance because of the way human minds readily connect some intentional actions with other intuitive systems. For instance, the agency detected by HADD receives processing by the Theory of Mind (ToM) regarding beliefs, desires, and intentions of the agent, that may be used as inputs by devices concerned with social exchanges. To consider one such connection, people's minds have a tendency to link events representing great fortune or misfortune with a mental tool we may call Intuitive Morality. Somehow, gods get pulled into the mix, too. Religious systems commonly refine and enforce moral intuitions, and explain great fortune or misfortune as related to the activity of superhuman agents. Why is this connection between morality and religion so recurrent?

First, humans have a strong propensity to search the environment for explanation and meaning. Causal reasoning is one of the activities at which our species excels. Mental tools such as Naïve Physics and Naïve Biology make first attempts at explaining many events, but when these explanatory systems fail to match non-reflective assumptions with the evidence at hand, our minds default to social or intentional causation. This is where HADD, Theory of Mind, and other mental tools kick in. We have a tendency to invoke social or intentional causes when obvious mechanical or biological causes appear insufficient or absent.

Second, salient events regarded as fortune or misfortune inevitably happen. People experience inexplicably good crops or famine, great wealth or sudden death. Intuitively, such unusual events demand an explanation. Reasoning that the event has arisen merely by chance is no substitute for an explanation.

Gods enter the story because of having particular sorts of minimally counterintuitive properties. Many have unusual powers or invisibility that would allow them to bring about the fortune or misfortune without being directly detected. Perhaps more importantly, their invisibility or super-knowledge gives them *strategic information* about what people do in secret. Hence, the gods could be acting to punish or reward moral failings that no human could know about. In this way, fortune or misfortune can be easily understood as the action of an agent, motivated by moral concerns. These moral concerns, too, are cross-culturally recurrent because of another mental tool: Intuitive Morality (Boyer, 2001).

Intuitive Morality generates non-reflective beliefs about what constitutes moral behavior. One author has suggested that from an early age, children appear intuitively to differentiate between moral codes and social conventions (Turiel, 1998). Though the precise catalog of moral intuitions is a matter of continued empirical research and debate, it appears as though individuals and groups converge upon general rules of behavior that typically frown on murder, adultery, theft, deception, treachery, and cowardice, especially as directed toward one's own group. These moral intuitions may have a different quality to people than mere regularities of behavior or useful guidelines that might be amended at a later date. Rather, people regard them as immutable (Boyer, 2001; Lewis, 1947; see also Katz, 2000 for suggested evolutionary origins of morality).

Couple with Intuitive Morality otherwise inexplicable fortune or misfortune, and an important explanatory niche arises that gods fill naturally. By working in concert with these non-reflective beliefs, god concepts gain reflective plausibility. The more non-reflective beliefs that converge upon a candidate reflective belief, in this case the belief that gods exist and act, the more likely it is to become reflectively believed.

Naturally, the intuitiveness of these relations helps motivate a wide range of religious actions that appeal to gods to bring about or prevent fortune or misfortune. If gods can bring about fortune and misfortune, perhaps we can appeal to them to bring us fortune and prevent misfortune for us. Such a notion is an entirely intuitive extension of belief in gods and our ordinary ideas about social causation and exchange.

Agency after Death

A tendency to detect agency readily, even given ambiguous inputs, dovetails with intuitive assumptions about death. Some recent research suggests that early-developing biological reasoning in children readily accommodates cessation of life. Biological functions cease. But children's understanding of minds allows and even encourages the idea that mental functions continue after death (Bering, 2002; Bering, Hernandez-Blasi, Bjorklund, 2005). Data from children and adults in different cultural settings suggest that two of our mental tools, Naïve Biology and Theory of Mind, offer conflicting non-reflective beliefs concerning death—perhaps especially the death of a loved one (Bering, 2002, Boyer, 2001).

When someone dies, Naïve Biology registers the non-reflective beliefs that biological functions cease. The person will no longer move, no longer require nourishment, and so forth. Theory of Mind, however, readily generates inferences about mental states, beliefs and desires, without biological considerations. Accustomed to reasoning without a body present, Theory of Mind finds the physical absence of a person of little consequence. This intuitive dualism non-reflectively makes people sympathetic to agency after death (Bloom, 2004).[11]

Couple hyperactive agency detection with a Theory of Mind tool that continues to treat the deceased person's mind as functioning, and you have a recipe for detecting agency after death. Traces or events agreeable to what the deceased might have wanted or might have done (via Theory of Mind activity) might be attributed to the deceased person. But such detection by HADD need not occur very often. Once an ancestor-ghost concept has been floated as a candidate reflective belief, its resonance with intuitive mental tools' associated non-reflective beliefs enhances its credibility and facilitates its transmission. These observations account for the robust recurrence of ancestor-ghost beliefs across cultures.

Why People Believe in Particular Divine Attributes

Thus far I have sketched an account of why people believe in religious entities generally. Belief in gods is encouraged by the dynamics of a number of intuitive inference systems I call *mental tools*. Minimally counterintuitive concepts enjoy a transmission advantage over other comparable concepts. Agent concepts in particular have tremendous inferential potential and get picked up by a number of receptive systems concerning morality, fortune, misfortune, and death. In the next section I will expand this "naturalness of religious belief" thesis to consider how belief in the divine attributes of a super god such as those in Judaism, Islam, and Christianity might, too, receive special support from cognitive structures.

So far I have emphasized factors that increase the likelihood of beliefs being spread *horizontally*—from person to person within and across groups. God concepts enjoy these transmission benefits. But super gods also benefit from cognitive developmental factors that boost *vertical transmission*—spread from one generation to the next.

Specifically, super knowledge, super perception, super power (especially to create natural things), and immortality all benefit from the operation of men-

---

11. Jesse Bering offers a different interpretation of the same data. He suggests that embracing the cessation of mental activities is difficult because of our inability to simulate not thinking or not feeling (2002). Bering may be correct that simulation difficulties play a key role. Conclusive data distinguishing these interpretations are not yet available. Nevertheless, both the conflicting beliefs theory and the simulation theory arrive at the same conclusion that mental activities continuing after death is very much intuitive.

tal tools in childhood development. In all four of these cases, the relevant mental tools seem to assume super abilities for all agents and then, through the course of development, restrict these abilities for people and other natural agents. Because children seem to assume that agents have super properties on these four dimensions (knowledge, perception, power, and mortality), they need not learn these divine attributes so much as have them simply affirmed or left unchallenged (Barrett & Richert, 2003).

Super Knowledge

In research concerning children's developing Theory of Mind, data strongly support the position that before around five-years of age (and sometimes later) children assume that everyone's beliefs about the world are infallible (e.g., Wellman, Cross & Watson, 2001). That is, if a three-year-old child knows that he has a coin in his pocket, he assumes that his mother, too, will know that he has a coin in his pocket. He will fail to consider that his mother might not have had the prerequisite perceptual information to form such a belief. Colleagues and I replicated this finding using versions of a paradigm that has come to be called a *false-belief task* (Barrett, Richert & Driesenga, 2001; Knight, Sousa, Barrett & Atran, 2004).

In one such study, experimenters showed three- through six-year-old American Protestant children a closed cracker box (Barrett, Richert & Driesenga, 2001). Experimenters then asked children what they thought was inside the box. Familiar with that sort of container, children all answered "crackers." After being shown the box actually contained rocks, the box was closed and the experimenter asked the children what their absent mothers would think was inside the box if they saw it for the first time. Consistent with previous research, the vast majority of three- and four-year-olds reported that their mother would think that the box contained rocks. But more than eighty percent of five- and six-year-olds reported that their mothers would think the box contained crackers. That is, not until age five did children tend to understand that their mothers would have a false belief. Asked about other potential observers (e.g., bear, elephant, tree), children answered essentially identically as for their mother. Four-year-olds assumed infallible beliefs but five-year-olds understood false beliefs. God proved an exception. When asked what God would think was inside the closed cracker box, children at all ages examined showed the same strong tendency to say that God would know the box contained rocks. That is, three- or six-year-olds "accurately" (theologically speaking) predicted God's infallible knowledge.

Experimenters replicated these sorts of results using different theory of mind tasks and different populations (Barrett, Newman & Richert, 2003,

Knight, et al, 2004). Importantly, Knight et al showed that Mayan children living on the Yucatan Peninsula differentiated among the probable knowledge of different deities in a way that closely mapped on to adult theological conceptions, providing additional evidence that children are not crude anthropomorphizers or simply confused. Cumulatively, these studies suggest that children find a super knowing god readily comprehended and used to generate predictions while they still struggle with understanding the boundaries on human (or animal) knowledge and beliefs. Children may find super knowing gods relatively easy to understand because of Theory of Mind's default assumption that agents are super knowing. Children must learn when this default does not apply with humans, but no such lessons need be learned for understanding God.

Super Perception

A similar account has emerged from research concerning children's understanding of others' perception. Three- and four-year-olds tend to assume others perceive objects as they themselves perceive them, whereas five- and six-year-olds tend to understand that this is not always the case. But children of all these ages tend to represent God as having perceptual access to everything (including smells, sounds, and sights) (Richert & Barrett, 2005). As with knowledge, children's default is to assume full perceptual access for other agents and through development they pare back these generous allowances. They need not pare back for super perceiving gods.

Super Power

Since Piaget, developmentalists have noted children's tendency to over-estimate the strength and power of adults, treating them as god-like (Piaget, 1929). I am aware of no recent data that challenge this claim. Rather, at least with regard to creative power, a formidable amount of research supports the view that children intuitively regard gods as the designers and creators of the natural world. As with knowledge and perception, children begin with high expectations of intentional agents and must then learn the limitations of humans. As the concept of a creator god or omnipotent god requires no comparable boundary learning, these developmental biases make these types of god concepts readily adopted by children.

From childhood, people are very sensitive to evidence of purposefulness in the environment and in objects. In fact, there may be a tendency to over-attribute design even when evidence is thin—a "promiscuous teleology" akin to hypersensitive agency detection (Kelemen, 2005). Deborah Kelemen has found that children tend to attribute design and purpose not only to biological kinds but also other natural kinds such as rocks. Rocks are pointy, for instance, to keep from being sat upon rather than because of some series of natural or random factors (Kelemen, 1999a, 1999b).

Not surprisingly, then, Margaret Evans' research on children's relative preferences for different origins accounts of animals has shown that children eagerly embrace creationist accounts and are very resistant to evolutionary accounts, even if their parents and schools advance evolutionary origins (Evans, 2001).

As mental tools encourage people to find design in the environment, the notion of a creator god receives tremendous intuitive, non-reflective support. It is no wonder that creator god concepts are so widespread. In fact, these factors are so powerful as to lead some to suggest that children are intuitive theists (Kelemen, 2005).

Immortality

As described above, two competing mental tools that generate conflicting non-reflective beliefs regarding human death complicate children's understanding of mortality. Not surprisingly, then, children begin understanding God's immortality before they have a robust understanding of human mortality. The default assumption that minds are not tied to biological death makes God (who is not a biological being) easily understood as immortal.

The Developmental Privileges of Some God Concepts

These biases in mental tools regarding knowledge, perception, creative power, and mortality provide additional transmission advantages to god concepts that have the divine attributes of being super knowing, super perceiving, a creator, and immortal. Once such concepts are introduced into a population, all else being equal, they are likely to spread well both horizontally and vertically. Perhaps this, in part, explains the success of Christian, Jewish, and Muslim god concepts.

Do not, however, misunderstand me as arguing that all attributes of the Abrahamic God have more "fitness" than those of other god concepts. Being non-temporal or a Trinity, for instance, are probably liabilities rather than assets. Further, I do not argue that strict monotheism is favored in any way. Neither the theory nor the data support such a claim. After all, even in the great monotheisms devils, angels, ghosts, and other superhuman agents (i.e., gods or minimally counterintuitive agents) populate adherents' belief systems.

Belief and Religious Actions

Belief in gods, and the motivation to act that such beliefs produce, changes ordinary action into religious action. Consequently, having some grasp of the factors that prompt religious belief serves as precondition for any cognitive treatment of religious ritual or any other classes of religious action.

Now that the naturalness of religious beliefs has been described, the reasons religious actions (such as rituals) arise might be obvious. Gods possess powers and knowledge that would prove useful for us in achieving our own ends. Having the gods against us could be disastrous.

Getting intentional agents to share their resources with us happens to be yet another gift that human possess by virtue of our cognitive endowment. We understand social relations and exchange very well and have non-reflective beliefs about how they should operate (Cosmides, Tooby & Barkow, 1992). It is no surprise then, that under the theological veneer, many religious rituals and petitions look very similar to how we would appeal to another human to get what we want (Barrett, 2001; Barrett & Lawson, 2001). Intuitively we expect that if we give the gods what they want, they will give us what we want. If we frustrate the desires of the gods, the gods might retaliate against us. Crimes are punished. Good deeds are rewarded.

Were gods represented as having wholly different sort of minds from those we assume humans have, we might expect a much more diverse range of religious actions, or even belief systems with no religious actions. But because gods' minds intuitively make sense to us, we naturally try to engage them through communication, verbal (e.g., prayer) and symbolic (e.g., ritual). Unsurprisingly, then, religious actions are not wholly invented but demonstrate predictable structural regularities because of their reliance on regular human cognition (Lawson & McCauley, 1990; McCauley & Lawson, 2002; Pyysiäinen, 2004; Whitehouse, 2001, 2004).

But religious actions do not merely represent responses to religious belief. Rather, they often play a critical role in reinforcing and transmitting religious belief. Recall that the greater the number of mental tools that provide outputs consistent with a reflective belief candidate, the more likely it is to become believed. These outputs might include memories relevant to any particular belief such as the thoughts and feelings associated with related religious actions. Salient explicit reasons or evidence (including memories) may count for or against an explicit belief. Religious actions often provide these outputs that fortify religious beliefs. Briefly, I offer four dynamics impacting belief via religious actions: social conformity, dissonance reduction, explicit transmission, and HADD experiences.

Social Testimony and Conformity Pressure

Corporate religious observances of all types implicitly communicate mutual commitment to the same belief system. When everyone else affirms the existence and activities of a deity through participation in a ceremony, rite, or ritual, those behaviors join the corpus of evidence in support of belief. It may be the case that a large proportion of participants harbor doubts but submit to the observance nevertheless. This submission creates the impression of more steadfast belief than might actually exist (initially). When people (implicitly or explicitly) tabulate reasons for belief, the non-reflective beliefs find themselves joined by the observation that "everyone else" believes. Such testimony plays no trivial role in reinforcing already intuitively plausible beliefs.

Dissonance Reduction

Social psychologists have shown that although attitudes and beliefs direct behaviors, it is also true that actions influence beliefs and attitudes as well. Once someone acts in a way consistent with a particular attitude or belief, that person is likely to revise his or her beliefs to be consistent with that action. Why? One way to explain this well-documented phenomenon is that the conflict between attitudes and action produces "cognitive dissonance" or internal conflict (Festinger, 1957). This conflict implicitly demands resolution. As the behavior, already committed, cannot be changed, the attitude must be changed to justify the behavior. (Why did I treat John so generously? I must like him very much.) But an explanation may be offered in terms of the nature of belief sketched above. In considering a candidate belief (e.g., I like John very much), a mind searches for supporting or disconfirming mental tool outputs. One salient output is the memory of having done something related to the belief (e.g., acting generously toward John). That memory helps tip the ledger in favor of a particular reflective belief.

In the context of religious actions, having performed a religious action, even if just acting as if one believed, may provide another piece of evidence in favor of the religious belief. For instance, in religious communities that demand converts to proselytize, the act of having proselytized may be counted in favor of belief. (I would not have done something so socially uncomfortable unless I really believed in what I was doing.)

Explicit Transmission

A common function or feature of corporate religious events is the explicit statement of theological beliefs. As Harvey Whitehouse has observed, the frequency with which religious leaders present some doctrinal teaching seems excessive for merely communicating ideas (Whitehouse, 2004). Among the number of consequences of this repetition, Whitehouse notes that this repetition is sure to help in the communication of concepts that are more than minimally counterintuitive. Concepts that are more difficult, cumbersome, or under-supported by mental tools require additional explicit or reflective reasons before they become plausible. That Jesus' death by crucifixion makes atonement for our sin, for instance, is an idea requiring a fair amount of unpacking to make it understood enough to be believed (in any meaningful sense). Further, explicitly drawing out implications of counterintuitive beliefs may be necessary to connect them with various mundane life experiences, other experiences and, hence, the exercise of more ordinary non-reflective beliefs, thereby improving plausibility. So, for example, Jesus' crucifixion might be compared to other cases of one person suffering or dying in the place of another so that it becomes more familiar, easily processed, and more connected to analogous ordinary occurrences. Frequent repetition keeps ideas and relations salient in listeners' minds.

Suppose a theological tradition advances the idea that at death, spirits leave bodies but then remain among and around their neighbors and family until they have communicated important truths about life to the living. Once successful, the spirits depart to another world. This modestly complex piece of doctrine would probably be a non-starter without its intuitive connections to mental tools' tendency to see minds continuing after death. Nevertheless, the details beyond simple life-after-death do not receive any obvious intuitive support. Consequently, such an idea is unlikely to transmit well and gain many successful adherents without other factors contributing. Conducting funeral rites consistent with this doctrine would help reinforce belief. Further, frequent explicit instruction about the fate of spirits after death and explanations that draw out implications of this doctrine would be likely to promote belief. For example, arguing that the end of grief is explained by the spirit no longer being present to keep its passing in the forefront of our minds would help connect the doctrine with real life experiences.

HADD Experiences

Perhaps a more powerful way that religious actions encourage belief is by providing opportunities for gods to be seen to act. Many religious acts serve as petitions for divine action. People pray or conduct rituals in order to express requests. These acts, which might be highly emotional, focus attention on potential divine activity. That is, agency detection is encouraged.

Consider the difference between someone who works hard hunting and has a successful hunt and someone who works hard, prays for help, and then has a successful hunt. The one who prayed is more likely to search for confirming evidence that the petitioned god contributed to success. The good hunt reaffirms divine activity. Psychologists call this strong tendency to attend selectively to evidence for preconceptions *confirmation bias* (Gilovich, 1991).

Similarly, consider the family which, returning from a funeral where the immortality of the spirit has been reaffirmed, finds that the deceased's favorite mug is out of place (they believe). Because HADD has been primed to find evidence of the deceased person's continued agency, something as simple as the placement of a mug could trigger agency detection. The preceding rite played an important role in this detection.

It does happen that religious activities may undermine religious belief as well. Whitehouse records the events of a splinter group's ritual attempts to bring back the ancestors. These rituals fail to bring about their determined ends and subsequently, the splinter group dissolves (Whitehouse, 1995). Especially dangerous are rituals that lack what McCauley and Lawson call *conceptual control*—the ability to withstand evidence of ritual failure (McCauley & Lawson, 2002). Rituals intended to bring about specific, easily measured ends run the risk of being demonstrable and indisputable failures. On the other hand, rituals that join people in marriage, forgive sins, welcome people into a community, or officially make a youth into an adult have good conceptual control. Ritual systems with good conceptual control may be an asset to the survival of accompanying belief systems whereas poor conceptual control may be a liability. As their central rituals do not serve practical, utilitarian aims, Islam and Christianity seem to be systems with strong conceptual control, perhaps partly explaining their remarkable spread and tenacity.

Conclusion

Beliefs generally form through the operation of implicit mental tools feeding their outputs to cognitive systems responsible for forming reflective beliefs. Beliefs consistent with the biases of mental tools seem plausible or intuitive on a reflective level and become believed.

By virtue of being minimally counterintuitive, god concepts transmit easily and retain general plausibility. By virtue of being agents, gods have tremendous inferential potential. They may be used to explain a broad range of phenomena important to people. This ability for gods to make sense non-reflectively of events in the world encourages belief in them.

Most gods who occupy central positions in religious systems have properties such as mind reading or invisibility that grant them strategic information. Such information allows them to know of the moral triumphs and failings of humans. Consequently, they may be invoked as plausible causes for otherwise inexplicable events such as cases of extreme fortune or misfortune. Death is no exception. Consequently, gods become connected with yet more mental tools that may produce god-consistent non-reflective beliefs.

Super properties of gods, if present, receive further encouragement from early emerging biases in mental tools to favor the attribution to agents of super knowledge, super perception, creative power, and immortality. Children's minds bias them toward understanding these divine properties but they must labor to learn human limitations along these same dimensions. Similarly, mental tools encourage children (and adults) to find design in the natural world. So, the suggestion that a god or gods account for the natural world carries great intuitive plausibility.

Taken as a whole, the way our minds work in historically prevalent natural and social environments prompts us to believe in gods. As intentional beings potentially possessing power and insights valuable to our survival and success, we likewise have motivation to attempt to engage these gods, to communicate and exchange with them. Developing religious actions including ceremonies, rituals, rites, and prayers springs naturally out of our tendencies to socially engage other people. These religious actions in turn fortify belief through conformity pressures, dissonance reductions, communication and persuasion, and prompting more opportunities for detecting gods at work in human affairs.

References

Atran, S. (1995) 'Causal constraints on categories and categorical constraints on biological reasoning across cultures' in Sperber, D., Premack D., & Premack A.J.,(eds.) *Causal Cognition: A multidisciplinary debate*, pp. 205–233. New York: Oxford University Press.

Baron-Cohen, S. (1995) *Mindblindness: An essay on autism and theory of mind*, Cambridge, MA: MIT Bradford.

Barrett, J. L. (1998) 'Cognitive constraints on Hindu concepts of the divine' *Journal for the Scientific Study of Religion, 37*, 608–619.

Barrett, J. L. (2001) 'How ordinary cognition informs petitionary prayer' *Journal of Cognition & Culture, 1*, 259–69.

Barrett, J. L. (2004) Why would anyone believe in God? *Walnut Creek, CA: AltaMira Press.*

Barrett, J.L., & Lawson, E.T. (2001) 'Ritual Intuitions: Cognitive contributions to judgments of ritual efficacy' in *Journal of Cognition & Culture, 1*(2), 183–201.

Barrett, J.L., Newman, R., & Richert, R.A. (2003) 'When seeing does not lead to believing: Children's understanding of the importance of background knowledge for interpreting visual displays' in *Journal of Cognition & Culture, 3*, 91–108.

Barrett, J.L., & Nyhof, M.A. (2001) 'Spreading non-natural concepts: The role of intuitive conceptual structures in memory and transmission of cultural materials' *Journal of Cognition & Culture, 1*, 69–100.

Barrett, J. L., & Richert, R.A. (2003) 'Anthropomorphism or preparedness? Exploring children's concept of God' *Review of Religious Research, 44*, 300–312.

Barrett, J.L., Richert, R.A., & Driesenga, A. (2001) 'God's beliefs versus mother's: The development of non-human agent concepts' *Child Development, 71*, 50–65.

Barrett, J. L. & VanOrman, B. (1996) 'The effects of image use in worship on God concepts' *Journal of Psychology and Christianity, 15*(1), 38–45.

Bering, J. (2002) 'Intuitive conceptions of dead agents' minds: The natural foundations of afterlife beliefs as phenomenological boundary' in *Journal of Cognition & Culture, 2*, 263–308.

Bering, J.M., Hernández-Blasi, C. Bjorklund, D F. (2005) 'The development of 'afterlife' beliefs in secularly and religiously schooled children' *British Journal of Developmental Psychology, 23*, 587–607.

Bloom, P. (2004) *Descartes' Baby: How the Science of Child Development Explains What Makes Us Human*, New York: Basic Books.

Boyer, P. (1994) *The Naturalness of Religious Ideas. A Cognitive Theory of Religion*, Berkeley: University of California Press.

Boyer, P. (2001) *Religion Explained: The Evolutionary Origins of Religious Thought*, New York: Basic Books.

Boyer, P. and Ramble, C. (2001) 'Cognitive templates for religious concepts: Cross-cultural evidence for recall of counter-intuitive representations' *Cognitive Science, 25,* 535–64.

Cosmides, L. Tooby, J. and Barkow, J. (1992) 'Evolutionary psychology and conceptual integration' In J. Barkow, L. Cosmides, & J. Tooby (eds.), *The adapted mind*: Evolutionary psychology and the generation of culture. New York: Oxford University Press.

Evans, E. M. (2001) 'Cognitive and contextual factors in the emergence of diverse belief systems: Creation versus evolution' *Cognitive Psychology, 42,* 217–266.

Festinger, L.(1957) *A Theory of Cognitive Dissonance,* Stanford: Stanford University Press.

Gazzaniga, M.S. Ivry, R.B. Mangun, G.R. (1998) *Cognitive Neurosciences*: The Biology of the Mind New York: W.W. Norton.

Gilovich, T. (1991) *How we know what isn't so: The fallibility of human reason in everyday life,* New York: Free Press.

Guthrie, S.E. (1993) *Faces in the Clouds: A new theory of religion.* New York: Oxford University Press.

Hirschfeld, L.A. (1996) *Race in the Making: Cognition, Culture, and the Child's Construction of Human Kinds,* Cambridge, MA: MIT Press.

Katz, L.D. (ed.) (2000) *Evolutionary origins of morality: Cross-disciplinary perspectives.* Thoverton, UK: Imprint Academic.

Kelemen, D. (1999a) 'Why are rocks pointy? Children's preference for teleological explanations of the natural world' *Developmental Psychology, 35,* 1440–53.

Kelemen, D. (1999b) 'Functions, goals, and intentions: Children's teleological reasoning about objects' *Trends in Cognitive Sciences, 12,* 461–468.

Kelemen, D. (2005) 'Are children "intuitive theists"? Reasoning about purpose and design in nature' *Psychological Science.*

Knight, N. Sousa, P. Barrett, J.L. Atran, S. (2004) 'Children's attributions of beliefs to humans and God: Cross-cultural evidence' *Cognitive Science, 28.*

Lawson, E.T. and McCauley, R.N. (1990) *Rethinking Religion: Connection Cognition and Culture,* Cambridge: Cambridge University Press.

Malley, B. (2004). *How the Bible Works: An Anthropological Study of Evangelical Biblicism*. Walnut Creek, CA: AltaMira.

McCauley, R. N. and Lawson, E. T. (2002) *Bringing Ritual to Mind: Psychological Foundations of Cultural Forms*, Cambridge: Cambridge University Press.

Piaget, J. (1929) *The Child's Conception of the World*, New York: Harcourt Brace.

Pinker, S. (1997) *How the Mind Works*, New York: W. W. Norton & Company.

Pyysiäinen, I. (2001) *How Religion Works: Towards a New Cognitive Science of Religion*, Leiden: Brill.

Pyysiäinen, I. (2004) *Magic, Miracles and Religion: A Scientist's Perspective*, Walnut Creek, CA: AltaMira Press.

Richert, R. A. and Barrett, J.L. (2005) 'Do you see what I see? Young children's assumptions about God's perceptual abilities' *International Journal for the Psychology of Religion*, 15, 283–295.

Rochat, P. Morgan,R. and Carpenter, M. (1997) 'Young infants' sensitivity to movement information specifying social causality' *Cognitive Development*, 12, 537–561.

Scholl, B.J. and Tremoulet, P.D. (2000) 'Perceptual causality and animacy' *Trends in Cognitive Sciences*, 4, 299–308.

Simons,D.J. and Keil, F.C. (1995) 'An abstract to concrete shift in development of biological thought: The insides story' *Cognition*, 56, 129–163.

Slone, D. J. (2004). *Theological Correctness: Why Religious People Believe What They Shouldn't*. New York: Oxford University Press.

Spelke, E. S. Phillips, A. and Woodward, A.L. (1995) 'Infant's knowledge of object motion and human action' In Sperber, D. Premack, D. and Premack, A. J (eds.) *Causal Cognition: A multidisciplinary debate*, pp. 44–78. New York: Oxford University Press.

Spelke, E.S. and Van de Walle, G. (1993) 'Perceiving and reasoning about objects: insights from infants' in Elian, N. Brewer, W. and McCarthy, R (eds.), *Spatial Representation*. New York: Blackwell.

Sperber, D. (1997) 'Intuitive and Reflective Beliefs' *Mind and Language*, 12, 67–83.

Turiel, E. (1998) 'The development of morality' In Damon, W.(ed.), *Handbook of Child Psychology*, (5th ed.) Vol. 3., pp. 863–932.

Wellman, H., Cross, D. and Watson, J. (2001) 'Meta-analysis of theory of mind development: The truth about false-belief' *Child Development*, *72(3)*, 655–684.

Whitehouse, H. (1995) *Inside the Cult: Religious innovation and transmission in Papua New Guinea*, Oxford: Clarendon Press.

Whitehouse, H. (2000) Arguments *and Icons: Divergent modes of religiosity*, Oxford: Oxford University Press.

Whitehouse, H. (2004*) Modes of Religiosity: a cognitive theory of religious transmission*, Walnut Creek, CA: AltaMira Press.

Whitehouse, H. and McCauley, R. N. (eds.) (2005) *Mind and Religion: Psychological and Cognitive Foundations of Religiosity*, Walnut Creek, CA: AltaMira Press.

PART THREE

SOCIAL ANTHROPOLOGY, RELIGION, AND THE COGNITIVE SCIENCES

CHAPTER EIGHT

A WELL-DISPOSED SOCIAL ANTHROPOLOGIST'S PROBLEMS WITH THE 'COGNITIVE SCIENCE OF RELIGION'[1]

James Laidlaw

What is true is that each action is explained, in the first place, by an individual's psychology; what is not true is that the individual's psychology is entirely explained by psychology. There are human sciences other than psychology, and there is not the slightest reason to suppose that one can understand humanity without them (Williams 1995: 86).

Since what follows will be critical of some aspects of the foregoing papers, and since it will argue that what its proponents call 'the cognitive science of religion' will not be able to fulfil some of their hopes and ambitions, at least in the form in which they are currently held, it might be helpful if I begin by making clear that I am not unsympathetic to the enterprise. I do not share with some of my fellow anthropologists any hostility to what they disparagingly call 'Western' science (or more specifically to biology, genetics, Darwin-

1. Apologies are due, for the liberty taken with the title, to Maurice Bloch (2005). Thanks are due, for comments on earlier drafts, to Peter Allen, Justin Barrett, Susan Bayly, Matei Candea, Stephen Hugh-Jones, Caroline Humphrey, Timothy Jenkins, Hallvard Lillehammer, Jonathan Mair, Matteo Mameli, Soumhya Venkatesan, and Harvey Whitehouse. It is more than usually true that while I have tried to address the comments and criticisms so generously offered by these colleagues and friends, I am sure I will not have succeeded to the satisfaction of them all, and none of course is responsible for the failings that remain.

ian evolutionary theory, or experimental cognitive psychology). I have no objection to the notion of human nature or to the thought that the cognitive architecture of the brain materially affects the ways in which humans learn, think, and behave. Further, it seems to me clear that developments in cognitive science in recent decades have included ideas and discoveries that are of real interest and consequence for social anthropology in general and the study of religion in particular.

However, in order that the most might be made of these advances, it is important that their extent not be exaggerated, and that the character of their interest and consequence not be mistaken. Some at least of the contributors to this volume clearly expect a complete revolution in the anthropology of religion and, in particular, the comprehensive superseding or encompassment of hermeneutic or interpretive by what they call scientific methods. I am sure that these expectations will be disappointed. There are aspects of religion for which cognitive science has begun to provide a persuasive explanatory account, and undoubtedly there is scope for further progress along similar lines. However, I shall argue that what this tells us about is only a very little of what we call religion, and that this limitation derives from the very nature of the cognitive-science enterprise. The idea that we are seeing the beginnings of a new discipline that could provide what hopeful protagonists call a 'complete explanation' of religion, even if it is imagined that others such as interpretive anthropologists might still have a role in the enterprise, is I think not well founded. I do not think that any such enterprise is in prospect, and if or to the extent that it were to be, cognitive science could not provide the conceptual basis for it. The claims I shall make are as follows:

1. Cognitive science, like any explanatory method, has blind spots as well as foci.

2. Explanation is intentional, so necessarily plural, and causal explanations in terms of mechanisms of cognitive processing cannot substitute for the contextual interpretation of thought and action, yet the ambition of an integrated 'cognitive science of religion' ignores this irreducible plurality.

3. While cognitive science can provide a causal account of some religious phenomena, this is not, as its practitioners claim, an explanation of 'religion'; because

4. much that is distinctive about religious traditions as traditions falls outside the definition of religion used by cognitive scientists; and in any case

5. religion is not an object, such that 'it' can be defined analytically rather than historically, and therefore is not a proper object for the kind of explanations cognitive science can provide.

6. What cognitive science can and to some extent has developed explanations for is what the Enlightenment called Natural Religion, and what both it and many religious authorities have called Superstition.

7. This being the case, the contribution cognitive science can make to any general understanding of religion or to the study of particular religious traditions is necessarily ancillary, and roughly equivalent to the contribution that technical knowledge about materials can make to aesthetics and the history of art.

8. The anti-humanist methodological exclusions on which cognitive science is founded are reflected in the way some if not all cognitive scientists of religion handle the concept of belief, which, even where this might be against their best intentions, involves implicit denial of the reality of human reason, imagination, and will.

The Necessary Partiality of Cognitive Science

Reviewing the range of possible explanations for religious concepts, Pascal Boyer (2002: 69), arguing for the value of the cognitive-science approach, observes that if we seek to explain the reason why people have a concept, we often assume that it must be, precisely, a reason; that is, a set of facts that make sense of the concept's import.

> When we say, 'People worry about the ancestors' reactions because [they believe] the ancestors are powerful,' we put these two facts together (a worry about ancestors, a belief in their power) because one seems to *make sense* in the context of the other.

But, he rightly observes,

> we must remember that many aspects of cognitive processing are explained by *causes* rather than *reasons*, that is, by functional processes that do not always make sense. We all have a very good memory for faces and a much poorer one for names. There is an explanation for that. But it is not that it makes more sense to recall faces than names. It is just the way human memory works.

This is a telling point, and it identifies most economically the description under which cognitive science understands human thought and conduct: it does so as and insofar as they are the subject of causes, as distinct from reasons. It is just insofar as thought can be conceived under the causal description—as the outcome of mechanisms of information processing—that cognitive science can comprehend it. But Boyer, in making his point, implicitly concedes that contrariwise there are aspects of our thinking that are explained by the reasons agents hold rather than the causes that affect them.[2] And these, by definition, cannot be part of a cognitive-science approach.

Before I go any further, let me be clear: I am not criticising cognitive science on the grounds that it makes this exclusion. Any research programme must be founded on conceiving its subject matter in a certain way. This will always involve exclusions. You cannot focus equally on everything at once, or you would not be focusing at all. The point is to understand the consequences of the decisions you make.

Although of course cognitive science and scientists come in a variety of forms, certain decisions are constitutive of the approach as such. The crucial decisions are the commitment to regarding thought as information processing and therefore to regarding humans (like other animals) as, in this respect, like certain machines.[3] One can concede the productivity of this point of view, while observing that it excludes much. It excludes, significantly for my purposes here, everything that humans think and do in the reflective exercise of the kinds of capacities I shall designate, in shorthand here, as reason, imagination, and will. To the extent that humans are possessed of such capacities—the extent itself is debatable (as of course is their correct delineation) and I will simply be assuming that it is not negligible—their con-

---

2. A terminological clarification is in order here. In following Boyer in distinguishing reasons from causes, I remain uncommitted on the question of whether reasons for acting are completely unrelated to causes (and therefore not amenable to causal explanation of any kind) or are a special type of cause (and therefore that explaining actions in terms of reasons is a species of causal explanation). There is no need to decide on this for my purposes here because the most persuasive arguments for the latter position (e.g. Davidson 1980) also entail that explaining intentional action differs from explanation in the natural sciences because the irreducible importance for the former of a normative concept of rationality means that the causal connections invoked in explaining action by reasons are not nomological. So whether reasons are causes or not, they remain different in the relevant way from any causes that a science of information processing mechanisms could reveal.

3. This may be, and increasingly is, combined with a principled insistence that since human beings are also animals, the mechanisms for cognitive processing of which their brains are composed are, and can be explained as, the outcome of natural selection. Thus, for most contributors to this volume, the cognitive science of religion is part of evolutionary psychology. For a brilliantly concise explanation of why many human psychological mechanisms are probably not adaptations and therefore not amenable to the kind of explanations evolutionary psychology proposes, see Mameli 2007.

duct will be inexplicable as the result of causal mechanisms of this kind. It will be inexplicable, to adapt the point from Boyer, except (also) in relation to reasons.

It is worth observing here—we shall return to the point later—that one of the things that the word 'religion' identifies is the media in which mankind has as it happens made many of its most sustained and concentrated attempts to exercise its reason, imagination, and will. The point that cognitive science therefore works, insofar as it does, by a methodological exclusion of much that we mean by religion, will be relevant to assessing the scope and likely prospects of the 'cognitive science of religion'.

The case here is comparable to the exclusion on which neo-classical economics is constituted. No one can doubt that economics, not least in its formal and more-or-less mathematical sub-disciplines, has developed, as cognitive science aims to do, a sophisticated body of theory founded on scientific method and assumptions. This is a body of theory that issues in precise, quantified, testable predictions. But as John Stuart Mill observed at the very foundation of the discipline in this form, there is a cost. Political Economy, he observed,

> does not treat of the whole of man's nature as modified by the social state, nor of the whole conduct of man in society. It is concerned with him solely as a being who desires to possess wealth, and who is capable of judging of the comparative efficacy of means for obtaining that end. It predicts only such of the phenomena of the social state as take place in consequence of the pursuit of wealth. It makes entire abstraction of every other human passion or motive (1864: 137).

This 'entire abstraction' is productive, so long as it does not lead its practitioners to suppose that 'every other human passion or motive' is on that account actually either absent or trivial in human affairs. But it is an easy over-extension of enthusiasm for a powerful method or technique to want to insist that only problems that it can be used to solve are real or well-formed problems. And some economists have indeed regarded human conduct as really being motivated by the single passion or motive their method can comprehend. These days, most economists probably recognise that their methods can throw light on only certain aspects of human conduct, and those too viewed from a certain point of view. But a range of reductive and imperialist 'economic theories' of human behaviour as such, or of love or law or war or religion or whatever, continue to be put forward in more or less popularising forms.

In cognitive science too, some practitioners and enthusiasts in various ways both explicitly and implicitly deny the consequences of the exclusions on which their discipline is founded. So several authors, including some contributors to this volume, express the hope or expectation that hermeneutic or humanistic methods in the study of religion will, progressively, be reduced in scope or even replaced as a natural consequence of the advance of cognitive science.[4] On this view, rival explanatory paradigms are conceived as being in a zero-sum game where to win would be to stand in sole possession of a single field, having successfully either excluded or 'reduced' one's opponents. Others, more liberally, imagine interpretive methods surviving, but only insofar as they are 'integrated' with cognitive-scientific approaches (see for instance the essays by Lanman and Whitehouse in this volume). Now two things might be meant here. One is that an interpretation should not logically contradict the conclusions of scientific research. That is unexceptionable, and could provide the basis for ongoing peaceful and distinct coexistence between humanistic and cognitive-science approaches. But often more is meant, namely the claims that the conclusions of cognitive and interpretive research will become substantively integrated, that such integration is indeed a criterion for the validity and rigour of the latter (evidence that it is not merely fanciful[5]), and that therefore ultimately they will merge into a single body of knowledge, which body of knowledge it will make sense to call, because the cognitive method is what will stand at its centre and give it shape, the 'cognitive science of religion'. The spirit of the proposal need not be hostile—I happen to know that in some cases it is genuinely open—but the stance is not compatible with acknowledging the limitations and blind-spots that follow, inescapably, from the exclusions on which the method is based. Humanist and

---

4. Thus for example Guthrie asserts in passing in his essay in this volume (pp. 49–50) that Durkheim's theory of religion is simply no longer needed, because we now have the theory of the over-extension of human attributes, which explains the same phenomena. But even if we are persuaded that the over-extension theory is indeed explanatory, does it answer all the same questions as are addressed by Durkheim's account? It must be a mistake to assume that because something 'scientific' has been said on a subject, nothing else that might be said is henceforth of any value.

5. Thus in one of many essentially similar recent programmatic essays by enthusiasts, whose ostensible purpose is to persuade ethnographers, historians, and others of that 'the emergence of the cognitive science of religion signals a new era in the field', Slone and Mort make the following winning observation: 'The gains in accuracy and understanding that the cognitive sciences can provide for the study of religion include limiting the epistemological freedoms of intuitive inference that hermeneuts ... now illegitimately enjoy' (2004: 159–60).

interpretive approaches to human thought and conduct do not make the same exclusions (they make others, of course). Yet the criterion of integration pre-supposes that scientific and humanist approaches are fundamentally the same enterprise, on the apparently reasonable grounds that they both seek to ex-plain the same thing, namely religion. But this apparently reasonable suppo-sition is, I want to insist, mistaken. Neither is it the case that the 'religion' they could conceivably give an account of is in fact the same thing, nor is it the case that what it would be for them to succeed in explaining 'it' is the same thing.

The Intentionality, and Therefore Plurality, of Explanation

First, let me address the question of the meaning of explanation. The hopes and expectations entertained by many in the cognitive science of religion of either the replacement of interpretive by cognitive-science accounts or their integration into a single scientific method only make sense if it is forgotten that explanation is interest-relative, and therefore a necessarily plural and het-erogeneous category.

To use one of Hilary Putnam's classic examples (1978: 42–3), it is unas-sailably true, but hopeless, to explain Professor's X's presence, naked at mid-night in the girls' dormitory, by saying that (a) he was naked in the girls' dor-mitory at midnight–∈, so that he could not exit the dormitory before midnight without exceeding the speed of light, and that (b—covering law) nothing (certainly not professors) can travel faster than light. This is hopeless as an explanation because although true, it is irrelevant to the interest we have in asking the question. It does correctly answer a question, but not as it hap-pens one that anyone has asked.

A why-question always presupposes and is motivated by a definite range of interests (in this case obviously we are interested in motives and inten-tions). An explanation is never simply and completely an explanation *of* any thing (or event, or process, or state of affairs, or series, etc.); it is an expla-nation of that thing from a certain point of view, in answer to a certain kind of question. We may approach the same phenomenon with more than one interest. Different explanations 'of the same thing' therefore might equally be valid, and not in competition, because they are answers to different ques-tions with respect to 'it'. So, to use another of Putnam's examples, the bank robber Willie Sutton's famous reply when asked 'Why do you rob banks?' — 'That's where the money is' — was a good explanation, and an answer to the question he had been asked, if we imagine his interlocutor to have been another crook, but it is not an explanation at all, and not an answer to the question, if we imagine the question to have been asked, as it were, by a priest.

So explanation is intentional. Whether and to what extent any account of a set of phenomena is explanatory depends in part on to whom it is addressed. This means that the idea of a *complete* explanation of a phenomenon is an incoherent one. How comprehensive or satisfactory an explanation is, is never entirely a matter of the phenomenon to be explained, but always also depends on the questions and interests the enquiry is answering. The point of Putnam's examples, and of my citing them, is not to show that one kind of explanation (in terms of reasons and motives) is better than another (reductive or causal), any more than the reverse, but just to show that they really are different, and that there are circumstances in which one cannot substitute for the other, however rigorous it might be.

Because cognitive science places human thought under the category of material cause, its why-questions are always roughly equivalent to asking of any incidence or pattern of representations or practices, 'through which mechanisms', or 'impelled by which forces', or 'under what selective pressure' did they arise? As Boyer rightly observes, causes of these kinds are quite independent of whether it *makes any sense* for anyone to hold these representations or engage in these practices rather than any others. By contrast a humanist study that took reason, imagination, and will seriously as constitutive of its subject matter would ask why-questions whose natural paraphrases would be quite different. Many, for instance, would be teleological. They would concern the ideals and values *towards* which the ideas or practices concerned are orientated. To recognise thought as exercise of reason, for instance, would be to acknowledge that it aims at truth, and would be to evaluate it accordingly. To ask for an explanation of religious thought and practice under these two sets of descriptions is therefore to ask quite distinct sets of questions. Now the answers to one might well be of interest or help to someone seeking answers to the other, and actual contradiction will not be possible between *true* answers to any of them. I shall return below to the question of what the proper relation between causal and interpretive accounts of religious life might be. For the moment, it suffices to say that there is no reason whatsoever to expect that the answers will ever be the same in substance, or that being in possession of answers to one set will obviate the interests that motivate the other.[6]

---

6. As with economics, cognitive science is not immune from scientism, by which I do not mean the desire to explain human behaviour in scientific terms, still less scientific practice, but the specific mistaken belief that physicalist and reductionist explanations are bet-

This is true in general terms of the humanistic and historical understanding of human affairs on the one hand and reductive or naturalistic understanding of human behaviour on the other. It is however especially vividly true as applied to the phenomena we call religion. I said above that religion as conceived by cognitive science is not the same thing as that conceived by humane study, and I turn now to the reasons why this must be so.

Explaining Some Widespread Religious Beliefs and Practices

The social and cultural anthropology of religion has for many decades overwhelmingly emphasised the diversity of religious beliefs and practices: diversity as between peoples and places and religions and, for the historical and literate 'world religions', as between official doctrines and the local variants within those traditions. It has been a bold move by the proponents of the cognitive science of religion (though one of course that was anticipated by Marxists and others) to insist that the supernatural beings and entities who popu-

---

ter than any other explanation *for all purposes and all subject matter* and that whenever such explanations can be given they render any other kind redundant. Thus Barrett, illustrating how our cognitive architecture forces on us an array of false beliefs we are not even aware of having, writes, 'opossums and raccoons are intuitively or non-reflectively thought to be more similar to each other than either is to horses or dogs or cows (Atran, 1995). Biologists tell us otherwise. As marsupials, opossums are more similar to kangaroos than raccoons and raccoons are more similar to bears than to opossums' (p. 185). But of course opossums are only more similar to kangaroos than raccoons from the point of view of how they reproduce, and their genetic make-up. They are not more similar, to use a criterion favoured on other occasions by Barrett himself, if you are distinguishing animals that might be a threat from those that are not, or for a host of other interests you might conceivably have. As Barrett is aware, genetic description is not simply and for all purposes 'more true' than other bases for description, and whether or not it is 'explanatory' depends on what you hope to understand or to do. Yet this example is used to illustrate the kind of 'errors' our cognitive processing mechanisms are prone to, to prepare the way for the claim that religious beliefs are formed as a result of similar cognitive mistakes. But it seems to me that in both instances (intuitive biology and religion) the alleged mistakes are so only in light of a disregard for the varieties of interest and purpose that inform the practices involved. I would not wish to suggest, however, that anthropologists are immune from similar errors. Anthropologists too often argue that there is only one legitimate, rigorous, or interesting mode of explanation. Often this is done for polemical purposes, but anthropologists, like everyone else, often end up believing their own rhetoric: e.g. Malinowski for functionalism against history, Lévi-Strauss for the structure of the mind, Geertz for interpretation, substantivists against formalists, and so on.

late the popular religious imagination right across the globe are in fact substantially similar, and then to offer a distinctive and persuasive explanation for why this should be so (Boyer 1994, 2001, Guthrie 1993). Similarly, they have argued that beneath the detailed variety of forms of religious ritual, there are a few basic types generated by reasonably simple and very general cognitive principles governing actions and interactions relating to these supernatural beings (Lawson & McCauley 1990; McCauley & Lawson 2002) and/or responses to the felt risk of danger in dealing with them (Boyer 2001; Boyer & Lienard in press). A further theme that has been developed with some success is to explore the ways in which the capacities and limitations of the mechanisms of human memory differentially constrain or enable the retention and transmission of different mental representations, so that some ideas are intrinsically very difficult for human minds to acquire and retain while others are much more easy and therefore are extremely widespread (Sperber 1985, 1996; Whitehouse 2000, 2004; see also Whitehouse & Laidlaw 2004).

The phenomena under discussion here are, it is convincingly claimed, so widespread in human populations because their causes—evolved mechanisms of cognitive architecture—are universal to humans. Thus they are to be seen, albeit in locally variable forms, everywhere. But if they are indeed very widely distributed across societies, and of incontestable importance, they do not come near to constituting all that we might reasonably call religion. This fact is partly disguised by, and possibly also from, practitioners of the cognitive science of religion by the virtually unanimous agreement among them in defining religion as beliefs and practices relating to spiritual or supernatural beings.

At first sight, to most anthropologists, this insistence on defining religion with reference to supernatural beings seems like a curious, merely anachronistic reversion to the Tylorian 'intellectualist' theories of the origin of religion from the end of the nineteenth century. Durkheim famously attacked definitions of that kind (1995 [1912]), Evans-Pritchard buried them (1965), and no one much has thought it worthwhile trying to resurrect them since.[7] But the matter is far from trivial. Durkheim's refutation emphasized Buddhism, which, as he rightly said, is not centrally concerned with deities at all. Guthrie (this volume) and others (Lawson & McCauley 1990; Boyer 1994, 2001) have replied by observing that throughout the Buddhist world popular devotional practice prominently features deities of various kinds. This is quite true. Pro-

---

7. Horton (1993) is one of the few. See discussion by Skorupski (1976) and Tambiah (1990).

pitiation of deities is indeed common, but no remotely reflective Buddhist, including those who spend time and resources participating in such rites, would confuse them for a moment with following the teachings of the Buddha. And whatever else Buddhism is, it surely must include that. Buddhists will certainly maintain so.

Now, to what do we apply the term religion in this situation? At one level, it does not matter. Anthropologists for generations have happily applied it both to the transmitted teachings of the Buddha and to Buddhists' beliefs and practices relating to gods and spirits. Some have indeed seen it as their calling to demonstrate that in any given local social context they form a single integrated complex whole (Leach 1968, Tambiah 1970).[8] But this has been of no serious consequence precisely because for these authors and for the interpretive enterprise they are engaged in the question of what counts as religion is of absolutely no theoretical importance. There is no such entity they have sought in any sense to explain. These authors' interpretive and functional holism embraces equally a good deal that no one would ever be seriously tempted to call religion. In these circumstances, no definitional question arises with respect to religion.

But this is not true for the self-declared cognitive science of religion. For this project, the definition of its subject matter is of considerable theoretical moment. Consider Guthrie's contribution to this volume. Although he begins by accepting, apparently, that the category religion is vague and has no indigenous equivalent in many societies, he nevertheless seeks an explanatory 'theory of religion'. So the question of what is and is not included in the *explanandum* is a recurring concern. He proceeds on the operating assumption that theories of religion are adequate if and only if they apply comprehensively and exclusively to 'it'. So, for instance, what he calls 'comfort theories' are rejected on the grounds that there are instances of 'religion' to which they do not apply. In Guthrie's own terms, this is indeed the correct way to proceed. A series of important questions about the evaluation of his own theory—its testability, its completeness, and the adequacy of his treatment of apparent counter-evidence—all depend on him being fastidious in just this way. I am not claiming that it is a fault in Guthrie that he seeks to define his object of study in this manner. On the contrary, it is a virtue. It is a problem, because it is a source of real potential confusion, only that he wants that object to be defined as 'religion'.

---

8. Notable and persuasive arguments to the contrary include Mumford (1989) and Humphrey (1996).

Religious Traditions as Traditions

Let me begin to illustrate why it is a serious problem by describing the traditions of Jainism and Theravada Buddhism. I choose these examples partly because I happen to know a certain amount about them, and partly because the features of them that elude a cognitive-science characterisation of religion are so prominent and clear.[9] But the general point applies in fact to all religions insofar as they are historical phenomena, which of course includes religions (such as those of so-called 'tribal' peoples) whose history has not (until recently) been written down.

Both Jainism and Theravada Buddhism are soteriologies, traditions that transmit and embody a distinctive project of self-fashioning, in pursuit of an ideal of liberation from embodied existence. These projects are systematically pursued only by ordained renouncers, who have never been more than a minority of the followers of these traditions. But the ways of life of their much more numerous lay followers have nevertheless been inflected by their renunciatory projects. Both projects took definite form at the same place and time (the Gangetic plain in eastern north India in the 5th to 4th centuries BC). In both cases they incorporate ideas, practices, and forms of organisation that were part of the general cultural milieu of that place and time, including a sombre view of every-day householder existence and an ideal of enlightened liberation from it, an abstractly formulated moral theory relating directly to the psychophysical individual, and forms of organisation for single-sex groups of religious professionals among which there were traditions of experimentation with practices—meditation, changes in diet, other forms of austerity—designed to effect psychological changes. But equally, in both cases, specific known individuals (Mahavir Swami and Gautam Buddha respectively) gave their respective projects qualities and a style which each still retains, though both have changed radically in various ways, through histories of schism, political patronage and persecution, encounter and competition with other traditions, changes in the composition and fortunes of their followers, and movements of self-conscious reform. The two traditions continue to bear the recognisable stamp of the thought and imagination of Mahavir and the Buddha respectively, and the distinctive ideas, concerns, practices, and institutions they bequeathed, and this makes them unmistakably distinctive forms

---

9. The account that follows synthesises a large and diverse literature, but is especially influenced by a brilliant paper by Carrithers (1990).

of life. This continuity is not to be accounted for in terms of there being simply consistent and continuous transmission of shared beliefs, but rather by what Carrithers calls a 'patterned flow of contingencies and aspirations, routines and imaginative responses' (Carrithers 1990: 141). As important to the transmission and content of the traditions as beliefs, are institutions, roles and relationships, practices (including and especially bodily techniques), narratives, and material culture including visual representations.

In these traditions, deities, ghosts, spirits, and magic are all part of the picture. As cognitive science would predict, renouncers and lay followers alike, along with the rest of the species, 'catch' these 'minimally counter-intuitive' or 'cognitively optimal' representations. But they are not what these projects are about, nor are they in any sense central or even, frankly, relevant to them. It would be highly eccentric not to call these traditions 'religion', if one is going to use the term analytically at all, but as practitioners will tell you, 'gods have nothing to do with it'.[10] So although if you look at life in a Jain or Buddhist community you will find 'religion' as cognitive science expects to find it—they are valid instances of the patterns it seeks to explain—this will all be at best peripheral to an understanding of these traditions *as traditions*. That is, cognitive science will tell us as much or as little about what Jains and Buddhists believe and why as it will of anyone else, but nothing at all about what they believe or do, distinctively, as Jains or Buddhists. To capture the sense in which these traditions are religious traditions, you would need at the very least to allow some aspects of a wholly different order from beliefs in the existence of gods and ghosts into your characterisation of religion. There are several ways one might sensibly go about this, but I hope it will be immediately apparent, for instance, how much more to the purpose is Jenkins' suggestion 'that religion be best understood as the expression of the desire to be human in a particular form' and therefore that religious traditions are different socially embodied conceptions of human flourishing (Jenkins 1999: 13).

This is why religious traditions centrally and constitutively include concepts that may have nothing necessarily to do with belief in supernatural beings, and of which cognitive science will find it extremely difficult to give any meaningful account. I mean concepts, such as shame or compassion or penitence—or, in the Jain case, *vairagya* which translates roughly as 'disgust (with the world)'—that refer to what it is to be a human subject, because they only have

---

10. Gombrich (1971: 46). The rest of the ethnography is full of reports of ordinary Buddhists and Jains saying this. See discussion in Southwold (1978) and Gellner (1990) for Buddhism, and, for Jainism, Laidlaw (1995) and Cort (2001).

meaning in relation to webs of other such complex psychological terms. Shame makes no sense without related notions, typically such as respect, tact, shyness, and reserve (not necessarily honour; see Wikan 1984). And because they are also inherently and strongly evaluative—judgements of worth are intrinsic to the meaning of these concepts and the judgements include second-order and self-reflective valuing *of values* and so on—they can only properly be predicates of a moral subject (Frankfurt 1988). As Williams (1995: 82) puts the point, the qualities described by such concepts,

> can be possessed only by a creature that *has a life*, where this implies, among other things, that its experience has a meaning for it and that features of its environment display salience, relevance, and so on, particularly in the light of what it sees as valuable.

Not all such concepts are overtly 'religious'. But one of the things religious traditions do is to propose whole webs of these strongly evaluative concepts.

If one thing religious traditions do is to propose strongly evaluative psychological concepts, another is to embody practices through which the qualities they describe are variously cultivated, elicited, and enforced. The reflective process of understanding and articulating one's experience in terms of these emotions, motivations, and qualities of character is never just to describe but always also to evaluate, and thus to affect. In understanding and articulating our experience in such terms, we necessarily act upon the self, because we ascribe not only content but *import* to the emotions or motivations or qualities of character so described. Such self-interpretations are constitutive (Taylor 1985: 45–76). It follows that, while we may in important ways be mistaken about our own thoughts, emotions, and motivations, our self-understandings are never *merely* mistakes, for they are part of the fact of the matter, part of what they seek to articulate. The articulation, even if partly mistaken or even actively self-deluding, is nevertheless part of its object. But further, it is important not to think of this constitutive self-interpretation as a merely psychological process, in the sense of it being internal to the individual. It takes place within institutions and relationships, and through instituted practices and language, and this is why although the claims I have made in this and the preceding paragraphs are unashamedly general claims about what human social life is like, and therefore about 'human nature', the precise forms in which human subjects are reflectively constituted are on this view historically variable.[11]

---

11. For an exceptional study not just of variability and change but of change being brought about, see Hacking 1995.

Each religious tradition has its own distinctive ways of describing, judging, and shaping character in relation to its historically created and developing conceptions of human wellbeing and worth. It is through instituted religious practices—forms of worship, confession, penance, celebration, interaction, ecstasy, and so on—that people come to have the emotions and self-understandings that make them Christian, Muslim, Buddhist, Jain, or whatever. And just as it is not possible to be a Jain, or to feel 'disgust (with the world)', without the language needed to form this self-interpretation, so the language and the emotion could not exist without the tradition and the institutions and practices through which it is cultivated and experienced. And because these emotions and motivations are historical products, invented and developed contingently in particular times and places, and sustained by particular practices and institutions, they cannot be adequately described purely in terms of cognitive mechanisms, internal to individual minds. They are particularly clear and strong examples of those aspects of language, meaning, and therefore thought and experience that are inter-subjective, which is to say 'not (only) in the head' (on which see Putnam 1975 and especially Pettit & McDowell 1986). Again, 'religious' traditions are not the only kind of contexts in which all this occurs, but overwhelmingly the most concentrated, sustained, influential, and enduring *patterned* ways in which humans have done this have been religious traditions. This is true, to repeat, of religious traditions as historical phenomena irrespective of whether or of the extent to which they are literate traditions. In the case of Jainism and Buddhism, moreover, it is very overtly and self-consciously what these traditions are about.

From Analytical to Historical Characterisation of Religion

Now, my purpose in setting out this aspect of the meaning of 'religion' is not to propose it as the basis for a definition, either to replace or even to complete those that focus on beliefs and practices relating to supernatural beings. Many have laboured, including many cognitive scientists, to develop a defensible analytical definition of religion (see for instance, and in many ways admirably, Saler 2000). While many brilliant and illuminating points have been made in the course of these discussions, the effort is misguided. It is not just malign accident that 'religion' in modern English has these (and other) disparate meanings. The word has a history that is inseparable from the fact that the phenomena it describes are historically constituted and variable. This history is a complex one, and there is neither reason nor space (nor am I competent) to try to tell it all here.[12] In any case neither telling it, nor any definitional fiat, can wish that history away. The most important point is that 'religion' as it is understood in the modern (post-) Christian West is not an object with a single origin, let alone a single essence that defines it, but a fairly local and contingent meeting up of several different questions and areas of concern. Seventeenth-century England was a crucial turning point for reasons that are lucidly summarised by Jenkins,

> In a period prior to the seventeenth century, theology had to do with everything, considered in the light of God's saving action and purposes, and the word 'religion' was a relatively unimportant term, concerning the right ordering of worship. In the seventeenth century, a mutation took place, whereby notions of cause and effect became important. 'God' then became the name for the final cause of everything, and 'religion' became what concerns God, that is, separated from the spheres of specific causalities in the world—the public sphere, politics, economics and so forth. This constituted a real reduction, since one can in fact do without a universal cause; 'religion' in this reduced sense was born to be irrelevant (Jenkins 1999: 9).

Every member of a modern, post-Enlightenment society is in some measure obliged to have beliefs about politics, economics, public morals, and science, and in these spheres is obliged further to have beliefs that they themselves believe, at least, are rationally grounded. Religion, by contrast, has become optional, a matter of personal subjective need—for meaning, comfort, identity, and so on. Before this transformation, as Asad in particular brings out (1993: 27–54), processes of shaping character and authorising judgements of truth and worth were much more prominent in the self-understanding of Christianity than they have become subsequently. It would not have been necessary or made so much sense then, as I have done here, to invoke Jainism and Buddhism in order to highlight their importance, relative to matters of internal mental state such as 'belief' or 'faith'. Although 'belief' has always been central to Christianity in ways that mark it out from other traditions (Ruel 1982), nevertheless the transformation in the sense of this, from public affirmation to internal state of mind, is distinctively modern, and it is anachronistic if simply applied elsewhere.[13] It is not so much that such a definition is wrong;

---

12. The most important sources I draw upon are Asad (1993; 2003), Dumont (1985), Harrison (1990), Lash (1996), Masuzawa (2005).

13. A particular concern of Asad's is the way in which accepting a modern, Western conception of religion defined by individual belief makes Islam, where there has not in gen-

it is rather that it is historically and ethnographically insensitive to regard it or any variation of it as the definition of a simply existing entity. There is no such entity to define.

This means that the effort to discover what religion really is—to get the definition of it definitively right—is based on a category error. The changing history of how the word 'religion' has been understood is, inseparably, the history of 'it' changing. We may contrast the word 'gold' which also has a history, and was used and had meaning before the subatomic composition of gold was discovered. But neither that discovery, nor any other change in human understanding or use or valuation of gold, had any effect on what gold is as a material substance. It is not in this sense an historical phenomenon, and this makes a difference to the kind of knowledge that can be hoped for of it. So a chemist can validly formulate theories and generalisations about gold, as it always has and always will be, and insist that it just is different from iron pyrites, whatever anyone has ever thought or done, mistaking one for the other. The history of human interactions with gold is neither here nor there. And just as it would be an error for an historian or social scientist not to acknowledge this, and not to respect the consequent limits to the applicability of his or her methods to genuinely natural facts (for an example of such error, see Latour 1998), so it is an error not to acknowledge and attend to the intrinsically historical character of religion.[14]

Rediscovering Natural Religion and Explaining Superstition

So the focus on supernatural beings, the focus on belief, and the fact that it is not historical all weaken cognitive science's definition of religion. Jenkins points out that the transformation from pre-Enlightenment theology to the post-Enlightenment disciplines of the 'study of religion' was built upon a re-

---

eral been the same separation from politics and the public sphere, appear to be an aberration. Given how fond cognitive scientists and evolutionary psychologists are of criticising Geertz, it is interesting how forcefully Asad's objection to Geertz's conception of religion applies also to their own. It is, he says, 'a modern, privatized Christian one because and to the extent that it emphasizes the priority of belief as a state of mind rather than as constituting activity in the world' (Asad 1993: 47).

14. For just two exemplary studies of the way religions have been profoundly modified by changes in self-understanding see Gombrich & Obeyesekere (1988) and Pennington (2005).

duction, from knowledge about everything, seen in a certain light (in the light, that is, of the most important facts there were), to a certain distinct subject matter. This reduction is a prerequisite for the modern idea of there being different 'religions', each a token of the general type ('religion'), where each is a different, logically equivalent set of beliefs, held by different people and/or in different times and places, about that same subject matter. The cognitive-science definition of religion presupposes just this transformation. It defines religion as sets of representations, and/or practices 'relating to' those representations, each with the same general kind of content. Once you have the idea of each 'religion' as a species of a genus or a token of a type, you have by implication the question of how much they share and the idea of the basic form of which they are all a variant. This was the problem constituted in the seventeenth and eighteenth centuries as that of 'Natural Religion': what did human reason, or human nature, require or incline man to believe? (Harrison 1990: 28–34).

It is not surprising that cognitive science has rediscovered basically this problem. It asks, first: what, given its architecture and mode of operation, is the human mind, as a cognitive processing device, disposed to believe?

That is to describe the subject matter of cognitive science from more or less within its own terms of reference, but there is another way to put the same thing, and I think this is worth spelling out, although it may not please either the cognitive scientists or (though for different reasons) many social and cultural anthropologists. This is to say that, as viewed from within some, perhaps even all, self-conscious religious traditions, what the cognitive science of religion gives us is an account of 'superstition': not the self-conscious products of reason, imagination, and will, not what the tradition is to itself, but rather the popular beliefs and practices which in particular the untutored and uncultivated are always prone to, which are at best incidental to a good, or pious, or virtuous, or enlightened life, and at worst highly destructive illusions or temptations. One of the reasons it is worth drawing attention to this coincidence of object is that cognitive science agrees at least with this: that the 'religion' it identifies and explains is built up from a series of observable mistakes: beliefs we can be shown to acquire not because the world is thus and so, but because our cognitive programming mechanisms pre-judge the matter and bias our perceptions. And, specifically of religion, cognitive science asks: which of the apparently infinitely many possible *erroneous* things of a certain kind (those in which supernatural beings or processes figure) is the human mind most disposed to believe?

This then is why supernatural, or as cognitive scientists often say 'non-empirical' beings, are essential to its definition of religion: the fact that these entities, though non-existent, nevertheless present themselves to human minds is an index of the extent to which the structure of the mind, rather than the content of the world, determines the representations humans come to have, and therefore of the extent to which the explanation of these beliefs and the associated behaviour must be in cognitive terms. If gods were admitted to exist, the role for cognitive science in explaining why we believe in them would of course seem less compelling. If such beings are what religion is defined as being about, the compelling relevance of the approach appears to apply to all of it.

The oft-cited distinction between a cognitive mechanism's 'proper' and 'actual' domain recasts this thought in terms of evolutionary psychology (Millikan 1984, Sperber 1997). It is not even, in evolutionary terms, useful that we have these representations. They are errors produced as by-products by mechanisms we have because those mechanisms were useful for other reasons—thus for instance our tendency to identify agents became hyperactive when we were Neolithic hunters (thus Barrett, Guthrie, and Cohen, all in this volume). It is partly because error is thus intrinsic to the cognitive-science *identification* and *definition* of religion that it coincides, in its understanding of its subject matter, with the religious category of superstition.

It is not to denigrate what the cognitive scientists have been doing to point this out. They have given us a new description of some general phenomena and a new explanation for them, one that includes an account of why the beliefs in question are so resistant to suppression and found among people who are not otherwise or in the more usual sense 'religious'. By this account, convinced atheists are no more able than the devout to resist 'catching' superstitious ideas, for we are all by nature highly susceptible to them. This brings out another more general point: for cognitive science, people are routinely mistaken about their own beliefs. Their thinking is guided, as Boyer insists, by causes (of which they are generally unaware) rather than any reasons they may consciously hold. And, to repeat, this is why, insofar as human thought is in fact guided by reflective reason, cognitive science has nothing to say about it. And this in turn is why cognitive science, while it can frame interesting hypotheses about cross-culturally recurrent tendencies, has been and will remain unable directly to explain any of the distinctive features of any specific religious tradition.

The Proper Study of Cognitive Science

We have seen why it makes sense to define the object of a cognitive science's inquiry with reference to belief in supernatural beings. For a generalizing science, popular religious-superstitious beliefs may be a satisfactory object of enquiry, and there can be no objection to those who wish to do so pursuing that inquiry. And no harm will be done in calling this enterprise the 'cognitive science of religion' so long as it is recognised that this is only a very constricted, indeed one must say an impoverished, idea of 'religion'. It excludes the history of religion as mankind's various more concentrated and sustained attempts to think and act out its conceptions of human value and worth, and the particular and varied achievements and follies that have resulted. Nothing cognitive science has any prospect of achieving will obviate the need to understand these, in humanist terms.

My argument is not that actual religions are complex and scientific explanations must simplify. The right kind of simplification is generally a necessary part of explanation, whether scientific or otherwise. The point is rather that no single kind of simplification is in this sense right for any and every kind of question or interest. Similarly, the argument is not that cognitive science cannot take contingently variable circumstances into account in formulating its generalisations. Nothing prevents this. What it cannot do, using its methods, is actually to *account* for the contingent historical creations of reason, imagination, and will. The attempt to use the methods of cognitive science to explain particular forms of religious life is in effect to deny that this is what they are.

Quite properly, since cognitive science generally seeks explanation of *recurrent* features of thought in terms of universal causal factors, its data are generally understood and enumerated as *instances* of the regularities they reveal. Its facts are statistical facts. To understand religious traditions as traditions is necessarily a qualitatively different exercise. For this, it matters that some things could happen only after specific other things, and some of them happened only once. Because and insofar as the phenomena we seek to understand are conceived as the products of human reason, imagination, and will, this exercise calls for the understanding of events, actions, beliefs, and practices not as instances of a regularity or as items in a series, but as meaningful contingencies, and it therefore understands them by means of contextualisation. To try to answer one of these two kinds of question, or to account for phenomena presented by one mode of understanding, using concepts, methods, and reasoning drawn from the other, is to be strictly irrelevant.[15]

---

15. The argument here and throughout is influenced by Michael Oakeshott's *Experience and its Modes*. In this context Oakeshott's critical remarks on the idea that anthropology might ever be a science, and his claim that it is properly a form of historical knowledge and experience (1933: 162–9), bear re-reading even after so much water has flowed under that particular bridge.

Humanist study, as pursued alike by history and anthropology, cannot ignore the fact that in religion people have *aimed* at certain values and virtues, including and especially truth. To study the way they have variously invented, discovered, criticised, amended, defended, and reformed the doctrines, practices, and institutions of their religion, and have tried, succeeded, and failed to live up to and according to them, is necessarily at least in part to ask whether and to what extent, in doing so, they have realised their values and ideals.[16] To seek instead to explain their beliefs and behaviour causally as the outcome of the mechanics of information processing, and largely with reference to processing errors, is just not to look them in the eye.[17] This is no way to achieve 'integration' of interpretive and scientific-explanatory accounts. In any case, the situation I have described calls not for integration but for a somewhat different kind of peaceful coexistence.

The difference between scientific and humanist understanding is not in itself or most importantly a difference in subject matter—the same events can figure in both—so much as it is a difference in the description under which subject matter is conceived, experienced, and understood. But this does mean that the objects of study in a humanist study—socio-historically embodied religious traditions—are simply not instances or cases of the entity that the cognitive science of religion seeks to understand. One can better think of the latter as a substrate, which, if and insofar as cognitive science has established

---

16. I should note here that cognitive science is not alone in construing human social life and institutions in such a way as to elide or to refuse to take seriously the claims to truth and value that are embodied in them. Anthropology and other 'social science' does so, whenever and insofar as it lapses into relativism. See Rabinow's excellent discussion of this (1983). I should also note, for the avoidance of doubt, that institutions and practices embodying reason, imagination, and will, are not of course confined to social élites. On this see classic discussions by Leach (1968), Brown (1981), Das (1984).

17. Although I do not sympathise with his tone, what Collingwood says is nonetheless true: 'In religion, we have people holding definite beliefs as to the nature of God. In conduct generally we have certain actions, individual or social, designed to attain ends of morality, utility, or the like; psychology will study these actions without asking whether they are right or wrong, but taking them merely as things done ... When a man makes a statement about the nature of God (or anything else) he is interested, not in the fact that he is making that statement, but in the belief, or hope, or fancy that it is true. If then the psychologist merely takes a note of the statement and declines to join in the question whether it is true ... *The mind, regarded in this external way, really ceases to be a mind at all* ... [psychology] cannot enter into the life it studies, because it refuses to look with it eye to eye; and it is left with the cold unreality of thought which is the thought of nothing, action with no purpose, and fact with no meaning' (Collingwood 1994: 40–2; my emphasis).

its case, we may regard as always present and part of the raw material from which self-conscious traditions—products of reason, imagination, and will— are fashioned. This is not to say that the cognitive science of religion cannot inform humane study of religious traditions.[18] Knowing about the 'substrate', the medium with which reason, imagination, and will are constrained to work, can undoubtedly be enlightening: but only in limited ways. It can explain why there are commonalities, but cannot provide a complete or satisfying account of any particular practice, belief, or institution in any particular time and place. Indeed, insofar as a practice, belief, or institution is indeed particular, it can have nothing relevant to say about it. It can no more form the basis of an account of any of the distinctive, historically embedded projects of human flourishing than a detailed study of metallurgy would constitute an adequate response to Donatello's David.

Now that comparison, I am aware, will sound highly evaluative. Am I saying that self-conscious products of reason and moral aspiration are nobler and more valuable than the unconscious reflexes we exhibit as by-products of the evolved architecture of our brains; that conscious and reflective thought and practice is more of a human achievement than the (mostly false) beliefs we can scarcely avoid or escape? Well, although it is quite incidental to my argument, I am happy to admit that I do indeed think this. Nothing follows from this analogy, of course, about the worth or difficulty of the respective disciplines that study these phenomena. Some things do follow, however, about the proper relations between them. Materials science is a serious and demanding science, and a good historian of sculpture will be well advised to acquaint him or herself with many of its findings, and to be open to the fact that insights will be gained into particular historical events or processes by doing so. At all times, the capacities and limitations of available materials will influence what sculptors have done; at some times, the availability of new materials or innovations with familiar ones will radically have affected what was possible; and fully understanding the achievements of the very greatest sculptors will often depend on being able to appreciate the technical mastery that informed their genius. For these reasons a whole host of facts uncovered by materials science might be relevant to the art historian. Some interpretations an art historian might otherwise wish to put forward could be ruled out, or shown to be trivial, by such facts; others might be suggested. But none of this makes the *questions* or the *methods* of material science the appropriate ones

---

18. For an anthropological use of some cognitive-science research, which treats it in this way as a substrate from which historical traditions make their own distinctive ways of thought and action, see Humphrey 1996.

around which to organise a study of Renaissance sculpture. And so it is with cognitive science and religion.

Methods and concepts that are suitable for identifying and explaining re-current cross-cultural regularities in religious and other concepts are at best very ancillary to any attempt to account for why specific religious traditions take the particular form they do, still less to an attempt to say what if anything we might learn from comparing them, or to the elucidation of concepts such as the Trinity, the Wheel of the Law, or the Dance of Siva. Scholars engaged in these exercises might well gain insights from reading the work of cognitive scientists. A demonstration for instance that on cognitive grounds such and such an idea is more intuitive than another one is an important and interest-ing finding, especially if cognitive science is able to be more precise and actu-ally quantify such claims,[19] but the way to *pursue an inquiry* into matters of these kinds is not by the methods of cognitive science. Insofar as the objects of study are the contingent products of human reason, imagination, and will, it will always be a category mistake to try to account for them, as cognitive science must, as instances of general tendencies. For these reasons, the exer-cises some of our contributors have been tempted into, of trying for instance to explain historical contingencies such as Semitic monotheism, witch-find-ing crazes, and Captain Cook's experiences in Hawaii, on the basis of univer-sal cognitive mechanisms, simply cannot succeed. While they could in prin-ciple offer specific insights into the general kinds of beliefs that are involved in each case—why witch beliefs differ cognitively from beliefs about sorcery for example—the methods they are using are irrelevant to the questions they would like to try to answer, which are questions about what has happened in

---

19. Appropriately, many of the central claims of cognitive science are quantitative, in-deed probabilistic, but few are actually stated in specifically quantified terms. A few ex-amples chosen at random from this volume: Barrett begins his contribution by saying, 'Below I sketch an account of why belief in superhuman agents is historically and cross-culturally so common by appealing to the naturally occurring properties of human minds operating in historically and cross-culturally common natural and social environments' (p. 182). A little later he continues, 'These mental tools automatically and non-reflectively con-struct perhaps most of our beliefs about the natural and social world' (p. 184). These claims, which might be made by almost any practitioner in the field, are intuitive enough, and plausible cases are made for them. But how common is 'so common' and how many are 'most' of our beliefs? Cohen, similarly, claims that counter-intuitive spirit concepts are widespread because to learn them, 'little novel information has to be learned and rehearsed in memory as the new concepts already largely fit with intuitive knowledge' (p. 147). It would no doubt be difficult to say how little is 'little' and how largely is 'largely' but is it conceptually impossible?

human history, not questions about any invariant things to which it has happened. The result of applying methods that are not suited to the question asked is bound to be either generalities that are true, insofar as they are true, of very much more than the specific object of inquiry, and on that account irrelevant to understanding its particularity, or a failure to engage with the details of the case, or both. Where cognitive science strays into trying to use probabilistic claims of general tendencies to account for unique particularities, it will be guilty of irrelevance, or *ignoratio elenchi* (Oakeshott 1933).

Beliefs, Reasons, and Causes

I began with the observation that in conceiving of human thought under the category of cause, to the exclusion of that of reason, cognitive science makes a powerful and productive methodological simplification, which is also a radical partiality. The consequences of this exclusion can be seen in some of the problems that arise with respect to the category of belief. Much of the complexity that has intrigued and frustrated philosophers and others about belief derives from its reflective character, from the fact that belief is both how we know and also an object of our knowing, which source of complexity is amplified where, as in Christianity, 'belief' is also a centrally important category of religious thought, introducing the notion that belief is distinct from knowledge because characterised by certainty, or by doubt, or by peculiar kinds of commitment. In an important essay that showed among other things how unwise a generation of anthropologists had been to neglect the writings of Lévy-Bruhl, Rodney Needham (1972) demonstrated that the category of belief does not correspond to a natural or universal psychological reality, but is instead a specifically post-Christian and not-so-post-Cartesian logical muddle: one that is no doubt now culturally inescapable, at least for users of English, but for all that a challenge rather than a useful tool for any attempt systematically to think about thought. But this is all generally side-stepped in much cognitive science, in favour of a conception of beliefs simply as the distinct mental entities that severally *cause* specific behaviour, and in favour of the associated practice of inferring the existence of beliefs, conceived in this way, from behaviour by reverse-engineering reasoning.

In an early paper (1982) Dan Sperber distinguished between what he called propositional and semi-propositional representations. He was interested in how to understand what is going on when people appear to hold and act upon apparently irrational beliefs (when a friend comes rushing to tell you of an opportunity to kill a dragon, for example). Sperber observed that there must be a difference in the manner in which we hold a belief (represent a representation) depending on whether or not we understand its meaning. We can hold and in some ways act upon a representation whose meaning we do not or only partly understand—a 'symbolic' or semi-propositional representation, in Sperber's terms—but just because we do not understand its meaning, the ways in which it can inform our thinking and behaviour, and interact with our other beliefs, will be restricted. We believe it in quotation marks: we can recognise the idea, but perhaps only in some forms, we can repeat it and affirm it, but we can only in very limited ways reason or innovate with it, or question it and see where it does and does not apply, and so on.

This paper of Sperber's is one of very few instances where cognitive scientists have addressed any of the complexities in the concept of belief, rather than taking it for granted, and Astuti's paper in this volume, in addressing the question of the context-dependency of belief, is another. Most serious thought about belief has been conducted outside the field of cognitive psychology. Paul Veyne's (1988) brilliant discussion of the terms in which ancient Greeks 'believed' in their myths is a case in point, and adds support to the general line of thought Astuti is opening up.

Veyne describes how for half a millennium Greek thinkers grappled with questions of what was and was not reliable in their myths. Noting that even Christians in the later part of his period, who of course denied the existence of the Olympian gods, never questioned the historicity of heroes such as Aeneas, Romulus, Theseus, Heracles, Achilles, or even Dionysus (1988: 40), he emphasises that scepticisms took different forms and were concerned with different matters from those we might expect. Both ancients and moderns, he observes, accept the basic historicity of the Trojan war, although what we know of it comes so overwhelmingly in narratives much of which we know must not be true, but we do so for different reasons.

> We believe because of its marvellous aspect; they believed in spite of it. For the Greeks, the Trojan War had existed because a war has nothing of the marvellous about it; if one takes the marvellous out of Homer, the war remains. For the moderns, the war is true because of the fabulous elements with which Homer surrounds it; only an authentic event that moved the national soul gives birth to epic and legend (1988: 60).

In their attempts to sort truth from fiction and lies, the learned of the time seem to us by turns sceptical and completely credulous. Veyne doubts that either bad faith or some notion of half belief explains this. Of course we are familiar with phenomena such as suspension of disbelief, but this again is neither of these. As he remarks, 'even if we consider Alice and the plays of Racine as fiction, while we are reading them we believe; we weep at the theater' (1988: 22). It is not that we half-believe or pretend to believe, but rather that we believe, in certain contexts, processes, or practices. And those learned Greeks, Veyne suggests, were similarly wavering or alternating between different criteria of truth (1988: 50). While they might often seem to have half-believed, it was rather that because they regarded myth as a mixed (or half-rotten) corpus, they hesitated between different ways in which they might find the uncorrupted truth in it (1988: 65). The problem was never solved, and in the end Christianization raised other concerns and made it possible to abandon it (1988: 111–2). All along then, argues Veyne, the question of whether and in what ways the Greeks believed in their myths was not a subjective or merely psychological question. Their modalities of belief were related to the definite, socially instituted ways in which truth could be pursued and possessed (1988: 27). People 'believed' as they participated in these ways of knowing.

Sperber's 1982 paper was at least an attempt to begin to address these matters in the language of cognitive science. The distinction he proposed between propositional and semi-propositional representations has however been largely neglected, in favour of a different one drawn by him in a later paper (1997), that between reflective and intuitive beliefs. Reflective beliefs are those we are consciously aware of holding, intuitive beliefs are those that our inherited cognitive architecture causes us to act upon, before and irrespective of any reflection in which we might engage. Barrett (this volume) adopts but rephrases this as the distinction between reflective and non-reflective beliefs. With this distinction, matters of qualified or half belief are lost, as is the whole question of context dependence, for in practice it becomes a distinction between what we think we believe and what we are inescapably caused to and therefore *really* believe, even if we do not know it.

The idea that we can believe something without knowing we do—indeed something that we believe we do not believe—is now so ingrained in our everyday thinking, largely (and perhaps embarrassingly for most cognitivists) through the influence of Freudianism, that the real force of the claims made with this distinction does not strike us as it should. For all the capacious ambiguity already evident in the concept, it must be doubtful that it is helpful to expand the extension of the word 'belief' to include postulated facts about the mind that are not on the face of it *representations* at all. In any case, even if we do allow these unconscious causes to be beliefs, this only re-emphasises Needham's point. We should not imagine that in saying something is a belief or that someone appears to believe a particular thing, one is saying anything very definite at all. Certainly, in attributing a belief one is not always doing the same thing. Some cognitive scientists, such as Boyer (2005: 26), have concluded that a cognitive study of religion should try to do without the concept of belief, as for different reasons Southwold suggested should anthropology (1983). This would have the advantage that the cognitive mechanisms postulated would not be confused with the mental phenomena they are supposed to explain.

Consider Barrett's discussion of the human propensity to 'believe' in racial stereotypes:

> For instance, research suggests it is quite natural to assume non-reflectively (automatically and without conscious awareness) that members of other human groups (e.g., racial, regional, or national) are more alike than people within one's own group (Hirschfeld, 1996). We refer to this "belief" as a tendency to stereotype. Reflectively we may become convinced that this non-reflective belief is flawed or inaccurate, but if so, the non-reflective belief nevertheless remains (pp. 183–4).

But what the research shows, in so far as it does, is in fact the *tendency*, and only that, to *reason* in an essentialist way. The idea that behind this observable tendency, and causing it, there lies a belief with propositional content is actually Barrett's interpretation,[20] and while he may have reasons for proffering this, it has costs. To begin with it leaves an ambiguity as to what it is that our cognitive architecture unalterably endows us with. Obviously it is not the particular content of racial stereotypes (the Chinese do this, Indians that); is it even the idea of race in the first place, or does that, like the rest of the content of the racial beliefs people have, come from elsewhere? By rephrasing a statistical tendency (rather than trying to quantify it) as a definite 'belief' we are all supposed to have, this crucial question (in addition to questions about the tendency's magnitude) is obscured. Secondly, the suggestion of definite propositional content makes it possible to think that this (all, as it were) 'nevertheless remains', unchanged and impervious to experience. Phrased as a statistical tendency, this would not seem so plausible. Thirdly, rather than pursuing the point that different beliefs may affect us in different situations (as Astuti begins to do), it arbitrarily regards some (those we may never profess, but for which cognitive science has a favoured explanation) as the real and permanent ones.

---

20. So it would be a more accurate exposition of his argument, I think, if Barrett were to say not, 'We refer to this "belief" as a tendency to stereotype', but instead, 'I refer to this tendency to stereotype as a "belief"'.

Another instructive example, also from Barrett (p. 191–2), is the following:

> It is HADD [hyperactive agency detection device] that makes us non-reflectively believe that our computers deliberately try to frustrate us, that strange sounds in a still house are evidence of intruders, and that light patterns on a television screen are people or animals with beliefs and desires. But more relevant to religious belief are situations in which a sheet on a clothesline or a wisp of mist gets recognized as a ghost or spirit.

There is probably no harm in saying, of someone who shakes his fist and shouts at his computer, that he 'believes' it is deliberately trying to frustrate him, or that the child who starts awake at an unfamiliar sound 'believes' what she hears is an intruder, or that the woman who laughs uproariously at a television programme 'believes' she is seeing people and animals being funny. There is positive confusion, however, if we imagine that these 'believings' are instances of the same thing. A rage that drives us to our habitual expression of anger, a momentary alarum that quickly passes when we collect our thoughts, and willing participation in institutionalized dramatic illusion are not the same kinds of mental operation. Their various relations to conventions, language, and instituted practices are obviously different. Postulating a faulty device that forces them all upon us does not seem to me to be a promising way to proceed. The fact is, indeed, that all these examples are to some degree conventional. Even if the same cognitive mechanism does turn out to be involved in them all, this would no more explain why they occur, or otherwise explain them, than would identifying the cognition involved in catching a ball explain the game of cricket.

It is a major problem for cognitive science (and especially when it uses reverse-engineering reasoning drawn from evolutionary psychology) that a form of observed behaviour may almost always be accounted for by more than one possible set of beliefs and intentions (Fodor 2005; see also Fodor 2000). So to seek to explain why people do what they do by postulating 'beliefs', as causal forces, for which there is no other direct evidence than the behaviour they are invoked to explain, is very narrowly circular. And if this is generally the case, it is even more so of much that pertains to religion, namely ritual action. One of the distinctive features of ritualised action, or so at least Caroline Humphrey and I have argued (Humphrey & Laidlaw 1994: Ch 7), is what we call a disconnection between meaning and form: the fact that different participants (or the same ones on different occasions) seek to attain quite different and even contradictory ends by performing the same ritual actions, because the meaning attributed to a ritualized action is radically underdetermined, as compared even to normal, unritualized action, by the physical form of what is done.[21]

Lanman, in his contribution to this volume, follows the logic of Barrett's distinction with admirable clarity. Since he regards cognitive-science methods of inferring beliefs from observed behaviour as 'meticulous' and 'robust' (we can concede at least that they are difficult to falsify), our knowledge of 're-flective beliefs' (those people do know they have) seems to him correspond-ingly flimsy, since all we have is their own reports. This is a common theme in the literature, and given a causal notion of belief, and the fact that of course the clearest examples of 'unreflective beliefs' come from instances of people behaving in ways that appear to conflict with their avowed beliefs, this is un-surprising. Lanman finds himself wondering,

> If people's self-reports of their reflective beliefs do not match up with their behaviors and other beliefs, do they actually "believe" what they say or are such statements now to be labeled as merely customary speech behaviors? (p. 127)[22]

The concerns about the reliability of people's self-reports that prompt this re-flection also motivate Lanman to question Astuti's experimental data on Vezo beliefs about the afterlife.[23] He conjectures (pp. 128–9) that some of the re-sponses informants gave to her questions were influenced by what are known as 'social desirability effects': that is, they said not what they 'really believed' but what they thought they ought to think.

Now of course there are cases where people do hypocritically report a be-lief they do not have, and that they might even despise, but which they know the powerful will reward them for expressing. But this is different from cases

---

21. See also on this point Bloch (2004). Ritual amplifies the effect of the general fea-ture of language and social practice that Putnam (1975) and Kripke (1980) refer to as the social division of labour in the generation of meaning, reference, and truth.

22. Here Lanman cites, as a reason for doubting people's self reports, not only cases where they do not apparently act as would seem to follow from their reported beliefs, but also cases where reported beliefs do not 'match up' with other self-reported beliefs. This is a complex matter, complexly related to the question of how we should treat apparent in-consistencies between belief reports and behaviour. I should note, however, that it is not obvious that people cannot 'really believe' mutually inconsistent things.

23. Astuti's results appear to contradict the claims of Jesse Bering and others (Bering 2002; Bering & Bjorklund 2004, Bering in press), cited in this volume by Guthrie, Barrett, and Whitehouse, to the effect that belief in psychological states persisting after death, and therefore in ghosts and souls, is an evolved 'default assumption' produced more or less in-escapably in young children by the 'Theory of Mind' module.

where people are genuinely *influenced* by the opinions of (certain) others, or regard the beliefs (certain) others express as a genuine *reason* for them to accept (or for that matter to reject) those beliefs. The notion of 'social desirability effects' treats these cases as equally suspicious: equally, as Lanman puts it, 'something that psychologists strive to eliminate from their studies'. But given that a high degree of the latter kind of deference is a prerequisite for anyone ever learning a language, for example, this may be an error of method.

There is no reason to suppose that it is exclusively the hypocritical kind of deference that is at work in the Vezo case. It is likely instead, to judge from the available ethnography, that Astuti's Vezo informants were telling her what they thought, on reflection, must be the case. They may find it a bit difficult to imagine exactly, and it is certainly not quite common sense, and perhaps it would not take very much to make them reconsider. Certainly, they are to some extent trusting tradition and received opinion in forming the view they do; perhaps they are even conscious that this is what they are doing. After all, they have little directly to go on themselves. This is not a strange or unreasonable position. In any case, none of this changes the fact that they are also exercising their reason and judgement, *in* deferring in this way. There is no reason to regard the result as not a 'genuine' belief, however much a robustly empiricist self image might be offended by the way it has been arrived at.

Maybe it is true that in some circumstances, under pressure, they act unthinkingly on instinct and common sense rather than reflective reason. That should be news to no one. But what do we conclude from it?

It depends, to revert to a point I have made before, on the interest that motivates inquiry. Lanman reports, accurately, that the response of many psychologists is to attempt to select out, or correct for, this tendency of people to exercise reflective reason and judgement in answering a question. Well, insofar as their interest is in the reductive explanation of human behaviour, as of a causal system, which, insofar as it is explained, is thereby amenable to prediction and control, this is a sensible response. But while the causal manipulation of behaviour is an alarmingly prevalent regulative concern in much psychological science,[24] it is not the only possible interest in understanding human thought. Eliminating the free exercise of reason from the purview of your inquiry is, fortunately, not the same as eliminating it from human affairs, and although this method might well achieve some statistically significant predictive measure of how people will behave (although, as I have observed, success in this regard does not in fact seem imminent and has certainly

---

24. On this see the powerful remarks in MacIntyre (1985).

not been achieved) this will not make it an exhaustive description of how in fact people do go on.

The important point is that re-classifying human thought and discourse as 'merely customary speech behaviors' is not, as it superficially appears to be, a conclusion indicated by experimental evidence. The hypothesis that human reason, imagination, and will are illusory, and that conscious thought and discourse are, as I have heard it put in cognitive-science circles, just the sound of lips flapping about, is instead implicit in the *premises* of cognitive science as a method. Lanman himself only raises this as a possibility, and does not endorse it as a conclusion, but other cognitive scientists (for instance Palmer and Steadman 2004) have argued for it as the only possible way forward. And it will indeed persistently suggest itself, unless the pragmatic working assumptions for the application of a method are consistently and clearly distinguished from description, or worse still criteria, of reality. As individuals, cognitive scientists can of course resist this alluring confusion of the real with the measurable. They may be as persuaded as anyone else of the reality of human freedom and reason. But if so, it would be well to acknowledge that the methods of cognitive science, since they assume them away, will not be of help in understanding them, and that these features of human life set the limits for the method.

Conclusion

Cognitive science can give us an account of some mental operations that are involved in religious thought and action. Just as we may be enlightened by a cognitive-scientific account of what it is to recognise a table or a raccoon, or to mistake an artefact for a living thing, or to see a mirage, or to remember a story, so the same methods can tell us how we remember what we have been told about gods or ghosts, and why we might sometimes think we have seen one. They have given us an intuitively plausible account of why ideas of gods, ghosts, and magic are so ubiquitous in human societies, by explaining why our minds might be highly prone to entertain and retain, and find it so easy to work with, these ideas. But for the evaluative concepts, emotions, and motivations that are not in this sense 'natural', but instead the historical products of particular traditions, an adequate account will have to include the history of the language and institutions and relationships and practices that sustain them, and the web of other such concepts on which they depend for their meanings. So if cognitive science can explain why we are disposed to a certain degree to believe in demons, it cannot explain why this demon takes this form in this tradition, or why we find him, say, pathetic. We are at the beginning of developing a scientific account of the computational aspects of human cognition, and this is valuable, interesting in itself, and also something about which students of religion should be informed: just as knowledge of the materials artists work with is useful for historians of art. But however complete and precise its description of those processes might become, cognitive science will never be more than ancillary to and will always be methodologically quite distinct from what anthropological and/or historical students of religion have to do. This means, as I have suggested, that while they can learn from each other's results, cognitive-scientific and humanist study of religion are qualitatively different modes of knowledge and experience, and that therefore there is no prospect that one will ever entirely replace the other, or that they might merge into anything other than confusion.

References

Asad, Talal. 1993. *Genealogies of Religion: Discipline and Reasons of Power in Christianity and Islam*. Baltimore: Johns Hopkins University Press.

——— 2003. *Formations of the Secular: Christianity, Islam, Modernity*. Palo Alto: Stanford University Press.

Bering, J. M. 2002. Intuitive Conceptions of Dead Agents' Minds: The Natural Foundations of Afterlife Beliefs as Phenomenological Boundary. *Journal of Cognition and Culture*, 2: 263–308.

——— In press. The Folk Psychology of Souls. *Behavioral & Brain Sciences*.

Bering, J. M. and D. F. Bjorklund. 2004. The Natural Emergence of Reasoning about the Afterlife as a Developmental Regularity. *Developmental Psychology*, 40: 217–233.

Bloch, Maurice. 2004. Ritual and Deference. In Harvey Whitehouse & James Laidlaw (eds), *Ritual and Memory: Toward a Comparative Anthropology of Religion*. Walnut Creek: AltaMira: 65–78.

——— 2005. A Well-Disposed Social Anthropologist's Problems with Memes. In *Essays on Cultural Transmission*. London: Berg: 87–102.

Boyer, Pascal. 1994. *The Naturalness of Religious Ideas: A Cognitive Theory of Religion*. Berkeley: University of California Press.

——— 2001. *Religion Explained: The Human Instincts that Fashion Gods, Spirits and Ancestors*. London: Heinemann.

——— 2002. Why do Gods and Spirits Matter at All? In Ilkka Pyysiäinen & Veikko Anttonen (eds), *Current Approaches in the Cognitive Science of Religion*. London: Continuum: 68–92.

———— 2005. A Reductionist Model of Distinct Modes of Religious Transmission. In Harvey Whitehouse & Robert McCauley (eds), *Mind and Religion: Psychological and Cognitive Foundations of Religiosity*. Walnut Creek: AltaMira: 3–29.

Boyer, Pascal and Pierre Lienard. In press (2007). Why Ritualized Behavior? Precaution Systems and Action-Parsing in Developmental, Pathological and Cultural Rituals. *Behavioral and Brain Sciences*.

Brown, Peter. 1981. *The Cult of the Saints: Its Rise and Function in Latin Christianity*. London: SCM Press.

Carrithers, Michael. 1990. Jainism and Buddhism as Enduring Historical Streams. *Journal of the Anthropological Society of Oxford*, 21/2: 141–63.

Collingwood, R. G. 1994 [1916] *Religion and Philosophy*. Bristol: Thoemmes Press.

Cort, John E. 2001. *Jains in the World: Religious Values and Ideology in India*. New York: Oxford University Press.

Davidson, Donald. 1980. *Essays on Actions and Events*. Oxford: Clarendon Press.

Das, Veena. 1984. Towards a Folk Theology and Theological Anthropology of Islam. *Contributions to Indian Sociology* (NS), 18: 239–305.

Dumont, Louis. 1985. A Modified View of Our Origins: The Christian Beginnings of Modern Individualism. In Michael Carrithers, Steven Collins, & Steven Lukes (eds) *The Category of the Person*. Cambridge: University Press: 93–122.

Durkheim, Emile. 1995 [1912] *The Elementary Forms of the Religious Life*. New York: Simon & Schuster.

Fodor, Jerry. 2000. *The Mind Doesn't Work That Way: The Scope and Limits of Computational Psychology*. Cambridge MA: MIT Press.

———— 2005. The Selfish Gene Pool: Mother Nature, Easter Bunnies and Other Common Mistakes. *Times Literary Supplement*, 29 July.

Frankfurt, Harry G. 1988. Freedom of the Will and the Concept of the Person. In *The Importance of What We Care About: Philosophical Essays*. Cambridge: University Press.

Gellner, David N. 1990. What is the Anthropology of Buddhism About? *Journal of the Anthropological Society of Oxford*, 21: 95–112.

Gombrich, Richard & Gananath Obeyesekere. 1988. *Buddhism Transformed: Religious Change in Sri Lanka*. Princeton: University Press.

Guthrie, Stewart. 1993. *Faces in the Clouds: A New Theory of Religion*. Oxford: University Press.

Hacking, Ian. 1995. *Rewriting the Soul: Multiple Personality and the Sciences of Memory*. Princeton: University Press.

Harrison, Peter. 1990. *'Religion' and the Religions in the English Enlightenment*. Cambridge: University Press.

Hirschfeld, Lawrence A. 1996. *Race in the Making: Cognition, Culture, and the Child's Construction of Human Kinds*. Cambridge MA: MIT Press.

Horton, Robin. 1993. *Patterns of Thought in Africa and the West: Essays on Magic, Religion, and Science*. Cambridge: University Press.

Humphrey, Caroline with Urgunge Onon. 1996. *Shamans and Elders: Experience, Knowledge, and Power among the Daur Mongols*. Oxford: Clarendon Press.

Humphrey, Caroline & James Laidlaw. 1994. *The Archetypal Actions of Ritual: A Theory of Ritual Illustrated by the Jain Rite of Worship*. Oxford: Clarendon Press.

Jenkins, Timothy. 1999. *Religion in English Everyday Life: An Ethnographic Approach*. Oxford: Berghahn.

Kripke, Saul. 1980 [1972]. *Naming and Necessity*. Oxford, Blackwell.

Laidlaw, James. 1995. *Riches and Renunciation: Religion, Economy, and Society among the Jains*. Oxford, Clarendon Press.

Lash, Nicholas. 1996. *The Beginning and the End of 'Religion'*. Cambridge: University Press.

Latour, Bruno. 1998. Ramses II, est-il mort de la tuberculose? *La Recherche*, 307.

Lawson, E. Thomas & Robert N. McCauley. 1990. *Rethinking Religion*. Cambridge: University Press.

Leach, E. R. (ed.) 1968. *Dialectic in Practical Religion*. Cambridge: University Press.

McCauley, Robert N. & E. Thomas Lawson. 2002. *Bringing Ritual to Mind*. Cambridge: University Press.

MacIntyre, Alasdair. 1985 [1981]. *After Virtue: A Study in Moral Theory*. London: Duckworth.

Mameli, Matteo. 2007. Evolution and Psychology in Philosophical Perspective. In R. Dunbar & L. Barrett (eds) *Oxford Handbook of Evolutionary Psychology*. Oxford: University Press.

Masuzawa, Tomoko. 2005. *The Invention of World Religions*. Chicago: University Press.

Mill, John Stuart. 1864. On the Definition of Political Economy. In *Essays on Some Unsettled Questions of Political Economy*. London: J. W. Parker.

Millikan, Ruth. 1984. *Language, Thought, and Other Biological Categories*. Cambridge, MA: MIT Press.

Mumford, Stan Royal. 1989. *Himalayan Dialogue: Tibetan Lamas and Gurung Shamans in Nepal*. Madison: University of Wisconsin Press.

Needham, Rodney. 1972. *Belief, Language, and Experience*. Oxford: Blackwell.

Oakeshott, Michael. 1933. *Experience and its Modes*. Cambridge: University Press.

Palmer, C. T. and L. B. Steadman. 2004. With or Without Belief: A New Evolutionary Approach to the Definition and Explanation of Religion. *Evolution and Cognition*, 10: 138–147.

Pennington, Brian K. 2005. *Was Hinduism Invented? Britons, Indians, and the Colonial Construction of Religion*. Oxford: University Press.

Pettit, Philip & John McDowell (eds) 1986. *Subject, Thought, and Context*. Oxford: Clarendon Press.

Putnam, Hilary. 1975. *Mind, Language, And Reality: Philosophical Papers. Volume 2*. Cambridge: University Press.

———— 1978. *Meaning and the Moral Sciences*. London: Routledge.

Rabinow, Paul. 1983. Humanism as Nihilism: The Bracketing of Truth and Seriousness in American Cultural Anthropology. In Norma Haas et al (eds) *Social Science as Moral Inquiry*. New York: Columbia University Press. 52–75.

Ruel, Malcolm. 1982. Christians as Believers. In J. Davis (ed.), *Religious Organization and Religious Experience*. London: Academic Press. 9–31.

Saler, Benson. 2000 [1993]. *Conceptualising Religion: Immanent Anthropologists, Transcendent Natives, and Unbounded Categories*. Oxford: Berghahn.

Skorupski, John. 1976. *Symbol and Theory: A Philosophical Study of Theories of Religion in Social Anthropology*. Cambridge: University Press.

Slone, D. Jason & Joel G. Mort. 2004. On the Epistemological Magic of Ethnographic Analysis. *Method & Theory in the Study of Religion*, 16: 149–63.

Southwold, Martin. 1978. Buddhism and the Definition of Religion. *Man* (NS), 13: 362–379.

———— 1979. Religious Belief. *Man* (NS), 14: 628–44.

———— 1983. *Buddhism in Life: The Anthropological Study of Religion and the Sinhalese Practice of Buddhism*. Manchester: University Press.

Sperber, Dan. 1982. Apparently Irrational Beliefs. In Steven Lukes & Martin Hollis (eds) *Rationality and Relativism*. Oxford: Blackwell: 149–80.

———— 1997. Intuitive and Reflective Beliefs. *Mind and Language*, 12: 67–83.

Tambiah, Stanley Jeyaraja. 1970. *Buddhism and the Spirit Cults in North-East Thailand*. Cambridge: University Press.

———— 1990. *Magic, Science, Religion, and the Scope of Rationality*. Cambridge: University Press.

Taylor, Charles. 1985. *Human Agency and Language: Philosophical Papers 1*. Cambridge: University Press.

Veyne, Paul. 1988. *Did the Greeks Believe in their Myths? An Essay on the Constitutive Imagination*. Chicago: University Press.

Whitehouse, Harvey. 2004. *Modes of Religiosity: A Cognitive Theory of Religious Transmission*. Walnut Creek: AltaMira.

Whitehouse, Harvey & James Laidlaw (eds.). 2004. *Ritual and Memory: Toward a Comparative Anthropology of Religion*. Walnut Creek: AltaMira.

Wikan, Unni. 1984. Shame and Honour: A Contestable Pair. *Man* (NS), 19: 635–52.

Williams, Bernard. 1995. *Making Sense of Humanity*. Cambridge: University Press.

CHAPTER NINE

TOWARDS AN INTEGRATION OF ETHNOGRAPHY, HISTORY, AND THE COGNITIVE SCIENCE OF RELIGION

Harvey Whitehouse

Scientific explanations and interpretive accounts of human behaviour, including religious behaviour, are different kinds of enterprise. It is tempting to think that although the questions asked by both scientists and humanist scholars look similar, they are actually incommensurate. Hilary Putnam's professor, caught with his trousers down in the girls' dormitory, may serve as an instructive illustration (Putnam 1978: 42–3; see Laidlaw, this volume). As Putnam observes, the question 'why was the professor there?' could be answered in a potentially infinite variety of ways, including that the professor was there so that he could not leave before midnight at a speed faster than light, given that nobody (certainly not professors) can travel faster than light. To the ethnographer or historian[1] it may seem that the answers suggested by scientific psychology have a similarly bizarre character, quite unrelated to the questions that matter to people in everyday life. Nothing could be further from the truth.

Cognitive scientists are typically interested in fundamentally the same problems that perplex interpretive anthropologists, as well as historians and others. In the scenario Putnam presents, all would be eager to know about the professor's motivations and intentions. The ethnographer or historian might seek to contextualize the professor's own account of his intentions within a web of locally and temporally variable values (e.g. whether this event occurred

---

1. Although this remark does not apply to Laidlaw, who recognizes to a considerable extent the value and relevance of scientific enquiry.

on a California campus in the 1960s or in a twenty-first century theological seminary). The question of how the professor's behaviour is judged in the prevailing cultural context (e.g. one that celebrates free love or one that counsels moral censure or litigation), is unquestionably relevant to understanding his predicament. But the cognitive scientist urges us to heed an *additional* set of questions. For instance (and this is only an example), what kinds of evolved human capacities govern processes of reputation management? How are these brought to bear when a transgression occurs?

Our closest relatives, the great apes, do not have to deal with such issues. Chimpanzee transgressions do not become the object of gossip or slander that might handicap their abilities to mobilize authority and resources in the future, even among strangers. But humans have to make immensely subtle calculations about such matters, resulting in a glorious repertoire of strategies for managing their reputations. Recent studies suggest, for example, that confession is widely used as a means of damage limitation in circumstances when exposure is a serious risk, based on the intuition that punishment will be less severe if the transgressor displays remorse. The greater the risk of exposure and the more serious its consequences the stronger the urge to confess becomes (at least by the statistical measures used in these kinds of studies). Consequently, meaning and context *matter*, even for cognitive scientists—in fact, *especially* for cognitive scientists. People, even professors, tend to lie when they think they have a low risk of detection and to confess when they fear discovery. But these strategies are carefully modulated by subtle features of context: how severe the punishments for a particular transgression are likely to be in a particular cultural setting, the extent to which forgiveness might be anticipated in response to displays of remorse and contrition, and so on. And these kinds of judgements come into play irrespective of actual guilt, for sometimes even the innocent confess (even innocent professors, if that is not a contradiction in terms).

If cognitive and interpretive anthropologists are really studying the same things, as I think they are, then the crunch question is whether the kinds of answers they provide could be *integrated*. Two extreme views on this matter may be distinguished. Hardline cognitivists maintain that conscious thought is merely a surface expression of processes outside our awareness, and that the latter processes shape and constrain our consciousness whereas it seldom (if ever) happens the other way around (e.g. Bering and Shackelford *in press*). For this reason asking people about their intentions or the meanings of their experiences and observations elicits no more than cryptic clues to the real causes of their behaviour. We ignore these clues at our peril, to be sure, but they do not constitute explanations in themselves. Hardline interpretivists in-

sist that meanings and reasons are only explainable in terms of other meanings and reasons, whether those of informants (the ethnographic gambit) or
of the interpreter (the hermeneutic gambit)[2]. Both forms of hardline interpretivism constitute a circular strategy (amusingly dubbed 'the hermeneutic
vortex'[3]) that accomplishes ever more elaborate stories but forecloses the possibility of ever explaining anything. An alternative to both extremes is available, based on a certain amount of compromise but also a large dose of messy-
world empirical enquiry.

There is now a mounting body of evidence that explicit representations, including many (if not all) the things go to make a religious tradition, are influenced by implicit cognition, about which we can only learn indirectly,
through experimental research (both laboratory-based and naturalistic). Such
findings have opened up the possibility of two major types of contribution to
core anthropological problems. The first type seeks to contribute to an explanation for cross-culturally recurrent features of religious thinking and behaviour, regardless of the specificities of local contexts and histories. Such a strategy proceeds on the basis that, all else being equal, certain kinds of religious
concepts (for instance) will be more widespread in human societies than others. Such claims pertain to statistical patterns of recurrence in the ethnographic record as a whole rather than to individual cases. The second potential contribution from this quarter, however, considers how specified
environmental conditions bias the activation of different types and configurations of cognitive mechanisms in predictable ways. How does the presence
of a particular institutional system trigger or inhibit implicit thinking, overt
behaviour and consequent patterns of cultural transmission? The latter question (which of course could be fractionated in a wide range of narrower variants), encompasses our concerns about Putnam's unfortunate Professor,
whose individual mental states and behaviour can only be fully understood in
their wider context. While a generalizing approach may accurately quantify
the likelihood of intended sexual transgressions on the part of half-naked men
in girls' dormitories, the more detail we provide about the context in which
such escapades occur the more precisely we can predict the psychological states
and behavioural choices of particular would-be transgressors. Lawyers do it.
So do anthropologists. But on the whole they do it by appeal to more or less

---

2. In the latter case, paradoxically, the conscious meanings attributed by the interpreter
are sometimes viewed as inaccessible to the actor, a state of affairs that may attributed to
a diversity of factors (e.g. collective unconscious, dynamic unconscious, false consciousness, mystification, hegemonic ideology, etc.).

3. Lawson and McCauley 1993.

implicit assumptions, stereotypes, or fashionable interpretive frameworks rather than with reference to testable theories of the way people actually think.

Implicit cognitive biases, even if situated in richly specified sociocultural contexts, may turn out to be only part of the story, however. Contrary to some cognitivist hardliners, I would argue that conscious reasoning and reflection also influence the way we behave, in turn shaping and constraining processes of cultural innovation and transmission. Experimental psychology provides just a fraction of the evidence needed to understand such processes. We must look also to the data commanded by ethnographers and historians, among others who catalogue the statements and deeds of our fellow human beings in their historically specific cultural habitats. For this reason, anthropologists must be part of the explanatory endeavour, in on the ground floor. Although we cannot (yet) measure the relative importance of implicit and explicit cognition in patterns of social behaviour and cultural efflorescence that is the direction in which I believe we need to go. Let us begin, however, by considering how far the cognitivist hardliners can take us.

Implicit Cognitive Constraints on Religious Transmission

A substantial and growing literature in the cognitive science of religion argues that religious transmission is shaped and constrained by implicit (unconscious) cognitive processes. A central feature of this approach is that it seeks to fractionate religious thinking and behaviour into myriad different components that are explainable in terms of a finite array of relatively discrete cognitive mechanisms. Sometimes construed as 'modules', or at least as 'domain-specific' systems, [4] these cognitive mechanisms are often assumed to have evolved in response to evolutionary pressures that are, at least in principle, discoverable by evolutionary psychologists, physical anthropologists, cognitive archaeologists, and other students of human evolution. But evolutionary arguments play a subsidiary role in the cognitive science of religion, since the main evidence for specialized, domain-specific cognitive systems comes from experimental research by developmental and cognitive psychologists (and to some extent also from neuroscientists and clinical psychologists). The strategy is to ask what effect these implicit mechanisms have on the transmission

---

4. For a cutting edge discussion of modularity theory and domain-specificity, and an account of the history of these terms, see Barrett and Kurzban (in press).

of culture, for instance in the area of religious thinking and behaviour. And what this requires, in practice, is a piecemeal approach to the phenomena of interest.

Religious behaviour is extremely complex, involving a huge diversity of cognitive systems. Nobody could study all of those things at once. So cognitive scientists have adopted the procedure of taking one cognitive mechanism (or cluster of mechanisms) at a time and asking what role it plays in the transmission of very specific kinds of religious information. Rather than asking, for instance, 'how are rituals in general transmitted?' cognitive scientists home in on some strikingly recurrent features of ritual behaviour around the world (e.g. the tendency to repeat nonsensical verbal formulae) and try to explain each component more or less in isolation, before moving on to explain other aspects of the same ritual behaviour (perhaps with reference to very different mechanisms). This way of proceeding can seem very puzzling if you are not used to it. Scholars trained in the grand theoretical traditions of Marxism, psychoanalysis, semiotics, or phenomenology may assume that theories of religion must always take the form of *general theories of religion as a whole*. Indeed, it may seem absurd to reduce religion to one puny little mechanism in the mind. But such reactions belie a basic misunderstanding. The aim is to build up a picture of the multiple causes of a huge variety of different components of, for instance, ritual behaviour *before* attempting to declare that we have something approaching a 'theory of ritual' as such.

The best way to illustrate this point is, perhaps, to look at a specific example of ritual behaviour and to reflect briefly on the range of cognitive mechanisms that would seem to shape and constrain its varied component features. Consider the following piece of ethnography deriving from my fieldwork among members of the Pomio Kivung religious movement in Papua New Guinea in the late 1980s, who daily laid out offerings to their ancestors in various kinds of temple (Whitehouse 1995: 67–68):

> The task of preparing offerings for the ancestors is supposed to be quite distinct from the task of secular food preparation. When handling offerings to the ancestors, the women should observe specified internal states. For example, the women should never think about eating the food as they prepare it for (although they may eventually eat their fill of it) the food at this stage belongs to the ancestors and must be prepared with a view to (in the local idiom) 'giving with the palm of the hand' (i.e. freely, generously, and unreservedly). If the cooks think of eating the food in the course of its preparation then it will come from 'the back of their hands' and the

ancestors will reject it. In actual fact, it is not the material substance of the food which the ancestors consume, but the respect, goodwill, generosity, deep faith, and devotion which the living supposedly put into its preparation and presentation. It follows that any breach of Kivung morality on the part of the cooks during food preparation renders the offering useless, because such breaches imply lack of devotion and respect (insofar as they 'injure' the ancestors in the sense of causing them offence) and lack of faith (insofar as a true believer would be too afraid to sin during the food preparation). A typical sin on the part of the cooks would be for two of them to gossip about the third's laziness, such gossip being seen (in the local idiom) as the 'theft' or 'killing' of the third person's good name. By cooking for the ancestors separately the women avoid squabbles or covert bad feeling about relative labour inputs. Under no circumstances should a menstruating woman work as cook (if she comes into contact with the food it will be polluted and unacceptable to the ancestors). Sickness and menstruation may reduce the labour power of the cooking group and this usually just means that less food is prepared.

At 2.30 p.m. the village bell is struck with a stick three times by anybody who knows the time ... Of the men who come to take the food from the cook house to the Cemetery Temple when the bell is struck, not all necessarily have set duties to perform, some acting merely as assistants. The men do not communicate with one another except by mouthing, gesticulating, or whispering and they are supposed to observe the same morally sound internal states as the cooks. They enter the Cemetery Temple one by one through the front door and place the food and drink (e.g. bottles of water) on a sideboard.

The temple is internally divided into two rooms. The first room, accessible through the front door, is dedicated to lower ranking ancestors and contains two tables with benches (one for deceased men and boys and the other for deceased women, girls and babies) and a sideboard for storing food. A team of designated (all-male) helpers lays the tables in this room with plates, cutlery and decorative flowers or leaves in vases. Other tasks include the final cleaning of crockery and other equipment with tea towels and the display of elaborate concern with neatness and tidiness in the room. Checks are also made on the provision of additional comforts for the ancestors who will come to 'eat', for example a blanket and pillow in case one of them is 'cold' or 'tired'. Finally, food is dished into plates on the tables.

Clearly, there are great many different things going on even in this relatively simple string of ritual procedures. The cognitivist strategy is to begin by plucking out certain features that are found in rituals more generally, for instance: the fear of menstrual pollution, the overt concern with cleanliness and neatness, the emphasis on rules that have no known function (e.g. the rigid adherence to a certain division of labour by sex, the requirement that the temple be entered in single file, the observation of routines carefully marked out by the chiming of the village bell, etc.). These are only part of what cemetery temple rituals entail, in the Kivung religious tradition, but at least we have a starting point. Could there be a single underlying mechanism that produces these particular features of ritualized behaviour, whether in the Kivung or in the many thousands of other ritual traditions that ethnographers have documented around the world?

Pascal Boyer and Pierre Lienard (2006) argue that certain characteristic features of culturally standardized rituals can be explained with recourse to the implicit operations of a cognitive system geared to the handling of potentially hazardous materials in the environment. This 'hazard-precaution system', they argue, involves three major levels of functioning. The first is described (following Szechtman and Woody 2004) as the 'security motivation system', the function of which is to identify potential hazards through the stepwise engagement of three kinds of neural mechanisms. One mechanism is concerned with the appraisal of potential threats. Its activation in turn triggers a motivational system geared to evaluating the nature and seriousness of the threats. And where the threats are deemed sufficiently serious a third system is activated that selects an appropriate response to the potential hazard from a limited repertoire of motor and visceral programmes. Activation of these programmes (leading to precautionary procedures, such as cleaning or isolating and arranging potentially contaminated objects) should normally feedback inhibitory signals to the appraisal mechanism. Boyer and Lienard point out, however, that Szechtman and Woody's model is not sufficient, as it stands, to account for some of the characteristic features of the precautionary procedures that are selected. For instance, why those particular procedures and not others? Why are they performed in a certain order rather than some other? To answer these questions, they introduce a second major system that responds to the elevated arousal occasioned by the security motivation system. At an experiential level, the operations of this second system produce a nonspecific sense of threat and a tendency to focus on minutiae rather than on overall patterns. This latter process places heavy burdens on working memory leading to a high degree of conscious attention to the performance of rigidly circumscribed procedures.

Boyer and Lienard argue that this model reveals why humans respond to perceived threats of contamination in highly stereotyped ways (i.e. conforming to rigid procedural rules), entailing such features as redundant repetition and a sense of obligation or compulsion. They argue further that these mechanisms are activated in slightly modified fashion in socially sanctioned rituals, on the one hand, and in the pathological condition known as 'obsessive-compulsive disorder' (or OCD), on the other. In the case of socially sanctioned rituals, the hazard-precaution system is only partially activated—that is, rituals that have become standardized in society serve to mimic some of the input conditions of the hazard-precaution system without necessarily triggering the arousal occasioned by potential hazards. In the case of OCD, the hazard-precaution system is activated in its entirety but due to the malfunctioning of certain parts of the system (which need not detain us here) anxiety levels occasioned by the potential hazard are modulated incorrectly and the system becomes trapped in a self-feedback loop that generates obsessive repetition of particular micro-procedures. Despite important differences between the behaviours found in socially sanctioned rituals and OCD patients respectively, Boyer and Lienard argue that this model helps explain many interesting similarities between the two.

The link between OCD and religious rituals had been considered in considerable detail in previous research, some of it inspired by Sigmund Freud's early speculations on the topic. The most impressive contribution to this area of research in modern times has arguably been Fiske and Haslam's (1997) comparison between OCD symptoms and traits found in socially sanctioned rituals based on an extensive survey of the ethnographic record. What Boyer and Lienard bring to this topic, however, is a plausible account of the precise mechanisms responsible for the similarities between the behaviours of OCD sufferers and some of the actions that widely recur in cultural rituals. Moreover, they set out an elegant model of how the specific behavioural traits arising from the activation of the hazard-precaution system would have been adaptive for our hominid ancestors.

In considering the evolutionary background to the relationship between psychological mechanisms and recurrent behavioural outputs[5] it is helpful to distinguish between the *proper* and *actual* domains of the mechanisms in-

---

5. As noted above, this is not a necessary requirement for cognitive approaches but may be seen as enriching the theoretical breadth of the enterprise, given that evolutionary biology constitutes one of the most robust sciences available to the study of human (and animal) behaviour.

volved.[6] The proper domain of hazard-precaution mechanisms would be hazardous materials in the ancestral environment, such as rotting meat, faeces, infected wounds, and other contaminants. These constitute threats to survival (and thus to reproductive success) from which our hazard-precaution mechanisms evolved to protect us and, consequently, these are the kinds of inputs that will typically serve to activate those dedicated mechanisms. But the same mechanisms could be set off by inputs that resemble contaminants, for instance because they are linked by association to feelings of disgust or nausea (some people feel that way about soft egg yoke or butter) or because we see other people handling them in a way that suggests that they are potentially dangerous (inasmuch as many objects used in religious settings, for instance, are treated with special care and attention they too are likely to set off our hazard-precaution mechanisms). These kinds of triggers, which may vary widely among individuals and across populations, do not actually target potential sources of contamination. Consequently they belong to the *actual* but not the *proper* domains of the mechanisms at issue.

If Boyer and Lienard are right, they appear to have gone some way to explaining why the Kivung ritual incorporates such a striking concern with the avoidance of contamination of the offerings, with straightening and arranging tasks, with arbitrary rules for the performance of sequencing of actions, and suchlike. The persuasiveness of their theory lies in the fact that it draws on such a broad range of scientific evidence: developmental, neurological, clinical, biological, and so on. But it is also a very modest theory, in the sense that it does not for a moment assume that it is capable of explaining rituals in general, or the entire range of behaviours entailed in any one particular ritual. Rather, it plucks out a rather narrow strand of the behavioural repertoire entailed in ritual performances and tries to explain that, and only that. This means, of course, that we are still left with the challenge of explaining many other things going on in our Kivung ritual. For instance, why are the men unable to speak normally inside the temple? Why do people suppose the ancestors will be offended if the women think about eating the food during its preparation? Even these two questions (and there are many more we could ask, as we shall soon see) suggest that we still have a long way to go in explaining the data before us.

To begin with the whispering of the men inside the temple, this would seem to be linked to the idea that the ancestors are invisibly present and should be treated respectfully. In this regard, their behaviour differs little (if at all) from

6. Millikan 1984; see also Sperber 1996.

the way visitors to a church in England might speak only in hushed tones upon entering. One of the psychological mechanisms responsible for this behaviour might be dubbed 'agency detection'. As with the hazard-precaution system significant work has been carried out on the neural and cognitive characteristics of agency detection, as well as its evolutionary foundations.[7] We also have a body of evidence suggesting that humans are easily primed to *overdetect* agents in their environments. Stewart Guthrie argues (1993 and in this volume) that, regardless of cultural differences, people everywhere require little encouragement to see signs of agency in almost any kind of situation. We curse our computers when they crash, we scream in the dark when an object unexpectedly brushes against us, and we are easily seduced by advertisements that display a vast range of products (from household detergents to Michelan tyres) behaving like people. Being sensitive to the presence of possible agents would have conferred considerable benefits in the conditions in which our ancestors evolved. Clearly, any failure to pay attention to signs that a predator is present would have been far more costly than the experience of innumerable false alarms (Guthrie 1980, 1993; Barrett 2000). So when my friends in Papua New Guinea lowered their voices to a whisper inside the temple, perhaps it was (partly) because their agency-detection systems were delivering powerful intuitions that there were ancestors around.

Perhaps. But still there is much more going on. Consider the food preparation problem (that the women shouldn't think about eating the food themselves). This is essentially a moral issue. Food that is prepared for the ancestors with thoughts of greed or hunger is considered by Kivung members to be harmful to the ancestors. Such behaviour is described as 'killing' the ancestors. In the local idiom, 'killing' refers not only to homicide but to all harm-causing behaviour. And as such its use elicits ideas of a moral nature that have universal foundations. Since Elliott Turiel's work in the 1980s, psychologists have realized that moral rules involve intuitions that are somewhat different from rules of mere convention. For a start, moral rules are fundamentally similar the world over, while conventional rules may differ very widely. One of the core features of moral rules is the intuition that causing *harm* to others is wrong. Moral violations everywhere are considered to be more serious than conventional violations. And, crucially, moral rules are felt to hold true whether or not they are upheld by a figure of authority (that is, people intuitively judge harming behaviour to be wrong even if it is condoned or not ex-

---

7. For overviews of work on agency-detection systems, see Scholl and Tremoulet 2000 and Barrett 2004.

plicitly forbidden by authorities). This appears to be the case even when we are talking about divine or supernatural authority. For instance, in a study of Amish teenagers, Nucci found that all participants considered that working on Sunday would be acceptable if God had not forbidden it but agreed that hitting people would be wrong whether or not God forbade it (Nucci 1986).

From Piaget onwards many psychologists have assumed that the development of moral thinking is a consequence of empathy towards others based on being able to imagine oneself in their shoes. But Shaun Nichols (2004) has shown that individuals who have very limited perspective-taking capacities (e.g. children under the age of four and people with autism) nevertheless are quite competent at distinguishing moral from conventional rules. In response to this kind of evidence, Blair (1995) has argued, following Lorenz (1966) that social animals like dogs and humans have evolved mechanisms of limiting aggression between individuals of the same species. For instance, dogs stop attacking in response to submission cues. Blair argues that in humans the activation of a 'violence inhibition mechanism' (VIM) in response to distress cues in others sets off a search for meaning, resulting in a negatively valenced interpretation of an event (i.e. the moral evaluation that what is happening is wrong). He has shown in a series of ingenious studies that psychopathic criminals do not respond to distress cues (in photographs) in the same way as normals and further that they cannot distinguish between morality and convention in the way most people can. He concludes from this that they have a defective VIM. But as Nichols (2004) has shown, the VIM account has a number of drawbacks. First, even though small children and people with autism have problems with perspective-taking, they are aware that people experience desires and suffer pain. We cannot therefore completely rule out the possibility that moral intuitions depend upon some rudimentary perspective-taking abilities. Second, the VIM notion cannot account for the sense that something is wrong as opposed to merely being regrettable. That is, even if we do feel bad when we see distress cues it doesn't follow that we judge what we see to be wrong. Seeing people have accidents or fall prey to natural disasters should activate VIM (if such a mechanism exists) but not lead us to conclude that what we have seen is morally wrong.

Nichols builds an alternative to both the Piagetian and VIM accounts, by offering a unique synthesis of both. His starting point is that in the course of development people acquire 'normative theories' consisting of sets of rules for how to behave. In order for these stipulations of convention to become moral rules, they must be emotionally valenced such that people *feel* it is wrong to break those rules. Such feelings are triggered when we witness people harming others. On this account, moral rules are rules of convention backed by affective systems. In support of this, Nichols has conducted experiments show-ing that affective systems concerned with themes other than causing harm produce intuitions of a moral kind that differ from those pertaining to more neutral conventional rules. For instance, he used behaviours that would be considered disgusting rather than harmful to demonstrate the point. As with harmful behaviours: 'The disgusting violations were regarded as less permis-sible, more serious, and less authority contingent than the neutral violations' (2004: 22). And just as Blair observed that psychopaths found it harder to dis-tinguish harmful behaviours (moral infractions) from violations of neutral norms (infractions of conventions), so Nichols found that people with a high tolerance for disgusting behaviour found it harder to distinguish disgusting behaviours (moral) from violations of neutral norms (conventions), in terms of our key parameters of seriousness, permissibility, and authority contin-gency. Thus, these parameters seem to be 'mediated by affective response' (2004: 24).

Nichols considers two possible ways in which normative rules might come to be emotionally valenced and thus *moral*. One possibility is that there is a developmental stage during which certain kinds of neural mechanisms start to be activated as a response to negatively valenced (e.g. harmful) actions. Once these responses become associated with particular norms, they result in stable moral attitudes (although the responses that kick-started them may pass, having been part of a transient developmental phase). A second possi-bility is that the emotional valence has to be present on-line in order to gen-erate moral responses. Various kinds of moral deficits, for instance as observed in criminal psychopaths, would thus be due either to abnormal development or due to the ongoing lack of some normal mechanism throughout life. Nichols also considers the possibility that the establishment of moral rules (or their failure to become established) may involve both developmental and on-line factors.

If the Nichols account, or something like it, turns out to be correct then the moral thinking system, like all other features of intuitive cognition, has an evolutionary history that needs to be unpacked. Although that is a task to be undertaken elsewhere, we should note that an obvious adaptive value of this system is that it serves to limit intra-species violence, a point made in some detail by Blair (see above). That function might belong to its proper do-main. But moral intuitions can also be activated in relation to other species, as happens among animal rights campaigners (see Milton 1993) or even in re-lation to non-empirical beings, such as the Pomio Kivung ancestors.

Rudimentary perspective-taking may, as Nichols proposes, be a necessary ingredient of moral thinking. But there are also mechanisms in normal adults that are capable of far more sophisticated forms of reflection on what other people may be thinking or feeling. Among experimental psychologists, these mechanisms are commonly referred to as 'theory of mind' (or ToM), the significance of which has also been stressed by many other contributors to this volume (most notably Astuti, Barrett, Bloch, Cohen, and Guthrie).[8]

Mature ToM mechanisms provide humans with the ability, indeed the nagging obligation, to generate inferences about intentional states that drive the behaviour of people around them. First-order ToM mechanisms deliver intuitions about the possible intentions of other actors, and they begin to emerge early in development. By around age four to five, children realize that people's behaviours are driven by intentions that may or may not be based on accurate information and that it is therefore possible to manipulate their behaviour through duplicity and deception. Second-order ToM mechanisms appear a little later, around age six or seven, allowing us to speculate not only on the intentional states of Jim and Mary but on the speculative inferences that they in turn might be making with regard to the states of mind accompanying our own behaviour. Second order ToM abilities enable us to construe behaviour as communicatively driven (Jim does x because he knows that Mary is likely to interpret x in a certain way).

In our Kivung ritual, every action that involves the agency-detection system has the potential to trigger ToM mechanisms as well. For instance, the preparation of food for the ancestors is carried out on the understanding not only that the ancestors are around (an intuition delivered by the agency-detection system) but that the ancestors can 'read' one's thoughts. These mindreading capacities attributed to the ancestors mean that even if a cook is careful never actually to eat any of the food being prepared, the ancestors will know immediately if she fantasizes about doing so. The idea that ancestors know what you are thinking carries important social consequences. Normally we predict the likely behaviours of others and calculate the risks of them finding out things we don't want them to know, on the assumption that people have an imperfect knowledge of what is going on and may not know things we do (or worse, may know things we don't). The idea that supernatural

---

8. Some of the most revealing studies of ToM come from developmental psychology, focusing on the emergence of mindreading capabilities in the course of childhood (Carey 1985, Gopnik and Meltzov 1997, Bloom 2000). Another important area focuses on deficits in ToM functioning among people with autism (Baron-Cohen 1995). In addition we now have an increasingly detailed picture of the neurological mechanisms involved in ToM (Baron-Cohen, Tager-Flusberg, and Cohen 2000; Williams, Whiten, Suddendorf and Perrett 2000).

agents, a group of ancestors in this case, have access to all our thoughts introduces a whole new level of complexity to these kinds of calculations. In particular if other people think that you think that the ancestors will find out and punish your wrongdoing (even when no earthly agent has any power to find out these things) then this has implications for your reputation in the eyes of others. A cook devoutly preparing offerings for the ancestors may accrue the respect and trust of others, or risk incurring censure and punishment, in ways that a cook preparing dinner for her husband may not.

Now, we could in principle go on like this for some time, picking out bits of the Kivung ritual that seem to satisfy the input conditions of various postulated domain-specific cognitive mechanisms. If we were to do that we would no doubt find that many behaviours require explanation with recourse to more than one (perhaps many) psychological mechanisms. After all, we have observed that it would be insufficient to explain the behaviour of cooks preparing offerings to the Kivung ancestors only with reference to, say, the agency-detection system. This same behaviour also involves ToM mechanisms since the ancestors are attributed special mindreading capabilities (and will know if one of the cooks even thinks about eating the food she is preparing). And we have also noted that this part of the ritual excites mechanisms dedicated to intuitive moralizing, since an offering given from the 'back of the hand' would harm the ancestors. But we need not stop there. Preparing food for the temple also involves the hazard-precaution system, since the idea of tainted offerings gives overt expression to pollution anxieties. And there are many more candidate mechanisms that could be implicated in one way or another in just this single feature of the ritual process.

It might be argued that if we were to persist in this type of exercise for long enough we would end up with an explanation for the Kivung ritual, and all other rituals that exhibit similar features. I have my doubts about that, however. Although we could certainly do a great deal more to explain our Kivung ritual (and millions of other recurrent behaviours like it, all around the world) by pursuing this strategy to its limits, we will eventually discover that there are important features of the observed behaviour that cannot be understood in that way, either because the approach is too narrow to encompass all the relevant facts (a problem of lack of comprehensiveness of the approach) or because the approach excludes more creative aspects of cognition responsible for the variability of thinking and behaviour from one cultural tradition to the next (a problem of lack of particularity of the approach). Both problems have always haunted the hardline cognitivist approach to explaining culture. But I will argue that they can also be overcome if we expand our conception of cognition to encompass processes that are often *conscious* and always *his-*

torically constituted. Herein, I believe, lie particularly fertile opportunities for the integration of cognitivist and interpretivist approaches.

Cognition and Religious Variation: Where Ethnography, History, and Science Meet

Hardline *interpretivism* envisages culture as an unstable (continuously contested, mediated, disrupted) network of meanings and inter-subjective states that hovers somewhat mysteriously above (or at least beyond) all other ontological levels of reality (e.g. the psychological or the biological) and is certainly irreducible to them. But I favour an alternative view of culture. We learn about other people's thoughts and feelings through empathetic dialogue and observation.[9] Over time, we can build up such a rich understanding of other people's construals of the world that they seem to assume a systemic quality more or less tentatively generalizable to others in their community, marking the group off from others living in different places or historical periods. The challenge for ethnographers and historians, it seems to me, is to characterize accurately such patterns among individuals and populations, present and past. Explaining how the patterns came into being certainly entails close tracking of the way they change over time or are spread through the movement of people and things across space. But in order for people to invent or spread their ways of thinking to others, within and across the generations, requires tools— not just physical artefacts, like books and buildings, but also mental tools, such as the ability to acquire new concepts and to recognize their potential applications. Such abilities certainly include the kinds of domain-specific cognitive mechanisms discussed in the last section and understanding such mechanisms takes us a long way in explaining the behaviour of most mammals, ourselves included. But the case of humans is complicated by the fact that we have an extraordinary capacity for innovation and learning and therefore for the transmission of cumulative bodies of *acquired knowledge.* Only some of our psychological mechanisms confer this advantage, as we shall see, but they do so in ways that have consequences for the operation of all the kinds of mechanisms discussed above.

---

9. Although, as should be clear from the discussion of so-called Theory of Mind in the last section (and in many other parts of this volume), cognitive science has contributed more than any other approach to the development of a theoretical understanding of empathy and its role in human communication and sociality.

To understand why, it is helpful to return to ethnographic case material. Our Kivung ritual does not end with the laying out of offerings. Once the tables have been carefully prepared, and various minor rites have been performed, everyone leaves the temple—except for one man, who remains inside. This man observes a vigil, listening and watching for signs that the ancestors are present (Whitehouse 1995: 70–73):

> The official who keeps a vigil in the Cemetery Temple (between approximately 1.50 p.m. and 3.45 p.m.) plays the part of a kind of observer. His Pidgin title of *kuskus* (literally 'clerk' or 'bookkeeper') associates him with Western government structure, particularly the officials who keep records on what is said at meetings. I will refer to the *kuskus* as a 'witness'.... After entering the temple, the witness goes to sit in a small cubicle, built in the corner of an external wall and a wall dividing the two rooms of the house. According to Kivung ideology, he remains seated until 3.45 p.m. During the period that he sits there, the witness may hear a knocking at the door indicating the arrival of the ancestors, or he may hear a faint clattering of plates, cutlery or bottles, or the creaking of a door. Such sounds are caused by the ancestors who have come to receive the offerings. Although they create noises, the ancestors are never visible. An analogy with the wind is often made, for just as the wind moves the branches of trees yet is itself invisible so the spiritual substance of the ancestors moves objects in the Cemetery Temple thereby creating noise. These noises always cease before 3.45 p.m. and their cessation may be marked by another sound of knocking on the door. When the noises have stopped, it means that the ancestors have finished 'eating' and have departed. Sometimes the witness hears nothing in the course of his vigil.
>
> The task of the witness is to keep a mental note of any noises that occur during his vigil, representing evidence that the ancestors came to receive the offerings. All the men who act as witnesses are supposed to possess considerable courage and moral fibre since proximity to spirits, even the 'good' ancestors, is held to be dangerous to those who possess inadequate conviction and faith and who therefore have reason to fear the wrath of God and the ancestors. The danger is twofold: in the face of presumptuous behaviour on the part of the morally weak, the ancestors may confer sickness upon them and also the fear of the morally weak can itself cause sickness.
>
> At 3.45 p.m. the village 'bell' is struck three times once again, indicating that it is time for those villagers wishing to eat and to hear

the news from the witness (this could be anybody in the community) to gather outside the front door of the Cemetery Temple. The man in charge of the boss's room is the first to arrive at the cemetery. He knocks on the door of the Cemetery Temple, announces his identity, then opens the door and enters. The witness remains seated in his cubicle while this man checks the plates containing food, first in the 'lower' room and then in the boss's room. He may find that the food has not been disturbed, or he may notice that the rim of one or more of the plates has been splashed with food or that there are other signs of disturbance (e.g. a hole in a taro tuber where a morsel of food has been removed). If such signs are discovered he will show them to the witness who, until that moment, presumably does not know of their existence. Meanwhile, a team of helpers removes the food from the house and places it on leaves and tables in the open air. Then the witness and man in charge of the boss's room emerge from the Cemetery Temple into the light to find another kind of official (an 'orator') standing there with his back to them, facing a gathering of some or all of the villagers (depending on who wanted to come). The man in charge of the boss's room goes to join the throng while the witness goes to stand a little to one side and behind the orator. The hushed chatter of those gathered sinks into silence while the witness whispers into the orator's ear, informing him either that the ancestors did not come or that he heard certain noises and the food was disturbed indicating that the ancestors did come. The orator in turn conveys this information to the gathering. If the ancestors did not come, it means that the living have committed some offence, thereby contaminating the offering and rendering it unacceptable to the ancestors. In such a case, the orator urges the people to consider how they have caused offence (it may be that all, some or just one of them is/are to blame). He tells them that a monetary collection must be performed soon to wipe the slate clean and restore moral purity in the village. He probably reiterates the impossibility of being reunited with the ancestors if evil continues to flourish among them, or he may focus on the horrors of damnation. If the ancestors have come, the orator relates the evidence to his audience and urges everyone to continue along the righteous path which they have evidently found and to strengthen themselves against corruption by Satan ... After brief applause, the orator, the witness and the whole gathering repeat together the Lord's Prayer, and everybody shakes hands. The Lord's Prayer has a special significance for Kivung members insofar as it seems to focus on the themes of returning ancestors ('Thy kingdom come ...), the harmony of the group ('... as we forgive those who trespass against us'), and other central principles of Kivung doctrine.

Many of the details of what happens in these additional parts of the ritual arguably involve the same psychological mechanisms we have already considered. For instance, the witness's agent-detection systems are highly primed for signs of ghostly presence, since observing these events is the ostensible purpose of his vigil. The evidence as to whether or not the ancestors came to 'eat' the offerings is taken as an indication of what the ancestors are thinking about the living and this requires the activation of ToM mechanisms. But there are also non-modular cognitive systems involved in all of this, one of which may be dubbed the 'cross-domain analogical thinking system' or 'CAT system'.

The CAT system is one of the most powerful mental tools in the human repertoire, since it enables us to borrow knowledge from one domain of experience and to use it to solve problems in completely different domains. Classic studies of analogical thinking present subjects with a problem and its solution and test the extent to which they are capable of applying this information to other kinds of problems. For instance, Gick and Holyoak (1980, 1983) would tell people a story about a military general who realized that he needed a large number of troops to storm a fortress. Unfortunately the roads leading to the fortress were all too narrow for him to deliver his troops to the target in sufficient numbers at one time. His solution was to divide his men up across the countryside so that they could all converge on the fortress at a pre-arranged time. Later, subjects in the experiment were told about the problem of a surgeon who needed to destroy a tumour but could not cut it out without damaging the surrounding organs. He had the idea of using a laser to attack the tumour in a more precise fashion but also realized that this would damage healthy tissue at the point of entry. The rationale is that subjects should use the general and fortress story to solve the surgeon's dilemma. They should propose that, just as the general attacked from several directions, the surgeon should direct the laser at the tumour from many different angles thus converging in a sufficiently powerful ray to destroy the growth but without causing any damage upon entry to the body. These kinds of studies have produced mixed results. Overall it is clear that people are more likely to produce spontaneous analogies to solve problems in real-world conditions than in artificial laboratory settings (Kokinov and Petrov 2001), a situation that has come to be known as the 'analogical paradox' (Dunbar 2001).

One possible explanation for this paradox may be summed up by the old adage that necessity is the mother of invention. Real generals and real surgeons have to find ways out of the problems they encounter whereas participants in a psychological study generally lack the motivation to draw analogies between inconsequential stories. In the real world, analogical thinking delivers solutions to problems thick and fast. When seeking to persuade others to their way of thinking people routinely produce a rich variety of analogies, usually with strong emotional overtones (Thagard and Shelley 2001). It is a commonplace stereotype that politicians mix their metaphors but this may be because politicians' analogies are so prolific that they are hard for their producers to track in working memory.

During my field research on the Pomio Kivung, I found that the discourse of religious adherents was replete with analogies (*tok piksa* or 'talk picture' in Pidgin). Consider, for instance, the role of the witness which was construed as analogous to the role of a bookkeeper in government meetings. This analogy had immense significance for Kivung followers, because they claimed that the ancestors formed a ghostly assembly, itself modelled on earthly governments. According to my informants, this other-worldly government would soon return to 'this world' establishing a new system of administration and a powerful industrial base in the heart of their rainforest environment. People had detailed ideas about why and how this would happen and their ritual practices, including the temple rituals, were seen as part of the normal functioning of the ghostly assembly by close analogy with the House of Assembly in Port Moresby (the capital of Papua New Guinea). Moreover, when orators delivered their sermons at the end of the temple rituals, they prided themselves on their capacity for impassioned rhetoric, especially the ability to summon up new and exciting analogies. As I noted in my original ethnography (Whitehouse 1995: 81):

> The orators stir up a deep horror of the Devil and his many wives (evil female spirits), by stressing how sinners are separated from their social universe and sucked into a wilderness of hunger, fear, and loneliness and by focusing on the horrors of eternal damnation. The orators speak in elaborate and grisly metaphors which capture the imagination and instil fear into would-be sinners. They employ rhetoric and raised voices, charged with emotion. In view of the frequency of these meetings, the key speakers have highly developed oratory skills and powers of persuasion.

The CAT system figures prominently not only in the speeches of accomplished orators but in the daily discourse of ordinary Kivung followers. My fieldnotes soon became filled with colourful analogies and elaborate metaphors used to illustrate and justify the movement's doctrines. Mark Turner (1996) has argued that this predilection for parable is fundamental to all human thought. The title of his intriguing book, *The Literary Mind*, amply makes the point. To the extent that this analogical impulse is a pervasive feature of human thought (even if somewhat muted in the laboratory) it is hard to envisage a domain of human behaviour that does not in some way provide grist for its mill.

According to archaeologist Steven Mithen (1996), the capacity to make analogical connections between domain-specific forms of intelligence was a somewhat recent evolutionary adaptation in the hominid lineage. Mithen assembles a range of evidence suggesting that Early Humans possessed advanced forms of specialized intelligence in the domains of social thinking, technology production and use, and natural history. But these specialized forms of intelligence were 'cut off' from each other, so that there was no means of using technical intelligence to solve social problems or of using knowledge of natural kinds to organize social categories and statuses. The 'joining up' of these specialized capacities in Modern Humans explains the sudden profusion, in the archaeological record, of artefacts used as social markers (e.g. worn as body decorations) and of more complex forms of social organization based on analogues with natural taxonomies. Once fully established, the CAT system was capable of linking the outputs of literally any other cognitive system. To distinguish this type of system (and we must bear in mind that there may turn out to be a number of them[10]) from those that are domain specific, I propose to refer to the latter as 'nuclear systems' and the former as 'global connection systems'.

Innovations delivered by creative thinking would be of limited value if they could not be passed on from one generation to the next. For that type of cumulative learning to take place, we require systems of information storage (including external mnemonics and technologies of the intellect) capable of encompassing at least some key features of the outputs of all the other mechanisms in our cognitive repertoire and of binding them together into relatively durable networks of information packets. One such evolved cognitive

---

10. The forging of creative connections between distant or previously unconnected domains of knowledge may involve cognitive systems other than analogy-formation. For instance, logical or analytic thinking is also capable of creating novel conceptual connections and appears to operate in ways that differ significantly from what is sometimes called 'insight-thinking' (which includes analogical thinking). Whereas progress towards novel connections is *gradual* in logical thinking, it appears to be more *sudden* in the Eureka moments of insight-thinking (Metcalfe 1986). And whereas verbalization can adversely affect insight-thinking, this seems not to be the case with logical thinking (Schooler and Melcher 1995). These sorts of differences suggest that logical thinking should be viewed as a separate cognitive system from analogical thinking, even though both are types of global connection systems.

system in humans is 'semantic memory'.[11] Semantic memory is typically defined in contrast with 'episodic memory'.[12] Episodic memory refers to our capacity to recall distinctive moments in our lives. All mammals and birds possess a significant capacity for episodic remembering, such that specific types of cues trigger recall for relevant information about past experience. In apes, this type of remembering is rather highly developed. Chimpanzees, for instance, can recall quite large volumes of information but only in ways that are tied to *concrete encoding experiences*. For this reason, Merlin Donald (1991) describes ape culture as 'episodic', meaning that all new information, even the sort that is acquired through creative innovation, is tied to unique situations or episodes. One of the most strikingly distinctive features of human cognition is the capacity to store *general knowledge* about the world (objects, stories, people, dates, sequences, theories, and so on) in a manner that is quite independent of episodic recall (indeed, in the case of much of our general knowledge, we are helpless to recall the circumstances in which we first acquired it). This is what we mean by 'semantic memory'. As Donald has argued in considerable detail, the evolution of semantic memory in the mental armoury of our ancestors constituted a major cognitive breakthrough of unrivalled significance for the cumulative storage of cultural information.

The extraordinary value of semantic memory is that it enables each one of us to become a walking, talking encyclopaedia—a storehouse for knowledge. The evolution of such a system means that we can stockpile many of our greatest creative inventions and discoveries and pass these on to future generations. In order to exploit that capacity, however, there are some costs. While much of the information in semantic memory would be gathered informally through everyday experience, expert knowledge must be built up through long-term study involving regular review and rehearsal of the information acquired. In modern urban environments this involves formal schooling and examinations and it also increasingly involves the use of external data storage devices (ranging from traditional libraries to advanced digital archives) to extend our limited cognitive capacities. In the ancestral environment in which semantic memory mechanisms evolved, however, the first emergence of even rather limited capacities for explicit (teachable) information storage would have been revolutionary. Instead of having to rely on the outputs of nuclear systems (such as the contamination avoidance repertoire) or even global connection systems (such as analogical thinking) to decide how to respond to new situa-

---

11. For an excellent overview, see Baddeley 1997: Chapter 13.
12. Following the distinction first made by Tulving 1972.

tions, our ancestors could begin to rely on the lessons learned by their fore-bears.[13]

This meant that the actual domains of all kinds of cognitive systems were greatly enlarged. In the case of our global connection systems—such as the CAT system—the expansion of potential inputs would have been vast. And as storage capacity became enlarged through the development of the semantic memory system, our access to creative innovations from the past would have grown accordingly. This expansion, however, would still have been structured and constrained in various ways by our nuclear systems. For instance, our capacity to store information about the natural environment would have been constrained by nuclear systems dedicated to the construction of taxo-

---

13. One of the most ambitious theories of the cognitive and evolutionary foundations of human culture to date is that proposed by Tomasello (1999; see also Tomasello, Kruger, and Ratner 1993). Tomasello, like me, wants to explain distinctively human capacities for cumulative cultural transmission, whereby the knowledge and skills of one generation can be passed on to the next (a process he and his colleagues have labelled the 'ratchet effect'). Tomasello argues that creativity is not the key to this, since other primates show highly innovative tendencies as well (1999: 5). Rather, it is that humans uniquely have developed ways of *preserving* the outcomes of innovation. Tomasello thinks that knowledge-preservation can be explained by a cluster of cognitive mechanisms, among which 'perspective-taking' (ToM) plays a leading role (1999: 5–12). The present argument differs from Tomasello's in two key respects. First, humans are strikingly more creative than other primates insofar as our innovative and creative ideas are activated and applied *across* domains, hence my referring to analogical thinking (and other methods of creating cross-domain connections) as 'global systems'. Second, the mechanisms Tomasello focuses on are implicated in only some aspects of the ratchet effect, and are certainly not sufficient to account for it. Perspective-taking, for instance, undoubtedly plays an important role in most (but by no means all) forms of cultural learning, enabling us to 'learn not just *from* the other but *through* the other' (Tomasello 1999: 6, original emphases). But this is not a crucial feature of all distinctively human types of learning. The malfunctioning of ToM mechanisms in people with autism does not, as Tomasello seems to imply, necessarily imply a catastrophic failure of cultural learning. On the contrary, people with autism often show above-average capacities for acquiring expert knowledge in a wide range of domains. And despite the handicaps of their condition, some autistic individuals have contributed immensely to the store of human knowledge. The most immediate and obvious cause of the ratchet effect is not our capacity to imagine the world through other people's eyes but rather our capacity to *store* the information acquired from others so that it is available to conscious inspection, evaluation, and creative modification in the future. Explicit memory and cross-domain creativity constitute the key to this revolution. To use the terminology developed in this article: perspective-taking, along with the other nuclear mechanisms discussed by Tomasello, contribute significantly only to *some* aspects of learning; our global systems, dedicated to connecting and storing information, play an essential role in *all* forms of cultural innovation and transmission.

nomic databases and our knowledge about potential contaminants would have been constrained by nuclear systems that were naturally aroused by things that look rotten or smell bad. As intuitive botanists and healers, our capacities to harness and extend natural processes and to protect ourselves from diseases were inevitably based more on trial and error than on well-founded theories. Yet trial and error, driven by intuitive nuclear systems, is still capable of producing prodigious bodies of knowledge. Informal hypotheses generated by global creative systems, and 'stored' in semantic memory, could now be passed on and developed over many generations. So successful has this process been in human history that modern theory-driven science, which seeks to transcend the constraints of our nuclear systems, nevertheless is increasingly demonstrating the efficacy of many traditional remedies.[14]

One of the areas of human striving in which the constraints of intuitive thinking are somewhat loosened is the domain of *religion*.[15] Speculations about entities that don't exist (or that we cannot prove exist) and about origins that are little understood (i.e. concerning which we have limited evidence) present us with seemingly unlimited opportunities for cosmological innovation. Armed with tools for creative reasoning, such as the CAT system, modern humans were free to develop belief systems of extraordinary diversity. Connections made between one cluster of ideas and another could now be fixed in semantic memory through regimes of teaching and rehearsal. This fixation of the implicational or analogical links between otherwise quite unconnected ideas allowed the first emergence of what might be called 'doctrinal systems'.[16]

We have to be very careful at this point in the argument, however, because we teeter on the brink of ontological error. A doctrinal system is not a unitary 'thing' out there in the world, still less a 'being' of some kind with intelligent purposes of its own, but rather a series of countless iterations and reiterations stored in semantic memory as a set of templates (commonly called 'schemas' or 'scripts' by psychologists) that inform and guide our thinking and behaviour

To return to our ethnographic example, Kivung followers all told me strikingly similar things about the origins of the world, the history of their strug-

---

14. For a rounded evaluation of the scientific evidence on this topic, see Fontanarosa 2000.

15. Elsewhere, I have described these aspects of religion as 'cognitively costly' (see especially Whitehouse 2004: chapter 3).

16. See Whitehouse 1992, 1995, 2000, 2004; Whitehouse and Laidlaw 2004, Whitehouse and Martin 2004, Whitehouse and McCauley 2005.

gles with neighbouring groups, their experiences of colonization by the Germans and then the Australians, about their hopes for deliverance by their ancestors, the sacrifices this entailed, the meanings of the rituals they had to perform, and so on. This amounted to a substantial body of knowledge that gradually filled up my fieldnotes, to a point where I began to realize that everything was connected to everything else either by implication or by analogy. That insight was not my own special discovery, for it was more or less explicitly illustrated by every sermon I ever heard delivered by the Kivung's orators and other officials (and I heard a lot of them). What the orators knew, long before I came to know it as well, was that the cosmology and doctrine of their religious tradition formed an integrated network of connections that could be explored in speech, often in genuinely creative ways, but only by traversing well-worn tracks between the component concepts and networks of concepts. What gave these tracks their relative fixity was, as with a real track, the fact that people went over them time and again rather than randomly deviating and criss-crossing them. In the Kivung, unauthorized innovation on matters of doctrine and narrative was socially sanctioned. And heresy could not be committed inadvertently since regular reiteration of the orthodox canon ensured that innovations would always be noticed. This is one of the great accomplishments of semantic memory—that it facilitates not just recall for individual items but for elaborate networks of connections among them. Since semantic memory capacities evolved as a means of domain-general information storage all recurrent patterns of events in the world constitute its proper domain, including all the outputs of nuclear and global connection systems. I shall refer to semantic memory as a 'global storage' system.

Thanks to the presence of global storage systems in the human cognitive repertoire, cultural innovation never starts from scratch. The case of Kivung religion shows, even when we focus only on one type of ritual performed in one of its temples, that nuclear and global connection systems shape and constrain what people say and do at every turn. But no matter how closely we focus on those systems they will never enable us to explain why the Kivung tradition embraces particular configurations of systems and outputs while another tradition elsewhere embraces another. What is it that gives religious traditions their local and historical particularity, even though their members are all equipped with the same cognitive toolkits? The answer lies in the operations of global storage systems like semantic memory that impose a degree of fixity on particular configurations of representations, resulting from cumulative past experiences.

In talking about 'a degree of fixity' I do not mean to suggest that cultural systems really are fixed—only that they are somewhat resistant to change.

Once an elaborate network of schemas has become distributed in the memories of a population, it can certainly be changed but if that process happens swiftly then people will notice and could object (and may well have more or less explicit methods of co-operatively punishing unauthorized innovators). Slower processes of change (over years or generations) would of course be less noticeable except when one deliberately reflects on the subject (as an historian, or when engaged in autobiographical rumination). There are of course many ways in which distributed semantic schemas can change but at least some gross features of historical transformation owe their existence to the dynamic interaction between nuclear systems, on the one hand, and global systems, on the other.

Every time a mental representation is activated there is a risk that it will be transformed. Insofar as rehearsal reduces the risks of memory distortion and decay, frequently-activated schemas in a population will tend to be more robust than irregularly-activated schemas. To the extent that frequency of activation is modulated by the presence of artefacts, such as texts and iconography, it makes some sense to understand semantic memory as augmented by 'extended' global storage systems.[17] And to the extent that we can rely on others to reproduce specialized knowledge on behalf of others, it makes sense also to talk about 'distributed' global storage systems (Hutchins 1995). But no matter how important external mnemonics and expert knowledge may be in the reproduction of cultural schemas, the persistence of those schemas over time depends crucially on regular rehearsal (if only among specialists). When transmissive frequency falls below a critical level, there will be a risk of distortion. Distortions, however, are never random. All else being equal, the filling of gaps in semantic memory will be influenced most directly by in-

---

17. Donald goes so far as to argue that extended cognition, or 'external symbolic storage', constitutes a one of three major transitions in hominid cognitive evolution that were necessary for the emergence of distinctively human culture (his other two transitions are, first, the emergence of mimetic capabilities, that is being able to re-enact events, which he argues first appears among *homo erectus* populations, and, second, the development of speech systems). Although it makes some sense to regard extended cognition as a global storage system (facilitating the accumulation of information that could not otherwise be available to recall), we should not forget that artefacts (including inscriptions and computers) have to be interpreted by internal cognition in order to 'store' anything. Moreover, for most of human history, external storage has played a comparitively modest role in cultural transmission. Even rudimentary writing systems are no more than about 6,000 years old and the massive data storage capabilities afforded by computers only began to be realized half a century ago. So we should be cautious in over-estimating the importance of external storage in cultural transmission from the viewpoints of *both* evolution *and* history.

tuitive 'nuclear' systems. This weighting of cultural innovation in favour of intuitive thinking has been dubbed the 'cognitive optimum effect'.[18] The idea is that people readily 'default' to the easiest ways of representing information, in the absence of strong inducements to engage in more cognitively challenging ways of thinking. Among American Christians, for instance, it has been shown that 'theologically correct' ideas about divine omnipresence are easily overridden by more intuitive notions that God can only respond to one prayer at a time (Barrett and Van Ormann 1996). And we have growing evidence that 'theologically incorrect' religious ideas (i.e. more intuitive versions of authoritative teachings) are much more pervasive among rank and file members of religious traditions than among religious experts (Slone 2004).

Arguably the most elaborated attempt so far to synthesize cognitivist and interpretive perspectives on religion is the theory of 'modes of religiosity', arising initially out of ethnographic observations[19] but subsequently modified and extended through extensive collaboration with anthropologists, historians, and cognitive scientists.[20] The essence of this theory is that the transmission of two very general patterns of religious thinking and behaviour depends on the exploitation of both nuclear and global cognitive systems. In order to achieve widespread credibility, for instance, religious representations must have at least some cognitively optimal features (that is, they must meet the inputs conditions of our nucleated, intuitive cognitive systems). This is in accord with the claims, summarized in the last section, that have been repeatedly made by the cognitivist camp (and that are favoured by many contributors to this volume). But the cultural and historical particularities of religious traditions arise from the creative application of global connection systems and their fixation by means of global storage systems.

The theory of modes of religiosity postulates broadly two routes to creativity and storage. One (the doctrinal mode) emphasizes frequent repetition of core concepts and the connections that bind them together in semantic memory. The other (imagistic mode) emphasizes rare, climactic religious experiences and the formation of epiphanic insights and exegetical innovations. These two modes of religiosity, often present within the same tradition, not only bring about (and reinforce) highly distinctive patterns of activation of cognitively optimal religious concepts but they also give rise to massively coun-

---

18. Boyer 1994 (see also Whitehouse 2004).
19. Whitehouse 1995, 2000, 2004.
20. Whitehouse and Laidlaw 2004; Whitehouse and Martin 2004; Whitehouse and McCauley 2005.

terintuitive religious knowledge, such as the 'theologically correct' concepts of doctrinal elites or the esoteric revelations of mystics and expert cosmologists.

Tensions between the 'theologically incorrect' outputs of nuclear systems and the more cognitively challenging concepts of religious experts figure prominently among the causes of religious reformations, not only in Christianity but it would seem in all doctrinal religions. Religious reform is always at least partly an attempt to rectify theological incorrectness by establishing an uncompromising vision of the one true doctrinal system subjecting adherents to an extraordinarily intensive regime of high-frequency repetition of its cardinal concepts. But heavy repetition also carries costs, not just in terms of time and labour but potentially also in terms of morale and the maintenance of authority. High-frequency repetition of religious doctrine and intolerance of competing perspectives can lead to disaffection and ultimately to the formation of religious splintering and sectarian division. In such cases, the influence of nuclear systems (e.g. concerned with coalition-formation and the punishment of defectors) may figure prominently but theological innovation is very often driven by the same kinds of global systems that animated the original movements of reform, rather than by the so-called 'cognitive optimum effect'. These different consequences of nuclear and global cognitive systems are capable in principle of being theorized systematically, ultimately holding out the possibility of a thoroughgoing synthesis of cognitivist and ethnographic/historiographical perspectives on culture in general, and religion in particular.

Conclusion

Social and cultural anthropologists who are interested in explaining religion have much to learn from cognitive approaches. The evidence that our minds are composed of numerous specialized tools for handling different types of information is supporting increasingly plausible claims about the shaping and constraining effects of cognition on the invention and spread of culture in general, and religion in particular. So far, the contributions of cognitive scientists have focused rather heavily on a small set of domain-specific cognitive specializations (what I have been calling 'nuclear systems') in generating *universal* features of religious thinking and behaviour. Children, it now seems, cannot be raised to believe just anything; nor can adults be converted to any type of ideological system. Religions must exploit certain fundamental universal human intuitive biases and predilections if they are to get a foothold. The cognitivist project has certainly been valuable in explaining why many features of religious thinking and behaviour are much the same everywhere.

But religions also *vary* significantly from one place to the next. They differ not only their myriad details but also at the level of what we might call a 'middle range' of generalization. For instance, patterns of communication and exchange with putative supernatural beings are readily grouped into loose families of similar types of acts (prayers, rites of passage, sacrificial rituals, and so on) that receive strikingly different emphasis from one religious tradition to the next. Likewise, systems of belief exhibit highly contrasting cosmological, theological, ethical, and aesthetic predilections and biases. Patterns of leadership and spread are also highly variable, based on diverse types, and combinations of types, of authority claims (e.g. messianic, prophetic, textual, revelatory, etc.). This kind of variation, which has been the traditional focus of *interpretive* approaches to the study of religion, is salient for the very obvious practical reason that apparent differences between religious traditions provide a basis for coalitional thinking and contestations of identity. But it may also be salient theoretically, insofar as we are able to devise plausible explanations for varying patterns of practice, belief, scale, and structure in the world's diverse religions.

I have argued that the most promising explanatory strategies will be those that combine cognitivist, ethnographic, and historiographical perspectives on religion. The theory of modes of religiosity is one such approach. According to this theory, any universal tendencies towards certain types of religious thinking and behaviour are heavily shaped and constrained by socially and historically constituted prior patterns of innovation and transmission. But, at the same time, those patterns of innovation and transmission depend upon the presence of cognitive systems capable of forging novel ideas (and networks of ideas) and of 'fixing' those ideas in collective memory. Such processes are clearly influenced by the extent to which knowledge can be distributed and combined among specialists and by the ways in which external mnemonics (such as inscribing practices or commemorative artefacts and *aides memoires*) are used and elaborated. The theory of modes of religiosity focuses on just some (arguably significant) variables influencing the creation and storage of religious ideas, specifically such factors as frequency of transmission and level of arousal in the area of ritualized behaviour. But we are (or should be) witnessing only the beginning, and not the end, of a new synthesis of perspectives.

References

Astington, J.W., Harris, P.L. and Olson, D. (eds.) (1988) *Developing Theories of Mind*, Cambridge: Cambridge University Press.

Atran, Scott (1990) *Cognitive Foundations of Natural History*, Cambridge: Cambridge University Press.

Baddeley, A. D. (1997) *Human Memory: Theory and Practice*, Hove: Psychology Press.

Barrett, H. C., and Kurzban, R. (in press), 'Modularity in cognition: Framing the debate' in *Psychological Review*, Vol. 113, No. 3.

Barrett, J.L. (2000) 'Exploring the natural foundations of religion' in *Trends in Cognitive Sciences*, 4, 29–34.

——— (2004) *Why Would Anyone Believe in God?* Walnut Creek, Calif.: AltaMira Press.

Barrett, J.L. and Van Orman, B. (1996) 'The effects of image use in worship on God concepts' in *Journal of Psychology and Christianity*, 15, 38–45.

Baron-Cohen, Simon (1995) *Mindblindness: an essay on autism and theory of mind*, Cambridge MA.: MIT press.

Baron-Cohen, S., Tager-Flusberg, H. and Cohen, D.J. (eds.) (2000) *Understanding Other Minds: Perspective from Developmental Cognitive Neuroscience*, Oxford: Oxford University Press.

Bering, J. M. and Shackelford, T. K. (in press). 'Consciousness, intentionality, and human psychological adaptations' in *Theoria et Historia Scientiarum*.

Blair, R. (1995) 'A Cognitive Developmental Approach to Morality: Investigating the Psychopath' in *Cognition*, 57: 1–29.

Bloom, P. (2000) *How Children Learn the Meaning of Words*, Cambridge MA: MIT Press.

Boyer, Pascal (1990) *Tradition As Truth and Communication*, Cambridge: Cambridge University Press.

——— (1994) The *Naturalness of Religious Ideas: A Cognitive Theory of Religion*, Berkeley: University of California Press.

Boyer, Pascal and Lienard, Pierre (in press) 'Why Do Humans Peform Rituals? Cultural Rituals and the Psychology of Ritual Behaviour' in *Behavioural and Brain Sciences*.

Brown, C. (1984) *Language and Living Things: Uniformities in Folks Classification and Naming*, New Brunswick, NJ: Rutgers University Press.

Carey, S. (1985) *Conceptual Change in Childhood*, Cambridge MA: MIT Press.

Chi, M.T.H. and Slotta, J.D. (1993) 'The Ontological Coherence of Intuitive Physics' in *Cognition and Instruction*, 10: 249–260.

Churchland, P.M. (1989) *The Neurocomputational Perspective*, Cambridge MA: MIT Press.

Donald, Merlin (1991) *Origins of the Modern Mind: Three Stages in the Evolution of Culture and Cognition*, Cambridge MA: Harvard University Press.

Dunbar, Kevin (2001) 'The Analogical Paradox: Why Analogy Is so Easy in Naturalistic Settings, Yet so Difficult in the Psychological Laboratory' in Gentner, Holyoak, K.J., and Kokinov, B.N. (eds.) *The Analogical Mind: Perspectives From Cognitive Science*, Cambridge MA: MIT Press.

Fontanarosa, P.B. (ed.) (2000) *Alternative Medicine: An Objective Assessment*, Washington DC: AMA Press.

Geertz, Clifford (1973) *The Interpretation of Cultures*, London: Hutchinson.

Gelman, R. (1990) 'First Principles Organize Attention and Learning About Relevant Data: number and the animate-inanimate distinction as examples' in *Cognitive Science*, 14: 79–106.

Gelman, S.A. (1988) 'The Development of Induction Within Natural Kind and Artefact Categories' in *Cognitive Psychology*, 20: 65–95.

Gelman, R. and Gallistel, C.R. (1978) *The Child's Understanding of Number*, Boston: Harvard University Press.

Gelman, S.A., Gottfried, G.M., and Coley, J. (1994) 'Essentialist Beliefs in Children: the acquisition of concepts and theories' in L. Hirschfeld and S.A. Gelman (eds.) *Mapping the Mind: domain specificity in cognition and culture*, Cambridge: Cambridge University Press.

Gick, M.L. and Holyoak, K.J. (1980) 'Analogical Problem Solving' in *Cognitive Psychology*, 12: 306–355.

Gick, M.L. and Holyoak, K.J. (1983) 'Schema Induction and Analogical Transfer' in *Cognitive Psychology*, 15: 1–38.

Gopnik, A. and Meltzov, A. (1997) *Words, Thoughts, and Theories*, Cambridge MA: MIT Press.

Guthrie, Stewart. (1980) 'A Cognitive Theory of Religion' in *Current Anthropology*, 21(2):181–203.

Guthrie, Stewart. (1993) *Faces in the Clouds: A New Theory of Religion*. New York: Oxford University.

Harris, Paul L. (1989) *Children and Emotion: the development of psychological understanding*, Oxford: Blackwell.

Hirschfeld, L. (1995) 'Do children have a theory of race?' in Cognition 54: 209–252.

Hirschfeld, L.A. (1996) *Race in the Making: Cognition, Culture, and the Child's Construction of Human Kinds*, Cambridge MA: MIT Press.

Hutchins, Edwin (1995) *Cognition in the Wild*, Cambridge, MA: MIT Press.

Jackendoff, R. (1992) Language of the Mind: Essays on Mental *Representation*, Cambridge, MA: MIT Press.

Kaiser, M.K. Jonides, J. and Alexander, J. (1986) 'Intuitive Reasoning about Abstract and Familiar Physics Problems' in *Memory and Cognition*, 14: 308–312.

Karmiloff-Smith, A. (1992) *Beyond Modularity: A Developmental Perspective on Cognitive Science*, Cambridge MA: MIT Press.

Kokinov, B.N. and Petrov, A.A. (2001) 'Integrating Memory and Reasoning in Analogy-Making: The AMBR Model' in Gentner, Holyoak, K.J., and Kokinov, B.N. (eds.) *The Analogical Mind: Perspectives From Cognitive Science*, Cambridge MA: MIT Press.

Lawson, E. Thomas and McCauley, Robert N. (1993) 'Crisis of Conscience, Riddle of Identity: making space for a cognitive approach to religious phenomena' in *Journal of the American Academy of Religion*, 61: 201–223

Lorenz, Konrad (1966) *On Aggression*, New York: Harcourt Brace Jovanovich.

Milton, Kay (ed.) (1993) *Environmentalism: The View from Anthropology*, London: Routledge.

Mithen, S.J. (1996) *The Prehistory of the Mind*, London: Thames and Hudson

Metcalfe, J. (1986) 'Feeling of Knowing in Memory and Problem Solving' in *Journal of Experimental Psychology: Learning, Memory, and Cognition*, 12(2): 228–294.

Millikan, Ruth (1984) *Language, Thought, and Other Biological Categories*, Cambridge, Mass.: MIT Press.

Nichols, Shaun (2004) *Sentimental Rules: On the Natural Foundations of Moral Judgment*, Oxford: Oxford University Press.

Nucci, L. (1986) 'Children's Conceptions of Morality, Social Conventions, and Religious Prescription' in C. Harding (ed.) *Moral Dilemmas: Philosophical and Psychological Reconsiderations of the Development of Moral Reasoning*, Chicago: President Press.

Parascandola, M. and Weed, D.L. (2001) 'Causation in Epidemiology' in *Journal of Epidemiology and Community Health*, 55: 905–912.

Proffitt. D.R. and Gilden, D.L. (1989) 'Understanding Natural Dynamics' in *Journal of Experimental Psychology: Human Perception and Performance,* 15: 384–393.

Ranney, M. and Thagard, P. (1988) 'Explanatory Coherence and Belief Revision in Naïve Physics' in *Proceedings of the Tenth Annual Conference of the Cognitive Science Society,* pp 11–117, Hillsdale, NJ: Lawrence Erlbaum.

Resnick, L.B. (1986) 'The Development of Mathematical Intuition' in M. Perlmutter (ed.) *Perspectives on Intellectual Development: Minnesota Symposia on Child Psychology,* Vol.19, Hillsdale, NJ: Lawrence Erlbaum.

Richert, R.A., Whitehouse, H. and Stewart, E.E.A. (2005) 'Memory and Analogical Thinking in High-Arousal Rituals' in Harvey Whitehouse and Robert N. McCauley (eds.) *Mind and Religion: Psychological and Cognitive Foundations of Religiosity.* Walnut Creek, Calif.: AltaMira Press.

Rothbart, M. and Taylor, M. (1990) 'Category Labels and Social Reality: Do We View Social Categories as Natural Kinds?' in G. Semin and K. Fiedler (eds.) *Language and Social Cognition,* London: Sage.

Scholl, B.J. and Tremoulet, P.D. (2000) 'Perceptual Causality and Animacy' in *Trends in Cognitive Sciences,* 4: 299–308.

Schooler, J.W. and Melcher, J. (1995) 'The Ineffability of Insight' in S.M. Smith, T.B. Ward, and R.A. Finke (eds.) *The Creative Cognition Approach,* pp 97–134, Cambridge, MA: MIT Press.

Slone, J. (2004) *Theological Incorrectness: Why Religious People Believe What They Shouldn't,* New York: Oxford University Press.

Spelke, E.S. (1991) 'Physical Knowledge in Infancy: Reflections on Piaget's Theory' in S. Carey and R. Gelman (eds.) *Epigenesis of the Mind: Essays in Biology and Knowledge,* Hillsdale, NJ: Lawrence Erlbaum.

Sperber, Dan (1985) 'Anthropology and Psychology: towards and epidemiology of representations' in *Man* (N.S.), 20: 73–89.

——— (1996) *Explaining Culture: a naturalistic approach,* London: Blackwells.

Strauss, Claudia and Quinn, Naomi (1997) *A Cognitive Theory of Cultural Meaning,* Cambridge: Cambridge University Press.

Szechtman, H. and Woody, E. (2004) 'Obsessive-Compulsive Disorder as a Disturbance of Security Motivation' in *Psychological Review,* 111(1): 111–127.

Thagard, Paul and Shelley, Cameron (2001) 'Emotional Analogies and Analogical Inference' in Gentner, Holyoak, K.J., and Kokinov, B.N. (eds.)

The Analogical Mind: Perspectives From Cognitive Science, Cambridge MA: MIT Press.

Tomasello, Michael (1999) *The Cultural Origins of Human Cognition*, Cambridge MA: Harvard University Press.

Tulving, E. (1972) 'Episodic and Semantic Memory' in E. Tulving & W. Donaldson (eds.) *Organization of Memory*, New York: Academic Press.

Turiel, Elliott (1983) *The Development of Social Knowledge: Morality and Convention*, Cambridge: Cambridge University Press.

Turner, Mark (1996) *The Literary Mind: the origins of thought and Language*, Oxford: Oxford University Press.

Wellman, Henry (1990) *The Child's Theory of Mind*, Cambridge MA.: MIT Press.

Whitehouse, H. (1992) 'Memorable Religions: transmission, codification, and change in divergent Melanesian contexts' in *Man* (N.S.), 27: 777–797.

——— (1995) *Inside the Cult: religious innovation and transmission in Papua New Guinea*, Oxford: Oxford University Press.

——— (2000) *Arguments and Icons: divergent modes of religiosity*, Oxford: Oxford University Press.

——— (2001) *The Debated Mind: Evolutionary Psychology Versus Ethnography*, Oxford: Berg.

——— (2004) *Modes of Religiosity: a cognitive theory of religious transmission*, Walnut Creek, Calif.: AltaMira Press.

——— (2005) 'Cognitive Historiography: when science meets art' in Luther H. Martin and Harvey Whitehouse (eds.) *History, Memory, and Cognition*, special issue of *Historical Reflections/ Reflexions Historiques*, Vol.31, No.2.

Whitehouse, Harvey, and James Laidlaw, (eds.) (2004) *Ritual and Memory: Towards a New Comparative Anthropology of Religion*, Walnut Creek, Calif.: AltaMira Press.

Whitehouse, Harvey, and Luther H. Martin, (eds.) (2004) *Theorizing Religions Past: Historical and Archaeological Perspectives*, Walnut Creek, Calif.: AltaMira Press.

Whitehouse, Harvey, and Robert N. McCauley (2005) *Mind and Religion: Psychological and Cognitive Foundations of Religiosity*. Walnut Creek, Calif.: AltaMira Press.

Williams, J.H.G., Whiten, A., Suddendorf, T. and Perrett, D.I. (2000) 'Imitation, Mirror Neurons, and Autism' in *Neuroscience and Behavioural Reviews*, 25: 287–295.

Subject Index

adaptation, 19, 70, 139, 266
Africa, 5, 31, 60, 136–137, 146, 148, 154,
    244
Afro-Brazilian magic, 28, 149–153
agency/agents, 11–12, 16–18, 24, 37,
    46–49, 50–52, 54–55, 57–59,
    87–90, 98, 100, 102–103, 118,
    125–126, 138, 140, 156, 177,
    179–180, 182–184, 188–195, 198,
    202–204, 214, 229, 233, 238, 242,
    246, 256
agency detection, 125–126, 182–184,
    189–192, 195, 198, 202, 238, 256,
    260
Akan, 147, 156
analogy, 15, 66, 79, 232, 262, 265, 270,
    276
analogical thinking/CAT system,
    264–269, 278
ancestors, 5, 14, 65, 74, 77, 93, 101,
    161–179, 202, 213, 242, 251–252,
    254–256, 258–260, 262–265,
    267–268, 270
anthropomorphism, 17, 37–62, 129, 204
art, 26, 47, 58, 159, 213, 232, 242, 279
Azande, 137, 146–152, 157

belief, 6, 22, 26, 32, 34, 40, 43, 52, 57,
    71, 74, 76, 81, 85, 94, 120, 122–127,
    143, 150, 154, 156, 161–162,
    164–165, 167–171, 173–176,
    178–192, 194–196, 199–203, 205,
    213, 218, 223, 226–227, 229,
    231–240, 245–246, 269, 274, 278

brain, 7, 18, 29, 59, 63, 68–69, 79,
    101–102, 130, 177, 182, 212,
    242–243, 275
Brazil, 149–153
Buddhism, 39, 220–223, 225–226, 243,
    245–246

causality, 39, 43, 52, 61, 88, 91, 99–102,
    115, 122, 141, 146, 153, 190–191,
    206, 214, 218, 226, 234, 262, 268, 278
China, 38
Christianity, 39, 58, 64, 76, 117, 158,
    165, 185, 195, 198, 202, 204,
    225–227, 234, 242–243, 273, 275
cognitive constraints, 129, 204, 250
cognitive science, 3–4, 7–10, 12–14,
    16–21, 23–27, 30–31, 38, 49, 55,
    59, 74, 78–79, 82, 87, 102, 105,
    116–117, 121, 131, 145, 156, 159,
    205–206, 211–247, 250, 261,
    276–279
comparison, 18, 72, 173, 232, 254
computers, 15, 48, 61, 189–190, 238,
    256, 271
concepts, 9, 17–19, 23–24, 30, 66, 68,
    81, 102, 106, 129, 137–138,
    141–142, 145–146, 154–155, 158,
    175, 179, 186–188, 192, 194–195,
    197–198, 201, 203–205, 213,
    223–224, 230, 233, 241, 249, 261,
    270, 272–273, 275–276
conformity, 125, 200, 203
Cook, Capt James, 21, 107–115, 117–121,
    123, 125–129, 131–132, 233

281

Author Index